Killing Kebble

For my parents, who set me on this path. Enjoy the naartjies.
And for Sean, who has taught me how to live and to love.

Killing Kebble

An Underworld Exposed

Mandy Wiener

MACMILLAN

First published in 2011 by Pan Macmillan South Africa
Private Bag X19, Northlands
Johannesburg, 2116

www.panmacmillan.co.za

ISBN 978-1-77010-132-6

*Every attempt has been made to ensure the accuracy of the de-
tails, facts, names, places and events mentioned in these pages,
but the publisher and author welcome any feedback, comments
and/or corrections on the content, which is based on numerous interviews, court documents, newspaper reports, author
experiences and other sources. In order to preserve authenticity
all tweets and SMS messages have been reproduced exactly as
originally received or sent.*

Editing by Valda Strauss and Andrea Nattrass
Proofreading by Lisa Compton
Design and typesetting by Triple M Design, Johannesburg
Cover design by K4
Front cover photograph of Mikey Schultz by Antoine de Ras
Author photograph by Lisa Skinner

Printed by Ultra Litho (Pty) Limited

'At a glance, or in the eye of the uninitiated, one may be excused of thinking or saying that this is a run of the mill case of murder and conspiracy to commit any other offence. This is not so. In my view this case is about hidden and/or sinister agendas perpetrated by shady characters as well as ostensibly crooked and/or greedy businesspersons. It is about corrupt civil servants as well as prominent politicians or politically connected people wining and dining with devils incarnate under cover of darkness.'

Judge Frans Kgomo
25 November 2010

Foreword

The Brett Kebble murder captured the imagination of an entire nation. A mining tycoon who was gunned down in the dead of night in what may, or may not, have been a hijacking, by people he may, or may not, have known.

A man of means who was politically connected, Brett Kebble had attracted a fair amount of negative publicity in the run-up to his untimely death.

The speculation about his killing mounted and the story dominated Eyewitness News for weeks on end. South Africa was intrigued.

Deciding that Mandy Wiener would be the reporter we would send to the scene and who would 'go live' into our prime-time bulletins was a quick decision. She was a good reporter who handled live questions and answers on the radio particularly well. She also lived close by and was therefore an obvious choice.

Who would have thought that deploying her to the scene of the crime would lead to years of investigative work on her part and that it would culminate in this book?

Over the years, Mandy fought to hold onto this story and covered almost every aspect of it as one sordid detail after the next began to emerge.

She spent months following the court proceedings and linking the protagonists of this murky underworld as Glenn Agliotti stood trial for Kebble's murder. It became a standing joke among her colleagues in the newsroom who would comment that she'd pitched a tent and taken a sleeping bag to court because 'that's where she's now living'.

Mandy cultivated excellent contacts and showed great flair in her reporting on new developments; her thorough investigations made her an expert on the subject and this book reveals the remarkable depth of her understanding of the events which unfolded. She was instrumental in helping to revolutionise the way news is reported on Twitter with her constant courtroom tweets.

Killing Kebble: An Underworld Exposed is very much in line with the Eyewitness News philosophy of not only breaking the news, but following the evolution of such stories to their natural conclusions. This book also reflects Mandy's brilliant journalistic instinct and reminds me of one of the first assignments I sent her on.

As a young intern Mandy and another junior were tasked with going door-to-door in Houghton to ask about recent water cuts in the area. A relatively simple and safe assignment one would think. They were in for a rude awakening though as they were held up at gunpoint.

Instead of panicking, Mandy kept her wits about her and simply pressed 'record' on her equipment – capturing the entire incident.

I knew at that moment that the young traffic intern who insisted on being a part of the newsroom had what it took to be a phenomenal journalist.

Those who followed the Eyewitness News coverage of the Brett Kebble murder will be intrigued by this in-depth account of one of the most dramatic stories of our country's recent history. The readers will experience first-hand how the 'good' reporter we sent out that September turned out to be the great reporter whose work you read in these pages.

Eyewitness News is extremely proud to be represented by Mandy as she tackled the story and is equally proud to see how she has taken her work in the newsroom and turned it into what we believe is an outstanding book.

Katy Katopodis
Editor-in-Chief, Eyewitness News

Prologue

Mikey Schultz's lean, ripped body reads like a memoir of his turbulent, hell-raising life.

I always wanted to have a tattoo, but I was boxing professionally. I didn't want one you could see on my body, because I didn't want people to think funny of me.

My first tattoo I got in Wales with my mate Anthony van Niekerk. It's on my arse. It was of a little Tazz drinking beer. I said I'd never have another one. Before I left Wales, I got another one on my leg. Brian Mitchell used to have this T-shirt of Tazz in boxing gloves. I got that on my leg.

On my left forearm, I've got a lot of tattoos that mean stuff. There's my best friend Jody's name and the date he died and my boetie, Donald, and his date.

And then those are my four kids' names. Demi-Lee, Kalynn, Michael and Matthew. Above that is two hands praying in boxing handwraps, ready to fight.

On my left shoulder is a red confederation flag with a skull in the middle and my name underneath it. Clint Nassif, Gary van Staden, David Smith ... he's also been dead for about seven years now ... there were six of us that got it done.

On my right chest is a memorial for Carlo. It says, 'Rest in Peace, Outlaws Forever'. If I had to tattoo all my friends' names who died, I wouldn't even have space left on my body. I still need to put Julio's name somewhere.

There's Jesus's face with red blood on my right forearm. I'm not that religious but it's to repent for all my sins, hey. To show all my regrets.

My sister Cathy's face is next to that. My sissy. She's like my second mom, you know.

I used to have a Hells Angels tattoo on my right shoulder. An '8' and a '1'. That's because 'H' and 'A' are the eighth and first letters of the alphabet. I also used to have 'AFFA', 'Angels Forever, Forever Angels'. I wasn't allowed to have it, but I done it anyway. I've covered them up now.

Leonie's name is big across my chest. I love my wife, 'Fatty'. I was always going to put 'Respect' there. I saved that space for Respect.

Then I have 'Outlaw' across my stomach. Me, Kappie, Carlo and Nigel, we were like the elite in Elite. We were willing to do the extra. I tattooed 'Outlaw' across my stomach and Kappie and Carlo both done it on their arms. We tried to get Nigel to do it, but he won't get a tattoo.

Now we're trying to convince Nigel to get a tattoo. Kappie and I.

We need to put a tattoo somewhere to remember how the three of us stood together. How our loyalty and friendship helped us survive killing Kebble.

ON 27 SEPTEMBER 2005 ANDREW MINAAR STEERED HIS WAY ROUND the bend past the imposing gates of the Inanda Club, the fortress of the country's mink-and-manure set replete with 40 acres of equestrian lawns, a terrace restaurant, 75 years of rich heritage and a reputation for dazzling polo internationals. He continued down Fifth Avenue. There was remarkably little traffic along the route, bar the odd taxi barrelling through a four-way stop, capitalising on the short cut from the highway to Katherine Street in Sandton. As he did every morning, the tall, gangly butler chuckled at the names of the estates paraded proudly on the turrets of the ten-foot-high walls.

It wasn't long before he turned into the driveway of Hoëveld House, the impressive property owned by Brett Kebble, and was serenely waved through by a familiar security guard. He would miss this drive in the mornings through the avenues of Inanda.

A few weeks earlier Brett had informed him that he had sold the house and was scaling down. All the staff had been effectively retrenched and believed they would be moved to John Stratton's home a few kilometres away. The butler knew that his employer had got himself ensnared in a horrendous financial trap and was on the seam of a nervous breakdown. He had heard rumblings about investigations, missing shares and millions of rands owed to him by Glenn Agliotti and had pieced together snippets of conversations he had overheard on the patio – it was difficult not to hear when Brett was holding court, even though he made a point of keeping quiet when the butler came within proximity of the dining table. He had also read in the newspaper that his principal had been deposed from the boards of his companies and the signs were ominous.

Andrew considered himself to be fairly astute and always believed he had unique insight into Brett's business dealings, but things were becoming more obscure. This time he couldn't establish just how profound his boss's troubles were or what exactly had gone wrong, but he knew it was severe. Together with Joyce, the domestic worker, and Joseph, Brett's trusted driver, Andrew had spent the past few weeks purging the house of documents. They had been tasked with burning the papers. Large swathes of documents were fed into the roaring fire which burned in the lounge, surrounded by an elaborately decorated facade that reportedly cost Brett over a million rand.

On that Tuesday morning, Andrew arrived at work at 07:00 as was the norm. Since he had begun working there three years earlier, the awkward, slightly skittish butler had always started his day at that time and knocked off when coffee was served after dinner. Alternatively, he would work until whatever time Brett required him. Guests would usually retire to the lounge at about 22:00 or 23:00 and then he'd head off home to Townsview, fifteen or so kilometres away in the less illustrious Southern suburbs of the city, disparagingly referred to as 'the South'.

His primary task at the residence was to manage Kebble's staff, arrange meetings with guests, maintain the property and cater for the ever-flowing stream of visitors. But of late, his employer had seemed to tire of entertaining and the accompanied fuss.

Brett usually arrived in Johannesburg at midday on a Tuesday, having flown in from Cape Town on his private jet. He spent the greater part of the week with Ingrid and the four kids at their home in Bishopscourt and would usually be in Gauteng for only three days. It was an uncomfortable arrangement necessitated by business but, ironically, he would rarely travel into the CBD where JCI's head office was located on Harrison Street. He preferred to set up his HQ at home in Inanda and the patio or lounge would regularly become an impromptu boardroom. Joseph would be dispatched at midday on a Tuesday to drive to Lanseria Airport in the west of the city. It was a drive that took a good 45 minutes from Sandton, what with congested highways and interminable roadworks. Brett still preferred that arrangement to the unreliability of commercial airlines and the frenetic Johannesburg International Airport, particularly now that his public profile was taking a thumping. His fall from grace had filled more column space than he cared to remember.

He would stay in Johannesburg until Thursday night when Joseph would ferry him back to Lanseria. Once a month or so, Police Commissioner Jackie Selebi and Glenn Agliotti would come for dinner and Brett would push his flight back, only leaving Inanda at around 23:00. This particular week, though, things were out of sync as Brett had flown in on the Monday morning, a decision indicative of the fact that things were not as they usually were.

Brett rarely broke his Tuesday-to-Thursday routine until a month prior to this particular visit. Many things had begun to change in the past few weeks. The house had become far quieter, fewer people seemed to be visiting the property and Brett would often spend time at the house on his own. It was unsettling that Brett, normally such a gregarious character who revelled in the company of others, had begun to live a house-bound lifestyle. Andrew also noticed that Brett had become quieter and that his eating habits had changed. There was also far less money lying around the house. In the past he would often leave a couple of thousand rand on a countertop. Yet he was the type of character who would leave five cents on a table and a week later want to know where the coin had disappeared to.

That Tuesday morning, Andrew set about laying the table for breakfast. He could never be certain who would make an unannounced arrival for a meal as things just 'were as they were' with Brett. While the butler's job description was to manage Brett's guests, he would rarely be informed of meetings. A captain of industry or a sunglasses-adorned young political turk would arrive on the doorstep and lunch would be expected. Brett's personal assistants tried persistently to get him to confirm meetings and arrangements, but he shrugged off their messages, only replying when he felt the need. Having set the table, Andrew began meticulously cleaning the lounge, which was remarkably undisturbed from the day before, except for one peculiarity.

On the table in the centre of the room were two dessert containers. In each bowl, rested against the lip of the container, was a dirty spoon. Andrew immediately thought how very odd that image was. It was extremely unusual for Brett to go to the fridge and help himself to food. He would never really do that. Andrew also found the image of two bowls incongruous. He cast his mind back to the night before, trying to establish who the second bowl might be attributed to. He knew that he had cleaned up after Brett had dined with journalist David Gleason, clearing away the prawn plates and the soiled serviettes. After Gleason left the house, Brett had also departed, jacket in hand. Andrew had overheard Brett telling the hack that he was going to meet his associate Sello Rasethaba. Sello was having trouble with his son, Lebo, and Brett was going to chat to him about that. He also had plans to meet up with one of his spin doctors, Dominic Ntsele. Brett left just before 20:00 and Andrew climbed into his car shortly after.

An incident from the night before had unsettled the butler. While driving down Fifth Avenue the previous evening, he had noticed Brett's silver Mercedes-Benz, with registration CA 8979, parked next to the pavement around 500 metres from the house. He couldn't see who the driver was, but he presumed it was Brett, as Joseph had already been given the night off. Another peculiarity of late, as Joseph drove him 99 per cent of the time. Andrew didn't stop and continued on his way home to the South.

Perplexed, Andrew asked the maid, Joyce, who had been at the house the previous evening, but she knew as little as he did. She told him that Brett had returned about fifteen minutes after he had left the house the night before, but she didn't know of any visitors. Andrew set aside his discomfort and concentrated on the morning errands.

It wasn't long before the gate alarm buzzed, announcing the day's first unexpected visitor. It was only 08:00. Andrew pressed the remote and the solid metal gates on Fifth Avenue rumbled open. A luxury vehicle crawled up the long curved driveway past the blooming arum lilies and came to a halt near the shaped flower beds. Dominic climbed out of the front seat and rapped the heavy brass lion-faced knocker on the door, announcing his arrival yet again. Andrew welcomed him into the lounge. Dominic's was a familiar face at the house and he would often arrive at this hour. Brett consulted extensively with Dominic about his turbulent media profile, as he did with others in the industry too, such as veteran publicist David Barritt and Gleason. Brett and Dominic had become firm friends over time and their relationship extended beyond the professional. Dominic would even occasionally sit on the edge of Brett's bed, chatting to him as the tycoon fought insomnia. Brett would often resort to sleeping pills to help him fall asleep.

The spin doctor had had plans to meet Brett the previous evening at a Japanese restaurant in nearby Norwood. After receiving a message from Brett saying he was running late, Dominic cancelled the meeting. Brett also scrapped his scheduled date with Sello the night before via SMS. Dominic and Brett had already exchanged messages that morning, but the conversation had come to an abrupt halt and Dominic assumed Brett may have dozed off again. At 07:04, Dominic's phone had beeped with an SMS from the magnate: '*Hi dom. I am not feeling well had bad biltong snacks last eve. Can we meet latr? Shud b nk by lunch. Apolgies.*' But Dominic had gone to Hoëveld House because he only read the message once he had arrived.

Andrew set a tray bearing a teapot and a cup and saucer on the table in front of Dominic. He fired off an SMS to his boss at 08:04: '*Mr kebble,mr ntsele is here*'. Brett didn't respond so Dominic scribbled a note saying, '*Hey Chum, I was here*'. With that, the visitor went on his way, to return later that night. A third party was due to join them at the morning meeting so Dominic cancelled via a text. He and Brett exchanged messages throughout the afternoon about the day's news agenda and political developments. Nothing about their discourse suggested things were out of the ordinary.

It was a relatively uneventful morning for Andrew, who spent much of the time wrestling with the riddle of the dessert bowls. Finally, at 11:30, Brett made an appearance downstairs, his shock of brownish-grey curls dishevelled and unruly. He was dressed in his normal uniform of smart trousers, collared shirt and slip-on loafers. Brett complained that he was feeling queasy and suggested it was because of the prawns that Andrew had prepared for him the night before, the sensitivities of the housekeeper inconsequential to his boss. Brett made little effort to endear himself to his house staff and, as a result, they considered him to be arrogant and even, at times, a bully. He turned down the offer of breakfast, waving away the butler's suggestion and the already set table. Instead, Brett blearily made his way over to the drinks cabinet and proceeded to pour himself three stiff gin and tonics in quick succession.

This unusual development added to Andrew's discomfort. It was strange for Brett to have a drink so early in the day. Andrew also found it odd that a person with an upset stomach would be drinking alcohol. However, Brett had begun to drink more and more heavily lately, although he did have an astonishing capacity for alcohol. He was always ahead of everyone else at the party. He would normally open the bar cabinet up around 17:00 and he and his guests would have wine or whisky as an aperitif before dinner. During the meal, he could consume two to three bottles of wine on his own and always drank the most out of everyone at the table. And then, after dinner, there would be a grappa or some or other liqueur as a nightcap. Despite this, three gin and tonics at 11:30 on a troubled stomach seemed odd.

Brett retired to his bedroom and whiled away the time watching rolling news channels and savouring the shade from the sprawling Belhambra tree that filled the bay window. Legend has it that the tree was planted by the initial owners of Hoëveld House from a seed brought to the country in statesman Jan Smuts's pocket. It's believed the seed was imported into South Africa from Italy, but Brett was never entirely convinced of the veracity of the legend. It is a tree of South American descent so the story is unlikely to be correct. Whatever the truth, the baronial tree provided good cover to the main bedroom from the spring sun. At 12:01 he received a message from Gulu, his term of endearment for Ingrid, his wife. '*Leaving 4 malagas now my love 2 you x*.' She was taking the kids to Lily Cottage, their weekend retreat on the banks of the Breede River in Malgas in the mountainous Overberg.

After reading the message, he arose to lunch with David Gleason, a continuation of his meeting with the journalist from the evening before. Also present on the patio was former stockbroker Martin Irish. It was not uncommon for Brett to entertain journalists at his home. The charm offensive was Brett's favourite *modus operandi* when it came to sceptical journalists who were writing spurious articles about him. Andrew served fish and pasta and left the trio to their talking. At 14:30 Gleason and Irish went on their way. As they walked down the driveway, Brett said something to Gleason that he had never said before. He urged him to 'take good care of yourself'. The veteran reporter would later reflect on that lunch and recall that he had the impression that while Brett was a bit subdued, he gave an indication that he was considering a raft of new plans. The businessman had been humiliated and disgraced but gave no hint that he was depressed.

Just fifteen minutes later the metal gate was rumbling open again. Sello Barini arrived from Tilus Security, the company that was mandated to run the systems at the house. The company was responsible for checking the beams and monitors as well as the telephone lines. Usually, one of Barini's staff members would be tasked with the job of checking the systems but occasionally he would do a house call himself. Barini also ran the IT work for JCI, so he was well known to Brett. The two went into the lounge and had a brief meeting. Barini was gone by 15:30, less than an hour after he had arrived.

When Brett checked his phone he saw that a message had come through from Gleason at 15:30 letting him know that Neal Froneman, his competitor at Aflease, had secured permission from the Reserve Bank to restructure the company. '*Aflease/SCR deal approved by SARB.*' Nine months earlier, Brett's company Randgold & Exploration had sold a 19 per cent stake in Aflease Gold and Uranium Resources, a year after nearly seizing control of the company. Froneman had driven the move to have Brett booted from the boards of his three companies, stating that shareholders had had enough and needed more transparency from public companies. There was another message from Rita Meininghuis, his PA in Cape Town: '*reminder abt yr dinner tonight with sello – 19h30, sello's home*' followed by the address. He shot off a quick message to business associate Lunga Ncwana who was a prominent ANC Youth League member. '*Pl ph me*'.

He made a brief call to Dominic and then spoke to his old friend and stockbroker Peter Gray, who had inherited his positions at JCI and Randgold & Exploration. Brett had spent the past year grooming Peter to take over his positions. At around 16:15, Brett chatted to Minister in the Presidency Essop Pahad. The two spoke about a multimillion-rand fundraising dinner which Pahad was organising in Timbuktu on behalf of President Thabo Mbeki, with tables going at R500 000 a pop. The magnate had committed to a R3 million donation to the museum project in Mali and Pahad was phoning to collect his debt. Eleven days earlier, Brett had sent a message to the high-ranking politician. '*Dear Essop sorry abt not getting back to u. Busy week. Wil fix mali event on Monday. Best to u and meg. Brett*'.

At 18:40 he received an SMS from another Youth League politician, Andile Nkuhlu. The message was written to Gray and copied to Brett: '*Peter ps call me its urgent. I need to share the bad news from lazarus*'. Lazarus Zim was the CEO of mining powerhouse Anglo American and had been supporting JCI through its recent tribulations. But the Anglo board had decided to turn down JCI's offer for shares which it held in Western Areas. The company wanted an additional R40 million which JCI simply could not afford. This would mean an intricate empowerment deal would collapse as a result. Yet more bad news for Brett.

Dusk began to envelope Inanda and the long shadows from the weeping willow tree in the garden brought sunset prematurely. The din from the rush-hour traffic beyond the high walls fought with the noise of the passing swallows and the abrasive hadedas for the soundtrack of upmarket suburbia. Brett strolled into the kitchen as he did on most days to discuss the evening meal with Andrew. Brett considered himself to be a fairly capable cook, and if he was not the producer of meals in the kitchen, then he was certainly the executive producer. He had a refined palate and enjoyed the culinary process. It was not unusual for him to haul the chef out from the kitchen of a Michelin star restaurant so that they could debate the merits of a dish. Some found it awkward but it endeared him to many, as underlying the perceived pretentiousness was a deep appreciation for food. Even the choice of jam at breakfast would not be a simple thing. There would be the option of at least twenty preserves and he would want his guests to taste them all, even if he did not do so himself. Breakfasts at Brett's house could easily be mistaken for those at an upmarket hotel – there would be crumpets, croissants, muffins and anything else one could possibly desire.

His wine pairing was equally exemplary and he would take great care in his choice of accompaniment with each evening meal. That night he selected a red wine to complement the steak and chips that Andrew was preparing for dinner. Brett had been invited for supper to Sello's house as the former Prime Minister of Namibia, Hage Geingob, was in town and was being courted by the mining industry players. Linda Makatini, an advocate, would also be there. Sello was the CEO of Orlyfunt Holdings, the latest BEE conglomeration to be created by Brett. He knew that Sello would have got caterers in and the food would have been standing on hot trays since four o'clock in the afternoon. He knew it would taste like 'a fucking chalkboard' and often told Dominic as much. With dinner production in full swing, Brett took a seat at his Steinway grand piano and began to play. He continued for quite some time, immersed in the brilliant beauty of each note and didn't even notice his friend standing at the doorway. Finally, Brett caught a glimpse of Dominic's shortish, stocky frame and broad grin and immediately his fingers fell from the keys. He never liked an audience, even though Dominic did not consider himself to be one.

The two men chatted in the lounge for a while before moving into the dining room and sitting down to dinner. The conversation traversed all manner of topics, including Mbeki's siege of his deputy, Jacob Zuma, and finally returned to Brett's piano playing. Dom would often implore Brett to play for him but he was always reluctant and shy about his ability. Finally he conceded, but only on the condition that Dominic would sing as he played. His friend had a rich baritone voice which was easy on the ear. They alternated their choice of songs and finally decided on 'Summertime', but argued over which version they would sing. They considered the Ella Fitzgerald interpretation, but settled on Mahalia Jackson's take on the Gershwin classic.

Brett played and Dominic sang but occasionally the host would belt out a 'Don't you cry'. The two-man concert ended with a chuckle and they returned to the couches in the lounge. Brett was reluctant about going to dinner at Sello's house. He had told his empowerment partner that he would be only going for dessert, but he was reticent nonetheless. He hated these schmoozy functions and attempted to cajole Dominic into going with him. Several times he asked his friend to drive him the few short kilometres to Sello's home, but Dominic had other commitments. Dominic got up to leave and Brett walked him out of the front door as he always did. Even if he was conducting a business meeting at the house, Brett would get up and walk him out. There was a slight chill in the spring air and Dominic shivered. His shirt sleeves, the cuffs embossed with the letters 'DOM' were buttoned at his wrists while Brett had the sleeves of his pale lilac-and-white checked shirt rolled up. They chatted briefly and Brett sent his friend off with a familiar parting remark: 'Take care of yourself, Dom.' It was the same comment he had made to Gleason earlier in the day. Dominic manoeuvred his way down the driveway and turned onto Fifth Avenue, taking the route past the Inanda Club, left at the traffic circle, down Pretoria Street and onto Katherine. He joined the highway heading north and shot through to Midrand.

Meanwhile, Brett shut the heavy front door behind him and walked through to his study. He sat down and wrote a letter before bellowing down the passage to Andrew to bring him an envelope. Once Andrew had found one he looked around for Brett and was shocked when he found his boss urinating in the garden under the Belhambra tree, casually holding onto a branch to keep himself steady. It was an inexplicable sight as the butler had never seen him do such a thing before. Brett read the letter before placing it in the envelope and sealing it. Curiously, he told Andrew the letter was addressed to cabinet minister Essop Pahad, but didn't reveal the content of the document. It was out of character for Brett to mention detail like that. And then something even more curious occurred – Brett complimented Andrew on the dinner he had cooked. It was a rare remark which the butler relished.

At 20:30, Brett got up to leave. Earlier in the night, whilst overseeing dinner, he gave Joseph the driver the night off again. It was the second day in a row he'd given the peculiar instruction and Joseph knocked off reluctantly. As a consequence, Brett would be driving himself to Sello's house in his Merc. As he left, Andrew noted that Brett still had his shirt sleeves rolled up and that he didn't have a jacket with him. He always had a jacket with him when he had a dinner appointment and there was still a cold chill in the air. He also wasn't carrying a gift for his host which was very unusual. Brett usually went to the pantry and collected a box of chocolates or a bottle of wine, but on this particular night he would be arriving empty-handed.

Brett left for Sello's and Andrew tied up a few loose ends before driving out shortly after him at around 20:45. The butler stopped for a cup of coffee at Italian franchise restaurant Mimmos and arrived home at 21:30, still feeling unsettled from the day.

Earlier, when Brett was walking out of his house, he had called John Stratton and they spoke for four minutes. While they were on the phone, Brett received a text message from his prayer partner, Trevor, at exactly 20:40: '*Thinking of u, up in the Crags, cold, raining now, nice sound on the roof. Just love God, He'll pull you thru. Let go + let God have his way. Luv u, t.*' A few months prior, Brett had been baptised in the swimming pool of his good friend Peter George's Cape Town home. A number of close friends had witnessed the spiritual rebirthing. George had provided Brett with guidance for years and assisted him in taking the plunge to be 'reborn'.

As he was driving past the Wanderers Club, Brett switched to his car phone and his 'slave card' on the device kicked in. At 20:45 he called the landline at Lily Cottage in Malgas. He steered his way through the tree-lined avenues of Birdhaven and Melrose, spending seven minutes on the phone to Gulu or one of his four children. The details of that conversation would never be made public, and it was the last call he would make.

Mikey

Live fast, die hard, hey. I lost a lot of good friends very young. Fuck, I've been to more funerals than most people would see in two lifetimes. Of close friends, who were shot. We lived fast and they died young. They lived like thugs and died like thugs. They died in murders and drive-by shootings. That's just the way the street is, hey. You live by the sword and you die by the sword.

M IKEY SCHULTZ WAS BORN AT THE QUEEN VICTORIA HOSPITAL AT the bottom of Braamfontein on 5 January 1975. He shares a birthday with his mother which he thinks is 'quite lekker'.

His childhood was rough – a product of the gritty working-class central Johannesburg suburbs of Bez Valley and Troyeville, where only the strongest and smartest survived. He lived on the fringes of Ellis Park stadium, near the public swimming pool. His parents had little money, with his mother the only breadwinner, while his drunk, dropout father did little to contribute to the family's meagre income.

'My toppie is a bit of a hobo, hey. My father drinks a lot and, ag, he stopped working and that and he used to terrorise my poor mother. He used to stay at home and get *dronk* every day,' Mikey recalls in his coarse, unsophisticated twang. 'We were very poor when I was young, so my mom would walk to work and back, from Troyeville to Jeppe and back again, just to save her bus fare so that she had money for bread and stuff like that.' His mother worked at a building society and when his father, a motor mechanic by training, did finally get a job, it was at the newly built Eastgate shopping centre. When it opened in 1981, he was the maintenance manager for the entire mall.

Mikey's family dynamic is complex. His half-sister's father is really his uncle. His mother was married to Mikey's uncle, but after he died she married Mikey's father. The two men were brothers.

Sitting in the lounge of the hardened hit man's family home in Meyersdal in Johannesburg's Southern suburbs, I can't help but think it's the background I anticipated he would come from: Born into borderline poverty, drunk father, stoic mother, rough neighbourhood, becomes a law-breaking thug in order to make dirty money and climb out of poverty. The lessons from his youth are also predictable, but moving nonetheless. He certainly has a lifestyle now that is far different from that which he grew up with. He drives a Lexus, which I tease him is an 'old man's car', his home is tastefully furnished with classic art prints and a large flat-screen TV and it's in a private estate. I am amused at the irony of this – the thought that Mikey, who is a man-myth in these parts, has chosen to live in secure suburbia out of fear of common criminals. But there's no belying his upbringing as he speaks with a fierce determination and a seriousness which is true to his tribulations.

'Growing up hard and that builds character, hey. I've got a few friends that have got money and stuff and I see the way their kids are brought up and they've just got no personality, you know? Growing up hard and that, I believe like in tough times I'll be ok because I've been there before, you know.' Despite the Hollywoodesque saccharinity of his reflections, there is something deeply real about the way Mikey talks about his youth.

With a largely absent paternal figure, Mikey looked to his older brother Donny as a mentor. His sister Cathy's husband at the time, WBA Super Featherweight titleholder Brian Mitchell, also filled in, teaching him to box and passing down old clothes. But their relationship would sour. Mikey has several stories about a fall-down-drunk Mitchell in polly shorts, tattered vest and takkies trying to shoot at him with a pocket .22 pistol.

Unsurprisingly, Mikey the adolescent ruffian did not take keenly to authority and school was not a happy place for him. He went to Jeppe Preparatory before donning the black and white of Jeppe High but he only made it to Standard Seven before they asked him to leave.

'It was a number of incidents that got me kicked out of school, like bunking and fighting at break. I was a bad student. The only person I really got along with at school was [World Cup-winning rugby coach] Jake White. He was my PT teacher and one of the main reasons is because James Dalton [former Springbok hooker] is my second cousin. His mother and my father are first cousins and his oupa and mine were brothers. Jake and him were close because he was like the best rugby player in our school and obviously, being related to James and also boxing and that, Jake liked me because I used to box.'

Mikey failed every term in Standards Six and Seven. He hated school and simply didn't want to be there. Finally, when the headmaster called him in and suggested he find another school, he agreed. 'I was like, "Lekker, took yous long enough, hey."' His familiar boyish grin stretches across his face and his piercing ice-blue eyes light up as he laughs. He left Jeppe and went to the Johannesburg Technical College to go and learn a trade. He got himself a little motorbike which made bunking class much easier.

While teenage Mikey didn't excel in the classroom, he did find success in the boxing ring. He first began to box when he was twelve years old. 'It was the only sport that I took to. I tried to play cricket and soccer and that, but it was just not me, hey. I wasn't really into team sports. I mean, boxing is very personal and one-on-one but it is quite a team sport because of the guys you train with and stuff like that, so you are actually a team,' he explains. He would receive provincial colours for Southern Transvaal and Western Transvaal and even qualify for the Commonwealth Games. His weathered hands also bear testament to his many rounds in the ring – white scars cover his fists between the tattoos on his misshapen, lumpy knuckles.

Boxing would also bring Mikey his first taste of celebrity. When he was sixteen, he and close friend Jody Edwards auditioned at a casting for the movie adaptation of celebrated author Bryce Courtenay's prolific novel *The Power of One*. Steven Dorff had been cast as adult PK, Morgan Freeman was black trainer Geel Piet, and the producers were looking for extras who could box. 'So it was myself, Jody, Bradley Lottering (who also boxed for Malvern with me) and another guy, Jannes Coetzee, who boxed for Newlands. The four of us got chosen, but they said to us, "Listen, you're going to have to cut your hair if you go there." I had long hair then. I was out of school and I was like a little scruffy hobo from Malvern,' he says, much to my amusement. Since I've known him, Mikey has had his blond hair cropped short, accentuating his sharp, angular jaw. 'We all flew over to Harare and we had a haircut and that. We helped them with some coordination with the fights and we helped with our English accents. We were there for like three weeks. We didn't get a lot of time on screen. We were paid R1 000 a week in South Africa, and we got paid R1 000 there a week for like expenses and stuff. In those days, R1 000 was a lot of money.' Mikey excitedly flicks on the big-screen TV to show me the clip of himself, scrawny and blond and wearing baggy blue shorts, boxing against his olive-skinned friend Jody.

Mikey never got his call-up papers for the army but volunteered to 'klaar in' anyway with one of his friends, Anthony 'Dumpie' van Niekerk, on condition they could both go to the same base. 'We're like brothers, Dumpie and I. We've been friends from five years old. What a lekker oke, hey. He's amazing,' Mikey says about his oldest buddy. They were assigned to an infantry unit in Potchefstroom and spent most of their service boxing for the SADF. Mikey believes he would have been a successful soldier and regrets not being deployed to the volatile townships in the early 1990s, during the height of the country's political instability. It was while Mikey was in the defence force that he met a girl, Aletta, who fell pregnant before he'd even left the army. Mikey was nineteen, had few prospects of employment and was about to become a dad.

I N THE EARLY TO MID-1990S, THE 'RAVE' SCENE WAS GATHERING momentum in South Africa – mega clubs booming out electronic dance music were opening in Johannesburg and samples of Ecstasy were filtering into the country. Crazy young things, dressed in psychedelic neon outfits and platform shoes, were dancing nights and days away, charged by stimulants and hallucinogens. As the club culture began to grow, so too did the demand for increased security at these nightspots. There had always been a need for bouncers to man the doors at bars and dance venues, but the dynamic was changing. With the introduction of drugs, the stakes were getting higher and the business was far more lucrative. Various bouncer groups that operated in the city at the turn of the 1980s had been fairly organised, as they only had the effects of alcohol to deal with, but the politics of the game altered as the variable of narcotics was introduced. Bouncers became enforcers and pivotal players in pushing the drugs.

Different bouncer 'crews' began to take control of sections of Johannesburg, based largely on geography, and ran their regions as their own personal fiefdoms. Gerard Strydom's Equinon Protection Services (EPS) and JC le Roux's crew duelled for control of the city's East Rand, focusing primarily on Boksburg. Viper and Diplomat, run by Graham Diedericks, emerged as the strongest players in the Northern and Central suburbs. The bouncers standing sentinel at club doors would not be personally responsible for pushing drugs in the clubs. That role was allegedly assumed by the Hells Angels, the international motorcycle-gang-cum-organised-crime-syndicate, who were importing and manufacturing the pills. The bouncers would get a cut for ensuring only 'authorised' drug runners could ply their trade in the clubs. Any other dealer caught selling in their domain would be beaten and thrown out, and their stash confiscated. He who controlled the club, controlled the drug trade.

Initially, Mikey wasn't involved in this business. He was attempting to launch his professional boxing career and had a young family at home.

'The whole time I was boxing, I was living a very clean life. I didn't really drink much and that,' he recalls. 'When I was younger, all my mates used to go out the whole time. Me and Anthony used to live next door to one another and, on a Wednesday night, I'd be lying in bed with the baby and the wife and they'd be going out. I'd hear them driving down the road with the music blaring on the way to the club. So like they were all jolling and going mad and stuff like that, and I was at home basically being a dad and I didn't really jol much.'

Mikey's big brother Donny was part of the club scene at the time, working as a bouncer at Presley's in City Deep. Occasionally, Mikey would go there with his friends but it would inevitably end in fisticuffs.

'After a fight, we'd go there to have a few drinks, get smashed and that. But we'd end up fighting there plenty, hey. We'd fight, we'd get banned and then the following week we'd go back and ask Chris, the owner, "Listen, we're sorry and can we come back?"' he recounts, giggling at his youthful exploits.

Attempting to break through into the professional arena, Mikey and Anthony took up contracts in Wales to box, but they struggled to get work permits authorised. Bored and homesick, the two whiled away their time clubbing, riding the crest of the booming rave scene.

'When I was in Wales, I tried Ecstasy and *flip*, you know, it was *lekker*,' admits Mikey, his now familiar grin as broad as can be. 'And when we were young, in this country, it wasn't really here yet. There they had rave clubs and everything like that. When we came back home, the rave scene was just starting and a few rave clubs like ESP opened. I started working at Brian Mitchell's gym and I met some okes and that, and they were like, "Hey, why don't you come to ESP?" and what what. And I was like, "Ja, whatever."

'Then the one night, Jody and myself went to the old Synergy down there in Fourways. We went there and we organised some pills and we got shit-faced and that was like ... fuck! That was like the best thing ever, hey,' he recalls, slamming his hand on his knee for effect.

'And then I started meeting people and stuff like that. There was this one guy that used to work at the gym where I worked. He used to be an aerobics instructor. He was a gay oke. He used to sell pills and he used to give us pills.'

Lured by the appeal of drugs, Mikey began to lose his way and his clean-living lifestyle was abandoned, along with his young family. He began to make friends with guys who were more experienced in life and more entrenched in the nightclub circuit, some of whom he met through Donny. 'I became good friends with Rocky Wainstein. He was in the Hells Angels. I actually met him at the gym. He knew my brother 'cause they were more or less the same age and they came from the same area and they boxed in the army together. They were always like the older generations, those okes, Rocky, Lionel and Mitsi – all the okes we've always looked up to and stuff.' Mitsi is Mitsi Matthyson, who was also a Hells Angels member, and Lionel is a reference to Lionel Hunter, a scrap parts dealer.

Hitting the clubs hard and with a regular pill-popping habit, something had to give, and it was Mikey's career as a professional boxer. 'I had another professional fight and I could feel it in me that I would rather worry about jolling more than training. So I said to myself, "Listen, if I'm not going to do this a hundred per cent, I'm not going to do it at all." And it's hard. It's a hard lifestyle being straight and I said, "Ah fuck, I'm not going to box any more."'

At the time, Mikey was working for his brother-in-law, Brian Mitchell, at a spare parts yard, trading used motor vehicle parts. But, having chosen drugs over boxing, that soon substituted as his profession. 'You know, you spend a lot of money chowing pills. So I knew the Angels guys could get the stuff a lot cheaper. So I was speaking to them and saying, "So listen, would you like, get us stuff?" and then, as we moved the stuff, I was like, "If you get it at R30, give it to us at R45 and I'll move it at R60" or whatever. That way we could keep up our habits and that as well.'

He also began to earn himself a fierce reputation as a street fighter. But he's surprisingly philosophical about why he became so ferocious.

'I was going into the clubs with Rocky and meeting all these other okes and I was pretty small at the time, like about 80 kilos. About the size I am now, but next to those okes that was like tiny. Maybe I had the feeling I had to prove myself now because I was the little oke and that. So, if there was ever shit, I was on the front line, fighting first. I ended up getting into a lot of like street fights.'

With Mikey's stature growing, Graham Diedericks offered him a job bouncing for the Diplomat outfit at mega-club ESP in the city centre. 'ESP was like our church, hey. We wouldn't miss it for nothing. Sunday morning we'd get up and get ready and go to church. Myself, my mate Gary van Staden and Clinton Nassif.'

It was near the end of Mikey's boxing career that he first met Clinton Nassif. Clint is of Lebanese descent and is a tough product of the streets of Mayfair. He's a towering man who is well over six foot tall with broad shoulders and a pointy chin. With his burly frame and gruff voice, he's not the kind of character you'd want to bump into in a dark alley in the middle of the night. Clint also owned a scrap metal business and Mikey was working at Mitchell's spare parts yard at the time. 'Obviously with us having a scrap yard and Lionel Hunter working for him, you know, we'd speak and that. Clint used to also chuck pills so we became friends and then Clint and I started working together in the scrap yard. Like, I buy your car that's been in an accident from insurance and then we strip it out, and whatever we can use, we sell that as second-hand spares.' Mikey skirts my questions about whether or not Clint was buying 'hot cars', hijacked vehicles, and selling parts as packages as other spares dealers were doing at the time.

Mikey separated from Aletta, who was his wife by then, after she gave birth to another baby girl, his family becoming collateral as his fast-paced life picked up speed. Clint had also separated from his wife and Clint and Mikey moved in together along with friend Gary van Staden, who Mikey describes as 'very clever, tall, good-looking, really the best kind of oke'. Together they were a force to be reckoned with. 'We lived together here in the South and we'd just go out jolling all the time!' He and Gary worked at the scrap yard by day and bounced for Diplomat by night, earning some extra cash.

Mikey recalls those heydays, when he and Clint 'were like brothers', with near-childish glee and fondness.

'Those days we were only chowing like Es and chowing a little bit of paper, like LSD. That was still my drug of choice and my favourite one out of all of them was LSD, hey. We used to love chowing chips and you just ... fucking ... getting lost, hey. You know? Myself, Nassif and Gary, we'd chow like at home and then we'd sit, we'd talk kak to one another and fucking see how deep we could go in. It was just pretty good, hey.'

As the club scene evolved, territorial disputes became more frequent. It was around this time that Mikey really began to meddle in the messy business of keeping the lines separate. 'Diplomat had a problem in the East Rand. This DJ who owned a club in Boksburg gave the contract to Graham. When Graham's okes went there, JC's okes went and fucked them up. So they put me and Gary there. It was very territorial, hey.'

But difficult assignments such as the one on the East Rand earned Mikey his stripes and street cred. Mikey nonchalantly lets on how the drug trade was set up in the city's nightclubs. 'That's how this whole thing started. It was Rob Reynolds and Peter Conway from the Angels,' he explains. Peter Conway was the leader of the Hells Angels in South Africa in the late 1990s and early 2000s. 'They had the okes in the clubs that were moving the stuff. We were getting five hundred rand a night from Conway to make sure that the other okes didn't move the stock, plus we were earning a shift, plus we had free reign over whatever we wanted, which was quite cool. So we were out jolling and having a big fucking jol and it wasn't costing us much.' I spent months attempting to track down Reynolds and Conway to verify this claim with them. Conway had last popped up in 2009, when police arrested him in Meyerton, south of Johannesburg, on drug-dealing charges. He had also been bust in 2005 for allegedly selling Ecstasy tablets on two occasions. I finally did find the ex-Hells Angels boss and offered him the opportunity to comment on Mikey's claims. He responded via SMS: '*I am VERY sure that you are nowhere near the truth! Obviously you are more interested in slander than the truth. Here is a comment "first we eat."*'

According to *The Times* newspaper, authorities in the US linked Conway and another Hells Angel, Michael 'Jethro' Hall, to an international drug-smuggling operation allegedly run by the motorcycle gang. In 2002, investigators in Arizona exposed a plot to smuggle amphetamines from South Africa to the US by Angels' members – both men were charged but were never extradited or prosecuted. Several American Hells Angels were charged and one senior member pleaded guilty and was sentenced to a fifteen-year jail term. Jethro was apparently killed during a break-in at his Johannesburg home while Conway has been flying under the radar.

Mikey became a 'prospect' for the Nomad chapter of the Hells Angels in 1999. The Angels, a gang with international reach, was beginning to entrench itself in the drug market in South Africa. They were looking for recruits who already had contacts in the clubs and who came with reputations. Despite the gang's apparent involvement in drugs, members of the organisation have continuously asserted that they are only a group of motorcycle enthusiasts who have joined to ride bikes together and to organise social events and fundraisers.

'There was potential in making lots of money there. It was about business,' says Mikey. 'They just started a new chapter called the Nomads. The

Nomads consisted of Red, a Dutch guy who had come from overseas and was wanted by Interpol for murder. He'd done a big drug deal and he was over here with a lot of cash. This is how the Angels started to take over the clubs and that. They had another guy, Jethro, who was wanted in the US. He was cooking Methamphetamine that side. He came over. He was the first oke to cook the crystal in this country and teach the okes and stuff like that. So it was the two of them.

'Rocky became the "sergeant-at-arms". They were looking to build, but they didn't want the usual Angels, the *domgatte* and shit like that. They wanted the okes that were in the clubs and okes that could do the things.'

Mikey's version is that he was approached by Conway who asked him to do a 'job' for him because he had done work for the Angels in the past. 'When they had problems, I'd fuck the okes up and that,' explains Mikey. 'He said to me, "Here's a job for yous okes. Make sure that only our stuff gets pushed and we'll give it to yous okes at X, yous can run it at Y and we'll split the balance." I was still part of Diplomat but being with the Angels, I was making more money because I didn't have to go and work shifts. I would go to all the clubs, make sure the okes were around. If they picked up someone who was selling, they would phone us; we'd corner the oke, catch him and take his stuff. So that's how we got involved starting to move the stuff in clubs.'

For Mikey, it was purely business. 'I must have been the worst Angel they ever had because I never paid my subs. They gave me a motorbike when I joined. When I left, I sold them the bike back for ten grand.'

FIAZAL 'KAPPIE' SMITH IS THE PERSONIFICATION OF HARD LIVING. He's a stocky, muscular, coloured man with a shaved head, thick arms and gappy grin, who was raised on the Cape Flats. He talks with the lilt of the Kaapse Klopse and a heavy lisp, a result of his missing teeth, which he lost courtesy of police brutality in the early 1990s. When Kappie extends a hand to greet someone new, it's always accompanied by a smile, a tipping of his baseball cap and a 'how-do-you-do' which often catches his new acquaintance off guard – one would expect this survivor and reformed gangster to snarl and snap instead of being overly polite and sincere.

He was born in Durban, but lived a relatively nomadic life before settling in Mitchells Plain in Cape Town for a few years with his grandmother. 'My parents split apart when I was very young,' he tells me in his heavily accented way. 'We were drifting from place to place.' Kappie's father was a labourer, a builder by trade. His mother met a singer while he was still fairly young and went off 'on the road' with him. 'We moved from pillar to post, we were dragged all over the show. I got a brother and sister and my brother 'til today is still very messed up. He's locked up again in prison. He's been spending six years of his life in prison. I think it's got to do with your home, where you come from you know?'

Kappie has insightful perceptions about his upbringing, acknowledging he could have travelled a different life path had his circumstances been altered. 'Then my grandmother took hold of me and I stayed there with her for a few years. I had a hard upbringing. There was no parents to guide me. I had a very good grandmother that looked after me, and aunties, but it's hard out there, hey. You need to make it on your own somewhere.'

As a teenager on the impoverished, crime-riddled Cape Flats, Kappie began to lose his way, meddling in gangsterism. He began to associate with members of one of the most dominant crews, the Hard Livings gang. 'I started interfering with other guys from the Hard Livings and hanging around with them and stuff like that there and it didn't work. I was hanging around that Checkers Centre in Mitchells Plain. Most of the guys were hanging around there.' Kappie explains to me that only the roughest kids would loiter outside the Checkers Centre, which was a notorious meeting point for criminals. 'At the time, I didn't know what I wanted. I was young, just wanted to fit in anywhere and live a comfortable life. And then I moved from Cape Town to Jo'burg.' By 'Jo'burg' he really means Nigel, a small industrial town near Springs on Johannesburg's East Rand. He never found his grounding there and continued to be rebellious and difficult.

Kappie tells me an anecdote about one of his first brushes with the law as a teenager in Nigel, which also gives an interesting insight into his motives. He saw himself as something of a Robin Hood, stealing from the rich to give to the poorest of the poor. He tells me this has always remained one of his predominant reasons for breaking the law, but any sceptic would laugh that off.

'One year, I was still very young, living in Nigel. I stole about 32 bicycles on Christmas and gave it to the kids. I stole the bicycles from OK Bazaars and from other guys in the street. I gave them to all the kids in my area where I was staying. The police said, "You think you Father Christmas!" I actually got six cuts for that at the courts in Nigel. They gave me lashes, with the whip,' he says, laughing as he recounts the tale. 'Ag, today I don't steal but I still do a lot of that,' he tells me, referring to the charity work which he's apparently become involved in. 'You know, if you see someone battling, you know where you come from. You know you can't just accept it and there's a lot of people that's got out there and doesn't give a cent.'

Unstable and restless, Kappie ran away from his home in Nigel at the age of sixteen. He was attracted to the bright lights of Johannesburg and found a temporary place of refuge at his uncle's home. He drifted around the city, finding piecework in construction, his father's trade, and 'making a plan here and there'. He befriended a crowd of boys known as 'The Playboys' who hailed from the predominantly coloured neighbourhoods of Newclare and Bosmont. Kappie's hearty humour and *joie de vivre* come to the fore as he recalls this time. 'We'd see who gripped the most women. Young chicks from school. We'd move from chick to chick and see how many we could grip. We were the Playboys and there were other guys, the Ivies, who used to be the dressers. You know, all the breakdances and all that stuff is what we used to do when we were younger. We had no time to cause trouble.'

Nigel and Mikey often tease Kappie, the father of six, about his womanising streak. Another favourite point of humour for Nigel and Mikey is Kappie's gangster past. They're quick to tease him about being a member of the 28s prison gang, which has a reputation for sorting out disputes in jail through sodomy. Kappie just grins and shakes his head at being the 'butt' of their jokes.

The progression from street 'skelm' to fully fledged criminal was a natural one and it wasn't long before Kappie 'started making a plan for money'.

'We started stealing. Hanging around doing the wrong things. Started hanging around with guys that stole cars for a living. They were selling the cars for a living and stuff like that. They were dealing spare parts and that. We were with the wrong crowd. We needed to make money so I started stealing cars. I didn't have parents giving me money.' At the age of eighteen or nineteen, he was arrested and sent to 'Sun City', Johannesburg's main prison that had been given the tongue-in-cheek nickname by criminals as a reference to Sun King Sol Kerzner's popular gambling resort in the homeland of Bophuthatswana.

'The longest I was locked up for was eight months with no bail in Sun City when it first opened in '85. It was hard. It was very tough. I saw a guy get killed there one night. They cut him up with a Manora blade,' he tells me nonchalantly. 'He was a gangster from Picassia. His name was Billy Makiet. I got locked up and had nobody to bail me out and I had to survive and eventually I got off the case.'

Kappie became a career criminal and graduated to more serious crimes such as house burglaries and bank robberies. He moved to Hillbrow, where he began moving with more experienced characters. He won't tell me just how serious the crimes were and is euphemistic about his involvement. However, he is adamant that at no point was he ever involved in drugs. He developed a reputation as a skilled getaway driver and adopted that position regularly. 'The cops were chasing me and on the highway I done a U-turn at 160 kilometres per hour,' he tells me, beaming with pride. I ask him if the police caught him and he appears offended. 'No they did not. As a youngster I could drive well. Till today too. Ja, that's why they gave me the name "The Driver".'

Kappie was in and out of prison often, encountering the most brutal police officers of the apartheid era. He can claim to be amongst those who were tortured by the infamous Brixton Murder and Robbery squad.

'My teeth were cracked in my gums and air was put in my mouth. I was shocked in the middle of the night there [he points to his groin] to tell them what I'd done. Then I'd tell them I'd go to the magistrate to take a statement at 3 o'clock in the morning and I'd come to the magistrate and tell them these guys are torturing me there and I'd come back and they'd torture me again. It was hard at the time, you know. It was then proper Brixton Murder and Robbery at the time. You were treated like a dog. I was tied with a chain and bitten. The one colonel bit me blue on my back. He bit me. I'll never forget him. Bit me blue. They shocked me during the night, yes. They turned me upside down and put me down a well with a plank behind my back and that. Put me in the well with water. They wanted me to tell them the truth. And I would tell them I don't know what you speaking about and that there. It was hard at that time.'

Kappie developed a phenomenal resilience and still today has no trust in law-enforcement officials. It's simply against his policy to squeal, or as he describes it in his vocabulary, to 'turn yellow'. 'No I never cracked. It's against my policy. I'd rather die than to do that.'

Kappie met Mikey Schultz around 1994 when he got a job working at a panel-beating shop in the south of Johannesburg that he now runs. 'We used to go and buy spares there at Mikey's shop. Then we started speaking. Then we started hanging around and started going to the nightclubs together where Mikey and Nigel were running the clubs. We didn't get involved with most of the other groups but we always had a bond between the three of us.'

MIKEY'S INFAMY IN BOUNCING CIRCLES BEGAN TO GROW AND HE built his network, meeting friends of friends and acquainting himself with other heavies in the industry. He started hanging out more in the clubs on Johannesburg's West Rand and became friendly with two other high-profile movers, Carlo Binner and Julio Bascelli, both of whom lived fast and would die young.

'Carlo was a really staunch, staunch guy. He was a bouncer. He also used to smaak chowing pills and stuff. So we'd hook up and we'd chow pills there at Hideout and get totally shit-faced. We became friends and we started "moving" together. Like I'd check him out jolling and that, and he'd say, "Listen, there's a move. Somebody needs to be clamped," and we'd two react to it.'

Mikey met Julio, a tow-truck driver, through his old friend Jody. Julio was closely aligned to the Israeli Mafia which was beginning to operate in Johannesburg.

Mikey also crossed paths with Nigel McGurk at the nightclub ESP. 'We were very close. Me, Carlo and Nigel and Julio. And then Kappie, he's like our street child. He's like been friends with all of us for years. That oke's more heart and soul you're not going to find in anyone, hey. He wasn't involved in the bouncing but he'd come jolling with us and if ever there was a fight, me, Kappie and Carlo were in the middle of the mix.'

BIG EARS. THAT'S THE TERM OF ENDEARMENT THAT MIKEY AND Kappie use to refer to Nigel McGurk. Nigel is a tall, imposing man with a receding hairline, genuine, toothy smile and weathered appearance. He does have big, cauliflower ears, a souvenir of his many years spent at the bottom of a rugby ruck. He's as well known for his sporting prowess as for his fiery, explosive temper. He's quick to anger and, when ignited, the redness stretches across his furrowed brow to the very tips of his ears. But while Nigel's fury is notorious, he is equally well known amongst his circle for his good humour and deep loyalty.

What has always struck me about Nigel McGurk is the fact that he doesn't come from the dangerous, crime-ridden streets of the Cape Flats. He didn't grow up with an alcoholic father in a working-class suburb not knowing where his next meal was coming from. He comes from a well-to-do middle-class suburb in Northern Johannesburg. He went to an exclusive all-boys' school that produces captains of industry and leaders of men. His parents weren't poor. Yet, despite his upbringing and background, he achieved notoriety for all the wrong reasons.

'I came from a very good home. I didn't have a bad upbringing. My mom was a nurse and my dad had his own printing business. Coming from the north, my dad and my mom gave me what they could and everything like that. They supported me always through everything, even when I was bad and naughty. They always supported me and they were always there for me,' he tells me in his husky voice.

Nigel proudly lists all of his rugby achievements upfront. It's as though he wants to ensure that I understand they define him and that at one stage in his life, he was famous for the right reasons. 'I went to school at KES [King Edward VII School] and I made Craven Week for two years where I played with James Dalton and everyone. I played centre. I wasn't too quick. I should have actually played flank. I was stronger. I was a good ball carrier.' His body is still muscular and I can quite easily visualise him on the edge of a scrum, where he should have played, with a white band strapped around his ears.

Nigel spent a year at Sandown High School in Sandton, repeating matric, as KES wouldn't allow him to redo his final year as they said he only wanted to stay behind to play rugby. He insists he only wanted to better his marks. Once he'd finished school, he began playing rugby for Wits

University, although he didn't actually study there. 'I just played for their club. Then I made Transvaal under 20s and I played there for two seasons and then from there I left Wits and I went to Roodepoort Rugby Club where Calla Botha and Ferdi Barnard played,' he says, referring to the infamous security branch policemen who crossed over to the other side of the law. 'People feared to play Roodepoort,' he says unsurprisingly. 'We had a very good team and being an English guy, a *Soutie*, you know, the Afrikaners didn't like it. But I managed to click in there. I played with very good players and then I played seven games for Transvaal.' Nigel played at senior provincial level and for Die Rooibokke, which was the province's B team. It was at the end of his rugby career, when the game was just starting to turn professional, that his life took a swerve in another direction.

'When it became professional, everyone started getting contracts and I didn't get a contract. I started going out and going to the clubs and basically rugby stopped there and then I started meeting my friends.'

With his large build, Nigel was perfectly suited to the role of doorman. He began bouncing at nightspots around the city. 'I started to work in the clubs. There was a club in town called ESP. It was sort of a rave club that everyone went to and I actually started working there bouncing. I knew of Mikey and then I met him properly there at ESP.' Nigel reminisces fondly about those days, when there was order in the industry. 'We looked up to people like Rocky, Lionel Hunter, guys like that, Mitsi. When we walked into a club, we stood at attention. You respected, you knew not to have a fight in that club. You knew you came here and you must have a good time. These days there's none of that. The whole structure's changed. And certain people had certain areas. Especially in those days, if you had these clubs and you worked for that boss, you worked these clubs and everything. Everyone knew where to fit in.'

He admits his involvement in drugs and how lucrative the industry was. 'Drugs were there all the time. We were involved with it. I'm not involved with it whatsoever any more, but at that time we were involved in it. You must remember at that stage all the raves had just hit South Africa in a big way. Everyone was at raves, everyone was taking Ecstasy in the nightclubs and at that time there was plenty nightclubs. Not the one or two that you can go to and everything like that. It was a huge market. We were controlling the clubs so we could control who's allowed to work there and who's allowed to deal there and who wasn't. That was our job.'

Mikey

My boetie, Donny, shot himself in the head on the sixth of September 1999. That fucked me up badly. I was like a loose cannon before that, but after that, I like really had nothing to live for and I just became like a mad thing, hey. He had a bad temper and he got into an argument with his ex-wife in the car. I think he gave her a smack or something like that and he pulled his gun on her. She got out the car and he turned the gun on himself. But it wasn't like a planned thing. He just had a fucking violent temper and he turned the gun on himself. He shot himself. When he died, the bitch didn't phone us, didn't tell us that he had shot himself. At the time, I wasn't speaking to my boetie because of her and I was very close to him. I went mad, hey. I fucking collapsed. I walked outside. I punched all the windows out of my fucking car and then I got in the car and raced from Corlett Drive all the way through to my sister's house in the South and, on the way, I phoned my sister and I was hysterical; I couldn't speak to her. And my sister thought I said I killed my girlfriend. My sister phoned Gary and Clint, they were still living together. So when I stopped there outside the house, Gary and Clint were there and they could control me. They took me, put me back in the car and took me to Mulbarton to go and get some injections to calm me down. Clint had known the doctor; he organised the injections. When we got to the hospital, I walked in and I saw the fucking bitch. Before we got there, she let them turn off the machines. I fucking went mad and I was going to shoot her and I said, 'I'm going to fucking kill yous now.' They fucking hit me with like twenty Valiums and shit. They put me in the car, drove me around Jo'burg three times and they managed to talk me out of it.

AT THE TURN OF THE MILLENNIUM, MIKEY WAS STILL REELING
from his brother's suicide. He was out clubbing more and more and
getting heavily involved in drugs and trouble. The landscape of the bouncing industry in Johannesburg was also changing. One of the most prominent crews, Viper, had split into two, spawning Omega. The established
groups were struggling to keep their hold over clubs and weren't paying
employees for shifts. As a result, they were increasingly relying on backup,
in the form of Mikey and his boys.

'Wherever there was shit, me, Carlo and Julio were running around
fucking fighting there. And then we decided that if we're going to be paid
to do the backup whenever there's shit, we'd just take it over and do it ourselves,' explains Mikey.

And so Elite Security Group was born. It would become the most powerful and influential crew to operate in Johannesburg and would build a
formidable reputation for violent beatings. Its reputation instilled terror
in nightclub owners and patrons alike as, week in and week out, reports of
attacks and brawls filled newspaper column space. Teenage victims would
crow about how burly bouncers had beaten them to a pulp for 'looking at
them funny' or for 'chatting up the wrong chick'. Somehow, the perpetrators would almost always manage to evade the long arm of the law. They
had friends in high places and cops on their contact lists.

The six founding members were Mikey Schultz, Carlo Binner, Julio
Bascelli, Theuns Grobler, Jacques Hugo and Ashley Ginder.

'Jacques was always around. He wasn't on the drugs. He was a good guy.
He'd come to the clubs and me and Carlo would be fucking off our faces,
laying fucked there, and Jacques would walk in and swear at us.

'Ashley was also just around. He used to bounce and that. He was also
a operator, a mover and shaker and that. And Theuns, Theuns was always
there with us, so we couldn't leave him out, hey. Freddy Fourie came in
later. He was my most loyal partner in Elite. He was always there by my
side when there was action. I call him "my loyal Dutchman".'

Nigel McGurk wasn't part of the original crew that started Elite but was
always on the periphery. He was working for clubs privately and meddled
in the drug trade. 'We were just friends and we stuck together. Mikey was
Elite and I worked at a club called The Lounge, a strip club there in town.
Basically, because of my relationship with everyone else they didn't want

to have a bouncing group there. I wasn't part of it, but with Mikey and I being friends and everything, we were always together anyway. When there was an Elite issue we were there.'

Ashley Ginder is credited with coming up with the name but there's no profound or meaningful story motivating the choice. In Mikey's version, the founding members were sitting around trying to think of a 'lekker' name and Ashley threw out Elite. He was effectively the CEO of the company, taking responsibility for running the day-to-day business while Carlo, Julio and Mikey were doing 'the backups'. If there was shit, they would go.

Mikey and Elite ended up taking control of all the clubs in Northern and Central Johannesburg. 'Elite chased all the other crews away. We were the strongest crew this country has ever seen. I promise you,' Mikey reminds me. At the same time, Mikey tells me, they were still ensuring that the Hells Angels' drugs were being pushed in the venues and claims they were receiving a cut from them. He explains that the Angels had refined the process of producing pills and were making a killing, literally.

'Red and them had brought in guys from Holland to make the stuff. They were making the stuff in Europe and it was costing them five pounds to make a pill. They were making it here in this country for five rand a pill. They brought a chemist out here, they learned how to make it and then they killed the oke and they got rid of his body. They bumped him off and got rid of his body. It's one of the okes that I've fucking been accused of killing.' Police have confirmed this is a case that is still being investigated.

But as Elite's control over clubs began to strengthen, so they became greedier. But they were always careful to keep drug peddling and bouncing separate, although it was the bouncers who enforced the terrain for the runners.

'We never wanna put the two things together because you don't want the bouncers to be caught with drugs. That's why you can go and look into my history and not one of my bouncers was ever caught with any drugs. You'd never put the two together. If you wanted to run, you ran. If you wanted to bounce, you bounced,' Mikey explains.

Mike Bolhuis is a former bouncer who found God and has spent years investigating the industry. My witty colleague Gill Gifford from *The Star* newspaper describes him as, 'A real urban cowboy with his "I'll shoot you dead, but God bless your brother" kind of attitude.' Bolhuis, with his Johnny Bravo haircut, isn't held in particularly high regard by those he investigates, with more than one of his subjects saying to me, 'How can you believe a guy with hair like that?' Some of his theories may be based in fiction, but he does know his subject. He is scathing about Elite and its operations.

'They sorted all their problems out either by violence, threats, intimidation, or by their connections. Thousands of people could have made cases against them but they had a name and reputation. So no one ever made a case against them, nothing happened. They would get intimidated in such a way that they drop and leave the cases,' he tells me.

At the height of Elite's reign, Bolhuis was interviewed by *The Star* about the depths and extent of the bouncer problem:

'These are the guys who go out and kneecap people who owe drug lords money, or get roped into turf wars between competing tow-truck operators. They are the feet and arms for all the dirty work that needs doing. The press makes a hoo-ha about all this steroid-induced violence at clubs, but it goes way beyond that. These guys are bad, man, really bad. All sorts of people are on their payrolls – businessmen, policemen, sports celebrities, even state prosecutors. Dockets disappear like you cannot believe. And intimidation, well, that's another story' (21 November 2004).

In 2003, an 'informant', John, also told the newspaper about how Elite's operations were being run: 'Basically, they go into a club and offer to take over the security. Then they put the price up from R350 per bouncer per night to about R850. And then they put ten guys on the door when you would only need two,' he said, explaining how club owners were forced into leaving or handing over control of their establishments to Elite. 'Then Elite basically runs the place and they can do what they want and kick out who they want. They take out smaller groups that threaten them and, if you don't follow their lead, you get the hiding of your life.'

When Elite was at its pinnacle, Nigel says, 'It was like the movies. Basically we could do what we wanted. We could go into clubs, we could drink for free, we were living that fast life. You didn't have responsibilities, we were young and we didn't think. Ja, we were reckless but we had such a bond amongst our friends that if one was in trouble, we all had to be in trouble. If one needed money then we'd all help to make sure he was alright. If someone was arrested and they were in jail we'd make sure that the family and the girlfriends and everything were taken care of and looked after.' He recalls how the band of brothers was effectively running the city. 'Nature works like that,' he tells me, invoking the analogy. 'The weaker animals, they get older but they get wiser. The young blood has to come through and that's the same that happens now. At that stage we had formed such a bond and a clique that the other groups had to back down and come away with it. But it didn't come without loss and everything. We lost a few friends along the way who were killed. We lost a lot of good people.'

Kappie never became involved in Elite but the unique bond he shared with Nigel and Mikey ensured that if there was ever trouble, he would be called into the fray. 'Elite was just not my cup of tea. It wasn't my line and also I had kids. If Mikey needed help, Nigel and I, we were there. We were more loyal to each other than anyone else.'

In 2002, at the height of the reign, Nigel imploded. His mother died and he flew off the rails. 'Ja, I did. It was a time in our lives where some of our friends had been killed and then my mom passing away, you know, I was just on a self-destruct path. If there's one thing I was scared of it was my mother. That's the one person I was scared of. And then thank goodness for my friends and everything. They brought me right and everything like that.'

Nigel also admits the wrong he did and a look of acknowledgement, and possibly shame, is etched on his weathered face. 'No, we were bad,' he says, nodding his head. 'But we weren't evil, if I can say that. Everyone says we come out and we bully. Mikey had plenty fights; Mikey was never a bully. Kappie's had plenty fights and we'd never let him go down. He would never lose. But if there's 'rawling or having a fight with someone or if there was a story he would say, "It's my fight. Just make sure no one else gets involved." That's what's missing these days. There's no order.'

There is one story I am repeatedly told by various people that illustrates the reign of terror that was conducted at the time. I hear how Mikey al-legedly killed a young man named Renier Groenewald outside the New Concepts nightclub in Blackheath. The story goes that Mikey stuffed the body in the boot of his car and drove around from club to club displaying the corpse as a threat to anyone who dared challenge his power.

As I often established, the truth invariably differs from the legend.

While Mikey won't explicitly speak about the 'Renier Incident', I piece together what seems to have happened.

A rival crew was pushing drugs at a club at Northcliff Corner and got into a brawl with Mikey's bouncers. They called him to the club as backup. When he arrived there was a massive punch-up and shots were fired in a chaotic scene. Mikey was using a friend's gun which proved to be unreliable. So unreliable that he accidentally discharged the firearm and shot his own toe that night. Most of the opposing crew had moved up the road to another venue and Mikey followed despite the hole in his foot. The showdown continued to play out with more beatings and bullets ricocheting at the second venue. Renier Groenewald, who was allegedly a 'runner', was inside a car parked outside the club. The doors were locked and Renier was trying to get a gear lock out from under his seat. For some reason, Mikey banged his unreliable gun on the window to get Renier's attention and the firearm accidentally went off. A bullet struck Renier in the stomach. In a fit of panic, Mikey, Julio, Nigel and a few others bundled Renier into a car and rushed him to the Roosevelt Park Fire Station because they knew they would never get him to the Milpark Hospital in time. They couldn't save him in time and Renier died. Mikey and the others were arrested but there were no witnesses and police ballistics tests apparently found the gun was volatile. All Mikey will say about this is that it's the one incident about which he has the most remorse.

Despite what I discover about Renier's shooting, the legend persists that Mikey murdered a man and drove around from club to club proudly displaying his body.

I ask Nigel just how bad the things were that he did when he was at his worst and I find his answer incredibly poignant. It's almost a revelation for me as I battle to reconcile how 'thugs' and 'gangsters' who defied the law with reckless abandon could be so genuinely friendly and compelling. 'There's evil and there's naughty and then there's bad,' Nigel explains. 'Bad and naughty, yes. Evil, no. There's a difference. There is honour in that.'

The Elite crew's power base began to grow and they became increasingly greedy. They began to push back against the Hells Angels. Both wanted the lucrative business and its revenue all to themselves. It would start with a few skirmishes and tongue-lashings in nightclubs but would develop into a fierce and bitter battle that would ultimately end in bloodshed.

I T'S A FRIDAY NIGHT IN NOVEMBER 2002, AND JAZZ TIME CAFÉ, A popular haunt in the Glen shopping centre in Southern Johannesburg, is teeming with people warming up for a night on the town. It's a sensible venue for a potentially volatile meeting between two trigger-happy men with everything to lose. There have already been two previous meetings between the two at the same venue which were largely incident free. This time, however, something is stirring inside the men and there is a sense the outcome may be different.

Mikey, his peroxide-blond hair crew cut, is sitting at a table inside the buzzing restaurant. He has brought Nigel as backup. Both of them are packing.

On the two previous occasions Mikey had met with Red, the Hells Angels international hit man on the run from Interpol, he had made sure he had security in place. He had called up policeman Wayne Kukard, who specialised in probing organised crime in the city, and had asked him to wait outside the restaurant. Kukard had done so as he wanted to build intel on the Hells Angels. All he managed to gather was pictures of a fleet of vehicles without number plates. Mikey had also recruited Kappie to come along and sit at a table in the restaurant with a few friends. He had a mean reputation and his friends were even meaner. But on the night in question, Kappie couldn't make it and Kukard was running late.

Red was a 'black and white', one of the Hells Angels' 'Filthy Few'. This meant he had killed for the club and was supposedly the man the club turned to when they needed another job done. Word was he was wanted for as many as nine murders in Europe. Red had been calling Mikey incessantly because he needed to 'sort out' tensions between Elite and the Hells Angels.

A few weeks previously, Mikey, Nigel and a crew of their cronies had beaten several members of the motorcycle gang to a pulp at Papillon, a strip club in the city. The man who took the brunt of the beating was Peter Conway, the leader of the Hells Angels. A lower-ranking Angel, 'Guy', had also been targeted. According to a member of Elite at the time, the incident had been sparked when Conway told Nigel he'd 'cut his tongue out'.

Elite had won that round, leaving Conway, Guy and the other Angels stabbed and bleeding on Papillon's floor. Mikey knew the Angels would want revenge and Red would be the man selected to hand it out. Relations between the two crews had deteriorated as they both fought for power and they were on the brink of all-out war.

The truth of what happened at Jazz Time Café at The Glen on that night in November 2002 has been eroded through deliberate attempts to manipulate the definitive version. It all depends on who you speak to and what their particular agenda is. Mikey, Nigel and Kappie won't talk to me about the incident as there is still an outstanding investigation into the matter. Renowned detective Piet Byleveld, who retired from the police service in 2010 as something of a local celebrity as a result of his prowess, was tasked with probing the case in 2007, along with several unsolved crimes involving Mikey and other bouncers. The reconstruction of the murky events of that night has come from pieces of information gleaned from sources, investigators and people in the know. These are two of the versions.

VERSION ONE:
Red walks into the restaurant and takes a seat at the table across from Mikey and Nigel while Guy waits at the door to the restaurant. There are greetings and small talk. Within seconds of his sitting down, Red reaches for his holster and pulls out his gun. Mikey, with the instinct and reflexes of a prize boxer, grabs the table and throws his full force against it, sending Red off balance. The customers in the restaurant swivel their heads in horror and hear a scream of, 'What the fuck do you think you're doing?' They then see the peroxide-haired bouncer pull out his weapon, aim it at the fallen Angel and pull the trigger. In an instant, the bouncer's friend is also reaching for his gun. The customers jump from their seats and rush from the restaurant, hysterical.

Mikey's shot hits Red in the chest while Nigel's hits him in the head.

Kukard arrives on the scene within minutes and handcuffs Mikey and Nigel. As they sit cuffed on the floor in Jazz Time, staring at the coagulating blood that has seeped from Red's body, they order a tray of 'Suitcases' and proceed to obliterate themselves with Jack Daniel's and passion fruit.

VERSION TWO:
Red and Guy walk into the restaurant and take a seat across from Mikey and Nigel. The two bouncers had deliberately chosen to sit at that particular table because strapped to the underside of the tabletop is an unlicensed

firearm. Without a flicker of hesitation, Mikey pulls out his own gun and shoots the Hells Angels hit man in cold blood. Red's sidekick Guy looks on in horror before fleeing the restaurant in a stampede of hysterical patrons.

Mikey pulls the unlicensed gun off from under the table and plants it on Red to back up his 'self-defence' argument. Kukard arrives on the scene within minutes and handcuffs Mikey and Nigel, but he's in on the gig so it's a given that the two men will walk free. The two are taken to Booysens Police Station but charges are dropped the following day.

I meet with Byleveld to ask him about this curious case and we discuss it at length as he nurses a cold pint of beer. It's he who tells me that the firearm was strapped under the table and planted on Red. 'When I took over the investigation, a lot of the investigation was done but there were a lot of loopholes as well. When I interviewed people, they changed their versions. My biggest concern was the firearm. The firearm was definitely planted under the table. Mikey and Nigel went to sit at a specific table where the meeting took place, and they claim the guy pulled out the gun and that's a load of crap.' Byleveld wears a snarl on his face when he spits out Mikey's name. He tells me that Guy observed the entire incident, but due to the Hells Angels' creed of not cooperating with the police, he won't be a witness and has changed his version of what happened that night.

The experienced investigator shocks me with another of his theories. He doesn't believe the Mikey vs Red shootout was just an Elite vs Hells Angels squabble. He suggests that Peter Conway hired Mikey to take out Red because he wanted to consolidate his hold on the club and Red was gathering too much power. 'The whole idea was to take out Red. Red was brought out from the Netherlands to sort some people out here. There was also a clash between Red and Peter Conway because Conway wants to control the Hells Angels in Johannesburg. He was deeply involved in drug-related things as well,' Byleveld explains. When I asked Conway via SMS about this incident, his response was enigmatic: '*Piet has never had a conviction on any of the Elite C C members, or much knowledge of anything. Are you sure that you are ready to publish? My darling you seem very eager to be the first to publish conjecture, why not try for the truth?*' Conway did not take up my offer for him to put his version of events forward.

Byleveld is suspicious of the police's handling of the crime scene.

'There's a bit of things on the crime scene by certain policemen which I'm not pleased with but I can't say for definite police were complicit. I can't prove it.'

Although he's now retired, Byleveld would still like to see Mikey and Nigel prosecuted for this crime. 'I think we're going to hold a formal inquest in open court, then they must come and testify. No ways; it's not too late. It can happen any time. There is some other witnesses, but yus, let's see what's coming out. It's going to be tough, Mandy, definitely, but I think it was solved. We know who they were. I'd love to have seen them prosecuted.'

In accordance with Hells Angels custom, there is apparently still a hit out for Mikey in retaliation for Red's murder. He's nonchalant about it and isn't constantly looking over his shoulder, waiting for a hit man in black and white leathers and HA colours to come and kill him.

THE GRAINY CCTV FOOTAGE SHOWS A MAN SPRINTING THROUGH the booms of the office park in Kyalami, running for his life. Close behind him is an assailant, tearing through the checkpoint seconds later. Behind him follow three more men. Two of them run into the parking lot, out of eyeshot. A third stays behind and chats to the security guards. It appears as though he's trying to distract them from what is going on just a few metres away. Moments later he also disappears out of view, walking inside the parking lot to join the others. Then, after just a few minutes, four men can be seen running out the building. Patrick Caetano is left behind, bleeding out on the parking lot floor.

Caetano, a doorman at a Boksburg nightclub, was bludgeoned to death with a butcher's knife in December 2002 in an apparent revenge attack. He had been chased into the parking lot of the Kyalami Estate Business Park after being accosted by four men at the Blueberry Grill in Midrand. Amongst the four was Guil Yahav, a well-known bouncing figure who was easily recognisable by his one glass eye. The glass eye was Caetano's fault. He'd damaged the eye during a brawl a few years previously. Guil Yahav wanted Caetano to pay for the damage he'd done, in more ways than one. He'd met with Caetano and told him to pay him R100 000 or face a hit. The doorman, who allegedly had a crack habit, couldn't raise the cash.

Yahav rallied his troops, including Jonathan Street, a brute of a man with big muscles and a collection of tattoos. He was bouncing for Elite at the time. They confronted Caetano at the Blueberry Grill and chased him into the parking lot across the road where he was assaulted and later died. They fled the country and security guards found Caetano's bloodied body.

Nigel McGurk was arrested later that night. He allegedly had with him a togbag filled with bloodied clothes and was believed to be the 'clean-up man' for the murder, but was not in any way involved in the actual crime. He was charged with defeating the ends of justice. It was just a month after Red was shot at The Glen and another brush with the law was the very last thing Nigel would have wanted. Police also questioned Big Brother reality TV star Bradford 'Bad Brad' Wood about the murder as he was a close friend of Yahav's.

At the time of the killing, Elite founder Ashley Ginder went on investigative journalism TV show *Carte Blanche* and insisted that Elite bouncers were 'good guys'. 'At the end of the day, our clubs are running smoothly.

We have incidents here and there. People are drinking all the time. We do have assaults here and there where a bouncer has gone out of control. We discipline them. We send them to the cop shop, they do their statements and everything is in order,' he told interviewer Tim Modise.

Nigel speaks to me about that dark December in 2002 when Patrick Caetano was murdered. He tells me how Yahav phoned him for backup on the night and he didn't take his call, but after the attack on Caetano, Yahav went straight to Nigel's house. 'He said this is what he's done, he thinks the oke is dead. We phoned someone that is a medic to find out. He said no, the guy's dead. Guil and Jonathan wanted to stay at my house and I said, "You guys can't stay at my house, I've got all of this stories with Red and all of that."' Nigel convinced them to get hold of a lawyer and go to a hotel.

The following day, Nigel went to pick up Yahav and Street from their hotel near the Wanderers to take them to see a lawyer. Nigel left the two at the lawyer's office on Anderson Street and headed back to the hotel to collect Yahav's Filofax and wallet. He'd need cash if he was going to get bail. As he was opening Yahav's boot, the police swooped.

'The next minute cops started coming out everywhere and then, I'll never forget that cop's name. It was Captain Fouché. And another coloured guy came up there and they said, "You're under arrest." They said this car's been involved in a murder. They even said they know that Guil and Jonathan were at the lawyers.'

The police found a bag in the boot of Guil's car, which Nigel insists he never had in his possession. 'They grabbed that bag and there was the stuff to do crack in and that. And that must have been from Patrick. I didn't know if it was Guil's bag or if it was Patrick's bag and they arrested me. They said there was bloody clothes but I don't know if it was Guil's jeans or whatever but I never saw it.'

The cops forced Nigel to drive to the lawyer's office in the CBD and ignore Yahav's repeated phone calls. By the time they reached the office, Yahav and Street had fled. 'Guil knew something was up so they had made a move.' Nigel was held in the cells at the Sandton Police Station, fighting for days to secure bail. Charges were ultimately withdrawn.

Both Yahav and Street left the country, with the latter joining the French Foreign Legion. Yahav turned state witness against Street thinking that he would never actually have to testify against his friend who was in France.

He pleaded guilty to assaulting Caetano and was fined R10 000. However, Street was kicked out of the army and had to return to South Africa. He was initially convicted on a charge of murder in the Johannesburg Magistrates Court. On appeal, the conviction was overturned and replaced with a charge of common assault and a fine of R6 000. The judge found that it was more likely that Yahav had murdered Caetano, but he couldn't be tried for the killing as he'd cut a deal with the state.

Effectively, no one was ever forced to pay for Caetano's murder as they manipulated the law in a double-jeopardy-style tactic and Caetano's family never truly saw justice being done. Street is still in jail though. In 2006, on the very night before he was first convicted for Caetano's murder, Street opened fire in a strip club in Edenvale, killing eighteen-year-old art student Kyle Norris with a bullet to the back of the head. Three other people were wounded. Street is still serving time for that crime.

Patrick Caetano's mother, Sandy, is the face of the victims of the brutal and lawless reign of violence unleashed by drug-fuelled bouncers and still bears the emotional scars of her son's horrendous murder. She tells me that she saw the post-mortem photographs, which she describes as 'horrific', and says that her son 'put up one hell of a fight'. She believes 'those bouncers were on steroids to make them big and strong'. Sandy is adamant that there has been a major miscarriage of justice in this case and I'm astonished when she tells me about a visit she received from the investigating officer. 'He came to our house on Christmas Day to apologise for not having the guts to pursue the case any further.' According to Sandy, 'He and his family were threatened. He claimed documents and files went missing all the time and I would like to tell you that, had I not been at a particular hearing, the case would have been thrown out of court.'

Patrick Caetano's violent murder is just one of a litany of crimes involving dubious characters associated with the bouncing business that have gone unsolved. Incredibly, the perpetrators always manage to evade conviction and live to walk the streets for another day.

Mikey

Caetano. That was just a personal vendetta between Guil Yahav and Caetano. Caetano was like a fucking hobo. He was a rock addict. Guil got on top of him with a knife and cut his face. Said, 'You fucking marked me for life, motherfucker, I'm going to mark you,' and cut him in the face. As he got off him, that wannabe fucking Jonathan Street, fucking idiot, grabbed the knife from Guil. Guil tried to stop him and he was like, 'I'll fucking kill you' and hit him and he stabbed him through the side. He was always a wannabe. I punched him one night outside one club. He's a wannabe. He's on the juice. Street stuck him through the side and pulled the knife out. Then Caetano died. No cameras had seen it happen. I phone Guil and he was so fucked. He was just like, 'Hey Goosey. Fucking, we done it.' So I say, 'Guil, you a fucking big deal now, hey? Tomorrow morning when you wake up and you're not fucking drunk and that,' I said, 'you know you going to jail for a long time.' He said to me, 'Ja, but Mike, I didn't do anything. I cut the oke in the face and that. I tried to stop Jonathan.' Nigel wasn't the clean-up guy. Nigel sat New Year's in jail because of that cunt. I promise you.

IN THE LATE 1990S, REPRESENTATIVES OF THE ISRAELI MAFIA'S notorious Ramat Amidar gang had infiltrated Johannesburg and were plying their trade in the shadows of the city, with the mostly Jewish suburb of Norwood emerging as their stronghold. During the apartheid era, the Israeli government had a covert partnership with the South African Defence Force and, if you overheard the guttural spitting of Hebrew on a Norwood pavement, it was more than likely that the subject in question had previously been 'working with the air force' or 'in diamonds' – a euphemism for dodgy illegal gem trading. Israelis smoking hookahs and playing backgammon at cafés on Grant Avenue were ubiquitous at the time. It also wasn't uncommon to witness a panel van screeching to a stop outside one of these restaurants with burly men wearing black T-shirts getting out and bundling a patron into the back of the vehicle before screaming off.

I lived on Grant Avenue around that time and clearly recall witnessing exactly such an incident, and trying to not think too much of it. As a relatively naive student, I didn't realise the implications of such an event but, over time, as I discovered more about the workings of Elite and the dynamics of their business, I became fascinated by how South Africa's own Mafia-type operations collaborated with the Israeli representation. The two were intimately involved, feeding each other deals and sharing staff and clients. Inevitably, the partnership would be severed as bodies piled up.

The Ramat Amidar gang was reportedly created by Yossi Harari, a reputed mob 'godfather' from Israel. Shai Avissar and Lior Saadt, who was originally from Georgia, arrived in Johannesburg in the 1990s along with a team of two dozen or so henchmen, including a dangerous former soldier by the name of Amir Moila, aka David Mulner, who was wanted in his homeland on charges of murder and bombing. Mulner, the son of a police officer, was a discharged combat soldier and knew about explosives. According to Israel's *Haaretz* newspaper, he's attributed with planting small but lethal explosive charges in seat headrests and under the vehicles of known crime bosses who were assassinated.

The men set up shop in Norwood.

Avissar had met wealthy socialite Hazel Crane and married her following a stormy love affair. The two took up residence in a wealthy Johannesburg suburb. Hazel became a regular on the social circuit and frequently appeared in the celebrity pages of the city's newspapers. She and Avissar became close to former first lady Winnie Madikizela-Mandela and even accompanied her as she appeared before the Truth and Reconciliation Commission's hearings. Avissar reportedly bought her the dress she wore to her husband Nelson Mandela's inauguration as President in 1994. But Avissar had an affair and he and Hazel separated, although they remained firm friends.

In 1998, the 'godfather' of the Mafia, Harari, came to inspect the business. When he left town, he appointed Avissar as his boss in South Africa. He was a surprising choice as he didn't have the violent reputation which Saadt and Moila advanced. It's suspected it was for this very reason that Harari put Avissar in control of the business arm of the gang in order to lend it legitimacy. At the time, Moila (aka Mulner) was tasked with the dirty dealings of the mob. Shortly after Harari returned to Israel, he was arrested and sentenced to five years in prison for the murder of gangland boss 'Rabbi' Simon Hadif. Mulner was also incriminated in that killing.

Two policemen, Wayne Kukard and John Kruger, began investigating the criminal involvement of Israelis in the country. Both Kukard and Kruger had been stationed at the infamous Brixton Serious and Violent Crimes Unit and Kukard had also served on popular policeman Bushie Engelbrecht's special investigations team. They spent years infiltrating the Israeli Mafia. Kruger, a hard man who does not suffer fools gladly, is no longer a cop. He now owns a boxing gym in Edenvale where Mikey Schultz trains. He says he doesn't believe there was ever really an 'Israeli Mafia' in South Africa. Instead, he tells me it was just a group of criminal Israelis extorting businessmen from their own community and they used Lior Saadt as an enforcer.

Mikey and his crew started working with this so-called Israeli Mafia, doing jobs for them. 'We were just moving with Lior. He was getting work for us and all sorts of stuff and we'd go and sit at the dam and have lunches. He was always talking Hebrew and at the end of the day we'd all get like two, three hundred US dollars and shit like that from Shai. We'd always make some money like that.

'Lior was always doing something. We done a lot of things with Lior. He apparently shot an oke in the knees 'cause the oke owed money and that, hey. He was a ruthless fuck. He didn't feel nothing.

'There was also this guy that came from Israel. We knew him as David Mulner. He was wanted by Interpol and he was actually a terrorist. He had blown up fucking judges and shit in Israel. He was like the real deal. He was some explosives expert in the army in Israel,' Mikey recalls.

Kappie never meddled with the Israelis despite being approached on several occasions. He can even speak a few words of Hebrew and caught me off guard once as he rattled off a greeting fluently. Kappie tells me he knew that was trouble he didn't want to touch. 'I was offered the opportunity at the time but I never got involved there. I met Lior before anybody else. It was actually a friend of mine, Mottie, that brought Lior here to South Africa, who he killed eventually. The vibe at the time was very different. I was working at the panel shop. He used to come there every day and say, "Come with me to do some work," and it wasn't *mooi* you know. And I said, "No, no." Sometimes you can sense something. You can pick it up very quickly. And I just stayed away. Otherwise I'd have been dead today.'

I tell him that, to be honest, with his track record, I am quite surprised he isn't dead today.

Meanwhile, Saadt wasn't happy with the way Harari had structured the South African branch of his organisation. He didn't like the idea of his boss, Shai Avissar, being so closely aligned to Madikizela-Mandela. He thought him to be too soft and was furious at the amount of money being channelled back to Harari in Israel. He wanted control of the gang for himself.

On 8 October 1999, Avissar was seen getting into a friend's car outside a restaurant in Norwood. It's thought he was dropped off a few blocks away but he was never seen again. At around 14:00 on that day, his cellphone was switched off. At 1.8 metres tall and weighing 98 kg, his disappearance in full public view would not easily have gone unnoticed.

Despite the couple having been divorced two years earlier, Hazel went into overdrive searching for her former husband. She placed photographs of Avissar in coffee-shop windows, infuriating Saadt. She implored the police to open a case and came clean about his illicit deals. At the time, she stated that her ex-husband had a number of influential people on his payroll, including police officers. The mobster's picture was circulated around Interpol and border checks were done. Police chased up a tip-off that his body had been dumped in a dam in Melrose but sniffer dogs found nothing. Hazel was warned she too was on a hit list but she pursued the apparent abduction relentlessly. Madikizela-Mandela weighed in and used her pull. She phoned the cop in charge of the investigation to apply pressure and is even said to have told her 'people' to search for Avissar in the city's townships.

Three months later, in January 2000, Avissar's decomposing body was found in a shallow grave on a smallholding near Erasmia. Coincidentally, the corpse was buried at the entrance to former apartheid-era death camp Vlakplaas. Avissar had apparently been bludgeoned to death with a bat in a house in Sunninghill before being dumped.

Around that time, Mikey explains, Saadt began to fall out with his close friend and founding Elite member Julio. Julio had allegedly witnessed him killing Jo'burg's 'biggest bouncer', Milton Resnik, who weighed in at 230 kg and was 1.9 metres tall. 'Julio was actually witness to Lior killing "Fat Milton" in Julio's tow-truck. Milton used to run with the bouncers in the old days there in Hillbrow. He was just some fat pig that used to run around from club to club. Lior shot him in the back. So they had a fallout. That's how Lior used to work. He'd bring someone in and then get rid of the next oke, and bring someone in and get rid of the next ou so that nobody had too much on him.' Lior Saadt has not answered to any of these allegations against him.

Mikey says Julio began to squeal to the police, spilling details to Wayne Kukard. It's a difficult topic for Mikey to talk about, but he begrudgingly recalls: 'He said to Kukard, "I'll give you what you want. You want Lior, you want Shai, you want Milton's body? I'll go give you Milton's body. I tell you we can help you with this."'

Julio turned state witness against Lior Saadt for Milton's murder. His body was dug out of a shallow grave in City Deep. But what Kukard was really after was a conviction for Avissar's gruesome death. Julio agreed to try and get his good mate Carlo to come clean about Avissar's murder. As Mikey reveals, Carlo was with Saadt when Avissar was beaten. 'They hit him with the baseball bat. Carlo told me once that when Lior hit Shai with the bat, Shai said to him, "Please stop, you're hurting me. Please take me to a doctor." And he klapped him. Hit him dead.'

Kruger, who investigated the case, tells me how he was led to Avissar's burial site. Carlo knew that he had to speak about the incident but wasn't willing to squeal himself. So one Saturday night, he took Elite co-founder Jacques Hugo to the plot near Erasmia and pointed out where Avissar had been buried. Hugo, in turn, told Kruger. Carlo turned state witness against Saadt and Hugo received a R200 000 informer fee which Hazel Crane had sponsored. Hugo split it with his colleagues and Carlo received a cut. This effectively meant he received indemnity and a payout for bludgeoning a man to death with a baseball bat. Ultimately, he would pay with his life.

With the police hot on his trail, Saadt fled the country.

Mikey

Lior got on a plane and left the country. Then he came back through Mozambique and he killed Carlo and he killed Julio. If I see Lior now, it would be him or me. If it ever came down to the two of us, between him or me, I'll kill him. I swear on my life, I'll kill him, hey. I'll strangle him 'til he's dead.

WHEN MIKEY, NIGEL AND KAPPIE REMINISCE ABOUT CARLO AND Julio their emotions vacillate from deep sorrow to light-hearted and animated as they banter about their antics during the heady days when they all believed they were immortal.

'If Carlo was still around today we would all be dead or in jail,' Kappie tells me, a rare look of fright on his face. 'Because he didn't give a shit, he'd shoot each one of the witnesses. He was a good guy, he had a good heart and everything, but just ...' Nigel interrupts to finish off Kappie's sentence. 'He got involved with the Israeli Mafia. And that's in a different league. He did things and he got himself into some serious trouble and to get out of it was a serious problem. It was a completely different ballgame.'

The first attempt on Carlo's life was outside Bourbon Street in October 2000. Mikey recalls the night vividly. 'This car drove past twice and then a "Floppy" got out the car and walked up to Carlo like this and he shot Carlo. He shot him through the arm, shot him through the leg, shot him through the stomach.' One bullet missed Carlo and hit Julio's sister. She was a South African rower and it was her first ever visit to a nightclub. Carlo managed to get his gun out and shoot back at his attacker. Mikey laughs hard as he recalls how, despite her gunshot wound, Julio's sister refused to get in his car because he drove so badly. 'You'd never see a better driver on the road, but a fucking mad thing. That oke was phenomenal. Phenomenal, phenomenal, phenomenal. Kappie can drive, but that oke was the boss.'

Mikey suspects that Saadt was behind the shooting but he cannot be sure. 'We'd also done a lot of bad things to a lot of people and that. We never knew, really, to be honest. But it was Lior. It eventually came out.' Nigel and Kappie also aren't absolutely convinced the Israeli was behind the attempt and echo Mikey's sentiment. 'We had done so many things and we had enemies with quite a few people that you can't be 100 per cent sure where it was coming from. It could have been from someone that he just had given a hiding to or had beaten up in a club and someone got someone to come in and sort him out. We'll never be 100 per cent sure,' Nigel tells me.

Having survived an attempt on his life, Carlo became invincible. 'The bastard Carlo made it, hey, and after that he became like bulletproof,' says Mikey. The trio giggle as they reminisce about Carlo's crazy antics. One incident was particularly incredible, Kappie tells me. He had walked out of a club with a drink in his hand when a group of cops from the flying squad threatened to arrest him for drinking on a pavement. Mikey recalls what happened next. 'Carlo walks out there, he pulls out his gun and cocks it and puts it against the cop's head like this [he gestures], in uniform. That's how Carlo was. He felt fuck all. Carlo would feel nothing to shoot anyone. He cocks his gun and puts it against the oke's head like this and says, "Fucking leave him." Then the other oke points him with a R5 and he points back. He feels fuck all, hey.' I am intrigued that this trio of characters, whose own antics have spawned embellished tales of legend, find such amusement at their friend's mad courage.

They tell me another story, which I find equally amazing and alarming. It involves a burly Zulu taxi driver, a unit of police officers and crazy Carlo. Mikey talks excitedly as he fills me in. 'This fucker turns into us and we nearly ride into him. So I jumped out the car, I punch the oke through the window and I pull his car keys out. He's a big Zulu boy. He hits my eye open, we having a full-on 'rawl. Carlo thinks he's WWE. He runs in and he *goois* like this on the ou's bonnet to the maximum. Nearly breaks his elbow. We don't check there's a whole lot of uniform cops across the road and they run up to stop the fight. What does Carlo do? Pulls his gun. Fucking five uniform cops and he pulls out his gun and points it at them.'

The story is beginning to sound like something out of a far-fetched Hollywood movie but it's not. It's set in End Street in Johannesburg and features an invincible bouncer.

As Mikey goes on, the account becomes even more surreal. 'So as he points, they all pointing him so I'm like, ah fuck. This is all we need. Carlo's swearing at them and they all pointing. Julio's in the driver's seat, I get in the back. Carlo walks and gets in the front. They tune us, "Pull over here! Pull over here!" And the next thing, the one comes there and opens the door like this and he says to Carlo get out. Carlo swears at him, you know, "Fuck you, kaffir!" whatever like that. As he says that, Julio revs that car and drops the clutch of that M3. We go out there sideways. It wasn't good enough that we running away from the cops all armed, pointing guns at us. Carlo leans out that window like this and tunes, "Here, catch this," and he starts shooting, "Bah! Bah! Bah!" Let's them have it, hey. Carlo, he was a fucking lunatic. He felt absolutely fuck all.'

I never met Carlo, but the more I hear about him the more he strikes me as exactly the type of lunatic who gave Elite and the general bouncer brigade a bad name. Nigel assures me that was not the case. 'He could go to the max. But he wasn't evil. You know he could walk into anyone's house and if there was a kid there the kid will go straight to Carlo without a doubt. He just had that ... if it was a dog, the dog would go straight to Carlo. He was a great guy and if you needed help, that guy would be there.' Again, I am struck by the intense loyalty which these men share and, clearly, Carlo was a part of that.

After the attempt on Carlo's life, they all had their guards up. Julio, who was talking to the police about Saadt's crimes, had become paranoid and there were very few people he trusted, with good reason. On 25 November 2000, Julio was lured to a petrol station near the Modderfontein off-ramp in Eastern Johannesburg and was shot and killed in his car. It's not a topic Mikey speaks about easily. 'Somebody was with him in the car because the cops pulled him over earlier and there was another person with him there in the car. Whoever was with him in the car shot him. They shot him three times in the head.' It's a difficult topic for Mikey to discuss, not only because his friend was killed, but also because he suspects another of his close friends of doing the killing. In this circle, that is inexcusable. A breach of the most valued trait they possess, loyalty.

Mikey believes either Lior or Carlo was responsible. 'It's a very sad thing for me to say this, but I think somehow Lior got Carlo involved in killing Julio. I don't want to believe it, but if you look at all the circumstances, I think Carlo could have been involved. Somebody punched him through the window. I believe that Lior went through the window. Julio died with his gun in between his legs. And his eyes, when I went to go and see his body the next day, his eyes were still looking to the right-hand side. Somebody pushed the gun into the back of his head and klapped in the first shot. The first shot came in at the top of his head. And then they shot him twice through the ear and right next to the ear, dead.'

After Julio's death, Carlo knew his time was up. He was pushing it to the edge. 'I think he felt that he was invincible. I think he definitely felt that. But I had conversations with him before his death and everything and he knew it was coming,' Kappie tells me. 'I spent the weekend before they shot him, with him in Cape Town. I went to Cape Town and he called me and said, "Where you?" I looked the next morning and he was there. He was sitting on the beach with his big gold chain, two guns and his stokies. He used to wear green stokies,' he tells me with a laugh and the image of a gangster wearing slippers on the beach plays out in my head. 'When we came back from Cape Town we went back the Friday, the Saturday they shot him.'

Carlo was shot outside the Gecko Lounge club on 1 April 2001, just four months after Julio was murdered. Mikey still carries the heavy weight of Carlo's death in his heart and his memory of the night his close friend was killed is remarkable. He recalls exact details about what he was wearing as he relives the experience.

'Me and Kappie were supposed to be with Carlo, but we had been to Gecko Lounge the night before and some oke came there with this MDMA and we got fucking shit-faced. It was pure, pure stuff and we were chowing this, me and Kappie, and the next day I ended up at my ex-chick's place. I needed a lift home and Carlo fetched me. He took me to his place. I still had the clothes from the night before. I put on my jeans and he gave me a vest and he dropped me off. He said to me, "Ok, I'll see you later." We were supposed to go on a jol that Saturday night. He phoned me, must have been half an hour before he died. He phoned me and said, "Hey Michael, you naai. Waa's jy?" he said to me.'

Mikey was asleep when he received a phone call from a 'runner' who worked at Gecko Lounge, telling him that Carlo had been shot. He wasn't overly alarmed as, bizarrely, it was not an uncommon event.

'I jumped in the car and I rushed through there. I'm thinking, "Ag, this ou's been shot again, fucking whoopee." When I got to Olivedale Clinic they had him on the table. He'd taken two in the body and in the leg. He was laying there and his eyes were like half-open and they had that bag on him. They couldn't revive him. They chased me out and the paramedics knew me. They tuned, "Mikey, please get out of here." The paramedic came and said, "No boetie, he didn't make it, hey." I told his mom and I went in and I closed his eyes. They had tubes inside and I pulled that out. He used to have this thick, thick gold chain. I went and I took his gold chain off his neck and his bracelet and I gave it to his mom. That was the end of Carlo, hey. He was a good oke.'

Mikey, Nigel and Kappie can't say for certain who killed Carlo but they are sure that it was a professional hit. 'They knew he went to the Gecko Lounge. They knew exactly when he walked into the club because he parked his car there. They knew everything,' Nigel explains. 'It was really professional. It wasn't like us with the gun jamming. Even the grouping on him. No, they got him hey.'

I ask them the obvious question. Do they think Carlo and Julio were killed because they were going to give evidence against Israeli mobster Lior Saadt? The answer reinforces why these men had been so resistant against becoming state witnesses. 'We will never know that. And that's what you must understand. If he got a 204 for whatever he was doing, then you can understand why we never wanted this. 'Cause when people make deals, that's what happens. That's a known fact,' says Nigel sternly. Kappie nods in agreement. 'You can go overseas to each and every country. You'll die if you're yellow,' he says.

With loyalty such a valued principle amongst these men, the thought of dying in retaliation for selling out a friend is a very real possibility. 'If you live like a gangster, then you got to take the punishment like a gangster and go to jail,' says Nigel. 'That's the story. But you can't go there and make a deal. You make a deal and you can rest assured that the guy knows his days are numbered.'

Shai Avissar's lieutenant Lior Saadt was finally arrested on the Mozambican border in April 2001 for his boss's killing. He was charged with murder, attempted murder and kidnapping as well as intimidation. But two of the state witnesses against him, Julio Bascelli and Carlo Binner, had already been taken out.

A S A CHILD IN CONFLICT-STRICKEN BELFAST IN THE 1950S, HAZEL
Crane would be made by her mother to sit for hours with her
strawberry-blonde hair tied up with strips of cloth so that she could achieve
perfect springy ringlets. But now the honey-tinted strands, which she had
taken to wearing coiffed and hair-sprayed in her middle age, lie matted
against her skull, thick with blood. The stark contrast of the crimson against
her lily-white Ulster skin is jarring and the striking vision will likely live on
in the memory of the first respondents on the scene for time immemorial.

A few seconds earlier she had shouted, 'Jesus Christ!' before the car's
side window exploded. Despite her passenger's shrieks urging her to put
pressure on the vehicle's brake, the message relayed from her brain to
her foot was suspended mid-passage and the white E320 Mercedes-Benz
rolled into a lamp post before coming to a stop at the corner of First Street
and Athol Oaklands Road, one of the busiest thoroughfares in the stately
suburb of Abbotsford near Houghton. Four bullets had been pumped into
her body – one each in her face, chest, arm and leg. Two others missed
their target, with one striking her passenger's hand. Collateral.

The olive-toned shooter calmly placed his .38 Special into his sling bag,
stepped away from his hiding place behind a dustbin and strolled across
the road to a waiting getaway car, a white Mercedes-Benz – his job done.

Hazel Crane was en route to the then Johannesburg High Court in the
city's central business district to attend the trial of her former husband's
alleged killer, Israeli Mafioso Lior Saadt, when she was assassinated. She
was shot just blocks away from where Brett Kebble would be gunned down
close on two years later and, at first blush, the *modus operandi* of the two
hits appeared to be staggeringly similar.

I have always been intrigued by Hazel Crane's mob-like murder and
the mystery which has continued to shroud the crime. A wealthy, high-
society figure with impressive political ties gunned down in broad daylight in a rich suburb by a Mafia hit man. It's a sexy story for any curious
newshound.

On the morning of 10 November 2003, Hazel had waited for her long-
time friend Margaret Turner to travel from Benoni to Abbotsford so that
she could accompany her to court. She had done so twice previously,
flanking the socialite on her right, whilst her close confidante and former
first lady of the country, Winnie Madikizela-Mandela, supported her on

the left. On the ill-fated day in question, Madikizela-Mandela was making her own way to the court in Pritchard Street and Margaret was sitting in the passenger seat of Hazel's Merc.

At a few minutes after 09:00, Hazel and Margaret left the socialite's double-storey home and travelled down First Street. Several years later, Margaret would recount to *Noseweek* what happened next:

I saw this fellow standing on the corner. He had sunglasses and I thought he was wearing a yarmulke, although it could have been a baseball cap. He looked lost and I said to Hazel: 'Who's that fellow on the corner?'

Hazel said: 'Oh, those are St John's lads; they take the bus from there to St John's [the pricey Johannesburg boys' school].'

Then, as we were going to turn left, I saw this fellow's right hand go into a satchel slung over his left shoulder. That's when I saw his curly black hair. He had a green bomber jacket. I saw his white hand going into that satchel – and I saw the gun.

Before you could do anything, he shot from my side. The passenger window exploded, then it was just gunshots and gunshots and gunshots. I must have put my left hand up to protect my face. My index and middle fingers were virtually blown off.

I heard Hazel say, 'Jesus Christ!' Then it was deathly silence. I can remember coming up from somewhere; I must have been under the dash. The car was rolling slowly diagonally across the road and I saw this lamp post coming towards us. I went, 'Hazel, brake! Brake! Brake!'

We just rolled into the post. Then I looked at Hazel. Her head was back, her little hands were next to her and I could see bubbles, but no blood, coming from her mouth. I realised her lungs must have been damaged.

There was blood everywhere. She had holes everywhere: her legs, her chest. One eye was gone. She was very badly damaged and couldn't speak. I think she was brain dead already. I didn't see the killer's face. He had sunglasses on (Issue 91, May 2007).

Hazel Crane was dead. She was the third state witness in the case against Lior Saadt to be assassinated.

Mikey

Robbie, my best friend, was a tow-truck driver. He phones me and says, 'Hey boet, they just fucking shot Hazel Crane dead here on the side of the road!' I jumped in my car and I phone Wayne. He won't take my call. I phone him and I phone him. He had three numbers. I phoned all the numbers and he doesn't take my call. I phone his wife. I phoned John Kruger, Wayne's partner. I said to John, 'Fuck boet, they just shot Hazel.' So I phone Wayne's wife and I said, 'Julie please, he must get hold of me urgently.' So Wayne phones me back. He says, 'What's going on?' and I said, 'They just shot Hazel.' He says, 'Don't fucking act.' I said to him, 'Hey, they just shot Hazel, she's fucking laying on the side of the road.' He said to me, 'You tell them they must take good care of her; she's got a lot of money. She's got the best medical aid; they must take her to the best hospital.' I said, 'I'm not there yet, but I'll tell Robbie.' By the time I got there, Hazel was gone already. It's exactly one kilometre from where Brett died. There was only one police van there. They were just busy bringing out their tape to cordon off the road. I got there before Kukard and them. I can't remember where I was when I got the call. I got there and then John got there. There was no bullet shells so they were shot with a revolver. I know there was no shells because I went to go and look and John went to go and look.

T HE GEM-ADORNED, DIMINUTIVE SOCIALITE HAD ATTENDED COURT proceedings religiously, always occupying the same seat in the public gallery, glaring at Lior Saadt, the man accused of murdering her erstwhile partner. On one occasion, she was overheard in the court corridors saying she feared for her life despite hiring round-the-clock personal protection. Six months before she was killed, an attempt was made on her life. A man in an Audi aimed a firearm at her and three associates outside her house. They ducked for cover but one of her companions was shot – ironically, the man she was talking to about stepping up her security. Despite this, Hazel declined Wayne Kukard's offer of witness protection. She was to testify against Saadt and clearly she knew too much.

But someone also wanted Saadt dead. A police van ferrying him to court was ambushed by a helmeted gunman on a motorbike in Mayfair near the Johannesburg CBD. The van was sprayed with bullets and Saadt was shot in the buttocks. Two others were wounded and one person died.

As I go about attempting to piece together the events surrounding Hazel Crane's death, there are some events that are particularly intriguing. This shooting of Saadt is one of them. I had often wondered who the enigmatic 'helmeted gunman' was. I ask those who I think may know and I'm intrigued by the responses.

'Mikey was definitely involved. That was my information,' Piet Byleveld tells me. For some reason, I had always thought that the assailant was a dodgy Mossad agent rather than someone so familiar. 'Then there's stories that Kappie or John Kruger was on the bike driving him. The information, there's no proof, no evidence,' says Byleveld. Kruger denies he was in any way involved.

A lawyer who was in Saadt's circle at the time of the incident also shares illuminating information with me, although he doesn't want to be named: 'Lior was getting into the police van and he saw Wayne Kukard talking to Mikey, pointing out to him where Lior was sitting. Lior grabbed one of the other prisoners, a black guy, and forced him to swap seats with him. The black guy was shot and killed. It was Mikey who shot him and Kappie or Nigel riding the bike.'

Byleveld is also suspicious about Mikey's involvement in Hazel Crane's shooting, although he has no real evidence to back it up. 'Why did Mikey Schultz pitch up at Milpark Hospital shortly after she was admitted?'

Byleveld asks me rhetorically. 'Mikey's description doesn't fit the person who shot her but why did he pitch up at the hospital? I have evidence to that effect.' I ask the investigator how that piece of information implicates Mikey and he's vague in his response. 'You get this information, you reach a certain extent. These people are witnesses but they're also not witnesses. They're all lying. You can't trust them or their versions. I don't want them as witnesses in a court case of mine, that's for sure. They must go to jail.'

Mikey's abhorrence of Byleveld is obvious when I tell him about the investigator's suspicions. 'Mr Poesface Byleveld! I never, never had anything to do with it. I had no reason to hurt her. I had no reason to hurt Shai,' he insists.

Kruger, who investigated the case with Kukard, also responds furiously when I tell him about Byleveld's suspicions. 'Super-sleuth Byleveld. He's so fucking clever,' comments Kruger sarcastically. The ex-cop tells me Mikey was never at Milpark Hospital, but rather, former apartheid hit man and provincial rugby player Calla Botha was. Kruger is suspicious of Botha's involvement in Hazel's murder although he never had any firm evidence to link him to the case. There was talk that Hazel had sold a stolen diamond on behalf of Botha and that she had short-changed him. 'It was the perfect "eyeblind". The perfect front. He could kill her and pass it off as this Israeli story,' says Kruger. He also explains to me that while Hazel died at the scene of the shooting, Kukard arranged with Milpark Hospital to put out a statement saying she was still alive but in a critical condition. The policemen wanted to see who would show up at the hospital before they stated publicly that she was dead.

Exactly why Avissar was killed remains a mystery although Kruger says there was mention of a shoebox filled with US$30 000 at the time. Also a riddle was the role of Amir Moila, aka David Mulner, Ramit Amidar's executive for crime in South Africa. It was widely suspected that he was the man in the green bomber jacket who shot Hazel.

Not long after Hazel's death, Mulner fled South Africa to the Mexican resort of Cancun. According to *Haaretz* newspaper, he established an enclave of exiled Israeli mob figures. He was deterred from returning to Israel because of the evidence of a witness who had ensured his mob boss Yossi Harari be sent to jail. In 2004, the witness was killed while sitting in his wheelchair watching television, allowing Mulner to return to his home country. Saadt also apparently settled his affairs and returned to Israel. Mulner's name periodically pops up in Israeli media – he was stabbed in a plush hotel in 2006 and brutally attacked in a Tel Aviv restaurant that same year, all part of ongoing gangland feuds.

Mikey certainly believes Mulner was the shooter. 'Hazel was in the driver's seat and the passenger was next to her. When she stopped that David Mulner walked up to the window and klapped her like that dead. He shot her four times. He shot the passenger. At the time, at the scene, she said she saw the shooter. She was right next to the ou's fucking face. She says it was David Mulner.'

It may have been simple jealousy or mobster rivalry. At the time, it was speculated that the killing was a result of a diamond deal gone very wrong. Avissar took a man's cash but didn't hand over the stones – he hired people to kill the businessman, but the target upped the stakes and gave the hit men more money to shoot the gangster. People in the diamond industry referred to Avissar as a 'diamond thief' rather than a dealer and many even celebrated his disappearance. Another theory was that he was taken out because of a 'black dollar' scam. In her posthumously released autobiography, *Queen of Diamonds*, Hazel Crane details her ex-husband's involvement in the scam. It entails duping victims into believing that pieces of black-coated paper can be turned into original bank notes, a relic from the Vietnam War when soldiers' salaries were shipped over in this camouflaged form to ensure they weren't stolen. Victims forked over hundreds of thousands of dollars for kits, consisting of note-sized, coated pieces of ordinary paper with all sorts of necessary chemicals. They quickly established the scheme was a deception when no real bank notes appeared.

Hazel made other astonishing revelations in her autobiography, but few were about her husband's murder. Rather, they were about her own life of crime. It was already known that the regular on the celeb circuit had been convicted for dealing in unpolished diamonds, but it had happened years before she became a frequent feature in the society pages. In her autobiography she revealed how, as a Northern Irish immigrant to then Rhodesia, she turned to crime when her first husband died. She made money smuggling emeralds and diamonds, making black-market currency deals, owning a striptease joint and selling hard-core pornography. She revealed how she would smuggle emeralds by tucking them into her beehive hairdo or packing them into her son's nappies.

But what brought Hazel Crane true infamy was the sensation of her gangland-style murder in an upmarket enclave of Johannesburg, and the indelible memory for many will be the mystery that continues to shroud the killing. It was a brazen assassination in broad daylight. Sensibly, organised crime groups usually try to keep a low profile but this was high risk and threw a great big glaring spotlight on what was going on in the festering underbelly of the city.

The Mafia was at play on the streets of Johannesburg's most upmarket suburbs, capitalising on the susceptibility of the country's cops to corruption at a time when the violent crime rate was soaring. Officers were turning dirty, vendettas were being settled by bloodshed and guilty men were walking free.

AFTER HAZEL'S MURDER, WITNESSES WITHDREW IN FEAR. THERE were only two people left to testify against Saadt – one of whom was Kukard, the investigating officer who had put him in jail. But then came the *coup de grâce*. Kukard died of a heart attack after collapsing at his home. He was only 36 years old. The coroner found no sign of foul play. Kukard was heavily obese but rumours of a potential poisoning persisted with speculation that Israelis had broken into his house and switched his medication. Before his death, the investigating officer was convinced he could still achieve a conviction despite his dwindling witness list.

Throughout my investigations, I can never quite put my finger on whether Kukard really was dirty or not. He had an uneasy closeness to his suspects and Mikey talks about his relationship with him with surprising intimacy. But was that just the result of a cop who was wholeheartedly invested in building his sources and cracking his cases or was it the result of a cop who was on the take and tipping off his suspects?

John Kruger is at pains to assure me his former partner was clean. 'We were branded. It was said, "Kukard was Mikey's guardian angel". Bullshit. If you look at the cases properly, there was no funny stories. Kukard was a nice guy, but difficult. You couldn't pull the wool over his eyes.'

Byleveld also isn't convinced Kukard was corrupt. 'I used to work with him at Murder and Robbery and I thought he was an excellent policeman; later stories came forward but I don't want to believe it.' I am also never entirely certain about whether Kukard's heart attack was sinister or not. Days after Kukard's death charges against Saadt were withdrawn. Swamped by bodyguards, he was escorted out of court to a safe house and was on the first plane out of the country to Israel. He was a marked man.

Kruger was the only man left standing. Bodies were piling up and no one had been convicted – it fell to him to probe the murders of Hazel Crane, Avissar, Carlo and Julio. To date, no one has been arrested for any of these crimes and Kruger is no longer a cop. Ironically, it was Kruger who coached Mikey Schultz for the two weeks prior to his testimony in court against Glenn Agliotti and who accompanied Schultz to Courtroom 4C each day to watch the show play out.

Johannesburg magistrate slams bouncers

The Star, 17 November 2004 at 08:04 a.m.
By Jonathan Ancer and Gill Gifford

A magistrate has blasted clubs and the bouncers who work at them. 'I'm tired of steroid-induced violent crowd-control,' magistrate Deon Pool said on Tuesday.

'This is the third incident before me this year involving a Rivonia club. It's time the police were more visible. Maybe it's time to close down some of these clubs. This is ridiculous.'

Pool was speaking at the appearance in the Randburg magistrate's court of bouncer Ashley Ginder in connection with the assault on Bradley Silberman and two other Wits students outside the Tiger Tiger club at the weekend.

Ginder was provisionally charged with assault with intent to do grievous bodily harm. He was granted bail of R10 000 and will appear again on December 15.

While Ginder was in the dock, Silberman was meant to be sitting for a Maths exam – instead the 22-year-old lay in hospital, his life in the balance.

Michelle Silberman on Tuesday said her son's condition had not changed and he remained critical but stable.

'Friends and family are at the hospital to lend support. It has been a rollercoaster ride but we are praying hard. The bouncer industry has to be controlled so that this doesn't happen to another child,' she said.

Tiger Tiger has offered to pay Silberman's medical bills.

In court, Pool warned Ginder: 'If this boy (Silberman) goes any further down the road, you're looking at culpable homicide.'

Two shaven-headed bouncers wearing matching 'No Fear' T-shirts were in court to support Ginder. They said the media gave bouncers a bad name.

Ginder's lawyer, Jannie Kruger, said his client, who denied being a bouncer, was a self-employed businessman, but Kruger was not certain what business. Kruger added that Ginder was not part of the Elite Security Group, which had been contracted by Tiger Tiger to provide its security.

However, The Star has learned that Ginder is actually a shareholder of Elite.

Tiger Tiger's manager, Denis Vaden, said Ginder had never worked for them, and that as a result of the incident, the club had ended its contract with Elite.

Meanwhile, a father, who asked not to be identified, said his son had been beaten up earlier in 2004 at a Midrand club, allegedly by members of Elite. 'He is totally traumatised. At night he patrols the house with a gun.'

Mikey

Clint said I must come work for him and get away from Elite because we were very much in the eyes with all the public, with stuff like Patrick Caetano and when Ashley knocked out that Bradley Silberman at Tiger Tiger. We were just so much in the public eye. So it was something I wanted to get done as well. It was around 2004. I left Elite totally when I went over to Clint and it basically collapsed after that. I just said to them, 'Listen, take my shares in the business. I'm moving on,' you know? But I used to always stay good friends with all of them, hey. I still talk to all of them. Out of all the okes, I'm the only oke who still talks to all of them. Ashley doesn't speak to Freddy and Freddy doesn't speak to Jacques and Theuns doesn't speak to Ashley.

Clint came to me and said he'd secured this contract for me from these okes from the mines and that. It was the Kebbles and Agliotti. He said he'll give them to us, but we have to give him a kickback every month. So I said that's fine, that's 100 per cent. Then he came to me and he said, no look, he wants to do it himself. And then he decided he wanted to grow the business and that's when he asked me to come over and help him in the running of the business. I'd be his partner doing security for the Kebbles.

Ja fuck, well I got into plenty fights because of Clint. And you know, Clint was like my older brother. If he said to me, 'Can you help me collect this money?' or if he said, 'Look, I've got a problem with this guy, he's giving this oke shit and that,' then I would help him. We ended up going around breaking a few heads and stuff like that.

THE CHERUB-LIKE TODDLER STOOD ON THE STRETCH OF ROAD A few kilometres outside the backwater town of Delmas, in the then Eastern Transvaal, and stared in bewilderment at the carnage surrounding him. His mother was sitting in the passenger seat of the Buick with the bulk of a V8 engine on her lap. His father, who had been driving when the family's vehicle had collided head-on with a car full of 'pissed' German tourists, was stumbling around semi-conscious with part of the steering wheel pierced through his cheekbone. The silver beading from the hooter stuck out past his eye, an item of decorative jewellery on an otherwise ghastly portrait. One of Glenn Agliotti's brothers, Frank, had been sent flying through the windscreen on impact and landed some distance down the road – he would have to have a metal plate implanted in his head. Another brother, Sydney, had both his legs crushed between the passenger and driver's seats.

Miraculously, Glenn emerged from the collision without a scratch, thanks largely to the quick-thinking action of his third brother, Basil, who had instinctively pushed him under his seat as the accident occurred. His family had been en route to Swaziland on their regular vacation – they would often make the trip to the homeland to visit the king and his hundred wives and would take ownership of the royal suite at the Royal Swazi Spa for the duration of the holiday.

But this holiday in 1959 had started in tragedy and the little boy stood on the side of the road, comforted by a complete stranger who had taken pity on him, as his family was dispersed across the region. His mother and brothers were rushed off to the Brenthurst Clinic in Johannesburg, while his father was taken to a nearby facility in Delmas for treatment. Three-year-old Glenn spent the night at the stranger's house in the small *dorp*.

It's early October 2010, and there's a hiatus in Agliotti's trial for the murder of Brett Kebble as the prosecution awaits Roger Kebble's recovery from a knee operation. Agliotti has spent the time holidaying with his family in Ballito on the KwaZulu-Natal coast, dodging tax charges and embracing his new-found hobby Twitter. He's also agreed to spend some time with me, recounting his version of his life story over lavish lunches.

We spend long hours chatting over bottles of expensive wine at some of his favourite restaurants, La Campagnola in Bryanston and Bellagio in Atholl. Lunch with this man is not a simple affair. It's always excessive, impressive wine is mandatory and at least five people stop by the table to greet him during each meal. The manager/owner is always his best friend and receives a kiss on each cheek and a hug. Agliotti is beyond generous and is a fabulous host but I'm under no illusion that it's all part of the act for the suave 'fixer', who is desperate to impress and wow. It's the same act that won over the country's former Police Commissioner Jackie Selebi. As far as he's concerned, it's 'just who he is'.

Agliotti, who is 53 years old and sports greying hair and a thick moustache, is also generous with his time, granting me several hours to pepper him with questions. Having covered Agliotti's movements for five years, I've come to know him very well. So well that he greets me with a kiss on the cheek when he sees me.

But I'm not entirely convinced one can really know Glenn Agliotti. A story is always a 'version' of events and there's always an agenda – a deal to be made, a benefit to reap. But that doesn't stop him from being a friendly man.

Agliotti's story starts with the recollection of the seminal moment that shaped his childhood. 'It was a mess. People were lying all over the road. It was traumatic. I was so scared and afraid and there I was, standing there in the middle of the road staring at this accident and there's some strange woman holding me who had stopped when she saw the accident.' But his memory of the event isn't entirely macabre, and he jokingly recounts how, even at such a young age, he had insight and wit. 'So while I'm standing there, I see my dad appear and I stare at him and I say, "Daddy, you can't fucking drive." And there he is with the steering wheel through his cheek!' I contemplate whether a three-year-old would have the word 'fucking' in his vocabulary.

The accident had a definitive impact on Glenn Agliotti's life path. His father became detached as he focused his attention on his brother, Frank, who had been horribly injured in the crash. 'You know, that's what really hurt me. My father never took time out for me; he would just say to me that, "Ja, you'll be fine." He spoilt my brother Frank, whom we called Porky, because he felt indirectly responsible for the accident.'

But in reports and various profiles over the years, other family members disagree and insist Glenn remained 'the apple of his father's eye', accompanying him to the horse races and elegant parties on the social scene at the time. His dad, Frank (Senior), owned two racehorses and was a regular punter at the Durban July.

Agliotti proudly explains that he is the offspring of Italian descendants – his grandfather having arrived from Calabria in Southern Italy in the early 1950s. His infatuation for all things 'Mafioso' has its roots in his heritage, although some who know him describe him as 'just an Afrikaner convincing himself he's Italian'. Agliotti easily refers to himself as 'The Don' or 'Al Capo' on Twitter, channelling his Italian ancestry. Grandfather Agliotti was brought out to South Africa by the government at the time because of his vast knowledge of clay and ceramics, giving birth to a symbiosis between family and state, which would be replicated in generations to come. He started Kempton Park Potteries and the family quickly bought up large tracts of land in the area, setting the scene for what would become one of the most infamous property deals in the country's history.

In 1965, Agliotti's Uncle Joseph bought 266 hectares of land in the space that is now OR Tambo International Airport. He paid just R95 000 for it and duly sold it five years later to the apartheid government for the hugely inflated price of R7.5 million, at a time when the share market was crashing and property prices were levelling off. Agliotti was paid the money, in full, just twenty hours after signing the deed of sale and had made a profit of almost 80 times his original investment. It immediately appeared as though he had colluded with the government to defraud the state. On the very day the *Sunday Times* broke the story, Prime Minister John Vorster appointed a Commission of Inquiry into the deal and Joseph Agliotti was forced to repay R5 million of the purchase price. He shot himself in the head a few years later.

Glenn Agliotti has largely unaffectionate memories of his childhood. He was born in Germiston on Johannesburg's East Rand on 22 November 1956 and spent the majority of his formative years at boarding schools, first at Nelson House in Middelburg and then at St Andrews in Bloemfontein. 'My parents were travelling a lot at the time. They were in the steel and property business and travelled locally, to Swaziland and Botswana and funny places like that,' he recalls.

He had one full brother, three half-brothers and a half-sister – the result of various marriages by both parents. He describes his mother as a 'delightful, stylish woman who still has her hair done twice a week' and endearingly reveals how she used to refer to him as 'my little china doll'. It's clear that he was always closer to his mother than his father, whom he paints as a largely unemotional figure.

But Agliotti did inherit his swagger and suave from his father who, from a young age, taught his son to speak his mind with little diplomacy.

'One year, we were on Durban South Beach at the "Little Top" and there's this baby competition. I was wearing this tiger-skin cozzie with my fat stomach sticking out and I had this long curly blond hair. I was a little barrel and my parents enter me in this baby competition. So I'm standing on a stage and this woman says, "What a beautiful little girl." So I say, "Fuck you!" pull down my cozzie and show her my willy!'

Despite these somewhat dubious lessons of his youth, Agliotti – always one to portray himself in the best possible light – maintains he was the model pupil. He claims never to have been sent to detention or to the headmaster's office, was a prefect and was in the first rugby team at school, playing loose head prop. 'I was an angelic fucking thing,' he insists. The decorum of boarding school appealed to him and, as a teenager, he bought into the pomp of tipping his basher as a lady walked past and keeping the middle button of his blazer firmly fastened.

It was all about appearances for him then, a tenet that the sharp-dressing, big-talking, wheeler-dealer still advocates today. He only wears the finest brands and the names of designer labels slip off his tongue. Despite his apparent 'angelic behaviour' and success at school, he dropped out in his final matric year, only achieving his Standard Nine.

Author Rod Mackenzie wrote about his high-school memories of Glenn 'Ugly Tsotsi' Agliotti in a column on news website Newstime. Mackenzie was a few years behind him at St Andrews:

Around that time Agliotti was in matric, a rugby hero, a prefect, and had the affectionate nickname Ugly Tsotsi. I stood in awe of his size and strength. One day he picked me up by the belt and lifted me up to his eye level. Grinning, he marched me across the dorm, then lifted me even higher and held me against the wall. Shoes dangling in mid-air, I stared down at him in astonishment at his might. That he was bullying me didn't matter. That was as common as stealing coins off the school chapel collection tray that went up and down the pews on a Sunday.

Agliotti became a prefect even though a year before, with his cro-
nies, he perfected another boarding school tradition: the Saturday night
bunk. He and his gang had disappeared into town after lights out, went
to a pub in civvies, mingled with varsity students, got drunk, crashed
a car and their housemaster was called by the police to come and col-
lect them from the cop station. That's standard operating procedure:
it's what really goes on in posh, boater-and-blazer boarding schools
and which gets hushed. It is as de rigueur *as corrupt arms deals and*
their censorship. The private boarding school setting just created a regi-
mented version of The Lord of the Flies *in school uniform. At school*
assembly that week the Ugly Tsotsi Gang's Saturday night crimes were
intoned from the podium by the headmaster while we juniors listened
with a worshipful silence befitting the school chapel. Then each hero got
six of the best whilst we listened solemnly to the example being set, and
each hero came out of the classroom after the thrashing with a fixed
smirk on his face for the show. That got our veneration even more; a
mere two cuts usually had us skivvies squirming and doing a war dance
that would have won the All Blacks' approval. The only other punish-
ment our champions got was that they were gated for the rest of the
year. They were not expelled, as they should have been, and the police
charges were dropped. The reason seemed to be that some of them were
first team rugby players, members of a crony elite (sound familiar?).
Two of them, because they were first team rugby players I assume, went
on to be prefects, including Agliotti. The justice system and ruling po-
litical factions in South Africa (and indeed, the world) today seem to
have learned their craft at school level: if, like Kebble and Agliotti you
have the right connections or are on the right team, you win, almost
regardless of the lack of morals involved (5 October 2010).

When I show this column to Agliotti, he's outraged. 'Crap! That was my
brother Frank. Check your source of info,' he tells me. Agliotti is convinced
that Mackenzie has him confused with the brother he nicknamed 'Porky'.

However, if Mackenzie does have it right, his recollection shows that
from a young age Agliotti was influential and always ensured he had the
right protection. A long-time associate of Agliotti's, who doesn't want to
be named, also points out this trend. 'Throughout his life, Agliotti always

had a "strongman" alongside him to do the dirty work. The pattern repeats itself, you'll see,' he tells me.

After dropping out of school, Agliotti was required by the laws of conscription to serve in the army and joined the Third Infantry Battalion in Potchefstroom, where he became a driver. 'I thought, "Fuck this, I'm not going to shoot people",' he says, and I immediately recognise the immense irony of that position from the man who would later be accused of hiring others to do the shooting for him.

After completing his National Service, an ambitious Agliotti began to go in search of the proverbial quick buck, 'selling all sorts of shit'. He started repping, selling steel lockers to mines and records for the music label MFP. Already, as a young man, he dabbled in various business interests, his vocation murky.

Paging through the *Sunday Times* newspaper, he spotted an advert for a position with a large Japanese trading house, Itochuu. The job spec offered world travel and a company car. But the candidate required 'chemical experience', of which Agliotti had none. That didn't stop him though.

'So I put my best suit on and went to the Trust Bank building at the corner of Fox and Eloff, on the fourteenth floor, for an interview. I looked fucking smart. There were six Japanese guys at the table and this hot secretary. They asked me if I knew about organic chemicals and inorganic chemicals and I said, "Of course, of course." I told them I played golf and they were very interested. I clicked immediately how I was going to get the job.'

Agliotti made it onto the shortlist and the next interview, with the head of the company's chemical and oil division, was at Glendower golf course. 'I played well and I got the job, with my own secretary and a Mazda 323. When I got to work, I had my own Mercedes and driver. I would fly first class.' Agliotti tributes his absent father with teaching him to sell himself.

The smooth-talking young broker hit the big time whilst working for the Japanese and, before long, he was cruising around in a Porsche and luxury Rolls-Royce, swimming in money. 'They taught me how to trade. They're the best traders in the world, the Japanese,' Agliotti advises. He recommends I take a look at *Noble House*, a Pierce Brosnan TV-series based on a James Clavell book about the largest and oldest trading house in Hong Kong in the 1960s.

With his pockets filled with cash, a fleet of flashy cars in the garage, a boat on the Mediterranean and a tongue lined with silver, Agliotti became a hit with women, despite his rotund physique. He met his first wife Vivian over the phone. She was working for Merchant Shippers at the time and Agliotti's friend had suggested he give her a call. He wooed her via telephone, their first conversation lasting 45 minutes. He met her and took her out, and on their first date informed her that he was going to marry her, which he duly did.

But then, on 10 October 1987, Agliotti began a duplicitous lifestyle, when a Hollywood-like production played itself out at the luxurious Hazyview resort of Casa do Sol. With Vivian at home in Hyde Park in Johannesburg waiting for her husband to return from a business trip, Agliotti 'wed' a second bride, Charlene Voget. Guests indulged in a three-day celebration, champagne flowed and a chopper whisked the happy couple away from their post-wedding breakfast. Couturiers were the well-known outfit The Boys; Fowden & Bailey did the retinue's hair; and there were kilograms of chocolate mousse gateau cakes from the Les Marquis restaurant.

But the ever-cunning Agliotti knew he wasn't really 'marrying' Charlene, as the legal formalities were never completed. Nevertheless, he set up a home for himself and Charlene in Kempton Park while maintaining his residence in Hyde Park with Viv. The ruse lasted for a year before his 'second' wife found out.

During one of Agliotti's many court appearances, a little missive landed in my inbox. It was sent, to my surprise, by the 'ex-wife' Charlene:

Sewer Rat, as my friends and I fondly refer to him as, is entirely without a conscience. Every action he sets about is only ever for self-gain. To sit down and engage with him, will be a delight. His fantastical stories and charm will transport you. You'll leave, thinking, 'What a lovely human being; sheesh! He could be my new best friend, would love to connect again'… And if there's something for SR to gain from the association, you'll be cosseted, and the gifts will be well-timed and carefully chosen, you'll be none the wiser, only more enamoured …

Sewer Rat is not to be underestimated. He's very smart in his art and he'll run circles around most of us. The reality is, he truly believes his fantastical undertakings and because of his 'innocent take on the truth', he always slips through the loop. Sewer Rat has the ability to play it both ways, ensuring he doesn't make an enemy that could compromise him in any way. He's very adept, and can run circles around most of us. The old adage, 'bullshit baffles brains', especially a sociopath.

It is safe to say – the man is a pathological liar. I can attest to his fantastical delusions, and how his self effacing behaviour serves him, but destroys others. All said, 'finish and klaar', it's not with bitterness that I write. In fact, when I'm asked to relay the 'story', amid the gasps and gaping, we all fall about laughing at the incredulity of it all! Then we call for another bottle of wine!!!

It's all really quite funny – time allowing for hindsight …

Twenty-three years on and Charlene still carries the heavy burden of that trauma. She had a miscarriage as a result and suffered a nervous break-down. 'It was such a horrific time. My husband wasn't my husband. I was fourteen weeks pregnant and lost my child. There was a sense of loss. I had to be admitted to a sanatorium for three weeks,' she confesses when I ask her about it. Charlene suspects that Agliotti hired a crowd for the lavish reception and he allegedly told his curious friends that it was just 'a fancy dress party'. He even told his bride that his 'blood godfather', a Mafia boss in Italy, had given them a fourteen-bedroom villa in Florence as a wedding gift. She has no doubt this was a fabrication of Agliotti's mob fantasy. Charlene claims that her so-called husband stalked her for years in an attempt to scare and intimidate her, showing up at her workplace and bombarding her with gifts. 'It was a complete obsession,' she says.

Agliotti is surprisingly candid about the episode, although he does attribute much of the blame to Charlene. 'I had a scene with Charlene, I'm not going to lie to you. She got her claws, paws, into me. This woman put so much pressure on me, her friends had expectations, and so she said, "Let's have a ceremony of some sorts." So we did. I did have a house in Kempton Park with her, a flat, and she knew about Viv. But Viv only found out about it later. Chiara [their daughter] was a year old when we got divorced, but Viv forgave me and she's still my best friend. Charlene's a born again Christian and she still can't forgive me. She's bitter and also had an affair,' Agliotti spits out before reflecting, 'It was one of my biggest mistakes and I'm not proud of it.'

While the money may have attracted the women, the appeal could not have lasted long as Agliotti suddenly hit rock bottom, or, as he puts it: 'And then I hit the fucking wall and lost my balls.'

Agliotti lost the fortune he'd amassed overnight. He'd left the Japanese trading house and had gone into business with his half-brother Sydney Baker in a printing and trading company.

'Sydney was also in business with a German guy selling arms to Colombians and I was told their silent partner was an apartheid-era cabinet minister,' recalls Agliotti. 'Sydney was arrested in New York for arms smuggling. The chick he was shagging was the FBI agent who arrested him. He cost me everything on lawyer's fees and I put a million dollars up to get him out when the shit hit the fan,' Agliotti says bitterly. 'Someone' smuggled Sydney out of the New York state penitentiary but Agliotti is elusive about the details.

Agliotti also had a fallout with another of his half-brothers, Julio, which ripped his family apart. As his father lay on his deathbed, he reportedly amended his will at the behest of Julio, leaving his millions, tied into numerous properties and a scrap metal business, to him. Agliotti and his mother got nothing. 'There was shit with my father's will. Julio manipulated it and we all knew it. He did us out of it when my father died,' is all he will say about that. This is irreconcilable with another version of his father's death that Agliotti peddles. He's told others that his dad died while he was still at school and he first heard about it during an assembly when the headmaster extended condolences in front of all the other pupils.

Down and out, driving a battered old Nissan Skyline and shopping at Edgars, Agliotti met the vivacious Dianne Muller who owned a marketing company. She would become his fiancée and he would become her downfall. Agliotti built his way back up again as he dove back into the trading game, buying and selling products, weaselling out a gap and grabbing opportunities. He would 'put deals together for people' and, in later court documents, his official job description would be 'commodity trader'.

There is little doubt the man has a brilliant business brain which is assisted by his uncanny ability to remember facts and details. But his critics don't see it quite the same way. 'Agliotti is a ruthless bastard. He'll take a gap anywhere and try and capitalise on it,' explains one man who has investigated him. 'A bald-faced liar and suave scumbag' was how the *Mail*

& Guardian first presented him to the public when they broke the story of Agliotti's friendship with Jackie Selebi in mid-2006.

Agliotti's murky dealings would not evade the keen eye of the law, however. In 1997, he and three Congolese nationals had fraud charges brought against them in the Johannesburg Magistrates Court after a shady cobalt deal went belly up. Agliotti had arranged for nearly 170 tons of refined cobalt to be shipped to buyers in the United States and United Kingdom. The buyers travelled to South Africa and inspected the cargo at a bonded warehouse. But the deal was dubious, due to the involvement of the apparent owners of the shipment, who seemed to have links with Mobutu Sese Seko's regime. Instead of receiving a shipment of the lustrous silver metal, the purchasers received containers filled with sand. The insurers refused to pay out and Agliotti and his co-accused stood trial. Two of his accomplices fled the country, the third died. Agliotti was acquitted, but a private arbitration found against him and the transport company he was affiliated to, Trans-Atlantic.

As Agliotti's wealth accumulated, he made friends in high places and began to move in illustrious, well-connected circles. He would ply friends and acquaintances (and even random strangers at times) with expensive gifts. It was his *modus operandi*, endearing himself to those around him. He is overly generous with his money and doesn't hesitate to hand out cash. I once saw him dish out R200 to a stranger who approached him during a court recess begging for money – though I suspect Agliotti may have given him the cash only for my benefit. 'He has no loyalty, he's charming as hell and he'll only pay when people are watching,' according to a man who has known him for many years.

A businessman who knew Agliotti before he occupied the headlines says he used to drive a black Mercedes s350 at the time but had pulled the badge off the car so that people would think it was a better model. The man also tells me that Agliotti kept a million rand in cash in a basket in his boot, immediately arousing suspicion that he was a contraband dealer. Agliotti's response to this claim is that it is 'crap'.

And in another story, a prominent lawyer recalls meeting Agliotti at a hotel resort in the early 1990s and recounts how the charmer would join numerous couples out for dinner each night, leaving his fiancée in their hotel room. 'Before you knew it, he'd picked up the bill for everyone around the table,' he says. 'Bullshit' is what Agliotti responds when I run this anecdote past him.

Agliotti even bought a pair of shoes for a police officer who couldn't afford trainers to run a marathon. He is the type of man who buys the most expensive perfumes for all the air hostesses in first class on a flight, just because he can. His generosity is glossed with his relaxed demeanour as he easily calls those around him 'baby', or urges buddies to 'show me love, my brother'.

Who better to advance his public standing and screen his illicit deal brokering than the country's National Police Commissioner? Agliotti first met Jackie Selebi in the early 1990s at the ANC headquarters, Shell House, at a time when Selebi was the organisation's head of Social Welfare and Development. Agliotti met with Selebi because he had a business proposal for him. He wanted to import second-hand clothing and sell it locally; a portion of the proceeds would go to assist the ANC in relocating exiles. No doubt swayed by Agliotti's charisma, Selebi confided in him about some of his own monetary problems, an unusual thing to do during a first meeting. He told Agliotti that he had an overdue medical bill for one of his children. Agliotti, in his version, offered to pay the account and promptly made out a cheque to the doctor. Selebi denies this.

The two men met again in 2000 when Agliotti approached Selebi, who was by then the Chief of Police, with another proposal. He was arranging a torch run, named 'African Hope', from Robben Island to parliament in Cape Town which would raise money for the Special Olympics. Hollywood actor Arnold Schwarzenegger was involved and Agliotti needed Selebi's help regarding security. His old friend and beneficiary happily obliged.

Moonlighting police reservist Paul Stemmet, who was Brett Kebble's head of security and the boss of a shady security operation called Palto, did the close protection for the 'Terminator'. It would later emerge that Palto was a murky security company that did work for the police and regularly invoked Police Chief Jackie Selebi's name to abuse the law.

From the torch run Agliotti and Selebi's mutually beneficial relationship blossomed, with Selebi receiving regular cash payments and expensive gifts, while Agliotti enjoyed the luxury of being able to call on his friend the police chief whenever it suited him. As is his way, Agliotti would refer to Selebi in the most endearing terms, calling him 'Jax' or

'Chief' and would liberally bandy his name about when in esteemed company. Agliotti would use the relationship to leverage credibility with Brett Kebble and other businessmen, charging them heavily for his access to the National Commissioner.

The captains of industry would go to Agliotti with a problem and for a fee of a few hundred thousand dollars he would deliver Selebi to meetings in Sandton hotel rooms. If they were lucky, dinner with the country's top police officer at their homes could be arranged. Selebi, of course, vehemently denies this, saying he was using these meetings to build sources and gather intelligence.

Ultimately, the relationship between Agliotti the operator and Selebi the top cop would be laid bare for all to see as every interaction and exchange was closely scrutinised in a court of law.

BRETT KEBBLE WAS BORN AND BRED ON THE DUSTY GOLD DUMPS that would one day make him a 'mining magnate'. His father, Roger, was a mine captain, a shift boss, who, by the nature of his job, was forced to live a relatively gypsy-like existence, migrating from one tumbleweed town on the reef to the next. Brett was born in Springs, a mining centre about an hour outside of Johannesburg, on 19 February 1964. Springs, which is now populated by over 100 000 people, was originally founded to house workers in the coal mines of the surrounding area but, at its peak, produced more gold than anywhere else in the world. It also boasted the first railroad line in South Africa – the Rand Tram, which ran between Springs and Johannesburg.

Those who know him well describe Roger as uncouth and coarse, as expected of a shift boss who endeared himself to his men by spending Sunday afternoons in their shebeens drinking the miners' brew, Black Label. Despite his apparent lack of sophistication and rough edges, Roger saw to it that his sons Brett and Guy were well schooled and enrolled them at his alma mater, the prestigious St Andrew's in Bloemfontein, the same institution attended by Glenn Agliotti who was a few years ahead of Brett. Brett was a boarder, spending holidays at home in Klerksdorp or Welkom or whatever town his parents had settled in. As a boarding school, St Andrews was a favourite of the successful farmers and miners from Viljoenskroon to Kroonstad, who packed their sons off to the big city to get an education and some discipline.

During an interview with me in December 2010, Roger reflected on his son's formative years and what kind of a boy he was. 'He was always a handful as a baby. He wasn't a guy that slept long hours, he tended not to digest his food well, but amongst all of that he showed an inclination towards things that wouldn't interest other children. He was always very mature as a youngster. He was a bit of loner. He played with some of the other kids and so on but he never got involved in the things that children do in the form of their sort of games. He was always on the upper level. At one stage he was drawing up organograms of what the country should look like politically, who should be in those posts, and so on. So he had a huge intellect. Over and above that he was a very good tennis player in his youth. He played a lot of junior tournaments and when he went to boarding school I think that side of him left. He played other sports but not particularly with a lot of gusto. He didn't achieve the heights that he thought he would, or we thought he would at school. We expected him to be a more senior prefect than he was and for whatever reason he didn't make it.'

A junior at St Andrew's School at the time, who doesn't want to be named, recalls being ill in the school sanatorium when a group of raucous older boys was admitted. Among them was Brett Kebble. 'He definitely was the life and soul of the party – there really didn't seem to be too much wrong with him or his compatriots who just seemed keen to bunk school.' The bed Brett occupied was next to the door. The cleaners came into the room – he threw back the covers and exposed his genitals.

'I was seven. I had no idea what had made the women shriek and run away giggling. I do recall thinking that if what Kebble had exposed was what I thought it was – bearing in mind that I had not ever seen anything that size in that state – we were all in serious trouble. I rolled over pretending to sleep and eventually drifted off. When I woke up he and his compatriots were gone. Their laughter had no doubt caused the san sister to see through their apparent illness and they were packed off back to school.' Even then, Brett was larger than life.

Columnist Rod Mackenzie, who so vividly recalled Glenn Agliotti's antics from his school days, also has recollections about a pre-pubescent Brett Kebble. He was a year ahead of Brett at boarding school and was about eleven when he first met him in junior school. He tells me that his first impressions of Brett were that he was 'nervous, hiding behind a big, cheesy, brave smile'. Mackenzie remembers the podgy youngster as being a straight-A student who was never very sporty and somehow never seemed to be punished. 'He was a very good boy who sucked up to the prefects,' explains the writer. In a column on news website Newstime, Mackenzie recounts one of his experiences with adolescent Brett:

He was very nervous about going into standard six. I was going through the traditional baptism of fire in that first year of high school. We were known as 'skivvies' and did all sorts of daft things to please the prefects, Nazis-in-training who made us warm their toilet seats and wash their rugby gear in the showers (more than one of us urinated on their clobber and sniggered when we watched them parade onto the rugby field the next Saturday). The prefects gave us 'hard labour': hours of digging in the school grounds from five in the morning as punishment for misdemeanours such as a small blemish on otherwise perfectly polished shoes at inspection. 'How bad is standard six?' Brett anxiously asked me, and I nonchalantly lied, 'It's not that bad; we get all kinds of privileges you guys don't have.' When Brett got to standard six he made sure he was friends with all the bullies, sucked up to the prefects, and became, even then, a master of forming the right connections for his own ends. Though supposedly of superior, standard seven status, I recall that snake-like grin of his while he stood with the rugger buggers he had got in with while they jeered at me: I was still at the coalface of weekend 'hard labour' punishment for leaving, say, a school memo just slightly skew on top of my otherwise neatly stacked books in my desk. Our friendship drifted apart (5 October 2010).

Mackenzie has another anecdote about Brett that he recounts to me, explaining that Brett liked to bully through other bullies without getting his own hands dirty. In Standard Seven, Mackenzie and a classmate were ready to 'knock the living daylights out of each other' for reasons which time has eroded from Mackenzie's memory. Brett appointed himself as 'boxing fight manager and referee' – he arranged a time and place for the bout. Mackenzie and his mate climbed into one another while Brett called over the 'big okes' to watch the spectacle, ingratiating himself with the older boys. 'It was an episode of his which has always stayed with me, seeing that grin on Brett's face as he watched the fight he had arranged. If a master had come and seen it, we would have got hidings but Brett would have got off scot-free even though he had "arranged" the fight and ensured he stayed out of harm's way,' Mackenzie recalls. 'How the child becomes the man!' he points out aptly.

Brett's brother Guy, who was a few years behind Brett at school, says he spent much of his time protecting his older brother. 'Brett was always two or three years older than his peers. That was a problem to the peers because Brett felt he was just that much better than everybody else and that's why he didn't become Head Prefect or even Head of House. The system was that they voted for the kids and Brett couldn't take that. That was just a serious issue to him. Thinking that he was so much better, believing that, only to be found out that the system doesn't work like that. If you don't play the rest of the game you'll come short.'

After matriculating, Brett dodged the army. While he was opposed to the apartheid regime, he was not a conscientious objector. He simply evaded his call-up by signing up to study law at the University of Cape Town and graduated with an LLB degree. He served three years as an articled clerk at the prominent firm Mallinicks, which was established in 1969 with a history rooted in human rights law in the 1970s and 80s. It later merged with the better-known Webber Wentzel Bowens. Amongst his colleagues at the mother city firm was Judy Moon, who would become known as Judy Sexwale, after marrying celebrity politician and mining supremo Tokyo Sexwale. Brett left Mallinicks under curious circumstances as he encountered what was to be the first of countless run-ins with the law. The details aren't entirely clear but it involved a breach of foreign-exchange law related to a diamond-dealing company and the help of reputable senior counsel Advocate Max Hodes was needed. Coincidently, Hodes's son Laurance, who is an equally capable and highly respected silk, would years later defend Glenn Agliotti for Brett's murder.

Before Brett left law he met Ingrid, a 'salt of the earth' girl. They became engaged but Brett called off the engagement temporarily before deciding to go ahead with it. They married and soon bought their first house. It was his first foray into what would become a burgeoning property portfolio. He recalled the experience in an interview with *The Property Magazine* which gave unique insight into Brett's mainstream lifestyle before the billions came:

I could afford to take out a mortgage on a house for the first time in 1989 when I was 25. Ingrid and I were soon to be married, so we wanted something near the Claremont Primary School where she was a teacher. The best bet seemed upper Claremont that I knew was a good area and from where Ingrid could still walk over the railway bridge to school. I scanned the property pages each weekend looking for a bargain, but of course you don't get one in that sort of area. Then one Sunday morning I happened to be driving in the area when I saw an agent's show board pointing to a house for sale in Lelia Road. It was a typical 1930s Cape Town southern suburbs house; solid with big rooms, two bedrooms and one bathroom. There was a large palm tree in front of it, which I think is gone now. I was the first to walk into the showhouse. In fact, it was not yet officially open. They were asking R160 000. I made an offer at the asking price immediately. By that evening we had our first home. We had a wonderful time there. What's important to me is when I walk into a house and sense whether it is happy or unhappy. This was definitely a happy house. Ingrid and I settled in well and made a few minor changes. I'm not one for knocking a house around. I prefer to buy a house that I can add on to. But soon after buying, I was beginning to look ahead to when we had a couple of children. Clearly this house with only two bedrooms was not going to be ideal. So, after one and a half very happy years, we put it on the market. Another thing about happy homes is they sell very quickly. And, as on the day I bought it, 8 Lelia Road was sold at the asking price of R280 000 by the time the show day ended (May 2004).

Brett and Ingrid would need the bigger house for their brood of four children: Mathew, Andrew, Hannah and Lily. Brett was a doting father who loved his kids dearly, according to those who knew him best. Laura Sham was Brett's personal assistant for three years, from 2002 until 2005, and was intimately involved in his daily affairs. She tells me that her boss spoke affectionately about his four children. 'He loved them very much. He did speak about them, especially the little one, Lily, that had the burn mark.' Sham is referring to a tragic incident that occurred in 2003 involving Brett and Ingrid's last-born, Elizabeth. The toddler climbed into a bath filled with boiling hot water and suffered third-degree burns on most of her body. 'They have to do skin grafts every year she grows,' Sham explains, as she recalls ointments sent from Australia and specialised treatment.

Messages on Brett's cellphone found after his death give insight into his relationship with his kids. On 15 September 2005, just less than two weeks before he was murdered, he received a message from Ingrid's phone: 'DEAR DAD IM 10 I feel great but it don't feel rite wish u wer here.' The message was from Hannah who was celebrating her birthday while Brett, no doubt, was on his weekly visit to Johannesburg. He replied to her message half an hour later: *'Dear Hannah. You are correct that I shud b w u tnite. Sorry my baby. I DO LOVE YOU.!Xxx Dad'.*

'Brett only had photos of the children on his desk, not of Ingrid,' says Sham. 'There were some of his business dealings. He had a picture of himself on a mine and one of him and Tokyo Sexwale.' The PA insists Brett was fastidious about keeping his private and business lives separate. 'Ingrid kept a very low profile and he kept her out the business. If she was coming to Jo'burg, I'd have to fix up the house and prepare for her. I don't think there was much affection. I never saw them together but from what I can gather, they got on very well. He was very private and he didn't want his private and family life to be involved in business.'

Journalist David Gleason came to know Ingrid fairly well over the years. 'Ingrid was nice if not difficult. She struggled to make sure Brett did not dominate her. Brett could be a very dominating character. She would get mad and kick up her heels if he would do so and Brett would find himself in difficult, awkward situations. I always had the impression there was a great deal of tension in their relationship.'

Brett also had deep affection for his mother, Julienne Fritelli. 'That's where Brett gets his musical genius from. She would come to the house and Brett would say, "Get us some lovely flowers, my mother's coming." When she came, everything had to be perfect. Andrew would have to go and buy the best big roses he could find. He loved his mother and only treated her with respect,' recalls Sham.

But Brett's relationship with his father Roger was fraught with friction, despite the facade portrayed by the Kebble media machine. Brett never referred to his father as 'Dad' or anything of the sort, preferring to call him 'Roger'. Brett, a sensitive soul with a passion for the arts, never endeared himself to Roger, a rugger bugger man's man. Brett's brother Guy, a prop forward who played provincial and Springbok rugby, earned the title of firm favourite from Roger, who allegedly even disparagingly referred to Brett as his 'other daughter'. Guy was a 'boykie', who once owned a pub and loved sport, while Brett was the complete opposite. Roger and Guy acknowledge they had complicated relationships with Brett but stress that they never made any attempt to ostracise him.

Brett's troubleshooter Dominic Ntsele can testify to Brett's sensitivity and kind nature. 'There was once an opening of parliament and Brett had had too much to drink because we had gone to a lunch before and this was a dinner. He had a big capacity for alcohol. So when Brett drinks and he's drunk and it shows, it's serious consumption. I decided that I was going to drive him home and it was pissing with rain. There's a lady in an old, very nicely kept Mercedes-Benz who had stopped, standing next to the car, but it was raining. Brett said to me I should stop. I stopped. He got out and took his shirt off and he took the wheel spanner. It was so hard to get the wheel spanner down, he stood on it to loosen it and changed the tyre for the lady and we escorted the lady home and when she was in the gate he said it was fine. The amount of water he brought back into the car with him was amazing. Now for me, stopping and helping a lady is one thing. Stopping and helping a lady at 1.00 a.m. and it's raining and you're not particularly sober says to me that your sense of kindness has come from a very special place. He didn't fail to impress me that way.'

It seemed to many that Brett was simply too soft for Roger. Both Brett's butler and PA witnessed the two men in fist fights, literally coming to blows, as their fractious relationship imploded. While giving evidence during Glenn Agliotti's trial, Andrew Minaar recounted a fight which erupted between the two one night during a board meeting. He told how he heard a commotion and later discovered that Brett and Roger had begun punching one another in full view of 'the Watson brothers', the trio of businessmen brothers from the Eastern Cape who have reputations for liberal activism. Minaar's testimony provided much amusement for the journalists in the public gallery as he recalled how an ornamental clay frog had been broken in the fight and was collateral damage. We speculated that the frog was probably worth more than all of our salaries combined and the unfortunate creature became something of a mascot for the duration of the trial. I had the good fortune of actually seeing the frog myself. It so happens that a gardener who witnessed the duel between father and son still works at the house in Inanda and kept every piece of the ornament, which was shattered in the fight. It doesn't actually look like a frog at all, but coincidently rather like a caricature cartoon of Brett! The gardener giggled as he recalled Roger's big right hook and Brett running off crying.

Laura Sham also had the misfortune of once witnessing the two men coming to blows. 'I saw it at the house one day. Roger and Brett were having a heated argument and they came to blows. It wasn't very pretty and Roger won, unfortunately. Brett wasn't a fighter, hey. He was a cultured man and was well brought up. I don't know what they were fighting over but Roger punched him. I was outside and they didn't know that I knew,' she tells me. Sham's colleague in Cape Town, Rita Meininghuis, witnessed a more infamous fight between Brett and his brother Guy at the JCI box at Newlands Stadium during a rugby match. Meininghuis, who has since died, told Sham about the punch-up. 'I heard the story from Rita, she was in the box with them at Newlands in Cape Town. Guy had a bit much to drink and he called John Stratton, "You turtle", and he said to Brett, "Faggot", in front of everybody in the box and he walked away. Brett was very embarrassed. Guy came back and said it a second time and things got out of hand. There was a bit of a shove and then Brett just left. It was very unpleasant.' Guy vociferously denies ever calling his brother a 'faggot' and both he and Roger insist they never thought Brett was gay. He also insists he called Stratton 'a cockroach' and not a turtle because 'there are two things that will survive a nuclear war – cockroaches and John Stratton.'

On the odd occasion when Guy would visit the JCI building, Brett would tell his PA to 'ask him to vacate the building'. 'He couldn't stand Guy,' says Sham. She explains that Roger would never walk into Brett's office, choosing rather to request her to tell Brett that his father was waiting to see him. 'They never saw eye to eye,' she says. 'Roger is as rough as a goat's knee while Brett was classy and well bred.'

Glenn Agliotti, who came to know both men well during his tenure at JCI, agrees. 'Brett's father and brother are as rough as a bear's arse. He made himself sophisticated, that's why I think he was so intelligent. Guy is nowhere near like Brett that way. That's why there was such a clash of personalities,' he tells me.

It seems as though Brett Kebble was always destined for greatness. He had thrown off the shackles of his working-class background. He set himself on a path embossed with gold and diamonds, which would lead him to glory and power. But it would be that same path that would ultimately lead him over the cusp and to his downfall.

'Always wind up with a good curtain, and bring it down before the public gets tired – or has had time to find you out.'

Barney Barnato, Randlord (1851–97)

BRETT KEBBLE ALWAYS BILLED HIMSELF AS THE NEW BARNEY Barnato, a modern-day Randlord in the mould of those entrepreneurs who controlled the mining industry in Johannesburg from its pioneer phase in the nineteenth century through its boom until the First World War. Barnato's is a rags-to-riches tale featuring a colourful, eccentric character who accumulated massive wealth and who rose to the pinnacle of the cut-throat mining game. The parallels between their stories are astonishing. Both tycoons died under eerily similar unnatural circumstances, with the dominant theory in both cases being suicide.

Born Barnett Isaacs, Barnato was the son of a Jewish second-hand clothes trader who eked out a living in the relatively impoverished suburb of Petticoat Lane in London's East End. Barney and his brother Harry became performers – Harry learned to juggle and do sleight-of-hand tricks whilst Barney's forte was acrobatics. According to legend, Harry always took the bow at the end of the show and the crowd would give him the loudest round of applause, at which point the theatre manager would scream, 'And Barney too!' from the wings. The brothers adopted 'Barnato' as their surname – it had an Italian ring to it and they didn't have to associate their family name with their comical performances.

The good fortune of one of his cousins tempted Barney to the diamond mines of the Cape. Pursuing a tip-off from an insightful geologist, Barney and his brother struck it lucky and, within a year, they had sold 100 000 pounds worth of diamonds.

With the success also came the emergence of a tempestuous rivalry with Cecil John Rhodes. A bidding war ensued as Rhodes needed to take control of the Kimberley diamond mines to fuel his imperial ambitions in Africa. Both men recklessly bought up land as they tried to outmanoeuvre each other but, finally, Rhodes emerged victorious. Barney agreed to sell out to Rhodes, resulting in the formation of the international mining conglomerate De Beers. The purchase cheque signed by Rhodes is believed to be the largest ever presented for payment at that time. Tempted by the gold rush on the reef, Barney moved up to the Johannesburg area in 1886 and started the Johannesburg Consolidated Investment company (JCI), which would be plundered by its CEO Brett Kebble over a century later.

In 1897, Barney and his family sailed for England aboard the *Scot*. The story goes that he was taking a walk on the deck with a Solly Joel, whom he had been in business with, when all of a sudden Barney ran to the railing and threw himself overboard somewhere near the island of Madeira. A crew member insisted he heard someone shout, 'Murder!' The coroner's report declared 'death by drowning while temporarily insane', but Barney's wife never believed he had taken his own life. Nine months later, one of Barney's heirs, Woolf Joel, was shot and killed in his office in Johannesburg by a German extortionist. Curiously, this now left Solly Joel in control of Barney's massive fortune, fuelling speculation about whether or not Barney really had killed himself.

And so you see the intriguing parallels between the stories of Barney Barnato and Brett Kebble, a Randlord of a different kind in a different era. Both men were flamboyant characters with very deep pockets who controlled massive stakes in the cut-throat mining industry. There is the obvious shared control of JCI, the company that Barney started and Brett plundered. Both had an affinity for the arts and harboured political ambitions. And, of course, both died under extremely unnatural circumstances at very similar ages, leaving a myriad questions unanswered.

'The mining industry is like no other sector in this country. It's one which attracts a certain kind of animal,' explains Kebble-watcher and Miningmx editor David McKay, who spent years writing about the businessman's dealings.

'The mining industry is the riskiest industry you can ever be involved in. Your assets are always depleting as soon as you buy them. There's huge pressure to reinvent yourself all the time, often through merger-and-acquisition activity, hence all these deals always going on. There's always long lead times for your projects. The budgets are always huge. So the risk element of the industry is massive. It attracts a person who feels that they want to take that on. These guys are always massive personalities; they have to have massive egos to be able to survive. Everyone is trying to get the next best deal and there are less and less deals going around, so it's a bit of a rat race,' says McKay.

Brett Kebble was amongst the most grandiose of personalities in the game. 'He was just full of it. He employed thousands of people, so there was the power side of it. You often think, "Why didn't Brett get out?" like early on, just get out. It was just not in his make-up. He was after the power and it was like a drug to be doing deals. It was a deal a day.'

As Chris Barron wrote in the *Sunday Times* after Brett Kebble's star had plummeted, Brett was a player and the game quickly became the consuming passion for the whizz-kid who thought 'slow was boring':

> *Analysts and journalists were swept along as much by his polished persona as by a gung-ho, devil-may-care attitude that made the local mining world as exciting as during the heady days of Barney Barnato. 'If they hadn't been so busy laughing at his jokes, admiring his fancy finger work on the ivories and his ability to quote Shakespeare, they might have been more sceptical and noticed vaguely disturbing signs.*

Brett's lifestyle was ostentatious and excessive. He had a broad property portfolio that included Fair Seat, his family mansion in Bishopscourt, the weekend retreat in Malgas on the banks of the Breede River and Hoëveld House in Inanda. Prior to that, he called Melrose House home. Brett would proudly claim that some of the Jameson raiders took refuge in the house's cellar. There were the two private jets – a Gulfstream II and a Lear – to add to the fleet of flashy sports cars, amongst them a clutch of Ferraris. Brett mostly drove in his Mercedes S600 and a Bentley, which he kept in the Hoëveld House garage. The other vehicles were largely investments and would only be taken out for a spin on the odd occasion.

Andrew Minaar, the butler, recalls how Brett once 'forgot' one of his sports cars in the garage of a house he had sold. Only when he received a call six months later about the abandoned multimillion-rand vehicle was it fetched. Brett collected Rolex watches by the armful and also struggled to keep track of the timepieces. 'Even when he moved from Houghton to Melrose House, there was a safe and he forgot the combination. Six months later I went back with the locksmith and there were all these Rolexes in the safe. He had so many watches. He'd take off a watch and just leave it on the table outside.'

The art aficionado had a veritable gallery in his house and wasn't shy to splash out on new pieces. 'His collection was vast, it was exceptionally vast,' says Minaar. 'The art dealers would come here and he'd go, "I'll take that and I'll take that and that and that and that." Like in five minutes. All his artwork was actually documented and what went on auction was maybe one Irma Stern. That 'Lost Orchid' which was in the dining room. He knew it was damaged and it fetched R3 million and it was actually the least valuable piece. So what happened to the rest is still a mystery,' Minaar says cryptically.

Overweight and gluttonous, a *bon vivant*, Brett had all his clothes tailor-made. 'He had a wardrobe in Johannesburg and Cape Town and they both looked like shops. The one day he was going overseas and I had to pack a bag and take him clothes in Cape Town. You'd swear the guy never had any clothes. He always used to wear Hermes ties, and he really only wore two pairs of shoes. He had others, but always wore these slip-ons, like loafers, and in winter he'd always wear corduroy pants and his favourite was red socks. He had a tailor who used to make his pants and jackets. But also he had thousands of ties. Thousands. He'd go to a shop and buy sixty shirts and he used to actually hide his shirts from his wife. His wife came here once and we had to hide his shirts!' says Minaar, laughing at the extravagance.

Despite the lavishness, Brett would 'fuss about two cents'. 'Once I opened up a packet of cheese and it was starting to go off. I had to send it back to Thrupps. And you're looking at like fifteen rand,' says Minaar, pointing out his erstwhile boss's peculiarities. 'In Cape Town, there was a massive palm tree and the guys would dig a hole and plant it. He'd come and say "I don't like it there," and he'd do it three times. He had a fine eye for detail. The guys who built his fireplace, he didn't like it so they had to chop it down and start from scratch.'

For Brett, it was all about appearances. A prominent lawyer told me once that he saw the magnate drop R16 000 on one bag of groceries at an upmarket store, Thrupps, in the Illovo Centre. All that was in the packet was French champagne, Parma ham and caviar. The bag fitted neatly into the boot of his Ferrari. Glenn Agliotti has a similar anecdote about a lavish lunch at the famed French Horn restaurant in Berkshire in the United Kingdom, where Brett nonchalantly splashed out several thousand pounds on a lunch of *foie gras* and red wine.

Brett's former media strategist Dominic Ntsele is full of praise for the man he saw as worldly and above all, generous. 'Brett was probably one of the most intelligent people I've ever met. Very knowledgeable, very interesting. There wasn't a subject you could touch on and Brett didn't have knowledge of. Very wide, always in touch with what's happening around the world, what's happening in the country and in many aspects, ahead of his time. Brett saw business as a form of social redress, ultimately. I have no doubt that if Brett had amassed a lot of wealth he would have spent a lot of time agonising about how to wisely give it away. No doubt'.

Laura Sham, Brett's PA, was a fervent supporter of his business style and is easily convincing about why he was so successful so early. 'Brett was very strong. He spoke and when he spoke everyone listened. He was very strong and he called the shots. He was incredible, such a charismatic person, such a jovial person. He'd entertain us at Christmas parties. He'd get up and sing in that beautiful deep voice of his, he didn't care, he was up there. He was so cultured. He knew a lot about everything, from cigars and wines to cheeses.'

So how did it all go wrong for the blue-eyed boy of the mining industry who was revelling in the glory and the power of it all?

Barron maintains it was 'unchecked arrogance' that finally got its man. McKay agrees it was a combination of hubris, greed and power. 'He treated the companies of which he was the CEO as if they were his own empire, his own domain. CEOs are supposed to serve shareholders and companies belong to the people who own the shares. That was the case with JCI and Randgold, both listed companies with independent shareholders. But Brett just did his own thing, as if the money was his. That was the fundamental ethical breach that cuts across everything and anything Brett did commercially. CEOs should run companies on behalf of their shareholders but Brett's basic error was that he felt he was a law answerable only to himself.'

BRETT KEBBLE ARRIVED ON THE MINING SCENE IN 1991, ON HIS father's coat-tails. Roger, the mining engineer, had retired and gone off to spend his twilight years on a wine farm in the Cape. But he got bored, took his cash and pumped it into a 65-year-old embattled mine called Rand Leases. Brett was credited with engineering the subsequent takeover of Randgold & Exploration. Chris Barron of the *Sunday Times* explains:

> *[Brett joined Roger] and gave early notice of his ability to charm, and to impress, with complex calculations when he persuaded London fund manager Julian Baring of Mercury Asset Management to back a takeover bid for Randgold. Considering the Kebbles were an unknown quantity with nothing but the paltry Rand Leases to their name, and Brett Kebble knew nothing about mining, this took considerable chutzpah. Thanks to Baring, the Kebbles managed to buy just enough Randgold shares to give them a foot in the boardroom door. He schmoozed the shareholders and got them to vote management out. Barely out of law school and hardly 30, he'd chalked up a hostile takeover in an industry he knew very little about. He was a player and the game quickly became his consuming passion. He was known in the industry as 'deal-a-day Kebble' as he collected one marginal mine after another.*

Journalists and analysts were blown away by the manoeuvre. McKay, an experienced reporter, admits that so too was he. 'I was impressed by him, make no mistake. I was a lot younger and for me it was flying quite close to the sun. Brett was always like, "We're going to do this and do that and change the shape of mining" and I'd sit there in awe of these plans. I've since learnt to realise to be more critical but in those days, it was like, "Wow, this guy is a mover and shaker."'

Laura Sham testifies to the 'deal-a-day' tag bestowed on her boss. 'He used to do business deals all day long. Different boardrooms, different offices. Five meetings at once. If there were five boardrooms, he would have six meetings. He was just so dynamic and so intelligent. He'd never write things down and had an absolutely amazing memory and was so fast. We had to be fast and keep up with him. He'd pick up the phone and say x, y and z and you'd have to keep up with him.'

Minaar agrees. 'I've always thought he was sharp. He never wrote notes, never worked on a computer, and he remembered everything that happened in his life. Even documents that were delivered to the house, he hardly ever read them. They would just lay there.' Brett was all about business and cracking deals. 'I don't think he had a life, he never done things that normal people would do,' Minaar explains. 'You never saw him relaxing, having friends over or going to a movie. Everything was business, from morning until night. Even when I was at his home in Cape Town in December, it was just business. It was very seldom you would see him in shorts or even having a swim.'

The only real account I have of Brett's light-hearted humour away from the business arena comes from David McKay. 'Brett could be a bit juvenile; he was a complex kind of guy. An executive tells a story of how he once saw Brett Kebble sitting in the business-class lounge at the airport, sitting on a whoopee cushion because he wanted to scandalise the people sitting around him. He was quite juvenile.'

Glenn Agliotti has a similar account to Minaar's of Brett's incredible intelligence and desire to do deals. 'Bretty never carried a diary. Business deals, stock prices, were all in his head. I think he was a genius, I think he was so brilliant. He could command the attention of a full room of people. He spoke so well and had such a broad knowledge that he could converse on any topic. Brett had this beautiful, deep speaking voice and people always took notice of him. If he walked into a restaurant people would say, "There is Brett Kebble." Now they say, "There is that gangster Glenn Agliotti!"'

Under Brett's control, Randgold's shares went sky high, growing 400 per cent to R1 billion in just two years. Much of this can also be attributed to the fact that Brett had a strong chairman in Peter Flak to keep him in check. McKay tells the story of being at a Randgold quarterly results presentation in those early years, and relates a particular anecdote which exemplifies Brett's need for control:

'I remember the Randgold presentations were very different. They would see journalists one by one and you'd sit in this waiting room. Like a dentist's waiting room. You'd go in and there would be the full board of directors sitting there at this mahogany table. It was terrifying. They'd just look at you with your hand trembling. Peter Flak, who was the chairman, was quite a disciplinarian and, to some extent, he kept Brett under quite close control. Brett always needed someone like that. As soon as he was out on his own, he had no one to rein him in. I remember Brett saying something about a deal and Peter patting his hand and saying, "We'll get to that later, Brett." Brett didn't like that and bristled at being held back. He needed a godfather to say, "Brett, haul back, easy now."'

As McKay explains, Brett wanted to get out of Randgold & Exploration and build his own empire. Unchecked and without a strong chairman, he was going to run riot and that's exactly what he did.

In 1994, with the dawn of democracy, Brett took his first foray into the lucrative world of empowerment deals which would lay the foundation for a decade's worth of schmoozing with the ruling ANC. Mining powerhouse Anglo American was looking to offload a 34.9 per cent stake in JCI, the company that Barney Barnato founded. Brett teamed up with former Robben Islander Mzi Khumalo and bankrolled him to take over the JCI stake in a complicated cross-shareholding deal that would become characteristic of Kebble's deal brokering in the future. It was tipped as the model empowerment deal but collapsed spectacularly. They had bought the stake at its peak at R54.50, but the share price plummeted to R16 with Mzi at the helm, and gold fell below US$300 an ounce. Brett pushed Mzi out and took control of the gold assets.

'I think Brett just got pissed off with Mzi and said he has to go. Brett was calling the shots,' explains McKay. 'They would have quite public fallouts. At one meeting they had some ridiculous bet of six beers riding on gold. They would address each other in public under this appearance of bonhomie, but actually, the two were fighting. The basic idea was Brett thought gold was going north and Mzi thought it was going south. Mzi was right and Brett was wrong. In fact, a summary of Brett's career was that he called gold wrong on two occasions. In a nutshell.'

The fallout with Mzi would provide the roots for Brett's political alignment and conspiracy theories about jockeying for power in the upper echelons of government. Speaking to financial journalist Nicky Smith just a month before his death, Brett reflected on the Mzi episode. Smith, who is now with Bloomberg, wrote about it in *The Star* at the time:

'A big disillusionment for me was the fallout with Mzi Khumalo on JCI and the way that was handled, and the results that it led to,' Kebble said *last month. 'Mzi was not interested in the social upliftment interests or issues that interested me. I can understand why. He had come out of Robben Island and he just wanted to make himself the best living that he could. Mzi went and got his supporters in government to basically boycott me, to ostracise me. Mzi was close to a few people, people like Bulelani (Ngcuka, the former director of public prosecutions), who made a point of really having a go at me,' Kebble said (28 September 2005).*

Brett's theory was that by backing certain factions within the ruling party, such as Youth League members and ANC MP and struggle stalwart Andrew Mlangeni, he had made himself unpopular in other circles. Brett attributed this to his fallout with Mzi over the Anglo deal. He believed Mzi was driving the faction in support of President Thabo Mbeki against Zuma and that Mzi, in fact, was the kingmaker.

There was intense speculation in the media at the time that Brett was bankrolling ousted Deputy President Jacob Zuma who at the time was mired in controversy for his alleged corrupt relationship with his financial adviser Schabir Shaik. It was fairly obvious that Brett's backing of a particular faction within the ruling party, at a time when the organisation was consumed by a bitter battle for power, had made him a target. But Brett did back both horses and befriended Essop Pahad, Mbeki's lieutenant in chief, who even spoke at his funeral. Jackie Selebi, the National Commissioner of Police who would go on trial for allegedly accepting money from Brett, was also seen as an Mbeki man.

In 2003, ex-prosecutions boss Bulelani Ngcuka 'outed' Brett at a hugely controversial off-the-record briefing with black editors, held to update them on the progress of the investigation into allegations against Zuma. Ngcuka suggested Brett was paying protection fees to the Youth League. Brett was furious, threatened to sue Ngcuka for defamation and reported him to the Public Protector. His main riposte was publicly to accuse Ngcuka and then Justice Minister Penuell Maduna of pursuing a private agenda. At the time, Brett and his father Roger were facing fraud charges and it was in his interest to discredit the prosecutions authority – this was also one of his motives for supporting Zuma in his claims that the National Prosecuting Authority (NPA) was being manipulated. Brett swiftly appointed Advocate Willem Heath to investigate abuses of power by Maduna and Ngcuka. Brett's accusations featured during the Hefer Commission of Inquiry into claims by Zuma allies that Ngcuka was an apartheid-era spy. It was a tumultuous time politically in the country.

Through Glenn Agliotti, Brett sought out the assistance of the police's top brass in his ongoing feud with Ngcuka and capitalised on the SAPS's own desire to source information about the prosecutions chief. Selebi arranged meetings between Brett and senior crime intelligence officers such as Rayman Lalla and Mulangi Mphego. One of these meetings, which took place in the spring of 2003, was videotaped and was the subject of a *Mail & Guardian* article:

> In the meeting, Kebble links Ngcuka to the same group of alleged power-brokers who were to emerge in the hoax email allegations and in the so-called Zuma tapes that scotched the Zuma prosecution. They include businessmen Saki Macozoma and Mzi Khumalo and Ngcuka's wife, Phumzile Mlambo-Ngcuka.
>
> Kebble makes it clear that he believes Ngcuka's investigation of cases against him and his father – over two separate cases of alleged corporate fraud – were legally unfounded and politically motivated.
>
> Kebble, who emerges from the two-hour meeting as an astute and polished communicator, tells Mphego and Lalla: 'I knew from a fairly early stage – because he came to tell me – that Mzi [Khumalo] had a close relationship with Ngcuka. He came and said, "You know these claims you've got against me [Kebble's company JCI was seeking to enforce a R30-million debt against Khumalo] ... I know Bulelani very well and maybe if we can settle this thing he won't be so hard on you ..."
>
> 'I then started to look very closely at who was around Ngcuka and found these guys had a pattern of operating. They would get together regularly – Mzi, Saki, Moss Ngoasheng [former President Thabo Mbeki's former economic adviser] ... and Bulelani and friends – get together and drink heavily every Friday night ... and hatch their plots ...' (4 June 2010)

Kebble goes on to explain his view that Macozoma was, indeed, using Ngcuka to advance his own presidential ambitions and that was why Kebble was being investigated.

'The reason for this attack [on me] is that Bulelani's office is being abused. The office is used not in pursuit of justice; it was used to settle scores, commercially and politically' (4 June 2010).

Brett made little secret of the fact that he made generous donations to the ANC. It was assumed this was to curry political favour and buy influence. He admitted to being one of the mystery donors who pumped half a million rand into the beleaguered Western Cape branch of the ruling party in the early 2000s. After this was exposed by the *Sunday Times*, Brett released a public statement saying he was 'a patriot who would continue providing financial assistance for the development of democracy'. The Democratic Alliance also admitted to accepting half a million rands worth of donations between 2001 and 2004.

Whatever his motivation, Brett was plying young, up-and-coming political players with cash and business deals. ANC Youth League members Lunga Ncwana, Andile Nkuhlu and current Sports Minister Fikile Mbalula were all regular visitors to Brett's homes. Andrew Minaar speaks about how Brett bought pay-as-you-go phones for the men and would only use specific handsets to communicate with them. 'Brett was coaching the ANC Youth League and those phones were particularly bought for a Youth League rally so Brett could stay in touch with them. In terms of what they'd say, how they'd say it, what would happen.' Minaar has scandalous recollections of the behaviour of Mbalula during visits to Brett's house.

'Fikile was here often. He'd come here and in like an hour he'd finished a bottle of Johnny Walker Blue Label. Flat. Flat,' Minaar tells me, his face betraying his incredulity. 'The one day they were all here, and they were going on. Brett was running late and they were going on in the lounge like children, laughing and banging on the piano. They were like children in the house. They'd always be looking for something to eat and would only drink champagne. They used to refer to Fikile as a "coconut" and he really had a problem with that. Even on the one Christmas party on this patio, it was like a children's party the way they were behaving. Fikile was quite arrogant. He treated me just like a thing,' he says about the man who is now an influential cabinet minister.

Laura Sham corroborates what Minaar tells me. 'They'd behave like they'd never seen anything. They'd be fine when they arrived, but the more they drank, they'd become hooligans. I knew Fikile drank quite a bit. They behaved like absolute hooligans,' she says. Sham never saw Brett actually giving any of them cash in envelopes but as the person who managed the tycoon's affairs, she knew the intricacies of his business dealings. 'I didn't see the cash; it would be handled through the companies. Lunga had cars from him, all of them had cars and homes and it was all funded by Brett.' Roger and Guy Kebble confirm the extent to which the young politicians were benefitting from Brett's generosity.

Brett had an interest in the ANCYL's investment arm, Lembede, and shareholders in some of his companies included politicians. Some Youth League members, like Nkhulu, also served as fronts for Brett's business dealings, ready recipients of his largesse. Sham is particularly vocal about one event involving her erstwhile boss and the Youth League. 'He gave them four million rand for their conference one year. Brett's name was a lot in the papers at the time and he wasn't looking good. They actually said to him please don't come to the conference after he funded their conference. I'll never forget it, Brett came into the office and he was so down-trodden. He said to me, "How quickly they forget." Those were his words. It was a slap in the face,' she recounts bitterly.

Other politicians and prominent figures were also regular features at Brett's Inanda home, according to Minaar and Sham. The PA says she witnessed a current, influential cabinet minister visiting Brett on at least one occasion. She also claims that she actually saw an expense statement for a high-profile member of a prolific ANC struggle family whose lifestyle was being funded by Brett. 'I had it in my hand. The expense statement. So there were all these funnies happening.'

After the Anglo episode and the public fallout with Mzi Khumalo came the great Western Areas debacle. In the meeting video recorded in 2003, Brett mentions the case of corporate fraud being pursued against him. That case had its roots in the Western Areas saga. In 2003, Brett was sitting in the CEO's office at Western Areas and wanted to make a bid for Randfontein Estates in order to consolidate his portfolio and list it on the Canadian stock exchange. But Harmony Gold, headed by Bernard Swanepoel – another big player in the market – also wanted Randfontein. So Brett manipulated shares in order to repel Harmony's takeover bid.

Brett made unauthorised loans of up to R100 million of Western Areas money to Durban Roodepoort Deep (DRD), of which his father was the chairman. The idea was that DRD was supposed to have bought Randfontein shares, thereby ballooning the share price up and beyond Harmony's reach. But Swanepoel outclassed Brett, who was shown up to be cavalier with shareholders' money. He was forced to resign from the Western Areas board but later resumed the position.

Cue Mark Wellesley-Wood, the man dubbed the 'pinstripe bandit' from London.

A S THE HEAD OF DRD IN THE MID-2000S, MARK WELLESLEY-WOOD
was one of the first to finger the Kebbles for corporate skulduggery
and went head to head with the father-and-son pairing in a series of law-
suits over money he believed was still owing to the mining house. The
irony is that Wellesley-Wood was actually Roger Kebble's idea. In 1999,
DRD needed to boost its corporate governance standards, so Roger suggested to shareholder Mercury Asset Management that they bring 'their
guy' in to sort it out. 'Their guy' was banker Mark Wellesley-Wood, who
was already sitting on the DRD board as Mercury's representative. David
McKay remembers the appointment: 'Wellesley-Wood always styled himself as a Mr Fix it. He's kind of like "The Ghost of Christmas Present", this
enormous, quite jovial, amiable British guy. Roger employed him to come
and fix the company and sort out the malfeasance and all the rest of it and,
after a bit of time, Wellesley-Wood said, "Well, it's you," to Roger and he
toppled him. There was a palace coup and Roger was kicked out,' recalls
the business editor.

In a directive to shareholders in 2003, Wellesley-Wood said that he had
'received information regarding possible irregularities in DRD of a very
serious nature and at a high level of management'. Wellesley-Wood told
analysts and media at a quarterly presentation that the company was finally rid of the 'K Factor', – according to McKay, Roger was sitting in the
audience and was ashen-faced and furious.

Thereafter a bitter feud ensued between the two that played out over the
following years, with both men muck raking against one another. A subsequent forensic investigation found that shares had been illegally issued and
that Roger had invested over R120 million in an Indonesian mine called
Rawas, which had absolutely no intrinsic value. Legal suits were brought
against Roger – he was arrested at the then Johannesburg International
Airport on 62 charges of fraud amounting to close on R7 million and kept
in prison overnight. He immediately cried foul, claiming his arrest was
unlawful and designed purely to humiliate and embarrass him. The allegation was that Roger, while on the board of DRD, had channelled money
through a close corporation he owned, called Skilled Labour Brokers, to
a labour consultancy and had siphoned off the money for himself. The
brawl between Roger Kebble and Wellesley-Wood turned ugly as McKay
explained on Miningmx:

The five-year relationship between Mark Wellesley-Wood, CEO of DRDGOLD, and Roger Kebble, chairman of Randgold & Exploration, is as incredible as it's acrimonious. The two men have sued and allegedly spied on each other; Kebble has been imprisoned (in a series of events allegedly orchestrated by Wellesley-Wood); Wellesley-Wood was deported (allegedly through Kebble's links with the Government's Home Affairs Department).

And all the while, both have gladly seized the opportunity to firmly place a hob-nailed boot to the other's scrotum – preferably in public. For example, who can forget Wellesley-Wood's dubbing as 'that pin-striped bandit' – an indelicate sobriquet invented by Brett Kebble, Roger's son, during one live radio interview during 2002?

But that's nothing. Wellesley-Wood has wreaked a different kind of reputation destruction on the Kebbles. It's now four years since Wellesley-Wood first accused Roger Kebble of fraud, an allegation from which the veteran miner has never recovered (4 April 2005).

Another irony, according to McKay, was that Wellesley-Wood had himself awarded enormous share bonuses unsupported by the company performance and, in the end, 'he raided DRD just like everyone else did. No one is a good guy in this story.' In an article McKay wrote for Miningmx.com, he observes that Wellesley-Wood took home a R3.7 million bonus in the 2007 financial year, even though DRDGOLD endured a 'precipitous decline in its share price' (31 October 2007). Wellesley-Wood hit back at the claims he received inflated bonuses, telling McKay, 'I can take bullets like the next man but ... you should put the record straight'.

The Kebbles allegedly set about digging for dirt on the banker-turned-miner and apparently came up with a pearl of a claim. McKay tells me that Brett loved to tell the story about what they supposedly uncovered. Brett used to tell anyone who cared to listen that they discovered that 'Wellesley-Wood' was not, in fact, his real name – his moniker was only Mark Wood but he'd added his wife's surname to convert his own into a double-barrelled formation for vanity's sake, to make it sound a bit grander. It's unclear whether anyone bothered to follow up to see if that was really true.

The tales of corporate espionage are astounding. In an interview on the

Australian TV show *4 Corners*, Wellesley-Wood revealed the extent of the precautions he was taking. 'I think perhaps because I did take preventive action i.e. you're talking about safe houses, changing your pattern of work, basically changing your travel schedules, etcetera, meant that it was very, I was making it difficult for them to quote unquote "pin me down".' He also speaks about how, after launching a multimillion-dollar lawsuit against Brett Kebble and John Stratton, he arrived at his office to find the safe had been blown open and that documents were missing.

As the feud unfolded Wellesley-Wood turned to private investigators to fight in his corner. He went to Warren Goldblatt of Associated Intelligence Networks (AIN). The Kebbles, in turn, went to Agliotti who recruited Clinton Nassif's Central National Security Group (CNSG) to do the dirty work of spying and profiling.

According to Agliotti, this was his 'in' with the Kebbles. He testified that he set about arranging meetings between Selebi's lieutenants, Lalla and Mphego, and Brett's representatives, Stratton and Advocate Willem Heath, to discuss the issues of Ngcuka, Wellesley-Wood and looming prosecutions.

As the brawl rolled on, Brett's interests increasingly turned from business to politics. Minaar recalls the shift. 'Initially, when I started with Brett, it was all business. Then it turned to Wellesley-Wood, and Bulelani Ngcuka was discussed openly. Politics was discussed. His whole life became very politically orientated. Totally shifted from business to politics and the battles they were fighting. It was always public relations work being done, Gleason, Dominic Ntsele, David Barritt were here,' says the butler, referring to the team of spin doctors and journalists that Brett used to sugarcoat his public image. 'He used to manipulate the press and manipulate people. Articles were written in the press and what was going in the press, there was draft copies of it here.' From Minaar's version of events, it appears as though things were turning from the strange to the bizarre. 'I would have to keep people away from one another, who couldn't be seen together at the house. When there were political people here. Sometimes people would come in the front door and others would exit outside the back.'

Sham also witnessed the morphing of Brett the businessman into Brett the political player. 'It turned more politically inclined. It was very scary.

We started seeing big political figures coming to meetings, sometimes at the house. He started turning away from the office, he came in less and less and less and demanded to work at the house. I worked via fax, via phone and would be called to the house as well,' recalls the vivacious middle-aged blonde. 'I actually started realising in July 2004 that things started changing. And then suddenly we had a Christmas function in December 2004 and Brett was announcing the Orlyfunt deal and then I realised this is all a load of nonsense,' she says, referring to Brett's last-gasp economic empowerment deal that was on the table in the months before his death. 'The things he was saying and the things I saw passing my desk just didn't tie up.'

She also noticed a worrying change in his demeanour. 'Brett was changed by then, his moods, he was withdrawn, he was jovial that Christmas party, but he became more withdrawn, more of a recluse. He was different, moody, arrogant, rude, and that's not how I knew him. I could see he was not himself. I think it was a bit of depression and desperation. I think from the time he came into the business he was killing fires and it just spiralled out of control. The downfall was people stopped believing, the shareholders walked away and then he had no one in his corner and it was difficult out there on his own. All the ANC people stopped visiting and he realised he's out there on his own. I don't think it was greed. He had everything he wanted. It was power. It was a power-play thing. Brett loved power. But also, he tried to save his family from disgrace and it just didn't work.'

Things were on a downhill slide for Brett Kebble and his business interests. His malfeasance extended far beyond what was in the prosecutors' scopes at the time and things were beginning to look ominous. Western Areas shares were dipping steeply and, as McKay explains, Brett was still fleecing shares from Randgold. They were being encumbered and used as collateral.

'I think in the latter stages he was just sort of shuffling paper around. As he became more and more desperate, it was just robbing Peter to pay Paul,' says McKay. 'There were lots of these shelf companies he created to house share deals he did. Scrip lending was a big issue. The reason for this is that banks wouldn't deal directly with Brett so he'd have to engineer all kinds of risky trading devices to generate cash. So with scrip lending, Brett would sell shares in a company Randgold owned, say Anglo, for shares in Sasol.

He'd then sell the Sasol shares into the market for more than he would have got for the original Anglo shares. Unfortunately for Brett, those Sasol shares would have to be returned to the merchant banker with whom he did the swap. Brett's hope was that he could buy back the Sasol shares from the open market for less than we swapped them. It must have been that Brett often, if not invariably, lost the bet. Since Randgold's financial situation had actually worsened, not improved, he had no choice but to repeat the process in a kind of tragic vortex.'

In February 2004, Brett wrote to financial journalist Deon Basson following a series of articles he'd penned about a subsidiary of JCI. Basson had discovered a 'blow hole' where Brett was hiding funds. The editor, who has since passed away, read the letter during a debate on investigative journalism:

> *From the age of 30, I have been involved in a series of business coups that brought me public prominence. Perhaps the apogee of my success over the past 10 years was when entrepreneur Mzi Khumalo and I bought control of mining company JCI from Anglo-American. In those days the media loved me. I was held as the new Barney Barnato and my family was lauded for our role in making it possible for a new breed of independent mining operators to revitalise marginal mines, saving thousands of jobs and creating profit for shareholders. I am still the person I was then, although the intervening decades have seen some grey streaks in my hair. But these days, if you believed everything you read, you could be forgiven for thinking very bad things about me. Those who have made enough money to forget their own time in the cut and thrust of fortune building, or who try and portray me as a dubious businessman, say that the companies I control are shaking and sooner or later the whole house of cards will come tumbling down as I buckle under the pile of mounting debt and I'm forced to sell my assets. There isn't a word of truth in the whole story …*

A top Scorpions investigator who spent years probing the quagmire of Brett Kebble's financial affairs once told me about a metaphor he uses to explain exactly how Brett landed himself in the dwang. And it goes something like this: 'Joe' is working as a clerk in a bank and every day he comes to his till and does his job. His books balance and there are no problems. But one day, Joe is short on cash and really wants to buy himself some lunch. He thinks, 'Oh well, let me just borrow R50 from the till and I'll pay it back tomorrow.' He takes a pink lion note out the register and off he goes to buy a sarmie. The next day, Joe has the R50 in his pocket to repay the loan but before he can get to his till, out steps his manager who has some news. Joe is moving departments and now has a new job. But Joe needs to get back to his till to repay the money he took out the day before. Joe's manager tells him he doesn't have time to go back to his office because he has a new desk to get to. The problem is, if Joe doesn't make it back to the till, the new guy taking over his job will notice that R50 is missing and that the books don't balance. Joe needs to keep control of the till or else he will be found out and that's exactly what happens.

The difference between Brett Kebble and Joe is that Brett wasn't just stealing from the bank's till. He was looting the coffers of major list- ed companies with long histories and huge reputations. He also wasn't just pocketing R50, but rather there were millions of dollars involved. Investigators wading through incredibly complex cross-shareholding schemes would take months to establish that R900 million had been hived off from the three companies that he treated as one and as his own. It was the sheer scale and width of the theft. However, the principles were the same. Brett still needed to be in control of the till to hide his crime.

So, in early 2005, when the house of cards was beginning to collapse around him and Brett was asked to relinquish his executive duties, he fought like hell to keep control. Western Areas was haemorrhaging money while JCI and Randgold were suspended from the JSE for failing to submit their annual results. Investors were willing to bail out the companies but only on one condition – Brett Kebble had to resign and effectively lose control of the till. Untrue to his predecessor Barney Barnato's mantra, he would not 'wind up with a good curtain', and he'd fail to bring it down before the public had time to find him out.

Mikey

The first time I knew Brett was in trouble was when Clint came to me originally and said to me, 'Listen, John and Brett have a hit list of people who had done them in, either in business or bad-mouthed them or done something wrong to the Kebble family and to John Stratton,' that they needed to be sorted out and these okes were willing to pay R2 million per person on this list. I never ever saw a list, like a written list, but he did tell me. The first person on this list was Mark Wellesley-Wood, which they wanted me to see if we could catch him. There was an oke down in Cape Town; I think his name was Nortier. I never ever met him. I just got given an address that I went to stake out. I asked Clint what was the problem with Wellesley-Wood and he said to me that Stratton told him that they'd done him in for R200 million on a DRD mine deal and he wanted him taken out for payback. I never saw Wellesley-Wood. If I did, I would have shot him.

'H E WAS THE TUNGSTEN TIP OF THE DRILL BIT AND KEBBLE WAS THE great, flabby weight behind it.' That's how one Brett Kebble associate described John Stratton to the *Mail & Guardian* newspaper when his close relationship to the mining aficionado first began to come to the fore in 2006. He was Brett's 'consigliore', adviser, right-hand man and confidant.

Stratton, an elderly businessman who was already 71 when Brett was killed, has a colourful background. He has held numerous directorships over his life and has sat on the boards of over 120 companies, a number of which have been deregistered and have imploded publicly. According to an official profile he is 'a director of various Australian companies' with 40 years of experience in the resource sector, who had managed joint-venture operations in the Persian Gulf, Papua New Guinea, the Solomon Islands, the United States, Mauritius and India.

The British-naturalised Australian was brought into the JCI stable by Brett Kebble in 1998 to assist with the troubles around DRD and became a director. He quickly wriggled his way into the Kebbles' inner circle. The *Mail & Guardian* reported on Stratton's closeness to Brett, both in proximity and access:

> 'His office had an inter-leading door to Brett's and in would float this crow, this wattled crane,' said one source, referring to Stratton's skinny and aging appearance. 'There was a list of who had to get paid every month, no matter how dire the [financial] situation, and Stratton was always on it. At least R500 000 per month to my knowledge,' said the same insider (15 December 2006).

Laura Sham claims credit for Stratton's nickname 'Turtle', which has stuck. 'We used to call him Turtle because he looks like a little turtle! I started it and Rita and all the girls in the office used to call him Turtle,' she tells me, laughing hard. I laugh too – having only seen pictures of Stratton, he really does look like a turtle.

'Stratton was Brett's henchman,' says business editor David McKay. 'When I first met him, he was this little old guy, not a threatening person to see or meet, a bit wizened, a bit squirty. He came across as a bit of a grandpa, with his waddle. But during the course of our interview, when I put to him criticisms Wellesley-Wood had made of him, he turned to me and coldly stated Wellesley-Wood ought to watch his step or bad things would happen. Stratton was vicious.'

Sham agrees there was something foreboding and peculiar about the guy. 'He always had his head down and never looked you in the eye. That to me is scaly, something is not right. He was always meeting with Brett behind closed doors. I thought he was dangerous. I really didn't want to befriend him. He was, in the end, the puppet master running the show.'

Dominic Ntsele, Brett Kebble's media strategist, is more scathing about Stratton. 'I suspect he arrived in the country with a strategy and he executed it. It was Stratton who led Brett to the underworld and introduced him to corporate espionage,' says Ntsele, not masking his dislike for the man in any way. Ntsele is also extremely suspicious of Stratton's history in the British secret service – he used to claim he had worked for Western intelligence agencies such as MI5 and apparently saw himself as a James Bond character. 'He was controlling and always scheming. He's too good to be true. He's the kind of guy who doesn't have a meeting at the Vatican, he has a meeting with the Pope, you know. He's that kind of guy,' says Ntsele.

'He was a shrewd businessman. A real "shrewdy",' says Andrew Minaar, who was often privy to the closed-doors meetings. 'If you think about it, Stratton was actually calling the shots, telling Brett how to do things. He was also involved in the Agliottis and Nassifs. That relationship was mostly maintained by Stratton, not Brett,' he says.

Both Minaar and Sham agree that the two men shared a father-son type of relationship, which likely inflamed Roger Kebble's jealousy. 'Brett and him were always together, constantly together,' says Minaar. Sham agrees. 'Brett and John were more like father and son than Roger was. They confided in one another and had secret meetings. Maybe that's why Roger and Brett fought so much.'

Glenn Agliotti also believes Stratton's closeness to Brett infuriated Roger. 'Brett had his own way of running his business, and it wasn't necessarily what Roger agreed with. Roger almost saw where Brett was going wrong and he was upset that John Stratton was leading him in that direction. They didn't want Roger to know anything. Stratton is highly intelligent. He really knew his shit when it came to putting business deals together. If you interpret that as being calculating, then it was.' Stratton would feature prominently in the forensic audit probes into JCI and Randgold & Exploration.

Those who knew him best describe John Stratton as the type of man who always made sure he sat in the highest chair with his muscle, his strongmen, around him. They say he was Brett's conduit to Glenn Agliotti, Clinton Nassif and the world of corporate espionage.

CLINTON NASSIF MET GLENN AGLIOTTI ON THE GOLF COURSE. IT was the end of 2003 and Nassif was setting up his private security firm Central National Security Group (CNSG). Agliotti was nurturing his chummy relationship with the country's most powerful policeman. The two men were well-suited bedfellows. Mid-swing, Agliotti told Nassif that he did work for the Kebbles. With characteristic swagger, he also told his new friend that he 'was working with Jackie Selebi' and that he was 'friends' with the National Commissioner. It was habitual for Agliotti to follow up introductions with claims of closeness to Selebi.

I am always amused by just what kinds of deals are struck on golf courses. Business transactions are secured, partnerships nurtured, but I never suspected a burly security boss from the South and a wannabe Mafia Don would be plotting illegal dealings and the corruption of a police chief on the fairways and manicured greens of the most exclusive of clubs.

A week or so after the golf game, Nassif called his new mate and set up a breakfast date in Sandton City where the duo spoke at length about the Kebbles and Agliotti's relationship with Selebi. Agliotti saw a gap – he knew that Brett Kebble and John Stratton were in the market for a new security chief as they were unhappy with the work being done by Paul Stemmet, his current security head. He also knew that JCI's troubles with Mark Wellesley-Wood were becoming untenable and needed to be appropriately handled. Agliotti suggested to Nassif that he start doing work for the Kebbles.

According to Nassif, a meeting between himself and John Stratton was set up in Cape Town. Before the meeting, Agliotti, the master of sweet talk, briefed Nassif on exactly what to say in order to win Stratton over. According to Nassif, he was told to say that he was 'part of Jackie's team, doing investigations and gathering intelligence'. Stratton was sold and he set about briefing Nassif about the company's soft spots and what work needed doing.

And so, according to Nassif and Agliotti, began a process of what is commonly known as 'knocking' in the industry of dirty tricks. Nassif and Agliotti were paid millions of rands by Brett Kebble and Stratton through shelf companies Spring Lights and Misty Mountains. In exchange, Nassif and Agliotti claim they promised to sell them access to Jackie Selebi and agreed to 'sort out' problems for them. By 'knocking' them, they would take the money, telling Brett and Stratton they were paying bribes, but the bribe money was not always passed on. Nassif explains the process in his sworn statement: 'Brett and Stratton would then authorise and make payments to me to bribe and pay those people. However, I would not pay or bribe the people but say that I had done so and then keep the money. This is commonly known as knocking. I deal hereunder with Spring Light 6 (Pty) Limited which is the company in which monies from JCI Group and Consolidated Mining Management Services were channelled, *inter alia* for the payments referred to above.' He continued: 'I think Brett and Stratton did not always trust us when we told them that we had people in the bag and paid them, as they particularly wanted to meet with Selebi, obviously to confirm for themselves that Selebi was, in fact, providing services to their benefit on account of payments said to have been made to him.'

It was not in Agliotti's or Nassif's interests for Brett and Stratton to meet Selebi personally. Agliotti explained to the South Gauteng High Court why not: 'I did not want them to have easy access to the accused because then they would no longer need me, or my services. So it was a decision that I took, a business decision.' He went on: 'I tried to prevent this, but there reached a time where they insisted and said if this did not happen, they would terminate my services with them. So I arranged a dinner with the accused, myself, Brett Kebble and John Stratton.'

A perfect example of 'knocking' by Nassif is the circumstances surrounding the suspicious withdrawal of criminal charges against Roger Kebble in January 2005. Kebble Senior was facing 62 charges of fraud, amounting to about R7 million related to the mining brawl with Wellesley-Wood. The prosecutor was Advocate Barry Roux, who also happens to be Nassif's advocate. The case had been postponed over a dozen times when Roux asked Magistrate Vivien Hawkins to give the state yet more time because 'new evidence' had emerged. A recently discovered invoice showed that an amount paid into Roger Kebble's account was a 'loan amount' and he needed a postponement to look at the evidence. The magistrate found the delays to be unreasonable and ordered the case struck off the roll.

During Glenn Agliotti's trial, Nassif testified that he had told the Kebbles and Stratton that he could 'take care of' the prosecutor Barry Roux, his junior Sandra Mart and the magistrate. Under duress, Nassif acknowledged that he told them it would take a 'couple of hundred thousand rand' to pay them off and finally conceded the amount was R200 000. Nassif is adamant the bribe was never actually paid over to Roux and he was lucky as the case 'fell his way'.

With all this knocking going on, Nassif's street smarts quickly reminded him that he'd need brawn and brains to back up his big talk.

His first recruit was Stephen Sander who became his business partner. Sander, a short, stocky man, has a history in the police's 'Special Branch'; he was a member of Koevoet, worked in Iraq and was previously employed by Kebble's rivals, AIN – the company contracted by Wellesley-Wood. Before he took the stand in Jackie Selebi's corruption trial, Sander was described to me as 'the stuff action movies are made of' and 'the most dangerous of them all' but he is surprisingly well spoken and is an excellent witness. He also provided the brains for Nassif as he had the ability to decipher tender documents and put together complex deals. Nassif told Sander that he needed him to do surveillance and investigative work and appointed him Operational Director of CNSG. He also explained to him that Police Chief Jackie Selebi was unhappy with the work being done by Palto, a private security firm that was doing work for the police, and they would be taking it over. They would be performing drug busts and illegal transportation of containers across borders and would have to set up an informer network. Sander set about employing ex-policemen to work for CNSG but also hired fully employed cops to moonlight for him. This would mean his company would have unbridled access to the SAPS's intelligence resources and subvert any potential red tape. In a bid to woo Selebi, Nassif also employed the police chief's alleged mistress and former secretary Ntombi Matshoba as a director.

Nassif then turned to his good friend Mikey Schultz to help him. Mikey was looking for an out from Elite anyway and Nassif knew he could convince him to leave the fast life. Nassif told Mikey that he'd landed a big contract with some billionaires who owned lots of businesses and mines. Part of Mikey's job description was to 'look after' VIP sites, which mainly meant supplying guards to the homes of JCI directors.

Nassif began buying up small security companies in order to expand his portfolio. One of those was First Watch, which employed Nigel McGurk. Mikey encouraged his long-time friend to go and work with him at CNSG. During Agliotti's 2010 trial, Nigel candidly explained to the court that he had been doing some dirty work for Nassif even before he was officially employed:

> McGURK: We used to do some work for him with certain things like going to collect money for him, intimidating people, doing just basically the dirty work for Clint.
>
> ADV MASHIANE: What do you mean collecting money and intimidating people?
>
> McGURK: Well there were people that had come up for Clint that had owed money and we would go there and do debt collections, intimidate certain people. Myself and Mikey had built up a reputation through the night-club industry as the, if you want to call it, the heavies.

It didn't take long for Nigel to work out that he wasn't being employed for his intelligence and insight:

> McGURK: After a while it became clear to me that myself and Mikey weren't really there to get the security contracts. We were basically there for the muscle.
>
> ADV MASHIANE: In what capacity did you join this CNSG?
>
> McGURK: My capacity, in inverted commas, was to get guarding contracts and entertainment venue contracts for CNSG, but it became clear to us after a while that we weren't there for that, we were there for muscle – to be Clint's muscle and to do collections and to also intimidate people.

And there was much dirty work to be done. Brett Kebble was becoming increasingly desperate and disillusioned. He was so desperate and so disillusioned that he was willing to turn to the underworld to 'take out' his opponents and detractors.

However, in a sworn statement to the Scorpions, Sander reveals that he took instruction from Stratton alone and not Brett. He also revealed how he gave instructions to his investigators to illegally tap telephones, bug rooms, place monitoring devices on motor cars, draw financial records and telephone statements, and extract information from computers.

He explains how he blackmailed a JCI employee into resigning by covertly establishing he was surfing child pornography on his work computer. Sander also reveals how he clandestinely tracked a JCI secretary to establish if she was selling information to competitors.

He admits to spying on Kebble rival Peter Skeat, and compiling a dossier of transcripts of his phone conversations. Skeat had pursued Brett through the courts for payment of R80 million which was owed to him for the purchase of shares in the company Aflease. Brett had tried to get out of making the payment by alleging Skeat was guilty of fraud. However, a High Court judgment exonerated him. Skeat was clapped in leg irons and arrested in September 2005, just weeks before his accuser was killed, and he's convinced that the trumped-up charges brought against him were the work of a vindictive Brett Kebble.

Sensationally, in the sworn statement, Sander also divulges that he spied on Brett, Roger and Guy Kebble.

He claims Nassif ordered him to spy on Guy Kebble, allegedly on Brett's request, because of 'bad blood between the two of them'. He says he consulted with Stratton about this, and arranged the surveillance on Guy. Stratton requested that he monitor Roger Kebble's movements because he wanted to establish if Roger was meeting with former security chief Paul Stemmet and ex-policeman Calla Botha. Then, in the beginning of 2005, according to Sander, he did a profile on Brett at the request of Stratton. He claims Stratton was very upset because 'Brett took R400 million out of the accounts without telling him'. To the best of his recollection, investigators obtained the bank statements of all Brett's accounts.

The climate was becoming increasingly tense as the paranoia mounted. Nassif claims a 'hit list' featuring all Brett's rivals was put together and that the 'hit list' was never written down. He testified that it was fluid, changing regularly according to who had 'done them in' on any particular day. A price was put on the targets' heads: R2 million per person to whoever would 'take them out'.

Wellesley-Wood was at the top of the list, followed by Randgold Resources CEO Dr Mark Bristow and Aflease financial director Jean

Daniel Nortier. Bristow was targeted because he was vocal about Brett's looting of Randgold & Exploration and Randgold Resources. Nortier was the Chief Financial Officer of an entity called Aflease. During 2004, he attempted to assist Randgold & Exploration with its financial woes and entered into a share-swap agreement. Brett never kept his side of the bargain and reneged on several payments despite numerous enquiries by Nortier. The CFO resorted to sending lawyers' letters asking where his money was and the Kebbles didn't like that. *Noseweek* editor Martin Weltz and *The Citizen* journalist Paul Kirk supposedly even cracked a spot on the hit list.

When I ask Mikey Schultz about the 'missions' he was sent on as part of the execution of this apparent hit list, he is matter of fact and candid. It's a mind-boggling thought – that a leading captain of industry, with political favour, recruited a gunman to scare or even to kill his corporate rivals. Mikey did testify about this in open court during Agliotti's 2010 trial, with both the prosecution and the defence agreeing the 'hit list' did exist. However, the claim of Stratton's involvement remains untested.

Mikey's most vivid recollection was his pursuit of Wellesley-Wood. He tells me quite nonchalantly how he and Stephen Sander battled to track down the British businessman but, if he had found him, he would have killed him.

'They wanted me to shoot him and when I went there I was armed on a few occasions, ready to shoot him, hey. I went to his business. Then he had offices in Empire Road and we tried to find him there and we could never find him. Sander and I went to his house on St Patrick Street, opposite KES High School, the bottom side of Houghton there. The one time Sander dressed up as a hobo and sat outside the school from early in the morning. Another time, he asked me to drive him there on a motorbike to see if we could maybe see the guy in traffic because we have never been able to see him. He was out of the country most of the time.'

Mikey's deep disdain for Glenn Agliotti is also apparent when he divulges details of how Agliotti and Nassif allegedly 'knocked' Brett Kebble as part of the pursuit of Wellesley-Wood. '[Wellesley-Wood] had a house in London. That's the same house that Clint and Agliotti went over for a jol in London and let the Kebbles pay for it. They went to the oke's address and took pictures and that standing outside the address. They stayed in a five-star hotel, first class, ten days I think in London, spending as much money as they could, every day. They came back and charged the Kebbles and they got the money for it. That's our clever friend, Mr Agliotti. He's a proper poes, hey.'

Mikey drove down to Durban to scout out journalist Paul Kirk's house but he assures me it was just a 'recce'. 'I drove down to Durban early in the morning. I got there, stopped at Westville shopping centre, bought a map book of Durban, found the address, went there, checked it out and didn't take any photos.' When he tells me this, I think that it doesn't sound like the most sophisticated of assassination attempts and again realise that Mikey is not a 'professional' hit man as such. He's a security agent who knows how to use a gun but has no real formal training. I suspect he also has a conscience.

When Mikey tells me about the job he was recruited to do on Aflease CFO Daniel Nortier, this suspicion is reinforced. He never shot Nortier because the man had children of a similar age to his own. 'With Nortier, Clint gave me an address and said to me I must please fly down to Cape Town. I parked around the corner from the house and took a walk around, had a look at the house to see if something had to happen to this guy at this place, there's a way in and out. If I had to shoot him in the driveway, I was just going to do some scouting. I looked at the place and I thought let me take some photos. I never had a camera, so I took a drive down to the chemist. I went and bought a disposable camera and came back. I took some photos of the house and while walking back around the block, the young kids came outside with the mother and that's when I decided against it. I said, "If that guy's got kids, I don't want to do it. Let me not have anything to do with it, hey."' When he got back to Jo'burg, Mikey told Nassif that he couldn't execute the hit. 'I said to Clint, "Look, this oke's got kids. They're the same age as Michael." He turned around and he said to me, "This is business, you can't take it personal." So I said I'm not doing nothing. Fuck, that *laaitie*'s the same age as my son. I said no.'

While Mikey was travelling around the country plotting the murders of businessmen and journalists, another plan to secure Brett Kebble's financial survival was being hatched. It was a plan that would see Mikey playing a central role and was not all that different from the jobs he was already executing.

Mikey

Clint then came to discuss Stephen Mildenhall with me. He said, 'Look, Stephen Mildenhall was causing problems for them because he was the one that was auditing Brett and they couldn't secure loans because they needed money to patch up holes because they had been stealing money.' That's what Clint told me. And they were on the verge of securing loans and this oke was the only oke that was in the way. If he was out the way, they then could carry on and secure the loan. So Brett wanted the oke shot dead. At first I was told we must kill Mildenhall, and then it changed so that we should just put him out of action. I would have done it for Clint but I said to him, 'If this person is taken out, who's going to fill his position in the company? Somebody will.' So he said to me, 'This is what Brett and John want.'

THE FRESH-FACED, ROSY-CHEEKED AUDITOR HUNG UP THE PHONE in his Waterfront office in Cape Town, pleased with the way he'd conducted himself during the radio interview. It had been a gruelling few months for Stephen Mildenhall, the Chief Investment Officer of Allan Gray, one of the most notable privately owned investment management companies in the country. He'd been going head to head with imposing challenger Brett Kebble, but he had finally managed to wrap up the deal the way he wanted it to happen.

JCI, Randgold & Exploration and Western Areas were crippled and limping along, having been raided by Kebble. JCI and Randgold & Exploration had failed to list results on the stock exchange and Western Areas, in particular, was in dire need of a bailout. It needed US$12 million to pay for its South Deep project. South Deep was a very large gold deposit, but was a developing mine that was taking longer to develop than expected and costing a lot more money than anticipated. JCI had substantial assets in the South Deep mine that was at risk of defaulting – that would have resulted in a 'fire sale' of assets, which would have meant that shareholders would have ended up with very little.

Investec was prepared to lend JCI the money it desperately needed but, because Allan Gray was the largest institutional investor in all three Kebble firms, the bank wanted the shareholder to approve the terms of the loan agreements. Mildenhall had a few conditions of his own. He wanted the boards of the three companies to be 'reconstituted in such a way that Mr Brett Kebble would in no way exercise future control over any of the three entities and that he furthermore resign as a director from the board of Western Areas'. In essence, Kebble's companies would only be bailed out if he quit.

Kebble relented and, on 30 August 2005, the deal went through.

The very next day, Mildenhall and Investec's CEO Stephen Koseff were invited to talk on the radio about the recapitalisation of JCI and reconstitution of the company's boards.

Mildenhall hung up the phone and then packed up for the day. He made his way to the parking lot of the Allan Gray building at the V & A Waterfront and climbed into his silver Audi. It didn't take him too long to drive home, arriving at his Claremont house at 19:10. He pushed the button on his remote and watched as the electronic gate slid open and then manoeuvred his vehicle into the carport, parking alongside his wife's car. Safety-conscious and wary of all-too-common suburban hijackings in the city, Mildenhall waited for the gate to close before getting out of his Audi. Slamming the door shut behind him, he noticed two men climbing out of a red car parked near the driveway of his house. The auditor wouldn't remember the make of the vehicle, but an alert neighbour would later tell police it was a red Polo, registration CA 640392. At that time of day in late August in Cape Town, it's fairly dark and the street lighting wasn't adequate. The two men, one of whom was wearing a blue beanie, ran up to the electronic gate and pushed through the pedestrian gate alongside it, each pointing a firearm at him. Mildenhall was taken aback as the pedestrian gate was always kept locked but, for some reason, the duo opened it with ease and ran into the carport. Holding him at gunpoint, both men asked Mildenhall to empty his pockets, which he instantaneously did. He took his wallet, cellphone and keys and threw them to Blue Beanie. Blue Beanie caught the keys and wallet but dropped the cellphone, which hit the floor and smashed into pieces. Blue Beanie ordered Mildenhall to go with them, which he did not want to do. Instead, he backed out of the carport and scrambled to the front of the parked cars. At that point, both gunmen opened fire. Mildenhall recounted the harrowing events of that day from the witness stand during Brett Kebble's murder trial:

MILDENHALL: *I backed away to the back of the carport and started making my way in front of the parked cars, my car and the car that my wife was driving. As I was doing that, both men shot me. I continued making my way around the cars and I fell to the ground between the wall of the carport and the car that my wife was driving, and I was shot again. So I was shot three times in total, twice in my right shoulder and arm, and once in my left shoulder. I then lay on the ground, hoping that they would go away, and just lay very still, and I waited for the car, until I heard the car drive away. And then I struggled to get up because both my arms were essentially not capable of doing anything at the time, and I*

made my way to the front door of the house which
I couldn't, I can't – but I shouted very loudly for my
wife, who was in the house and she came down-
stairs, and drove me to Claremont Hospital to the
emergency unit, and I was treated for my injuries
there. I was admitted to ICU for – I believe I was in
ICU for I think was three days, and I was eventu-
ally released from hospital, I think was on the 8th
of September, so eight days after the incident.

In the days following the shooting, as he lay in his hospital bed in Claremont, Stephen Mildenhall mulled over the possibility that the shooting could have had something to do with the Kebble saga. He had noticed that Blue Beanie's gun had a silencer attached to it but, on second thoughts, realised it could have just been a long silver barrel. The timing of the incident was also obviously suspicious. Allan Gray appointed investigators to look into the shooting, but they concluded it was 'probably a normal crime incident' and Mildenhall put the idea of a link to Kebble into storage until a few years later. The shooting did not affect the deal struck with Kebble's companies as it had occurred a day too late. The announcement had come out the previous day and the loan agreements had been finalised in the two weeks prior to the attack. What Mildenhall didn't know until he took the stand in the South Gauteng High Court was the detail of the planning and execution of his shooting by a band of so-called 'bumbling assassins'.

I N MID-AUGUST 2005 BRETT KEBBLE WAS FEELING THE FULL WEIGHT of Allan Gray and Investec. Clinton Nassif says it was at this time that John Stratton summoned him to Cape Town. Nassif was accompanied by his partner, the ex-Koevoet agent Stephen Sander. At previous meetings with Stratton and Agliotti, Nassif claims he was regularly reminded that Stephen Mildenhall was becoming a big, big problem for JCI and some-thing had to be done about it. As Nassif and Agliotti had decided that they weren't going to kill anybody and were effectively 'knocking' Brett and Stratton, Nassif did little about 'taking care of the problem'.

But it was at the bizarre meeting at Stratton's house in Cape Town, which I like to call the 'Sushi Knife Incident', when Nassif was backed into a corner by 'The Turtle'. Nassif was cross-examined extensively about the meeting during Agliotti's trial. He told the court that at the meeting, Stratton allegedly gave him Mildenhall's address in Claremont and slid a small sushi knife across the table towards him, insisting the job must be done immediately and properly. I am amused at the image of the tortoise-like Stratton sliding a tiny sushi knife across the table with sinister intent and a visual of the seven-foot-tall hulk with the blade in his paw-like hand attempting to stab the auditor to death with a kitchen utensil!

Nassif, however, wasn't willing to get his own hands dirty. His version is that he drove past the address that Stratton gave him that night, looked at the house and then flew back to Jo'burg. He 'wasn't willing to take on the job of killing Mildenhall'. On his return, he met with Agliotti and told him there was no chance Mildenhall would be killed but, he testified, that Stratton and Brett were anxious. Time passed and Nassif claims Stratton was getting antsy. Nassif told the court that at a follow-up meeting, it was agreed that Mildenhall would be 'shut up for a couple of months' and not killed. Nassif said he told Stratton he would do the job but it would cost him R1 million and he needed R200 000 upfront to cover his overheads. Nassif insisted the cash was paid to him via Agliotti although Agliotti has always insisted he never knew anything about the Mildenhall job.

Nassif, unwilling to put himself in any kind of danger, turned to Mikey to carry out the project and paid the R200 000 over to him. Stephen Sander gave Mikey a piece of paper bearing Mildenhall's work and home addresses, his car registration and a brief description of him. And so would begin a series of comedic events that would read like the script of a Coen brothers' movie and which would reinforce the perception of the 'bumbling assassins'.

I always point to the Mildenhall shooting and the humorous circumstances that led to it when I'm asked if Mikey, Nigel and Kappie really are evil and are professional 'cleaners'. The entire operation was almost derailed by Bambi and an innocent, unsuspecting resident of Claremont was very nearly taken out because he happened to have a similar address and drive the same car as the target. It also took so long for the shooting to finally happen, that when it did, it was too late.

Mikey tells me that when he was first approached by Nassif about Mildenhall he didn't really take him seriously. 'At first I thought, "Ag, it was just another person on this hit list," so I was like, "Ja, ok cool." I just thought that some of these guys didn't really know how it works because people who don't know how it works always talk about how they got a hit put on them and how they're going to have somebody whack them,' says Mikey. 'It's not as easy and clear-cut as sitting and talking about it. It takes a lot of planning. But when Clint asked me to start staking out Mark Wellesley-Wood, I started realising that these guys were for real and they have got problems with these people and that, and they wanted them sorted out. It didn't sound like Brett was desperate at that time. It sounded like he was still on top of his game. But the story of Mildenhall, he did sound very desperate.'

Mikey was reluctant to shoot Mildenhall because his logic told him that, in the chain of command, if the top man gets taken out, the next lieutenant will simply fill his shoes. He didn't think the action would have the desired effect. As a result, he tried his best to get out of the job. 'I didn't really take Mildenhall to *kop* at first and then Clint started putting pressure on me. I tried to get out of it at first, hey. I said to him, "Listen, I know okes down in Cape Town. I'll get hold of them there and sort it out."'

Mikey could no longer absorb the pressure from Nassif and eventually relented, agreeing to shoot Mildenhall. 'A few days went by and Clint came to me and said to me, "Have you gotten hold of those people in Cape Town?" I said, "No, I can't get hold of them." But I hadn't even tried,' Mikey admits to me. 'He says to me, "I need you to go and sort this out for me, man." I said, "OK."'

Mikey then approached his loyal crew, Kappie and Nigel, to assist him with the job. As usual, they were willing to help one another out. 'I went and approached Kappie. I said to him, "Listen, will you come with me down there and help me sort this out?" He said, "No, sweet, no problem." So we then approached Nigel and said, "Nigel, will you come down with us?" Because Kappie knows a lot of people down there, he was going to help us find some people and we decided that if we can't find the people that need to do it, we'll do it ourselves. Three is better than two. Obviously. Two can do the job, one can drive. Then we left.'

Not wanting to be traced, the trio set off on a road trip from Jo'burg to Cape Town in a borrowed gold BMW X5 and left their cellphones at home. Kappie was driving and was packing a 40 Smith and Wesson handgun which he had 'organised in Yeoville'. Nigel was napping on the back seat. Just before Colesburg they ran over a 'little buck' and damaged the BMW's radiator so the car began to overheat. The car just made it to a nearby petrol station but the hired hit men had to hitchhike a lift into the nearby sleepy town of Colesburg and check in to a B&B under pseudonyms. One can only imagine what was going through the mind of the truck driver who gave them a ride and the look on the face of the owner of the B&B.

As they didn't have cellphones on them, Mikey had to use a payphone to phone his friend, tow-truck operator Robbie Cosanie, and ask him to travel to the Northern Cape to fetch the broken BMW. Cosanie had been the best man at Mikey's wedding and one of his most trusted friends. He also needed Cosanie to phone Nassif because he didn't want phone records to show any association between them. After what was no doubt a roaring night in Colesburg, the trio met Nassif and Cosanie the next morning. They all climbed into Nassif's M5 and off they went to hire a Citi Golf to carry out the rest of the job. Mikey returned with Nassif and Cosanie to Jo'burg to sort out the borrowed car which was now smashed and Nigel and Kappie carried on to Cape Town with the R200 000.

When they arrived in Cape Town, the two took a drive past the residential address that was on the piece of paper handed to them by Sander, so that they could 'familiarise' themselves with the surroundings before checking in to a Holiday Inn.

The next morning, Nigel and Kappie took a drive to Claremont to recruit shooters to do the job on Mildenhall for them. Nigel euphemistically explains that they went to 'meet some coloured people Kappie knows'.

Kappie says they went 'to see a family member' of his named Sikaram. The 'family member' took the duo to a nearby taxi rank where he introduced them to two men who were hired for the hit on the auditor. Remarkably, the two men have never been properly identified or investigated for the shooting and all we know is that the one's name was Ben. Ben may or may not be Blue Beanie. They were paid R150 000 (R50 000 upfront and R100 000 on completion) for the job and Kappie supplied the Smith and Wesson. Nigel and Kappie took the two to the address which they had, showed them the house which they'd identified the night before and then took them to the Allan Gray building at the Waterfront, where one of the shooters identified Mildenhall's Audi. They decided they would make their move in the morning when the businessman was leaving home for work.

For days, the hired hit men staked out the house waiting for the target to appear. Mildenhall never left the house and never returned.

Finally, Ben/Blue Beanie had an epiphany and decided to follow Mildenhall in his Audi as he left work. As a result of this stroke of brilliance, they discovered that the house they were staking out was not Mildenhall's. He lived a few blocks away at exactly the same number house, but the street was a 'Road' and not a 'Drive'. The shooters had spent days parked outside the wrong house. There was another glitch though – Mildenhall lived opposite a school, so the attack could not be done in the morning as children could be harmed and there was too much attention, so they decided on the evening instead. Nigel and Kappie waited at Allan Gray's offices and, as they saw the Audi drive out, they called Ben/Blue Beanie on pay-as-you-go phones to let them know the target was on its way. A while later, Nigel and Kappie received a call telling them the job had been done. The duo took a drive past the house to see for themselves and when they arrived, security vehicles and a police van were already parked on the street outside. They phoned Mikey to inform him of the success of the operation.

Nigel and Kappie met the shooters in Sea Point to pay over the outstanding amount owed to them. Ben/Blue Beanie handed Nigel Mildenhall's wallet and a bunch of keys to prove they had been successful. Kappie dismantled the gun and threw bits of it into the ocean. In another comedic development, the butt of the gun refused to sink because it was plastic, so Kappie had to pocket it and dispose of it later. On their trip back to

Jo'burg, Kappie and Nigel stopped on the side of the road and lit a bonfire under a bridge to destroy the wallet, gold credit cards and gun butt. Mildenhall's house keys were thrown out of the car window somewhere in the middle of the Karoo. They kept Mildenhall's driver's licence and handed it to Nassif, who testified that he, in turn, gave it to Stratton as proof.

Kappie made it home just in time to fetch his son from school.

Mikey

After Mildenhall, Clint came to me and said the story with the shooting in Cape Town didn't work and Brett wanted to kill himself. I was really against it, hey. I said to him, 'You keep on telling me how close you and Brett have become, but now you want to have the oke shot?' He said, 'No, it's not me. He needs to have it done.' So I said, 'Fuck, this oke's got money man. He can run away. He can run to Brazil or somewhere where there's no extradition. He's got ammo. He's going to be ok.' He said no, Brett didn't want to be remembered as the thief, he wanted to be remembered as the martyr to the black people and he wanted to do this in such a way that threw egg on the government's face, on the ANC's face. Clint started making plans straight away. We discussed with Clint how we going to do it. Clint wanted him to get shot outside a restaurant. I said, 'No, no fucking chance.' Then he wanted to get whacked on the side of the road. Thrown out the car or something. I didn't want to do that 'cause I would have to drive in the same car as the oke, and I didn't want to talk to him and then shoot him. I never knew him. I never met him. The first night I met him was the night that we shot him. Clint was coming with all these different things and, on maybe four occasions, me and Clint had arguments about it. Then I eventually said to him, 'Listen, tell that cunt he must shoot himself then. Tell him I'm not going to do it.' I said, 'Fuck, I'm not going to do this and get myself into shit. Fuck that. For what? Who's going to take care of my family?' I said, 'Fuck that.' I said, 'If he wants to die so badly, let the motherfucker shoot himself.'

THE EVENTS LEADING UP TO AND INCLUDING 22, 26 AND 27 September 2005 are in dispute and were the subject of captivating, tempestuous cross-examination during Glenn Agliotti's 2010 trial in the South Gauteng High Court. Each man has his version; some details are corroborated while others are not. I have compiled the version that follows from the testimony heard in court, affidavits signed by witnesses, interviews conducted with central characters and, crucially, phone records that pinpoint locations and length of calls. However, if anything has emerged it is that every man has an agenda and phone records can lie.

I N CLINTON NASSIF'S VERSION, WEEKS BEFORE STEPHEN MILDENHALL had three bullets pumped into his shoulders, John Stratton approached him about a job of a different kind.

According to Nassif's evidence in court, Stratton allegedly wanted a tablet 'that somebody could take or give to somebody and they won't pick it up in the autopsy when they die'. Nassif testified that he was also asked to get a second tablet for a pilot. The pill had to induce a heart attack and be untraceable. Nassif admitted he spun Stratton along, telling him he would try and source him such a tablet. He claimed Agliotti also repeatedly pressed him about whether or not he had managed to find the medication. The extent of his efforts amounted to asking his colleague Stephen Sander if he knew of such a pill. Nassif suspected that with Sander's background, if anyone knew, it would be him. Sander couldn't help and Nassif stopped trying.

After the Mildenhall incident, Nassif claims he went to a meeting at Brett's house – Agliotti and Stratton were both present on his account; however, Nassif's version of events vacillated while under cross-examination. During his evidence in chief, when he was led through his testimony by the state prosecutor, he specifically mentioned Agliotti's involvement in the plan:

NASSIF: *Some time passed, all the way up to Mildenhall being shot, and afterwards the pill wasn't available. I went to a meeting at Brett's house in Illovo. When I got there, Glenn was there and John was there. They told me that this pill was actually for Brett. I was like totally taken aback by it; I didn't understand it, what was going on. We then went into the dining room and had something to eat with Brett and John and Glenn. John told Brett that the pill wasn't available and I was battling to get it. He pleaded at me and asked me, please, I must really, really try and get it, he is at the end of his wits with all this trouble at JCI and if he doesn't do this, he will either end up in a mental institution or prison, meaning if he doesn't take this way out. While he was talking to me and telling me, John was there, shaking his head, saying it must be done, it must be done. I don't know what trouble these guys got themselves into really, but they pushed the issue and John, Mr Brett Kebble was very convincing and when he had his mind set on something, that is the way it was.*

However, under cross-examination, Laurance Hodes SC, Agliotti's advocate, pointed out that Nassif never mentioned his client at all, in a sworn statement he had signed three years previously:

ADV HODES: *So you give a detailed account of what transpired in the meeting, and you attribute nothing to Mr Agliotti. Sir, do you agree with me?*

NASSIF: *Well yes.*

ADV HODES: *Right. How then did you suddenly remember, some three years later when you compiled your second statement, that Mr Agliotti was at the meeting and may have played a significant role?*

NASSIF: *When I did the second statement there was most probably a certain aspect that I had to address, who was exactly at that meeting, what did they talk about. Even in the second statement, I mean Agliotti was there, but I mean he never contributed to it. I mean, when we walked in John Stratton was there with Mr Agliotti and John asked me if I got the pill yet. I said no. Then John told me what it was for. I think I was just as shocked as Glenn was.*

ADV HODES: *Sir, you could never have been as shocked as Glenn because, in your version, he knew about it.*

That night, Nassif claims he left the meeting and immediately picked up the phone to call Brett's father, Roger, despite the late hour. Nassif went past Roger's house and told him about Brett's 'crazy' plan. According to Nassif, Roger 'freaked out and cursed him' before telling the security man that since Brett was a teenager, whenever things got hard, Brett always 'threatened this'. Hearing Roger's comments about his son's claims of suicide drove home the extent of the tenuous relationship between father and son for me. Brett was emotional and Roger was dismissive of his son's sensitivities.

The next morning, Nassif says he was summoned by Stratton to Brett's house and Brett, Stratton and Agliotti were all waiting when he arrived. He later testified that 'Brett blasted me from a dizzy height because I told his father and his father apparently phoned him and he came down on him'. At first, Nassif denied telling Roger but he knew that was a 'stupid way out'. He says Brett explained to him that it had to be done, and a solution had to be found. If the pill couldn't be traced, then perhaps a hijacking would be an option. Nassif's version is that he met with Brett and Stratton at a later date, where they even suggested shooting him outside a restaurant.

The veracity of this entire Roger Kebble incident is in doubt – Roger avoided testifying in court, earning him the nickname 'Roger the Dodger' in the press at the time. This meant Nassif's version was never properly tested. However, on the day Nassif made the claim from the witness box that Roger knew of his son's plan to kill himself before he died, I phoned the ex-mining boss and asked him for an interview. On tape, he exploded and rubbished Nassif's allegation. A furious Kebble said Nassif did tell him that his son was looking for a pill that could arrest one's heart, but never mentioned anything about an assisted suicide. 'He is talking absolute rubbish. He did not indicate to me that Brett was about to commit suicide and I don't believe that he did,' Roger told me. He said he did confront his son about it, who told him he was 'just joking around with idiots'.

Nassif claims numerous meetings featuring Brett, Stratton, Agliotti and himself were allegedly held during September 2005. The singular topic on the agenda: How best to kill Brett.

Nassif approached 'the expert' Mikey Schultz to discuss the options with him. Schultz, by his own admission, thought the idea was insane.

'First, I said to Clint he must talk him out of it. I did think it was crazy and fuck, you know, there was a part of me that didn't actually believe that the oke would go through with it. Maybe he was just blowing hot air,' recalls Mikey.

Mikey confided in Kappie and Nigel about the prospect of killing Brett.

It was a conversation that, if you know the trio well, could be interpreted as bizarrely amusing.

Mikey was driving on a highway with Kappie when he broached the subject. 'I went to go speak to Kappie. We never talk on the phone, so we went to go and have a meeting. I remember it. I said to him, "Hey Kaps, that story in Cape Town. Brett wants to go." He's like, "Where does he want to go to?" I said, "No, he wants to go." He says, "Go where?" I said, "He wants to fucking sail!" He says, "Sail where?" Then I explained to him. I said that thing in Cape Town hasn't worked. Brett wants to be shot because everything around him is crumbling. He's going through a lot of shit.' Only once Kappie finally worked out that Brett Kebble wanted to be killed, and not go on a sailing trip, did he agree to help out Mikey. Initially, Mikey wanted to make use of the same men who had shot Mildenhall in Cape Town, but Kappie didn't want any comebacks. They spoke to Nigel and he also agreed to help.

All that was left to sort out was the logistics and the money. 'We all agreed on 500 grand each because Nassif, when he approached me, he said Brett was willing to pay two bar per person shot on that list. So fucking he probably paid four million because if I know Clint, the way the cunt worked. So he said to me, "How do I want to split it?" So I said to him, "We'll split it four ways. We each take 500 grand." We agreed on that,' says Mikey. They debated how the job would be done and ultimately it was Brett's suggestion to do it on the quiet road near 'the bird sanctuary' which emerged as the most viable.

A date was set. Brett was to be shot on the evening of Thursday 22 September.

Mikey [the 22nd]

We got to work that day and Clint said me and Nigel we must go for a ride and familiarise ourselves with Brett's car. We drove there to his house, pulled into his driveway, parked behind it and Clint said, 'Come inside.' I was still saying to him, 'Speak this oke out of it.' He said to me, 'Come inside and come meet this oke and hear for yourself.' I said, 'No, I won't, I don't want to speak to the oke and then have to kill him.'

That evening, I was busy getting ready to go and sort it out. My phone was on charge and I was going to leave my phone at home. I still said to Leonie, 'If anybody phones just answer,' so then at least it looks like there's movement on my phone at the house. Maybe about an hour or half an hour or so before we were supposed to go and do it, the phone rings and it was Kerry Nassif. She said Clint had phoned her. Clint said that we must call the meeting off. I must let Nigel and Kappie know that the meeting's off for the night. There was only one meeting and that was the thing to go and shoot Brett. The next thing I know is Glenn phoned me and said, 'Call the boys off.'

IN THE WEEK OF 22 SEPTEMBER 2005, BRETT KEBBLE BROKE ROUTINE. He usually travelled back to Cape Town on a Thursday but that week he changed his plans and scheduled his return flight for the following day. A message from his PA Rita Meininghuis to his cellphone at 15:40 confirmed this: '*viz yr msg to jill earlier today that you wont return tonight (+ take off time uknown for tmrw), I'v advised aviation co unlikely tht you're flying tonight*'.

Brett's inbox gives unique insight into his psyche and circumstances during those last few days. It's well known that he always had several phones and specific handsets for certain people, so a reading of his messages is a snapshot of his life.

Just after noon on the 22nd, a message arrived from a UK number and was signed by a 'Malcolm'. '*Brett Things are now getting desperate. Please return our calls, or transfer monies to our account, ASAP. Malcolm*'. Perhaps an indication of just how financially strapped Brett was at the time?

At 15:15, Ingrid, Brett's wife, texted him. '*There is so much I hav 2 say 2 u I look 4ward 2 the wkd I love u brett x*'. Evidence that she had no inkling as to what was unfolding in Inanda … that her husband was plotting his own demise? At 21:19 that night she sent a follow-up message: '*R u finished your meeting? Can you fone me now I really need 2 speak with you please! Love ingi x*' . One could detect an insightful urgency in her tone if one was looking for it.

By Thursday afternoon, the day of the scheduled shooting, no money had yet changed hands. Nassif claims he and Agliotti then took a decision not to go ahead with the hit because they had not been paid. When I ask Agliotti what his version is about this, he responds that it's 'kak'.

A flurry of phone calls was made on the night of the 22nd in the 'Call off the Boys' episode. The contention is that Agliotti phoned Mikey and Nigel and ordered them to abandon the hit by saying, 'Call off the Boys'. However, Agliotti's version is that he didn't know the weight of the words he was instructed to relay by Nassif. The media pack following the trial unanimously agreed that the slogan 'Call off the Boys' would come a close second to 'Show me Love', Agliotti's favourite phrase, if ever we were to have T-shirt mementos printed of our time in Courtroom 4C.

The exchange of calls on the evening of the 22nd is arguably one of the strongest pieces of evidence that the state produced against Glenn Agliotti and is best illustrated through actual cellphone records compiled by the prosecution. It is, however, important to know that these phone records are sanitised and only the parts that support the state have been extracted.

Throughout the afternoon, numerous calls are made between Stratton, Agliotti, Brett and Nassif. Mauro Sabbatini, Nassif's close colleague, also features regularly. The record lights up after 18:30:

18:42 Kerry Nassif, Clint's wife, phones Mikey Schultz and tells him that Nassif is in a meeting but she has a message to pass on. She says Nassif wants him to contact Nigel and Kappie to tell them the 'meeting is off'. Mikey knows there's only one 'meeting' that is scheduled for the night and that's the one he is due to have on a quiet road outside the bird sanctuary with Brett Kebble. Nassif testifies that he was 'sleeping' at the time because his job was exhausting.

18:44 Glenn Agliotti phones Mikey Schultz. The call lasts just six seconds. Long enough for him to say 'Call off the Boys'.

18:47 Glenn Agliotti phones Nigel McGurk – Nigel misses the call because he's in the shower getting ready to go and shoot Brett. He phones Agliotti back later.

Between 18:49 and 18:53 Agliotti speaks to Mikey again, as well as to Mauro Sabbatini and Stephen Sander, raising the possibility of some kind of complicity.

18:52 Nigel returns Agliotti's call. Agliotti tells him to 'Call off the Boys'. Nigel, known for his explosive temper, is furious that Agliotti knows about the plan. He takes Agliotti's instruction to be a direct reference to the scheduled shooting of Brett Kebble. Nigel is furious because no one outside the circle is supposed to know about the plan 'especially Glenn Agliotti'. Nigel doesn't like Agliotti 'because he talks too much and acts like we're always his boys'. Nigel says, 'He is the last person that I wanted to know' about what he was about to go and do.

20:01 Nigel McGurk phones Clint Nassif in a rage asking why Agliotti knew about the planned event. Nassif tells Nigel to 'take it easy' and he'll speak to him the following day. The call lasts two minutes seven seconds.

20:19 Mikey Schultz speaks to Clint Nassif. They agree not to talk on their phones and to discuss the evening's events in the morning. Mikey has also spoken to a livid Nigel and to Kappie and assured them he will take the issue of Glenn's involvement up with Clint in the morning.

The technology, as presented by the prosecution, tells a story and that is that Glenn Agliotti was pulling the strings, giving instructions and handing out orders. However, what is *not* shown on the state's compilation of phone records, but *does* appear on Agliotti's itemised billing, is a call that he received from Nassif's friend Mauro Sabbatini just three minutes before the 'Call off the Boys' calls were made. Agliotti's claim is that Clint phoned him from Mauro's handset and gave the initial instruction. He was simply innocently relaying the message. But no one is likely to ever know the exact content of that conversation.

Mikey Schultz has his own opinions about just how much Agliotti knew and how involved he was. 'In a way, I knew that Glenn knew. I knew that Glenn knew because him and Clint were always together. They were always together with Brett and everything. Clint said to me it was only us that knew. But I knew. I knew that Glenn knew because he and Clint were always together by the Kebbles. He knew about the Mildenhall thing. He didn't organise it, no, but he had exactly the same role as Clint. He didn't organise it. He himself didn't go and sit with Brett and organise to tell Clint, no. He, Clint and Brett sat together, and John, they sat together, the four of them concocted the same plan. Clint just set up Glenn to take the rap.'

Another anomaly around the events of the evening of 22 September 2005 is the version put forward by Brett's butler, Andrew Minaar. He insists that in the late afternoon on that day Brett had a short dinner with Stratton, Agliotti and Nassif. According to him, the men ate a pasta dish which he either prepared or bought, but he has no receipt to prove this. The reason the meal stuck in his mind was because 'Brett was edgy that night' and Stratton convinced Nassif to stay for dinner. Minaar says Nassif never ate at Brett's house, so this was unusual. The dinner was also much earlier than usual, at 18:30 or so, and then Brett retired to his bedroom very early, before 20:00. Minaar's most severe problem is that phone records show he cannot possibly be telling the truth. The data puts Agliotti in Khyber Rock and Nassif in the South near the Wemmer cellphone tower and Forest Hills at the time of the supposed dinner. Despite this, Minaar is adamant that the dinner meeting happened.

The following morning, Nassif had his hands full as Nigel and Mikey wanted to know how Agliotti had come to know about the plan. Nassif told them Agliotti was 'helping them to arrange the money' and that he worked closely with the man so he couldn't be excluded. Nigel told Nassif to relay a message to Agliotti – that he should never call him again. Nigel's temper is notorious; he turns tomato red to the tips of his ears and struggles to express himself properly, which frustrates him further. If he didn't like Agliotti, Agliotti would have known about it.

Having dealt with his foot patrol, Nassif then had to appease his master. According to Nassif's testimony, he was called to a meeting at Brett's Inanda house, along with Agliotti. The ubiquitous Stratton was also present. Andrew Minaar recalls it was a very short meeting. The men didn't even sit down and it took place 'between the lounge and the entrance hall'.

At that meeting, Nassif says Brett told Agliotti and him that he was in financial ruin and that he had no money to pay them for his own murder. 'He was a desperate man,' testified Nassif. 'Uncle John was also at that meeting. He put his hand on Uncle John's shoulder and he said, "The old man will take care of you guys, this has to be done, it has to be taken care of." So when Glenn and myself left there, we decided to help him, knowing full well that there most probably won't be any payment for it, but we had to help the guy. We have been working with him long enough and he has looked after us, you know. He looked after us. He gave us a lot of work and, ja, he took care of us and we took care of him, you know.'

It was agreed the shooting would take place the following Monday, 26 September. Brett flew home to Cape Town with Stratton and returned to Jo'burg again at midday on Monday.

On that Friday afternoon as he was en route to Cape Town, Brett received an SMS telling him his rival Peter Skeat had been arrested on fraud charges and been granted R500 000 bail. Skeat suspected that Stratton and Nassif's team had supplied evidence to investigators which resulted in his high-profile arrest. According to subsequent media reports, Stratton and Brett had boasted to others that they had access to Jackie Selebi and would use their influence with the commissioner to deal with their adversary.

Some time after Kebble's murder, Skeat told the *Financial Mail* (15 December 2005): 'My arrest was manipulated by Kebble, and possibly others, because Kebble was angry that he had lost the court case in which he was obliged to pay me a lot of money. He was trying to punish me in his way. The State dropped the charges because they had clearly been trumped up.'

Another message that popped into Brett's inbox that weekend is a reminder of the global events that were unfolding while the prospect of Brett's own murder was marinating in his mind. '*Bush just announced on CNN that the floods in New Orleans are believed to be the work of a suicide plumber from Iraq J* read the message from 'Eborall'. TV networks were running wall-to-wall coverage of the severe flooding in The Big Easy. Earlier in the month, when the natural catastrophe was at its worst, Gulu also took the time to send Brett a message making light of the event. '*A spokesman for sixties rock group The Animals has issued an apology ... apparently there is no House in New Orleans.*'

At midday on Monday, when Brett arrived back at Hoëveld House, Nassif and Agliotti were already waiting and sat with him on his patio for a few minutes. 'He assured us this is the only route out for him and he is very thankful to us for helping him and seeing this through,' recalled Nassif from the witness box. Nassif gave the instruction to Mikey that Brett would be driving up and down Central Road in Inanda waiting for him that night. They were to follow Brett as planned and then flash their lights at him or pull over when they thought the timing and location were appropriate. Mikey was told by Nassif there 'would be no resistance from Mr Kebble'. Nassif also assured Mikey that he would be protected by the National Police Commissioner Jackie Selebi. 'He said that if all goes as planned, Jackie Selebi will be in charge, the Police Commissioner will be in charge of the shooting. He said that Jackie Selebi was going to commission [Clint's men] to investigate and to assist with the investigation. He said by this we would at all times know exactly where the investigation was and, if there was any heat coming, we could derail the police,' Mikey testified. He was instructed to leave no evidence, such as bullet shells, and should not be seen or caught.

Right: Mikey Schultz boxing on the set of *The Power of One*.
(MIKEY SCHULTZ)

Below: In friendlier times, Mikey Schultz holding Clinton Nassif's son Sheldon, with Clinton and Gary van Staden at the house they shared in Bassonia in 1998.
(MIKEY SCHULTZ)

Below: Mikey Schultz, Fiazal 'Kappie' Smith and Nigel McGurk in their heyday in 2000 at Nigel's house.
(MIKEY SCHULTZ)

Top: Fiazal 'Kappie' Smith, Mikey Schultz and Nigel McGurk at Mikey and Leonie Schultz's wedding in 2003 at Shumba Valley Lodge. (MIKEY SCHULTZ)

Bottom: Tow truck driver Robbie Cosanie, Nigel McGurk, Guil Yahav and Mikey Schultz at footballer Marc Batchelor's wedding in 2002 at Avianto. (MIKEY SCHULTZ)

Above: Nigel McGurk is arrested for his alleged involvement in the murder of Patrick Caetano on 20 January 2003. His lawyer Ian Small-Smith walks behind him. (INDEPENDENT NEWSPAPERS)

Police arrest Guil Yahav on 21 August 2003, who had been on the run since January of the same year for allegedly killing Patrick Caetano. (BOXER NGWENYA, INDEPENDENT NEWSPAPERS)

Jonathan Street, who was involved in the murder of Patrick Caetano at the Kyalami Business Park with Guil Yahav. (INDEPENDENT NEWSPAPERS)

Above: Hazel Crane, supported by Winnie Madikizela-Mandela, at one of Lior Saadt's court appearances in October 2003, a month before Crane's death. (INDEPENDENT NEWSPAPERS)

Left: Police investigators retrieve evidence from the scene where Hazel Crane was shot, metres from her house in Abbotsford. The killer hid behind the concrete refuse bin in the foreground. Policeman Wayne Kukard can be seen in the white shirt on the right. (DEBBIE YAZBEK, INDEPENDENT NEWSPAPERS)

Above left: A police picture of Lior Saadt. (INDEPENDENT NEWSPAPERS)

Above right: Amir Moila, also known as David Mulner, who police suspected of killing Hazel Crane. (INDEPENDENT NEWSPAPERS)

Left: Police investigators work to retrieve bullets from the door panel of Hazel Crane's Mercedes. (DEBBIE YAZBEK, INDEPENDENT NEWSPAPERS)

Above left: A young Brett Kebble with his two siblings. (GUY KEBBLE)

Above: Brett on the beach, in the black-and-white swimming costume. (GUY KEBBLE)

Left: Brett at a dinner party, on the far right. (GUY KEBBLE)

Above: Glenn Agliotti and Charlene Voget at their lavish 'wedding' at the Casa do Sol resort in Hazyview in 1987. (CHARLENE VOGET)

Right: Charlene's designer wedding gown created by The Boys. (CHARLENE VOGET)

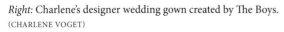

Top: Then National Police Commissioner Jackie Selebi holds aloft one of the thousands of bags of mandrax capsules recovered during the controversial bust involving Palto in January 2002.
(KIM LUDBROOK, INDEPENDENT NEWSPAPERS)

Bottom: Arnold Schwarzenegger and Jackie Selebi during the 'African Hope' torch run organised in 2000 by Glenn Agliotti and Dianne Muller.
(LEON MULLER, INDEPENDENT NEWSPAPERS)

Top: Rand Gold Chairman Roger Kebble, Phikoloso Mining's Lunga Ncwana and Brett Kebble celebrate an empowerment deal between the two mining groups in July 2003.
(JOHN WOODROOF, INDEPENDENT NEWSPAPERS)

Centre: Brett Kebble's car, as it came to rest on the Melrose bridge over the M1 highway on 27 September 2005.
(JOHN WOODROOF, INDEPENDENT NEWSPAPERS)

Bottom left: Roger and Guy Kebble speak to members of the media at a press conference in Inanda soon after Brett's death.
(THYS DULLAART, INDEPENDENT NEWSPAPERS)

Bottom right: A rare file image of John Stratton.
(INDEPENDENT NEWSPAPERS)

Above: Brett Kebble's coffin is carried from St George's Cathedral.
(ANDREW INGRAM, INDEPENDENT NEWSPAPERS)

Centre: Ingrid Kebble with her mother and her children Andrew, Matthew, Elizabeth (in Ingrid's arms) and Hannah at Brett's funeral at St George's Cathedral.
(ANDREW INGRAM, INDEPENDENT NEWSPAPERS)

Right: Glenn Agliotti walks with Roger Kebble, Guy Kebble and other family members to Brett's funeral.
(ANDREW INGRAM, INDEPENDENT NEWSPAPERS)

Mikey [the 26th]

On the 26th, I got home and waited for the time to pass. I picked up Kappie and we went to fetch Nigel in the north. On the way, the car started overheating, but we had been having a bit of trouble with the car for a week. It was Leonie's car, my wife's car. I pulled the number plates off. It was a black Golf. We drove up the hill to get to the place where the car started overheating bad. We stopped at a restaurant and put in water. We were late by the time we got there. As we drove down the road, Brett was driving up. We went in behind him and we flashed him. He started driving very slow. We followed him all the way past the golf course and that, left, right at the circle, down. By the time we got there, we decided we were not going to do the job because the car was overheating lank and we weren't sure if we would be able to get away. We got to the stop street. Brett took a right. We took a left. We were ready to do it. To be honest, I wanted to get it done because of the anxiety and the build-up.

O N THE EVENING OF 26 SEPTEMBER, BRETT DINED WITH JOURNAL-
IST David Gleason on a meal of prawns. At 18:06, Brett's phone
beeped with an SMS from Trish Beale, the JCI company secretary: '*Hi
Brett, we've moved the JCI board meeting from this Wednesday to Tuesday
11 October. We'll send out the change of date tomorrow and hope you ok
with the date? Bye T*'. The message to Brett was mere semantics – Brett
had been booted from the JCI board and no longer had a say over the
date of its meetings.

According to Andrew Minaar, Brett left home just before 20:00. At
19:48, Brett made a call from his car phone to Stratton. It lasted nearly
eight minutes and was picked up by the Chislehurston tower which is
within a kilometre of Hoëveld House. That call to Stratton is consistent
with Mikey's contention that Brett's last call before he was to be shot would
be to Stratton, so that whoever would find his body would dial the last-
called number and so establish his identity.

While on the phone to Stratton, Brett was driving to what he anticipated would be his death. The arrangement was that he would meet the
gunmen on Central Road in Inanda, they would follow him and then flash
their car lights when they thought the time was right. Brett saw them flash
their lights and they began to follow. But what he didn't know was that the
plan was falling apart because the car the shooters were travelling in was
overheating. Mikey, Nigel and Kappie weighed their options and decided
to abandon the attempt as they couldn't be sure they could make a getaway
in an unreliable car. The trio turned left into Melrose Street, while Brett
turned right into Greenacres Avenue.

Unaware that the shooters had aborted the operation, Brett assumed
he'd picked up the wrong tail and frantically drove the streets of suburbia, hunting down his would-be killers. At 19:58, he made the first of a
stream of phone calls to Glenn Agliotti, who was on a boys' night out at
nearby Assaggi restaurant. The prosecution would use this series of calls
in an attempt to prove Agliotti was the architect of Brett's assisted suicide.
He was the man Brett phoned when things were not going according to
plan. It also supported the state's contention of a hierarchy of instruction.
Immediately after Agliotti received the call, he dialled Clinton Nassif's
number and spoke to him for 30 seconds. For the next hour and a half
there would be a flurry of calls between Brett, Agliotti and Nassif as the

'target' drove around what would be the scene of his murder the following night.

While Brett was searching for his killers, his friends Dominic Ntsele and Sello Rasethaba were both independently waiting for him to arrive for their scheduled arrangements at 20:00. At around 20:10, Brett fired the same SMS off to both men: *'I am running late'*. Dominic replied, *'Ok I am at the restaurent'*. There was another exchange of messages between the two. Brett texted, *'Order so long and I wil join u. Sori to b late. I hate it'* and Dominic said, *'Don't worry U told me upfront that U are going to be hectic'*. Meanwhile, Sello tried three times to get hold of Brett on his cellphone, within a two-minute period, and each time Brett allowed the calls to go to voicemail. He had other priorities.

Lanky, assured restaurateur Alexis Christopher, who owns Willoughby Restaurant in Hyde Park and part-owns Assaggi in Illovo, was having dinner with Agliotti at Assaggi that night. They ate together most Monday nights. The two had met a few years previously when an employee of Christopher's drove into the back of Agliotti's then wife Vivian's car. Coincidentally, Christopher also knew Brett because he had grown up with him in Welkom in the Free State and they had been next-door neighbours. The restaurateur would be called as a witness for the state to testify about the series of calls that Agliotti received from Brett on the night in question.

CHRISTOPHER:	*Well, Glenn started getting, receiving calls, a numerous amount of calls, that prompted me to ask him who was calling, and he said it was Brett phoning him.*
ADV GCALEKA:	*He said that was Brett calling him, and what happened?*
CHRISTOPHER:	*Well, he was taking some of the calls out of the restaurant, and then approximately an hour later or I can't really remember the time, but about an hour later, he left and he said he is going to see Brett.*
COURT:	*Yes.*
ADV GCALEKA:	*At the time when you were having dinner together, how did he appear to you?*

CHRISTOPHER:	Well, he looked irritated with all the calls coming in.
ADV GCALEKA:	You mentioned that you were having dinner together. At the time when the accused left, had he finished his food?
CHRISTOPHER:	No, he left before his was – before he had eaten his dinner.

Christopher and the other 'boys' went out together to a strip club, The Lounge, where Agliotti met them later in the evening after he'd been to see Brett. Agliotti's version is that he spent some time at Hoëveld House drinking wine with Brett. He told Christopher that Brett owed him some money and he was just trying to sort it out.

For the second night in a week, Brett Kebble's assisted suicide had been planned and aborted.

Mikey [the 27th]

I remember it pretty well, hey. It was the morning after we had the dry run, the night before with the car overheating. The next morning I woke up. I had spoken to Clinton the night before when the phone rang. I told him that, 'Listen, the job wasn't done,' I'd speak to him in the morning.

That morning I got up, as usual, at home in the South, in Oakdene. When I woke up and that, I was actually hoping that the night before had actually scared him away and that it wasn't gonna happen. But the oke was in dire straits and he wanted to go on. I showered. I went to work at CNSG in Selby, south of Johannesburg. Clint came to me in the office. It was just him and myself in the office. I couldn't give a fuck whether he was upset. He asked me what had happened the night before. I then explained to him. I said to him we were driving. I said the car overheated and stuff. He then said to me that he had spoken to Brett and Brett was pissed off because he said we don't know what we had put him through. He said, Brett said to me that we don't know what we're putting him through and that after he turned right and we turned left down Melrose, he had gone driving around to look to see if he could find us because he thought we had maybe picked up the wrong tail and he was unhappy about it. I didn't really feel bad; I'll be honest, because it was a hell of a lot of pressure that was put onto us and by it not happening it was a bit of a relief. So it was like a 'cool, ok it didn't actually happen,' you know? And there was some chance of them calling it off that day.

Clint came back later on that day. He then confronted me again there in the office and he said to me, 'Listen, it's going to happen tonight.' So I said to him that, 'Ok cool, that's not a hassle. It can happen that night, but tell Brett not to meet us on Central Road there close to his house where we did the night before. He must meet us there in North Road, where that night we turned right.' And I made it an hour later. At the time we were meeting the night before, there was a lot of cars and stuff like that on the road and stuff. And also, at the time we were meeting, someone would drive past and see us or something stupid like that, so we said meet us back there by Planet Fitness in North Road. Later on he said to me, 'Look, everything is sorted out for an hour later.' I then went home.

I was trying to amp myself and get myself up for it again. That was the shit thing about the night before. We were all amped up and all ready to do it and boom, it didn't happen. A big anticlimax. So the next night, I got showered and got ready and that. Nigel came by to come fetch me. I can't give you the exact time. It must have been about seven o'clock or something. I had a black top on, I took gloves with and I must have had tracksuit pants or jeans. We drove to Kappie's panel-beating shop, which is in Robertsham. Kappie had organised another car for us to go with. We parked Nigel's car in there. So we drove up to the shop there, took the bag with the gun and everything in there and got in the Golf which Kappie said we were going to use. It was a black Citi Golf Velocity. It was a 1300 or 1600. It belonged to one of his clients. We decided we'll leave the plates on and stuff. The bag was just any old kitbag that I had. We had the gun in there. The gun I got from Jethro when I was prospecting for the Hells Angels. I got this gun from him when he went overseas and he asked me to keep it for safekeeping. When I left the Hells Angels, I didn't give it back to him and he was murdered so he never asked for it back. So I used a dead man's gun. Basically. Dead men tell no lies. They tell no stories.

Kappie was driving, Nigel was sitting in the front, I was in the back. I sat on the left and the kitbag was on the right. We got off at Athol Oaklands and turned left. I just wanted to get this fucking over with because of the anxiety. It's a total fuckup, hey. We then got on through that circle up North Road there by Planet Fitness. There's a garage on your left, and Planet Fitness on your right. As we came up, Brett came down. We recognised his car as it had Cape Town registration plates. We made a U-turn, flashed him lights; he acknowledged us. We drove down to the circle. He took the second exit down Edgewood again. We followed him. He was driving slow. It was a bit later so the roads were a lot more quiet. At the bottom of Edgewood, the road takes a right kink. As we went through the kink, it was quiet. There was nobody at the houses; there was no cars on the road. We flashed lights at him. 'Cause we agreed, I told Kappie this is the place. We pulled over, pulled next to him. We pulled up, my window and his window was in line. That was the first time I'd ever seen Brett. Brett looked at me. I positioned myself. I like leaned out and climbed out the window like that with my knee on the seat. I pointed, I pointed the gun at Brett and Brett looked at me like this, lifted his right shoulder like that. We never said one word to each other. I lifted the gun like this and pulled the trigger and the gun didn't go off.

My first thought was that the gun hadn't gone off because I had it in a plastic bag because Clint had given me instructions: You mustn't be seen there. We must make sure that we get off the scene. We mustn't leave evidence. We must leave our phones at home.

I climbed back into the car. Because the firing mechanism is on the side, the safety mechanism. So I thought to myself that obviously the bag pushed on that and it didn't fire. So I pulled the gun out the bag. By this time, Kappie had already turned left into Melrose Street. The first time I tried to shoot him, I tried to shoot him in the head because Clint also told me that we mustn't let the oke suffer and we must make sure that he dies. So now we turned left into Melrose Street. I pulled the gun a couple of times, checked that the gun's fine and the safety was on 'fire'. Kappie stopped in the middle of the road and Brett then came and stopped next to us. He stopped obviously with his window and mine in line. Once again, I leaned out the window, aimed the gun at him and pulled the trigger. The gun didn't fire the second time. As I pulled the trigger and the gun didn't fire, from nerves and anxiety I said to him, 'Wait here, we're coming now.'

He didn't say anything. Kappie then drove off. Nigel was swearing at me and going mad in the front. Like 'Ah fuck'. We call him a pressure cooker for specific reasons. He was just going off and swearing. He was going, 'Ah fuck it! I told you about that gun!' He jinxed that gun. He said to me, 'This gun's from fucking World War Two, what you going to use that gun for?' And I took the gun and I test fired it and it was fine. The gun wasn't really from World War Two. Nigel jinxed it.

So now we're driving up Melrose now towards the M1 bridge. We made a U-turn on the bridge. By that time I had taken the magazine out the gun. I cleared the chamber. I had taken the chamber drum out. I'd put the magazine back and the chamber with a new round. Brett hadn't waited where we told him to wait. He also, in fact, had made a U-turn back to the intersection there by Edgewood and Greenacres and Melrose. We drove up and saw flashing lights and we made a U-turn. We drove back to the same place where we had the second attempt. He then came down the road and he stopped like quite violently, and he looked at me to say, 'What the fuck are you doing? Please get this over with.' Like, you could see he was not in a good place.

On every attempt, every time I pointed the gun at him and pulled the trigger, he lifted his right shoulder a little bit. This time, I leaned out the window and I didn't aim at his head. I aimed at his body. I had to make sure. I pulled the trigger once and it started to go off. I just carried on firing. I just saw Brett taking bullets and he had this painful look on his face and he didn't make a noise. He didn't make a 'ah, ooh' anything like that. He was just like that with his shoulder up and as the bullets were hitting him. I kept on firing and Kappie pulled away and the last bullet missed him and went in the back window and Kappie said, 'Enough.'

I sat back into the car. I put the gun back in the bag. I looked over my right shoulder, back at where we had just shot him. Nigel was also looking back and said, 'Fuck, there's somebody following us,' and as I looked back, I seen Brett's car move forward. Obviously it was an automatic, it was in Drive and his foot had come off the brake and the car went into the pavement on the left-hand side. It hit the pavement, there's like a little wall there, and continued to follow us on the way to the bridge. At that time, I was ready to take the gun out the bag, which I had done because we couldn't leave any witnesses or anything like that. If it meant that we had to do that to ... to get away, then we would have done it, I would have shot them.

Realising that Nigel had mistaken Brett for somebody else following us, I put the gun back in. Kappie drove to the T-junction. Took a left down, took left back onto the highway and we went down the M1 south. We drove slowly. We didn't speak much. We just all commented on what balls the oke had and how he came there ... fucking that's ... something else. We drove back to the panel-beating shop. We weren't stressed or panicked. We were relieved. I was relieved this was over with now; because the build-up to it and the emotion and stuff like that to put yourself through, to actually go and do it and stuff like that ... it's ... it's a hard thing to do. I mean, if you just take out a gun and just shoot someone is a different thing. To plan it and go through your mind and if this goes wrong and what if this and that ... and it's quite a thing to do.

I took the bag out the car. I took the magazine out. I took the chamber drum out. Went back into the car and took the other bullet out off the floor that hadn't fired, and threw it in the bag. There were no shells. I was leaning. All the shells were falling and were left on the street. I gave the gun to Kappie. Kappie went to get a setaline torch. It's one that blows fire and pushes oxygen. It turns the flame from red to blue, like a concentrated flame. Kaps cut off the gun, cut off the barrel. He started cutting it into like three pieces. As he cut further down the barrel, the frame that the barrel and the slider and all that fitted on to was made out of ceramic. He finished cutting it up into pieces and he took them and threw it into a bucket of water there. Then he took it and gooied it back in the bag. He said, look, he's going to get rid of that. We said, "Ok cool." Nige and myself jumped back into Nigel's car. He then drove me back to my house where he fetched me.

I was working at night and stuff like that at clubs and stuff like that so I didn't have to explain to my wife where I had been. I've got a good relationship with my wife and she doesn't really question me and stuff. So I went and got into bed and, to be honest, I think that was the first night that I actually slept well. The anxiety and the whole build-up with this flipping thing to do and it was like, it's done now, it's ok. So I actually slept well that night.

Nigel went home and Kappie went to dispose of the gun, which he took to the Klip River, and threw it over the bridge over the Klip River and he threw pieces out there.

And that was the end of Brett, hey.

THE POLICE RADIO CRACKLED TO LIFE AS AN URGENT ALERT WAS sent through from the 10111 call centre. It was easily recognisable above the din of the busy restaurant in the Balfour Park shopping centre near Highlands North in Johannesburg. '023 Alpha. Suspected hijacking in Melrose. Two people shot.' The two police reservists, dressed in full uniform, threw down their dinner and ran for the parking lot and their marked cop car. It was 21:15 on a Tuesday night and their shift had been uneventful thus far. Little did they know that they would be the first two people on the scene of a murder that would rock the country.

One of the reservists, who was a constable stationed at Sandringham Police Station in September 2005, has recounted the events of that night to me on condition of anonymity. I will call him 'Constable'.

Constable and his partner arrived on the Melrose bridge crossing over the M1 highway within minutes of receiving the call on the radio. On their arrival, they found a silver Mercedes-Benz, which had come to rest with its nose crumpled against the barrier. The driver was dead – his shirt was ripped open and he was covered in blood. His body was leaning over onto the passenger side of the vehicle, his full weight resting on his left elbow. The driver's window was rolled down – a peculiarity on a chilly night in a city known to have one of the highest hijack rates in the world. The initial call centre alert had instructed that two people had been shot, but when Constable inspected the scene there was no other potential victim in sight. In fact, the scene was dead quiet. There were no passing pedestrians and no other cars travelling the route except for a second police car that arrived from the Sandton side of the overpass, almost simultaneously. It also seemed as though no paramedics had been on the scene at all. 'I always wonder who called in the incident,' Constable confides. 'There was not one person on the scene and the victim was dead, there was no two ways about it.'

It would later emerge that two people did drive past the scene of Brett Kebble's murder but did not stop – one was an attorney by the name of David Cahn. The other, incredibly, was Anthony Crane, Hazel Crane's son. By sheer coincidence, he was one of the very first people to spot the mining tycoon lying lifeless in his car just a few hundred metres from where his own mother had been assassinated less than two years previously. Anthony was on his way home, to the house from which Hazel had departed on the day of her murder. I am flummoxed every time I think of what a coincidence that is.

Constable admits that at the time he had absolutely no idea who Brett Kebble was and did not recognise him at all. I'm not entirely surprised by this admission as it does seem as though Kebble has achieved more notoriety through his death than through his life. 'I handled it like a normal, normal scene. I got on the radio and called it in. We found his wallet – I can't remember exactly where. It was either on the dashboard, in the cubbyhole or on the seat next to him. That's how we immediately knew it wasn't a hijacking.'

He got back onto his radio and requested detectives, a mortuary van and a duty officer to go out to the scene. Another officer suggested Constable run the licence plate of the Merc through the system and it came back as registered in the name of RB Kebble. Constable still didn't have a clue as to the enormity of the crime. 'One of the Sandton guys heard me testing the licence and asked me who the car belongs to. I told them it's a "Kebble". They told me, "This is big. This is really big. He's a multimillionaire, big-time bloke."'

More police officers began to arrive. Constable handed over the scene and went with some colleagues to see if they could find any evidence of bullet casings down the road.

'We walked for a few hundred metres until the road splits. We looked all over and couldn't find anything. It's quite dark and it was like looking for a needle in a haystack. We couldn't find any casings or anything,' he recalls. There were also no eyewitnesses, no one had stopped to help and the area they were searching in was extensive.

Constable recalls that it was around that time that the scene began to buzz, media started swarming the area and Brett's friends and colleagues began appearing. So too did the police top brass. 'Out of the blue, all Kebble's colleagues started arriving. Guys in suits and ties. Black guys and white guys. They were like shocked, saying that they had plans to meet him for dinner and he never arrived. Gauteng Police Commissioner Perumal Naidoo was there. All these high-brass people were on the scene, people you wouldn't normally expect.'

Sello Rasethaba could be overheard telling teary colleagues, 'He was on his way to have dinner with me,' before dismissing waiting reporters with a shout of 'Just let us grieve.' With police tape flapping in the wind, Commissioner Naidoo fed the media machine with a brief statement. 'It might have been a hit, but we will be investigating all possible leads,' he told the cameras. A crime-scene photographer was busy snapping pics of a long skid mark left by Kebble's car – an indication, perhaps, that he was trying to flee his attackers? A lamp post that had been hit by the car had been cordoned off and tracks showed that he'd clipped the pavement as he drove up the bridge. Ten orange cones marked vital pieces of evidence. Journalists could overhear a man making several muffled calls on his cellphone: 'Roger, it is close to Athol Oaklands Road. Yes, the police have confirmed that he had been shot.' They had little doubt that the Roger in question was Brett's father, who received the news while on holiday in Paris.

Amongst those arriving on the Melrose bridge were Glenn Agliotti and Clinton Nassif. I am almost certain that the man making the call to Roger on the bridge was Agliotti, ironic considering he was ultimately charged with the murder. Mid-trial, during one of our lunches, I asked Agliotti to recount the events of that night the way he remembers them:

'On the night of the murder, I was having dinner with my wife, Lelani, and a friend in Dainfern and I didn't have a fucking clue what was going on. Robert van der Merwe, a police reservist, phoned me. He phoned to tell me that Roger had been killed,' Glenn recalls vividly. 'I knew that Roger was in Paris at the time so I said I would check it out.'

Glenn explains to me that Roger's Mercedes-Benz S600 was a brownish, gunmetal colour while Brett's was silver so he wanted a description of the car. He also knew that Roger was in France at the time so the information could not be accurate. 'I said to Lani that this is bullshit,' he says, using his pet name for his wife. 'I phoned Brett once or twice and got his voicemail. This was about half past nine. Lani said, "Let's go to Brett's house." I got there and I asked the security guard if Brett was home and he said that he'd gone out.'

Glenn tells me that Robert van der Merwe had initially told him that the shooting had occurred near The Wilds sanctuary, which is on the border of the elite suburb of Houghton and the city's CBD.

'I hopped on the highway and got off at Harrow Road. I saw a police van with a blue flashing light and my heart sunk. But it was just a bumper bashing.' Agliotti explains what happened next: 'As I arrived, Selebi phoned me to say, "Have you heard Brett's been shot?" The media had called him.

I told him that I had heard it was Roger.' Selebi had publicly stated that he first found out that Brett had been shot from newspaper editor Jovial Rantao, and not from his friend Glenn Agliotti, as initially speculated by the media. That detail would have been far more salacious had Agliotti actually told the police chief that Brett Kebble had died.

As Agliotti was approaching The Wilds, he asked Lelani to phone Kerry Nassif, Clint's wife, to give him the news. 'I said to Lani, "Phone Kerry." Kerry said he'd taken a sleeping tablet and that he was sleeping. Lani told her to go wake him up and tell him Brett has been shot. He then phoned me back.' Phone records show a call lasting 2 minutes and 30 seconds from Lelani's phone to Kerry Nassif at 23:01, close on two hours after Brett was shot.

From here on things get very murky.

This is a major point of contention between Nassif and Agliotti. In Agliotti's version, when he spoke to Nassif, Agliotti was already en route to Melrose and it only took him a few minutes to get there. Nassif's wife, Kerry, claimed Clint was fast asleep when the call came through from Lelani. Somehow, Nassif made it to the crime scene from his home in Southern Johannesburg in his black Mercedes SL65 sports car before Agliotti and had managed to pick up Sander in that time. Agliotti says Nassif must be lying. 'So there I am, up and running, the adrenalin's pumping, I take Athol Oaklands off-ramp and he's fucking ahead of me. How the fuck did he get there before me? It's impossible!' Agliotti insists.

Nassif's version, according to his statement, is that the call from Agliotti came through at about nine o'clock and he was fast asleep at the time. He then picked up Sander before making his way to the overpass. But he was ripped apart by Agliotti's advocate, Laurance Hodes, during cross-examination – phone records show he was using his phone repeatedly before and after nine o'clock at his home near the Camaro Road tower. There were a number of calls to a jewellery dealer by the name of George Mihalevic and Nassif also spoke to Mauro Sabbatini and Sander. There is no way Nassif could have been asleep at the time.

Nassif says that on his way to the scene, he rallied his investigators and ordered them to Melrose. These included Henry Beukes, Dick Diederichs, Jan Bothma and André Burger. When he arrived in Melrose, Sander went to identify Brett but Nassif didn't want to 'see Brett like that'.

Agliotti says he too went to identify Brett's bloodied body in the car. He recalls what was happening that night on the Melrose bridge: 'Selebi phoned me and I said to him, "Please you've got to help us." He told me to hand the phone to the investigating officer, a black captain from Norwood, and they spoke. You know everybody said, "Ja, Selebi helped me out and covered up." That's a lot of fucking crap.' Initial reports suggested Agliotti phoned the National Commissioner from the scene but Agliotti insists it was vice versa.

Agliotti spent much of the night with his phone stuck to his ear. 'I spoke to Roger fifty fucking times – well, it felt like fifty times. He was in Paris. He was almost hysterical screaming, "What's happened to Brett?" I kept saying, "Roger, I'll phone you back." I said to him, "Bretty's been shot and I don't know what's going on." It was almost like chaos.'

Captain Johan Diedricks was the standby duty group officer that night. His responsibility was to attend to all serious crime incidents in the Johannesburg area. He had 32 years of service under his belt, 22 of which had been spent at the Serious and Violent crime unit formerly known as the Brixton Murder and Robbery unit. He had been involved in investigating and solving numerous murder cases prosecuted in high courts across the country. Late that night he received a call from the radio control centre instructing him to attend to a murder on the Melrose bridge.

'On my arrival at the scene I noticed that the scene was cordoned off with red police official tape,' he tells me. It is the first time he has ever spoken out about what exactly happened in the hours after Brett Kebble's murder. I am hoping his decision finally to break his silence will provide clarity on a situation mired in confusion. 'Outside of the cordon were a lot of people including Agliotti who introduced himself. Also on the scene was Commissioner [Mulangi] Mphego. The Provincial Commissioner Naidoo arrived. I was also introduced to Nassif who was with Beukes, Burger, Joshua [Dick] Diedericks and other unknown persons and was told that they did some security work for the deceased Kebble. I also met Sello Rasethaba who Kebble would have had dinner with that night.'

Captain Diedericks walked through the crime scene and was met by Superintendent Frank Murray from the Local Crime Scene Centre, commonly known as the fingerprint office. He was responsible for the forensic investigation on the scene and on Brett's vehicle. Professor Hendrik Scholtz from the Medico-Legal Laboratory was also there.

Diedericks explains what he saw: 'I noticed the deceased inside his vehicle and he was identified on the scene to me by Agliotti. The vehicle had collided with the side of the bridge. It was clear to me that the deceased was shot elsewhere and not on the scene. I requested other SAPS members to walk down in the street in the direction of the park and look for possible exhibits as it was clear the vehicle was from that direction. I also requested Beukes and them to assist the SAPS members as they are known to me as ex-SAPS members. The street was poorly lit and manpower was needed to do a proper inspection of the area.'

This is consistent with the version Nassif told in court five years later. He testified that Captain Diedericks, the investigating officer, asked CNSG employee Dick Diedericks to take a walk down the road past the bridge to see if he could find any evidence. Nassif claimed Dick Diedericks found cartridges about 500 or 600 metres down the road. Commissioner Naidoo and Henry Beukes got into a car and drove the half a kilometre to the location of the shells. Six 9-mm shells were recovered, according to the police report.

Captain Diedericks corroborates this. 'Whilst on the scene Beukes reported to me that they found empty cartridge casings at the entrance of the park about 500 metres from the scene on the same road. Because I was still busy at the scene, I sent Constable Danie Nortje to secure that scene. He was accompanied by Beukes and Commissioner Naidoo to the park.'

In the interim Captain Diedericks and Superintendent Murray inspected the Mercedes for fingerprints and other exhibits. Brett's body was removed to the government mortuary. Only once that was completed did the two policemen make their way to the entrance of the Ethel and Gray Park, where the casings were discovered.

'Myself and Sup. Murray went to the scene where the cartridges were recovered at the entrance of the park where he took photos and marked the spots where the exhibits were recovered. He then took the exhibits one at a time and sealed it apart in exhibit bags and marked it as procedures required,' explains Diedericks, emphasing the procedure which he had done hundreds of times before. He is at pains to prove everything was done by the book.

I've always found the discovery of the shells dubious, to say the least, and Nassif's version does not sit well with me. A theory I've heard from a high-ranking cop on the scene is that the bullet casings were moved the 500 metres or so from the bridge, down the road, to distort the forensics and throw off investigators. This would also answer another pressing question that had bothered me as well as an accident reconstruction specialist who had contacted the media at the time. How did Brett's car manage to travel as far as it apparently did, several hundred metres and around a bend, after he'd been shot? Could it be that the car didn't move, but rather that the bullets did? Mikey is dismissive of this idea. He's pointed out where he shot Brett and says his target drove several hundred metres up the road as his adrenalin must have been pumping.

However, in his book *Steeped in Blood: The Life and Times of a Forensic Scientist*, David Klatzow, who was employed by Judge Willem Heath to do a private investigation of the murder on behalf of Roger Kebble, has his own theory:

> Kebble did not die after the first shots were fired. Using eyewitness reports and my knowledge of anatomy and physiology, as well as the forensic detail regarding the shots, I could reconstruct the last minutes of Kebble's life. He left home and drove down a deserted road. He stopped the car in the dip of the road and was shot whilst stationary, probably with six shots. The theory at the time was that he was hijacked. Kebble drove the short way up a hill and around a slight bend (about 400 metres) after having been shot. His car then left the road and gently rammed its nose into the balustrade where the bridge crosses the M1 motorway. There was very little damage to the front of his vehicle and to the railing into which the car had bumped (p.232).

Klatzow goes on to explain the science of his interpretation:

> A bullet that slams into your spinal column will generally result in immediate flaccid paralysis. This means that Kebble would not have been able to drive or steer the car after the shot into his neck was fired, as all the nerves that controlled his arm and leg muscles would have been paralysed by the force of the bullet hitting the spinal column. So this shot couldn't have been one of the first shots fired in the dip of the road: it must have been the final shot. A dying Kebble had driven up the hill and someone had followed him there, where he had finished him off – a kind of coup de grâce (p.232).

Mikey Schultz, the shooter, rubbishes Klatzow's analysis, saying he didn't follow Brett up the road to 'finish him off'. Captain Diedericks also disagrees. 'After he was shot he escaped from the scene to the spot where his vehicle collided with the bridge. There was no evidence that he was finished off at the bridge.'

Klatzow also suggests, contrary to Captain Diedericks's version, that a policeman on the scene picked up all the cartridge cases and put them in his pocket without marking where they had fallen. He describes the mistake as a 'major blunder' as crucial evidence was lost as a result.

Klatzow was very right early on about the type of gun and bullets used. He established that the shooter must have been someone in the security industry or with a guarding or anti-hijacking interest. He worked this out after interviewing a domestic worker at a house 200 to 300 metres away from the bridge. The woman was standing talking outside in the garden and 'had seen a big car drive slowly down the hill and come to a stop before she heard a succession of shots'. Klatzow says she described the shots as 'bang, bang, bang' which told him that the weapon was cycling – firing one shot after another – as opposed to 'bang, reload, bang, reload'. Although the woman didn't actually witness anything of substance, Klatzow says her description of what she heard helped him narrow down the field of suspects.

Mikey proudly displays photographs of the Tec-9 semi-automatic pistol he used to shoot Brett, but Nigel is dismissive of the gun, saying it's 'like something out of World War Two'. According to a write-up Mikey showed me, the assault pistol 'bears the dubious distinction of being one of the most widely used "criminal" guns in the USA'. It was used in several mass murder cases, as well as in an unknown but definitely large number of street fights and other violent crimes. The review suggests the gun is unreliable – which explains why it jammed twice. Mikey also tells me that he used 9-mm 'subsonic' bullets, which is consistent with Klatzow's finding that bullets which were 'slowed down' were used by the shooter.

Police crime-scene photographs also show that officers recovered an Energade bottle, tissues, sweets wrappers and eleven cigarette butts. The recovery of the stompies led to initial suggestions by Kebble-watcher Barry Sergeant that the gunman had waited on the bridge for Brett, smoking Camels until he arrived. In his book *Brett Kebble: The Inside Story*

Sergeant theorises about the tycoon's murder, claiming it was as a result of a diamond deal gone wrong, enigmatically referring to a 'Mr X':

> At the loneliest point of the leafy, fairly well-lit street, with the bird sanctuary on his left, Kebble brought the big Mercedes to a gentle halt and pressed the button to open the window to his right. Two men stepped out from their hiding place under one of the big bluegum trees on the left, close to where the park fence had been cut. They must have been waiting for a while. Police later recovered at least ten Camel cigarette butts from the ground under the tree. A third man held vigil in the VW Polo, out of sight. Two members of the trio had arrived in South Africa very recently, after a circuitous journey that included Mozambique as the last leg. The third was from Pretoria. But would anyone ever know who had paid for the evening's deadly events? Was it, as some have speculated, Kebble himself? (p.5)

Mikey tells me that after reading Sergeant's reconstruction of the events of that night, his friend ex-policeman John Kruger sent the author an angry letter telling him in no uncertain terms what he thought of his conspiracy theory.

But there is also another critical piece of evidence that dismisses some established misconceptions about what happened on that chilly September night in 2005: a never-before-seen video of Brett Kebble's corpse collapsed in his car. Constable captured it on his cellphone and before now has not made it public.

At our meeting, he switches on his laptop and hits play. The image is grainy but the visual of the tycoon's bloodied body slumped to the left, a serene look on his face, is instantly recognisable. His collared shirt is ripped to the midriff and appears as though it's been partially pulled off him, revealing his right shoulder. Flashing blue lights illuminate the picture, a bullet hole through the back left-door window is perfectly framed and the chatter of policemen speaking about the cold weather serves as a soundtrack.

The video dispels a myth, which has been bothering me for some time. I'd repeatedly heard from other policemen and potential conspiracy theorists that there was a smear of blood on the bonnet of Brett's car which had been wiped off. Klatzow was also concerned about this smear after apparently seeing it on TV footage, and the *Cape Argus* newspaper claimed to have seen two photographs of the reddish-brown splatter. The video, shot literally minutes after the murder, showed no blood on the bonnet of the car. Constable also dismisses the theory, saying he never noticed anything of the sort. However, Constable is unsettled by other aspects of the scene, most notably by Brett's torn shirt. This is also plaguing me and I agree with him that it doesn't entirely make sense. He was the first person to arrive on the scene and no paramedics had been there. But Brett's shirt is torn open as if he had been worked on. Mikey tells me he never noticed anything unusual about Brett's shirt and vehemently denies ever touching him.

The day after the shooting, the *Cape Times* newspaper quoted 'a witness who arrived on the scene before the police on Tuesday night' as saying, 'There was blood everywhere. Someone wanted him dead – there can be no doubt. The car was riddled with bullet holes.' The 'witness' declined to be named. So who exactly did the newspaper quote? Perhaps it was Anthony Crane or attorney David Cahn, the two men who had driven past the murder scene.

In the early hours of Wednesday 28 September, Brett Kebble's bloodied Mercedes-Benz was loaded onto a flatbed truck and removed from the overpass. It was taken to Wynberg Police Station in Alexandra but it didn't stay there long. It was controversially removed from police custody and moved to Danmar Autobody in Booysens in downtown Jo'burg, which coincidently is owned by Mikey Schultz's brother-in-law Mark Groenewald. Clint Nassif explains in his statement how that came to be:

> The captain that was in control of the investigation phoned Beukes and asked him to move the car from Wynberg Police Station as they had done their checks, and he feared that the car would be stripped at the pound at the police depot. I told Beukes I did not want that car near my yard and requested him to take it through to Danmar Auto Body as I knew Mark Groenewald.

This meant that the holy 'chain of evidence' had been compromised – any evidence recovered from the car could not be used.

In late 2006, Danmar issued a media statement clarifying the events surrounding Brett's car. The panel beaters confirmed that Nassif had phoned Groenewald the morning after Brett's murder and asked him to collect the car from the police's Serious and Violent Crimes Unit in Wynberg, along with Henry Beukes. JJ Towing transported the car to Danmar on Friday afternoon.

Nassif then gave Groenewald an instruction to valet the vehicle because Roger Kebble wanted to inspect the car. Groenewald advised Nassif that before he could execute this request, he would require the instructions of the insurer of the vehicle, who would in all probability require inspection of the car before the valet could be authorised. Danmar confirmed that the insurers instructed Groenewald that the company should not touch or deal with the vehicle in any way as they had not as yet received any claim details. The panel beaters placed a plastic cover over the car and the words 'Do Not Touch. Investigation' were placed on the cover. Danmar insists the car was never cleaned as claimed in the media and was not handled by any of its employees. The company said that it refused to release the car to CNSG and only after receiving advice from the NPA was the vehicle released to Investigating Officer Johan Diedericks a week later.

Nassif initially denied giving the order to remove the car but later conceded that he did issue the request. He has, however, always maintained that he never asked that the vehicle be valeted.

Klatzow says alarm bells started going off for him when three days after the shooting he discovered the police had not properly examined the car. He immediately requested Major Leonie Ras, from the police's forensic department, to take him to the car. Klatzow says he was struck by the fact that there was very little evidence at all in the vehicle and the 'car could not render us as much information as it might have had it been left untouched'. None of Brett's three or so cellphones were recovered and the infamous reddish-brown blood smear on the bonnet was nowhere to be found.

It was also confirmed in media reports at the time that 'flocks of people' visited the car during its eight-day stay at Danmar and several of those people were allowed to take photographs of the vehicle. Danmar Director Peter Richardson was quoted in *The Star* as saying, 'We parked the car and put a plastic sheet over it, as we do with all new arrivals. We were completely oblivious as to whose car it was. Nobody told us not to touch it. Nobody said anything.' He said that the day after the vehicle was received, he found groups of people, including ANC Youth League members, inspecting the car and rifling through the cubbyhole. He was also quoted as saying that a man identifying himself as Brett's driver had removed items from the cubbyhole.

The person ultimately responsible for allowing the removal of the car was Captain Johan Diedericks, the investigating officer. He is frustrated by years of speculation about the circumstances and finally wants to set the record straight. He explains that on the Melrose bridge, the forensics investigator Superintendent Murray told him he had finished with inspecting the vehicle and it could be released.

'He is the forensic expert and responsible for the forensic part of investigations and is a highly qualified and experienced officer. Because there was no next of kin of the deceased on the scene it was decided that the SAPS would safeguard the vehicle until the next day when a decision will be made. From experience I knew that it is possible that the vehicle could be damaged or stripped in the SAPS impound by corrupt SAPS members and decided that it would be better to keep it at my office in Wynberg because it is guarded. The vehicle was removed to my office.

'The next day Sup. Murray decided to call the crime scene management from the forensic lab in Pretoria to re-examine the vehicle to be on the sure side because of the publicity. The vehicle was re-examined by the unit and nothing new was found. Their commander Superintendent Koekemoer than gave permission for the vehicle to be released. This was done to Beukes as there was no reason why the SAPS should have kept it any longer.'

As far as Diedericks is concerned, there was no malicious or sinister intent and no negligence in allowing the car to be released.

'I learned that Klatzow and the media made a big deal out of it. The Head of Forensic Services Commissioner Piet du Toit reclaimed the vehicle from the panel beaters for further investigation and as far as I can remember it was in vain,' he says.

In the wake of Brett's death, there was a firm belief that one of the most pivotal pieces of evidence in this high-profile murder investigation had been compromised. This added to mounting criticism of the fact that the actual scene had not been properly cordoned off on the night of the shooting and reporters and photographers were able to walk alongside detectives as they collected evidence.

Five hours after the shooting, investigators abandoned the scene on the overpass in Melrose. Police were satisfied that all possible evidence had been recovered. It would later emerge that this may have been short-sighted.

One full week after the murder, police returned to the bridge in Melrose in desperate search of evidence. Amongst them were high-ranking officers such as Head of the Serious and Violent Crimes Unit Sharon Schutte, Commissioner Piet du Toit and Major Leonie Ras. Divers carrying metal detectors searched a spruit about twenty metres from the shooting site in the hope that they'd recover the murder weapon. City Parks employees were called in to chop down trees and cut through reeds to allow officials to search the small stream. Members of the Explosives Unit scoured the area but came up empty-handed. Teams of officers spraypainted marks where they suspected spent cartridges had been picked up.

Captain Diedericks insists there was nothing unusual about this. 'The scene was visited several times after the initial investigation. There is nothing strange about that. Several people in the vicinity were questioned. Divers checked the water for possible exhibits.'

All of this seemed to be in vain though – even if fresh evidence was found it would be compromised as the scene had been left unattended for days. The police were floundering. There was effectively no forensic evidence at their disposal.

News of Brett Kebble's murder spread like wildfire as the shock reverberated through the city. An hour after his time of death, his phone was buzzing and voicemails were piling up. His dinner date Sello Rasethaba called at 22:15 as Brett had not yet arrived at his house as scheduled. Three minutes later, spokesperson David Barritt phoned. Glenn Agliotti called Brett twice, at 22:27 and 22:41, no doubt as he was racing from Dainfern to The Wilds. John Stratton also dialled Brett's number despite having already been informed by Clint Nassif that Brett was dead. Nassif would later state that he told Stratton 'his brother was gone' but that the old man was extremely calm. One of Brett's consultants, Clement Jackson, who used to serve as a senior detective in the diamond and gold branch, tried to get through to the magnate several times but there was no answer. Just before 23:00, as the media were beginning to gather on the poorly lit bridge over the highway in Melrose, journalist Nicky Smith rang Kebble's phone in an attempt to confirm the rumours. When her call went through to voicemail, she sent an SMS: '*Heard an absurd rumour that you had been killed! Pls call me the Star is trying to confirm the story ...*'

Business Day editor Peter Bruce also tried to call in an attempt to confirm what he'd heard. Dominic Ntsele, the spin doctor who had dined with Brett on the night of his death, had left his phone on silent as he slept that night, as he usually did. When he awoke at 04:00 to go to the toilet, he checked his handset and was shocked to discover dozens of missed calls and text messages received through the night asking and telling him about Brett's death.

Over the next few days, as Brett's body was being scrutinised in the clinical cold of the mortuary, his phone continued to buzz. Those who loved Brett used it as a conduit for their mourning, sending messages to the afterlife and listening to his voicemail.

On Wednesday evening, less than 24 hours after his death, a cryptic message came through on Brett's phone from his secretary Rita Meininghuis: '*johan, we're right! I know it! I cannot convince my inner voice of any other scenario – I keep coming back to his. Hugs rita*'.

Just before 10:00 the following morning, a poignant message came from Gulu's phone, probably sent by one of Brett's four children: '*Dear dad we all mis u so much.*' And then half an hour later, an eloquent farewell from a friend, typed in poetic Italian. '*Ciao Brett ci vediamo in paradiso per la ultima carbonara. Dio dia forza alla tua famiglia e la consoli nei dolore fanin.'* [Goodbye Brett. We will meet in paradise for the last carbonara. God give strength to your family that they may be consoled in their time of sadness at the end.]

The responsibility for identifying Brett's body fell, ironically, to Glenn Agliotti as Roger was still en route back to South Africa from Paris and Stratton was travelling from Cape Town. Agliotti clearly remembers the morning after the night before.

'I was up very early. I remember Stratton flew in and I ended up at Nassif's office. I didn't know where the morgue was and I had to identify his body. I phoned JCI to speak to Jill to get Brett's ID number and André Burger took me to the morgue to show me where it was,' he recounts. 'I identified the body and it was so kak, hey. Firstly it's such a stark, cold, fucking government building. You walk in and there's this window with a curtain. They wheeled the stretcher in and he was still in a black body bag and they unzipped the bag. He was still full of blood and they hadn't touched his body. At least that's what it looked like to me. And I remember the look on his face and it will stay with me forever. He had this smile on his face almost as if he was at peace with himself.'

After identifying Brett's body, Agliotti returned to the Inanda house where everyone was still in a state of panic. 'Nassif was running around getting bodyguards on everybody, bodyguards on Stratton and everyone. They were scared of threats; they didn't know who had killed Brett.' It would appear from the testimony, however, that they did know exactly who had killed Brett and the frantic running around was for appearance's sake.

Amidst the doom and drama, there was a moment of lightness, at least for me. Very early on the morning after the shooting, I began doing live crossings from the overpass in Melrose, reporting on the morning drive shows. The talk stations had wall-to-wall coverage of the event, kick-starting what would be years of speculation about what had really happened to Brett Kebble. With dawn still breaking, I had parked the red RunX I was driving at the time in a dirt clearing alongside the dump, parallel to the James and Ethel Gray Park, and was listening to John Robbie taking calls: Was it a hit? A hijacking gone wrong? Unacceptable crime rate in the country, something must be done! And then a panicked caller came through on air: 'John, I've just driven past the murder scene. There's a red RunX parked there now and it was there last night when I drove past. It's very suspicious, you should get the cops there immediately.' In hysterics, I immediately called the studio and quelled the alarm, telling them the suspicious red RunX was mine and no, I was not the murderer. John, never one to miss an opportunity for humour, immediately went on air and made light of the situation. The curse of the radio journalist – always the first to arrive and the last to leave a scene.

Later that day, a report broke on financial website Moneyweb that the mining magnate's death was the result of a failed car hijacking and not an assassination. It quoted 'reliable sources' as saying two vagrants had witnessed the murder and it appeared as though the alleged hijackers had relied on a 'classic' technique in which a man laid down on the road to force the vehicle to a halt. Moneyweb said that, according to its information, the vagrants saw the two men approaching Kebble's Mercedes, witnessed a scuffle, heard loud shouting and then the assailants began shooting the side windows of the car. Police immediately dismissed the report with Senior Superintendent Chris Wilken saying, 'A lot of people are making up stories about witnesses.'

The media was in overdrive as Roger Kebble arrived back in South Africa from Paris. In the hope of avoiding the prying cameras, Glenn Agliotti phoned Jackie Selebi and asked him to make arrangements so that he could meet Roger on the airport's apron. 'We were scared of the press,' Agliotti explains to me. 'So I said to Nassif, bring your guys and so this is the irony right. He gets Mikey and Sander to come and sit in the VIP lounge. I go in a BMW and drive onto the apron to a British Airways flight, which has landed on the tarmac. I meet Roger at the bottom of the stairs and we put him in the car and drive him back to the VIP area. And there's Mikey and all the guys waiting for him in the lounge having killed Brett the night before. How fucking ironic.'

Death Register No.: 2037/05
Medico-Legal Autopsy Report

I, Hendrik Johannes Scholtz, hereby certify that I examined the body
of a Caucasian male adult on the 28th day of September 2005 at the
Medico-Legal Laboratory, Johannesburg, beginning at 09h00.

Length: 1,77m
Mass: 128kg
Build: Muscular
Nutritional State: Overweight

Crime scene examination:
The body was seated in the driver's seat of a recent model S-Class
Mercedes Benz and was slightly slumped to the left. Rigor mortis was
starting to form in the muscles of the fingers, but was absent in the large
muscles across the large joints. Blotchy lividity was starting to form
appropriately in the left flank area. The ambient temperature was 9°
Celsius and the body temperature was 31,3° Celsius. This is consistent
with the reported time of the incident at approximately 21h00.

The body is received in a body bag. The body is clothed in a lilac col-
oured and white check long sleeve shirt, a pair of charcoal coloured
trousers with a black belt, grey underpants and black leather slip-on
shoes. The right shoe has a slightly illegible ink inscription on the in-
side of the shoe containing what appears to be numbers and the name
"Kipling". The shirt is blood-soaked and torn, circular or turn defects
are present in the right sleeve and shoulder area, the left shoulder area
and on the right side of the shirt. Some minor blood staining is present
on the trousers. The body is cold to the touch after refrigeration.

Chest and Diaphragm: Two entrance gunshot wound defects are present
in the 6th right intercostals space and exit wound defects are present in
the 9th and 11th left intercostals spaces. 300ml Blood is present in the
right chest cavity.

Large Blood vessels: The aorta is perforated at the level of the renal arteries. The left carotid artery is lacerated 6cm above its origin.
Abdominal Cavity: Contains 1100ml blood.
Stomach: Contains 450g of partially digested food consisting of proteinaceous material such as beef or chicken and vegetable matter including mushrooms, potato and peas and leafy vegetable material such as lettuce.
Liver and Gallbladder: The liver is enlarged and pale with a fatty appearance and perforated twice by gunshot wound tracks.
Genitalia: Normal circumcised male genitalia.

Two days after the initial autopsy was carried out by state forensic pathologist Professor Hendrik Scholtz, Brett's family decided they were not going to take any chances and were going to be thorough. Professor Jan Botha, a forensic pathologist at the University of the Free State in Bloemfontein, received a phone call, asking him to conduct a second autopsy on Brett's body, which had already been handed to his family.

But curiously, the call to Botha, on the morning of Thursday 29 September, came from Tamo Vink, who was then in the employ of Clinton Nassif's CNSG. Vink had worked with Botha at the state prosecutor's office in the past. On Friday morning, 30 September, Botha flew to Johannesburg and was met by Henry Beukes, Nassif's employee. He was taken to the crime scene on the Melrose bridge over the M1 highway, where he met Advocate Willem Heath. Later that morning, he was accompanied to the mortuary where, in the presence of Professor Scholtz, he carried out a second post-mortem:

Summary of Injuries:
The deceased was struck by seven bullets fired through the open window of the vehicle. The presence of tattooing over the right cheek and shoulder indicated that some, if not all, the shots were fired at close range, probably within 50 cm of the deceased. The assailant was standing immediately to the right of the deceased. During the shooting, the deceased raised his right arm in a flexed position as a defensive action, and turned to his left away from the assailant while the shooting was in progress. Three of the gunshot wounds were superficial in nature and

did not result in any significant injury. The remaining four gunshot wounds each individually resulted in severe injuries. All seven shots were fired from the right and directed at the torso. No shots were directed at the anterior chest or head. Any shooting incident is a dynamic event with the victim attempting evasive action and the assailant may also move while trying to maintain his arm. Consequently, while it is not possible to indicate the sequences of the shots with any certainty, it is probably that the gunshot wound over the mastoid process represented the final shot, given the tendency of a handgun to lift when fired in rapid sequence. The deceased did not die immediately but would have rapidly lost consciousness due to a combination of blood loss resulting from vascular injuries, inadequate blood flow to the brain due to direct trauma to the left common carotid artery and probably also the right vertebral artery and pressure on the upper cervical segment of the spinal cord due to local injury. The abrasion and surrounding contusion over the right lower jaw was strongly suggestive of an additional assault on the deceased, almost certainly caused by blunt force due to the muzzle of the firearm. If standard 9mm parabellum ammunition with a full metal jacket was used, it is surprising that all four bullets which penetrated the body were retained in the tissues as in the vast majority of cases bullets of this type perforate the body without undergoing deflection or disintegration.

Main Postmortem Findings:
Multiple gunshot wounds to trunk and neck with associated injuries to the right lung, liver, abdominal aorta, spleen, left common carotid artery and spinal column and concomitant blood loss.

Cause of Death:
Multiple gunshot wounds.

The post-mortems largely corroborate Mikey's version of events about what happened during the shooting. They are consistent with his claim that he shot at Brett's torso and not his head. They confirm Klatzow's suspicions that 'slowed down' bullets were used as they were 'retained in the tissues'. What I find most fascinating about the post-mortem report, besides Brett Kebble's true weight and what he had had for dinner, is the suggestion that he may have been assaulted by blunt force 'due to the muzzle of the firearm'. Mikey is adamant that he never touched Brett and certainly did not hit him with his gun.

THE BULKY FRAME OF PROP FORWARD GUY KEBBLE, STANDING WITH his hands thrust deep into his pockets, loomed large at the top of the stairs leading into St George's Cathedral. Alongside him, on either side of the balustrades, stood khaki-clad ANC marshals wearing berets, their fists clenched in a black-power salute. The thickset Guy was indifferent to the inclement weather and lashing rain, which besieged Cape Town that day and, unlike many mourners around him, did not hold an umbrella in his hand. He looked on as his father Roger struggled his way up the steps to the church, each stair appearing to demand huge effort and exertion, as though he were resisting what he would find at the top. Alongside Roger, escorting the haggard ex-mine boss up the stairs and into his son's funeral, was Glenn Agliotti. The irony of Agliotti playing the role of the compassionate friend would be lost on most who witnessed the image, but that visual would be replayed on national television at every opportunity in years to come.

Despite not having been granted an official state funeral, Brett Kebble's coffin was draped in a South African flag as it was carried up the steps of the cathedral. The pall-bearers, donning dark suits and large knotted orange-and-purple ties, were senior officials of the ANC Youth League with whom Brett had nurtured strong ties by empowering them in lucrative deals. Amongst them were Youth League President at the time Fikile Mbalula; business partners Lunga Ncwana and Andile Nkuhlu; Songezo Mjongile; and Sharif Pandor, the husband of then Education Minister Naledi Pandor.

Amongst the luminaries who crowded the cathedral on that Tuesday were business leaders including Tokyo Sexwale, property doyenne Pam Golding, mining pioneer and entrepreneur Bridgette Radebe and an unlikely mourner, Saki Macozoma, whom Brett had repeatedly accused publicly of spearheading a plot to stunt Jacob Zuma's ascendancy to the presidency. Also seated amongst the pews were Cape Town Mayor Nomaindia Mfeketo; Western Cape Premier Ebrahim Rasool; Schabir Shaik's brother and sleuth Mo Shaik; ANC staffers James Ngculu and Mcebisi Skwatsha; rugby player James Dalton; TV personality Dali Tambo; and Minister in the Presidency Essop Pahad. There were the *nouveau riche*, graduates from the empowerment class, whom Brett had lubricated with generous cash loans and enticing business deals. Then there was the old money with whom Brett rubbed shoulders, dressed in hats and sporting stiff upper lips. Brett's wife Ingrid hid behind dark glasses during this rare public appearance whilst his children arrived in school uniform.

Roger and Guy stood at the helm of the coffin as the national anthem boomed through the pipes of the cathedral's organ before they walked to the front of the chamber.

Five-year-old Lily Kebble sat in the front row dressed in red shoes and a black velvet dress decorated with red hearts as her three older siblings stood at the pulpit to deliver their heartfelt eulogy to their murdered father.

Brett's oldest son Matt tearfully recalled how his dad was 'extraordinarily talented', how he would cook Sunday lunch for the family 'like a chef', 'played the piano like a pro' and loved working in the garden. 'Some of my best memories were of him making my mom tea in bed and also of him making crumpets and pancakes for my friends and I.' Every moment of the limited time the four siblings had spent with their father would be deeply valued.

The teenager recounted how his dad had 'put everyone before himself'. 'My dad was a soft-hearted person. My dad was a family man. Some people made negative comments about him, but they didn't know him as well as we and his friends did.' But, in his adolescent wisdom, Matt observed that not all the people surrounding his father had been his allies or supporters. 'A few weren't. We have witnessed unspeakable actions of those few. Knowing my dad, he would probably forgive those who harmed him.' What stood out the most for him, he eulogised, was the way his father was generous, kind, caring and compassionate 'even to his own detriment'. Nine-year-old Hannah described her father as a 'loving father and husband' and affectionately spoke of his love for 'cracking jokes' and his brilliant sense of humour. Little Lily listened on attentively from her seat.

Following the funeral, Brett's wife and children disappeared from the public eye – they chose not to comment on developments around his murder and ignored media requests for interviews. The address from the pulpit was their final word.

The nave was thick with pungent incense as Roger Kebble, his eyebrows furrowed, rose and made his way to the podium, leaning heavily on Guy.

'Of one thing, I am sure, I will do all within my power to get to the bottom of Brett's death,' he vowed, before it all became too much for him. Old family friend and journalist David Gleason took the eulogy from Roger and read it on his behalf.

He spoke of the 'monstrous act' that had robbed the country of a 'brilliant mind' whose achievements had become 'part of legend'. He paid tribute to his son's contribution to the mining industry, explaining that Brett always understood that empowerment was a non-negotiable essential and 'every subsequent initiative he embarked on incorporated empowerment'. His son had made many enemies, but had never allowed personal allegiances to influence him. Gleason tailed off Roger's eulogy to Brett with the words from Rudyard Kipling's poem 'If'.

The mourners listened as others stood to speak, praising Brett as a 'real man', a 'patriot' and 'a warrior' who had led the charge for black economic empowerment and the building of a black 'economic citadel'. He was lauded for his support of the arts and for financing a feeding scheme for thousands of school children.

Youth Leaguer and business associate Andile Nkuhlu relied on the words of Tennyson and referred to Brett as his 'captain', describing him as a 'humble and passionate man who sometimes cut a lonely figure in his determination'. He remarked how Brett's 'outstretched hand became the ultimate bridge to experience and maturity in a world where youth and inexperience were shunned'.

But it was the bizarre address from Essop Pahad that filled column space in newspapers the following day, as politicos and Kebble-watchers alike attempted to unscramble the minister's words. He implored mourners to keep whatever information Brett had shared with them secret. 'Now that he's gone, these things must remain private.'

He railed against the media, saying some journalists were ignoring Brett's fundamental right to be presumed innocent until proven guilty and that his murder had thrown the relationship between rights and responsibilities under the Constitution into sharp relief. Pahad complained that the country had witnessed media speculation about Brett that seemed to border on the obsessive and which appeared to be trying to convict the magnate of past wrongdoing. He noted that in a constitutional democracy such as South Africa's, one was presumed innocent until proven guilty and accorded the right to a fair trial in an impartial court of law. 'Brett, it appears in death, was not accorded these fundamental human rights.' Of course, it was Pahad's remarks about keeping secrets secret that raised eyebrows. There was immediate speculation in the media that Pahad, a senior

lieutenant of President Thabo Mbeki, might have been circuitously referring to the millions that Brett had pumped into funding the ANC, which
the party would have liked to remain a secret. I'm still baffled by Pahad's
odd remarks and the curiosity persists today about just how deeply entrenched Brett was in the ruling party and what secrets he had to reveal.

As the haze of incense settled and Agliotti escorted an ashen Roger out
the cathedral once more, the eloquence of the praise and tributes rang out.
Brett's media hawks, who had spent years playing the game for him, had
continued to spin, even in death. Not all hacks were sold, however, and in
the wake of the murder, it was an editorial in the weekly *Sunday Times* that
appeared to speak most unequivocally:

> We will not join in the cacophony of eulogies to a man who has been
> described by some as a patriot and a great South African. Even though
> convention requires that we speak well of the dead, we will not be part
> of the lie. Brett Kebble was not a good South African. He was the great
> corrupter, a dirty businessman who had little respect for the law or
> codes of good practice. He corrupted politicians and created a para-
> sitical network of politically connected beneficiaries who affectionately
> called him 'umlungu wethu – our white man'. That is the reality of the
> man's legacy … That is the reality of the man's legacy …
>
> On his death, speculation of a hit was immediately followed by
> thoughts of the long list of people who would have wanted him dead.
> His business dealings were clearly not always above board, nor were
> they fair. He had openly crossed swords with numerous prominent
> people. Many of these battles ended up with legal action.
>
> His spokesman said that there had been threats in the past. But it
> would be wrong to assume that all high-profile businessmen have en-
> emies. Kebble's list was indeed long.
>
> Kebble is perhaps best summed up in the words of his father and
> business partner, Roger, who said his son had the 'intellectual capac-
> ity of a giant and the spirit of a warrior'. More tellingly, though, he
> also said that his son had been difficult to guide 'in terms of the Ten
> Commandments of life'.
>
> So today we say farewell to the Great Corrupter. May no more like
> you be born (2 October 2005).

ROGER KEBBLE HAD VOWED TO DO WHATEVER NECESSARY TO GET to the bottom of his son's murder. His consultant, Judge Willem Heath, who had a solid reputation having headed up government's Special Investigative Unit, led the private investigation and appointed David Klatzow to probe the murder. The recruitment of the private pathologist Dr Jan Botha was also part of this strategy.

However, within weeks of his appointment, Klatzow was pulled off the case on the instruction of Commissioner Jackie Selebi. A year after the murder, the police chief told Scorpions head Leonard McCarthy in an official interview that he had, in fact, met with Roger Kebble 'to find out from him does he want the police to investigate this or not'. Selebi told Kebble Senior that if he chose to have the crime investigated privately, then the police would 'pull back'. It was an astonishing admission by Selebi who had initially claimed in the media that he had no idea who Heath and Klatzow were. Klatzow had, perhaps, scratched too close to the wound.

During Klatzow's probe, he had established numerous peculiarities. He had discovered that Brett had taken out two large life-cover policies valued at R30 million just a few months prior to his death and his wife was the beneficiary. Brett had 'found the Lord' in his friend Peter George's swimming pool in a baptism just a short while before he died and there were photos to prove it. In the run-up to the shooting, Brett phoned his nemesis Peter Skeat to 'make amends and seek forgiveness', according to Klatzow. A High Court prosecutor also told the forensic scientist that a warrant for Brett's arrest had been issued in the weeks prior to his death. Added to these revelations were the peculiarities of Brett's behaviour on the night of his murder, pointed out by butler Andrew Minaar. Brett didn't take his customary dinner jacket with him and he left home without a gift for his host, Sello Rasethaba. After he was booted from the case and was not paid for his services, Klatzow did what he does best – he went to the media. He has a reputation for being media-indulgent and has often clashed with authorities as a result. He told the press, 'This is one of the most appalling police investigations I have had the misfortune to be involved in.' Klatzow went public with his suspicions about an assisted suicide, saying on national TV that he suspected Brett staged his own murder after taking out insurance policies. He also pointed to the fact that Brett's window had been rolled down on the night of the shooting and that the bullets used were of a type used only by security personnel.

Guy Kebble was furious about Klatzow's claim and came on the radio. He said that Klatzow was 'just looking to get his name in the press' and 'if he has something to say he must say it to the cops, otherwise just let them get on with the investigation'. At that stage, the Kebble family still had full faith in the police.

Despite Klatzow's discoveries, the trail was going cold for the police and theories about who may have wanted Brett Kebble dead mounted. The businessman evoked strong emotion in people and there were many who may have wanted to kill him. There were suspicions that it could have been a diamond deal gone wrong, a political hit or a desperate attempt to regain financial liquidity, which had ended in bloodshed. There was much talk about Russian hit men being involved who had travelled into the country via Mozambique.

Investigating Officer Johan Diedericks had numerous options to consider. 'As in any murder case one had to look at motive,' he explains to me. 'There were no eyewitnesses on the scene. According to bystanders, a vagrant in the park saw something but he could not be traced. The motive for the killing was unknown and all avenues needed to be explored. At this stage I gathered some background on Kebble and possible motives could have been: attempted car hijacking, one or other criminal deal went wrong, a political murder, a business-related murder as the deceased swindled huge sums of money from a lot of people, or by somebody known to him.'

Diedericks did not think it likely that Brett Kebble was killed as part of an assisted suicide plot as Klatzow alleged. 'I found it strange that this was an assisted suicide as Kebble was wounded several times. One would expect if this was the case, a normal person would have made sure that the first bullet counts so as not to suffer pain.'

Brett's last film interview surfaced, lending credence to the theory of a political assassination. In the interview with independent producer Liesl Gottert, who would later become President Jacob Zuma's media adviser, Brett 'laid bare a plot within the ANC to oust Zuma'. Gottert claimed at the time that 'Kebble was the only one with the guts to say what he thought on camera'.

In February 2006, in a desperate attempt to make arrests, the police investigating team recklessly stormed two Johannesburg flats in early-morning raids. Members of the elite Special Task Force from Pretoria raided the apartments in Birdhaven and Melrose simultaneously at 04:00 after receiving 'sound and solid information'. Embarrassingly, the cops arrested the wrong man. They took a 28-year-old advertising agent into custody. His girlfriend told Talk Radio 702 that day that the officers had accused her boyfriend of being Kebble's killer and claimed he had pictures of the murder scene. She overheard policemen say in Afrikaans that they had the wrong person. Officers were chasing down dead ends.

While on holiday in Zanzibar at the end of 2006, I coincidently met a Johannesburg father who told me that he too had been taken in for questioning in connection with Brett Kebble's murder. To my amusement, he told me that he was part of a medieval wartime re-enactment club – members dress up in outfits and reconstruct battles. Oddly, police had reason to believe that Brett Kebble's shooting was the work of a peculiar, albeit harmless, group of war enthusiasts.

Andrew Minaar, the butler with an appreciation for conspiracy theories, has a suggestion as to why police may have pursued this avenue. He reveals that Brett kept a dagger in his cupboard accompanied by a strange list. 'The dagger had like spider things on it, but in the pouch was this rolled-up piece of paper, with like a whole lot of people's names on it as if it was like a "brotherhood",' Minaar tells me with a glint of excitement in his eye. 'It was Stratton's name, it was Brett's name, Roger's name, Vaughn Brey, George Pool, Hennie Buitendag,' he says, rattling off a list of Brett Kebble's business associates. But the story gets far stranger. In addition to the dagger, Minaar also discovered a 'ceremonial sword' stashed in the back of Brett's dressing room. 'Right at the back, we found this ceremonial sword which was in the dressing room and it went to Roger. It was right on the top shelf right at the back. I'd never seen it before. When I took it out the pouch it had some sort of substance at the bottom. Dried blood or mud. It wasn't the kind of sword you'd go into the shop and buy,' he tells me.

To top it all off, Minaar, in his matter-of-fact way, tells me about one further odd development that occurred in the weeks after the tycoon's murder. 'The gun that was found in the garden, that was also strange.'

'What gun?' I ask, immediately intrigued.

'About three weeks after his death, the gardener came to me and said they'd found a rusted gun at the bottom of the garden. A 38. Who knows, it was strange because it was an area that had been cleaned constantly. So it hadn't been there very long. Diedericks [Captain Diedericks, the investigating officer] was supposed to come pick it up but Roger gave it to Karel, his security guy, and he took it away. It's just strange. Maybe somebody threw it over the wall.'

Brett Kebble's murder was a conspiracy theorist's dream with dead ends and wild goose trails occupying the police's time and resources. Clearly, investigators were no closer to solving what was emerging as the worst-kept crime riddle in Johannesburg.

WHILE THE POLICE UNIT TASKED WITH PROBING KEBBLE'S murder was chasing down dead ends, two events occurred which would prove to be crucial catalysts in the involvement of the Directorate of Special Operations, aka the Scorpions.

In November 2005, members of that police team were summoned to Commissioner Jackie Selebi's office in Wagthuis in Pretoria for an update on the progress of their investigation. Selebi was furious. The SAPS had been publicly vilified for apparently botching the crime scene and he was specifically irate about how Kebble's car had been allowed to be released from the scene without proper forensics being done. It was an embarrassment that he simply couldn't afford.

Amongst the team briefing Selebi was Chief Forensic Investigator Paula Roeland, who had been in the service since 1984 – a career policewoman with expertise in cellphone technology and tracking. Her job was to analyse phone calls of suspects involved in bank robberies, murders and other crimes, and track them down through their cellular footprint. Also in the meeting in Selebi's office was Roeland's direct superior, Sharon Schutte; Commissioner Johan de Beer, the head of detectives in the police; Commissioner Tim Williams; and Director Leonie Ras. Schutte had been responsible for handing over Kebble's phone numbers to Roeland to kick-start the telephone tracking, and together the two women had put together a PowerPoint presentation and a timeline dissecting the phone calls.

Roeland had established two peculiarities regarding cellphone activity surrounding the murder. She was able to place Kebble on the exact spot where he was murdered, on Monday 26 September, the night before the shooting took place. There had been a flurry of phone calls between Kebble and Glenn Agliotti – seven calls in total. But the next day, Agliotti's phone became dormant and Roeland suspected that he had switched it off. The participants in the meeting discussed the possibility of Kebble having had a third phone, as they only had two numbers that they were tracking. They also considered whether Agliotti could have another number that he was using on the day of the shooting. In their conversations, the name of a police reservist, Erasmus, popped up, as he had been one of the first on the scene of the crime.

And then, in Roeland's version of events, as told during Selebi's subsequent corruption trial, the most astonishing event occurred. The National Police Commissioner reached into his bag, pulled out his cellphone, dialled a number and said: 'Hello, Glenn. What is that story you told me about the reservist?'

Roeland testified that the Commissioner spoke to the person on the other end of the line for a short while and then ended the call by saying, 'Okay, bye,' before placing his cellphone back into his bag. As Roeland had been struggling to track down an active number for Agliotti, she immediately asked her boss, 'Commissioner, was that Glenn Agliotti?'

He didn't answer her; he simply ignored her question. She followed up with a request for the number he had just dialled, to which Selebi responded, 'I don't know numbers.' Roeland says that's how the conversation ended: abruptly. After the meeting, she spoke with Schutte and Ras about how very 'strange' that incident had been.

Roeland resigned a few weeks later.

During his time on the stand in his corruption trial, Selebi accused Roeland of blatantly lying. He claims he phoned Agliotti during the meeting to ask him who removed the car from the crime scene. He added that there was no way Roeland could have asked for the phone number because she had already written it on a whiteboard in the meeting room.

Mention of this bizarre meeting made its way to Scorpions Head of Special Projects and Chief Investigator Andrew Leask. His interest was immediately piqued.

Then, in January 2006, just a few weeks after the meeting, a letter landed in the inbox of the Gauteng regional head of the Scorpions, Advocate Gerrie Nel. It was from Gauteng's Director of Public Prosecutions Charin de Beer, and was labelled 'Top Secret'.

De Beer was the plucky blonde advocate who had led the prosecution against Jacob Zuma on a charge of rape and had been publicly denigrated for daring to bring such a case against him, which ultimately resulted in his acquittal. With this letter, requesting an investigation into the murder of Kebble, De Beer was consciously cracking open another mammoth can of worms. The letter was the result of a meeting with Kebble Investigating Officer Johan Diedericks, who had complained to De Beer and her deputy, Gerrit Roberts, about difficulties he was experiencing in getting hold of cellphone records.

Her letter read:

1. *I attach a document addressed to the National Prosecuting Authority for your attention. The letter is self-explanatory.*

2. *From the content of the letter, it is clear that a very close relationship exists inter alia between Messrs G Agliotti; C Nassif; J Selebi and B Kebble.*

3. *In order to verify these allegations, it is of the utmost importance that the cellphone records of the abovementioned persons be obtained and secured as evidence.*

4. *As you are aware, the cellphone service providers only keep the data for five months. After this period has lapsed, the information is lost. This period will lapse within a week.*

5. *A list of possible cellphone numbers is also attached. It is suggested that billing for these numbers be obtained.*

There was urgency in De Beer's letter to Nel – if the investigators didn't act swiftly, the cellphone records of the suspects named would be lost and a successful prosecution would be near impossible. Ironically, the cellphone records would never actually have held up as evidence in court. Nel and Leask were now sitting with a tip-off about a suspicious meeting in which Selebi had phoned a suspect in a murder investigation, the letter from Advocate De Beer urging that a probe be opened and information that was filtering in 'from the street'. They were hearing that Mikey Schultz was somehow involved in drugs, that Clinton Nassif had suddenly become very rich and that Glenn Agliotti was becoming increasingly flamboyant, portraying an image of a 'Mafioso'. There was enough suspicion to launch an investigation.

Mikey

I don't read newspapers. Kappie taught me that. He said, 'Fucking don't read because if you read you drive yourself mad,' you know? And everybody under the sun has got their own theory and version of what happened and everybody knows exactly what happened and there was many a time we'd sit in company of people who were saying, 'Fuck, ja, I heard this is what happened to Brett Kebble,' and, 'No, I heard this happened and no this is what happened,' and fucking nobody was remotely close. And you just say, 'Is it? Ja, no that sounds right,' or 'Ja, that's very plausible,' you know? I didn't lose any sleep after doing it for the simple reason that that man wanted to die. He came, I saw it with my own eyes, he came back and back and fucking back again, the night before, the night of the shooting and I could see that the oke really wanted to fucking do this, hey. I can't say I didn't think about it; we had thought about it a lot and we were just trying to keep tabs via Clint to find out where they are in the investigation. Clint would keep me updated and say, 'They don't know nothing, they don't know nothing, they don't know nothing.'

ANDREW LEASK WILL TELL ANY REPORTER WHO ASKS THAT HIS surname is 'Leask' and not 'Leaks'. He is an old-school investigator who subscribes to the mantra of 'sticking to the basics' and playing by the book when pursuing a suspect. With his large build, flushed cheeks, slimline moustache and temperate, unflappable demeanour, he's the kind of cop who always gets his man. Fastidious in his planning and strategic in his execution, he has worked on a litany of high-profile crimes since he became a police officer in 1983.

He grew up in the shadow of the mine dumps on Johannesburg's West Rand and his first placement as a policeman was in Westonaria. After enrolling, he went to college for a year as part of a special programme employed by the SAPS, which produced the youngest sergeants in the history of the service. Leask went to the 'border' for a year and returned to join the detectives unit, having spent less than twelve months in uniform.

He worked under Johan Steyn, the commander of the infamous Brixton murder and robbery unit, which was a crack unit in the police with a reputation for brutal interrogation techniques. Leask was assigned to apartheid-era assassins Ferdi Barnard and Calla Botha's first murder case. Both Barnard and Botha were members of the Civil Cooperation Bureau (CCB), a government-sponsored hit squad. Barnard, a former sergeant in the Narcotics Bureau of the police in Krugersdorp in 1982, was investigating several break-ins at pharmacies on the West Rand when he shot and killed a suspect, Peter Ward, and wounded another, Edward Joffe. Barnard was subsequently sentenced to six years behind bars for the crimes as a result of Leask's work. Barnard would go on to kill anti-apartheid activist David Webster and be convicted and sentenced to two life sentences in prison. He later claimed Botha had assisted him in carrying out the murder.

Just before the country's first democratic elections in 1994, there was an outbreak of violence in the Afrikaner stronghold of Ventersdorp – members of the right-wing Afrikaner Weerstandsbeweging (AWB) stopped cars, shot at occupants randomly and cut off their ears. An indication of the high regard in which he was held, Leask was tasked with probing the killings at a time when the country was at a tipping point and the possibility of the elections being scuppered was very real. Leask secured 32 death sentences in the case.

He was then given the mammoth task of leading the inquiry into the Shell House massacre in 1994. The incident had rocked the country while in its most vulnerable state. Eight Inkatha Freedom Party members were killed and at least twenty others injured when security guards outside the ANC's headquarters in Jeppe Street in the Johannesburg CBD opened fire on a crowd of 20 000, mostly Zulu, protesters. In the aftermath, accusations were slung from all directions about predetermined political motives and it was Leask's task to establish the truth. He spent two years recreating the entire chaotic day's violence, interviewing every victim and taxi driver implicated, going to each hospital that took in patients and even gleaned information from tribal headmen in KwaZulu-Natal about who had returned home wounded and who had not. Following that, Leask worked on investigating crimes relating to the Truth and Reconciliation Commission as part of then Transvaal Attorney-General Jan D'Oliveira's Special Investigations Unit.

In 1998, Leask heard that another crack elite unit was on the cards, called the Directorate of Special Operations (DSO), with the sexier marketing brand of 'the Scorpions', which would fall under the control of the National Prosecuting Authority. It followed a unique 'troika' model, which would see investigators, analysts and prosecutors working together. It was established in order to deal with national priority crimes such as high-level corruption and organised crime. Public confidence in the SAPS was at a low and President Mbeki announced that new machinery was required to battle organised crime.

Leask had known prosecutor Gerrie Nel from numerous cases that they had worked on together over the years and it was apparent the duo made a formidable team. Both men signed up as 'Scorpions' in September 1999, as soon as the unit was announced by the President. Leask's first big breakthrough at the unit was when he famously arrested Sir Mark Thatcher in his nightdress at his Cape Town home on coup charges, while Nel became the founding head of the unit in Gauteng.

Nel, who grew up in the Limpopo platteland in then Potgietersrus, is a *regte egte boereseun* and it takes very little stretch of the imagination to visualise a young Gerrie running around mealie fields barefoot in khaki shorts. Fit and agile, it's not uncommon to see Nel leaping across benches during court recess and slouching in the box with his feet up on a desk.

A state advocate endearingly recalls how, when she first became a junior prosecutor in Johannesburg in the late 1990s, she was very curious about 'this funny, short man who would rush through the DPP's office during teatime with his arms filled with files, his gown flapping behind him and a bevy of policemen trailing in his wake'. It turns out that Nel was cutting his tea break short because he was claustrophobic and wouldn't catch the lifts in the building. He needed the time to run up the stairs to make it to court promptly. This same colleague says she first recognised Nel's abilities when an old lady sitting in the public gallery approached her to tell her that it was the first time in years she'd seen someone argue with the same passion and conviction as Gerrie Nel.

Nel is a relentless prosecutor who argues with such intensity and sense of justice that it's apparent he is personally invested in his cases. He employs an admirable attention to detail and taunts his victims with sarcasm and wit to the point of infuriation and is thus deeply despised by those he has brought down. He is curt, pithy and largely unemotive. He earned his stripes as a junior prosecutor for the state against former Conservative Party MP Clive Derby-Lewis and right-wing Polish immigrant Janus Walusz, who were convicted of assassinating South African Communist Party leader Chris Hani at his home in 1993. The murder was part of a plot to attempt to derail negotiations to end the apartheid regime.

After Nel was sensationally arrested by the SAPS in a pre-dawn raid on his Pretoria home on trumped-up charges in 2008, the NPA was forced to issue a statement denying the prosecutor had ever been part of any 'riot cases', as claimed in the media at the time. The organisation also denied he had ever been a member of the Broederbond or any secret right-wing organisation.

The third member of the team that was tasked with investigating Brett Kebble's murder in early 2006 was Andrea Johnson. The petite, fiery prosecutor, who marches through court with barrels of gumption, her Durban Indian accented voice announcing her impending arrival, credits Nel as her mentor and even 'father figure'. Johnson, who was schooled in the small KwaZulu-Natal town of Scottburgh, was quickly promoted through the echelons of the civil service. Her first job was prosecuting in Alberton before doing a short stint in the district courts, where she was the first ever junior advocate to secure a life sentence at the time. She became a senior state advocate in 1999 and was amongst the first batch of prosecutors assigned to the DSO on 1 December 1999 and has worked closely in tandem with Nel since.

The trio, assisted initially by Thanda Mngwengwe, Special Director of Public Prosecutions in the DSO, began following up potential leads, unaware of the entangled web they would unravel. Their investigation would run parallel to that of the SAPS and the acrimonious relationship between the two law-enforcement agencies would escalate as they independently pursued Kebble's killers. Police officers and Scorpions investigators did not like one another.

AFTER OFFICIALLY COMING INTO OPERATION IN 1999, THE Directorate of Special Operations (The Scorpions) quickly earned a reputation for successful and effective prosecutions. They were independent and fearless and became giant-slayers. With their 'Hollywood-style' raids, slick media machine, swollen budget and flamboyant tactics, the Scorpions went after big ANC political players like the party's chief whip in parliament, the flashy Tony Yengeni, who was convicted of corruption relating to the controversial multibillion-rand arms deal. The infamous deal kept the unit in the spotlight as they pursued other politicians who had allegedly benefited improperly, most notably Jacob Zuma and his financial adviser Schabir Shaik who was also convicted of corruption and fraud related to the arms deal. Former Limpopo Premier Ngoako Ramatlhodi and ex-Transport Minister Mac Maharaj were also not exempt from the prying eyes of the Scorpions investigators.

Brett Kebble hated the unit as passionately as any of the politicians who were being investigated as he too was in their scopes. The Scorpions were probing the Kebbles' business dealings and Brett responded with a full-scale offensive. He was adamant the unit was being manipulated as part of the political feud between the factions within the ruling party. He pointed his finger at NPA head Bulelani Ngcuka who he maintained was using the state agency to quash Zuma's growing power base and pursue Saki Macozoma's presidential ambitions. Kebble closely aligned himself with the top police brass as a result. Agliotti testified that in 2003, he arranged a meeting between Kebble and John Stratton and high-ranking officers Mulangi Mphego and Rayman Lalla. They used the platform to air their conspiracy theories about Ngcuka and the Scorpions.

The more successful the Scorpions became, the more hated they were by those they targeted. The police also developed a particular dislike for the unit which reached a peak in August 2005 when black-clad agents raided Zuma's Forest Town home resulting in a standoff with the VIP protection police officers guarding the home. I was outside Zuma's home that day as the Scorpions' vehicles screeched to a halt and I had visions of an almighty shootout between the two sides. It was a miracle it was avoided. Bloodshed as a result of a firefight between two organs of state would have been unthinkable. In another unprecedented move, the Scorpions also had agents raid the Union Buildings and the Office of the Presidency to search for evidence against Zuma. The raids had not been sanctioned by the police and infuriated the SAPS officials. They were astonished at the arrogance and disregard displayed by the Scorpions, who were accused of using unvetted staff to raid the most powerful office in the land.

Despite their growing list of critics, the Scorpions' public profile grew exponentially and the DSO enjoyed significant support largely due to its successful use of the media through talented and able spin doctors such as Sipho Ngwema and Makhosini Nkosi. They had a high success rate because they got to pick and choose their cases and their guns were bigger and flashier. Police officers gave them the nickname 'Pick and Choose' for only selecting cases that promised successful prosecutions. It wasn't difficult for cops on the ground to dislike them.

In the year Brett Kebble was murdered, President Thabo Mbeki appointed a Commission of Inquiry headed by High Court Judge Sisi Khampepe to probe the unit's future. Khampepe's official mandate was determining whether the unit should remain under the NPA as its role was investigation rather than prosecution – the police were pushing for the DSO to be incorporated into the SAPS. Mbeki wanted Khampepe to look at its relationship with the SAPS and the overlap that existed between the two. He was concerned about rising tensions between political principals responsible for the two arms of law enforcement. ANC luminaries were unhappy with the autonomy of the Scorpions and Mbeki was acting accordingly.

Khampepe's hearings were held at a conference centre in Eastern Pretoria. Selebi pushed hard for the unit to be amalgamated into the SAPS and was supported by Billy Masethla, the Director of the National Intelligence Agency. Justice Minister Bridgette Mabandla, under whose ambit the unit fell politically, also suggested the DSO be relocated. Her argument was that South Africa no longer faced the same crime threat that it had when the Scorpions was established.

Leonard McCarthy, the head of the DSO, led the offensive in favour of the unit's survival. He blamed territorial jealousy and personality clashes between the heads of the police and the Scorpions for the strained relationships between the two units. He argued for the DSO to remain under the control of the NPA, but acknowledged that the country's laws needed to be amended in order to improve the efficiency of the directorate. McCarthy was backed up by Vusi Pikoli, the head of the NPA, who insisted the matter was 'bigger than individuals'. Intelligence Minister Ronnie Kasrils was also in support of the Scorpions remaining under the prosecuting authority. So too were two NGOs, the Foundation for Human Rights and the Institute for Security Studies, which argued that many of the reasons for locating the Scorpions 'beyond the organisational walls of the police service remained'.

Khampepe's recommendations were made public in June 2006 but the full report was kept under wraps for another two years and only released in 2008. The judge found that the location of the Scorpions was constitutional and that the DSO should be retained within the NPA. However, she advised that the political oversight of the law-enforcement component should reside with the Minister of Safety and Security rather than the Minister of Justice. This would improve oversight over investigative operations while the prosecutors would remain accountable to the Justice Ministry.

Khampepe was critical of both Jackie Selebi and Vusi Pikoli – the heads of the rival organisations. Pikoli was lashed for failing to ensure investigators were properly vetted while Selebi was also blamed for the deteriorating relationship between the two units. Khampepe recommended both be disciplined. 'It may be necessary for a reprimand by the president and/or parliament as a mark of displeasure. The institutional tensions that are explained by the personalities that head these institutions are regrettable in the extreme.' Khampepe recommended the Scorpions stop publicising their investigations and suggested a special committee be set up comprising the Police Commissioner, the Scorpions and other security cluster representatives to act as a troubleshooting mechanism.

Ironically, despite Khampepe's recommendations, the Scorpions no longer exist. In December 2007 a resolution was passed by the ruling party to amalgamate the unit into the SAPS. In October 2008, parliament voted to disband the DSO and replace it with a unit located within the police named the Directorate of Priority Crime Investigation, nicknamed 'the Hawks'. The criticism in the media was swift, with an outcry that Zuma's faction of the ANC, referred to as 'the coalition of the wounded' in the press, had succeeded in scrapping the Scorpions.

THE SCORPIONS TEAM ASSIGNED TO THE KEBBLE MURDER GOT cracking with their investigation. But first they needed a case name.

A feature of working in the DSO was that investigators could attribute their own names to cases they were working on, instead of being assigned generic, mundane titles. Nel remarked to Leask that the investigation was about organised crime, high-ranking officers and corruption, and the name had to sync with all that. They believed early on that they weren't only investigating a murder, but rather that the killing of Brett Kebble was just one small aspect of a far more complicated set of crimes, none of which could be precluded. Kebble's murder was simply the mistake that blew the lid on the syndicate. It was a stepping stone into 'their world' and a device for Leask and Nel to get into a position of authority.

While surfing the web in pursuit of something clever, Leask printed out a cartoon sketch of a little gangster, with a fedora hat and a Tommy gun in one hand. Nel took one look at the picture and quipped, 'Hey, that looks like a bad guy.' The men realised that this was exactly what they were dealing with in this case: Bad Guys. And the name stuck. There was nothing elusive or subtle about it, but that was Leask's style of operating. He would get in his suspects' faces early on.

In a signed affidavit, DSO head Leonard McCarthy would reveal the full scope of the operation, which was officially authorised on 28 March 2006:

> It is an investigation into an organised crime network operating both in South Africa and abroad. I have been in the DSO for five years and I can confirm that this is one of the most extensive, complex and sensitive investigations that the DSO has ever undertaken. The investigation focuses on the offences of drug dealing, racketeering, money laundering, corruption and murder. Some of the allegations that are being investigated include: allegations of targeted corruption of senior law enforcement personnel; laundering of large amounts of local and foreign currency through at least seven destinations worldwide; smuggling of drugs from Europe through South Africa and on to other foreign destinations; the smuggling of large-scale contraband and counterfeit goods into South Africa and the assassination of individuals who do not subscribe to the code of the criminal network.

The primary task of the team probing Bad Guys was to establish the veracity of the rumours they'd heard about the myriad phone calls linking Kebble, Agliotti and Selebi. There was talk that Agliotti had called the Police Commissioner from near the murder scene and there were also other senior officers on the Melrose bridge on the night of the hit. Investigators went in search of the detailed billing phone records, which were specifically pointed out by Advocate De Beer in her letter requesting an investigation be launched. But the Scorpions would receive little to no cooperation in their pursuits. According to an investigator, many of the executives in cellphone companies were extremely reluctant to help as they were former police officers themselves. 'There was just a concerted effort that no one should scratch where they shouldn't. We wanted all those police generals' detailed billings and, when we asked for Selebi's, they were shocked that we could expect them to hand those over.'

Top-level meetings were even set up between Scorpions leadership and CEOs of cellphone companies as they went to great lengths to get hold of the records. One of the members of the police's investigation team had succeeded, through well-placed contacts, to get hold of a portion of the documentation, but he was subsequently fired under the pretext that the information had been acquired illegally. Despite the hurdles, the Scorpions team managed to confirm that the strange Selebi meeting with Paula Roeland and the peculiar phone calls did indeed happen.

By March 2006, investigators were starting to accumulate information about Glenn Agliotti from official and unofficial sources. What they suspected was that Agliotti was transporting containers illegally, that he was involved in below-the-line tobacco running and that he may have been moving contraband narcotics as well. They also knew about his association with Zimbabwean tobacco trader Brian Baxter, who Agliotti later admitted he knew through illegal cigarette smuggling.

Then, on 9 March 2006, there was a crucial breakthrough. Scorpions investigators were able to turn shady police reservist, karate specialist and security expert Paul Stemmet, and he gave a statement detailing his relationship with both Agliotti and Selebi. Stemmet had been in charge of Brett Kebble's security before Clinton Nassif was employed. In fact, Agliotti had been introduced to the Kebbles through Stemmet. Selebi had met the security consultant during the Special Olympics promotion in Cape Town in July 2001, which Agliotti had approached the Police Commissioner about. It was Stemmet who acted as Arnold Schwarzenegger's bodyguard during the Special Olympics torch run.

I have never personally met Paul Stemmet despite his name lurking like the elephant in the room in every development in this convoluted story. He somehow managed to avoid testifying in both Jackie Selebi's and Glenn Agliotti's trials and has kept a relatively low media profile despite his evidence constituting an invaluable part of the arsenal in the Scorpions' weaponry. He's never been successfully prosecuted himself. According to those who have had dealings with him, he used to be 'big like a bodybuilder but the steroids worked themselves out of his body and he's now a big blob'. During consultations with him in the Bad Guys investigation it was remarked that, 'There is nothing intimidating or impressive about how he now looks. He is also rather slow. Whilst he speaks well enough he did not strike me as being bright – he clearly lived up to his name that he was muscle and hence people feared him but he was not known for his wit or charm.'

Stemmet's affidavit, and others corroborating his evidence, would be widely publicised in the *Mail & Guardian* newspaper in 2006 and the weekly would, over the next few months, reveal astonishing details about his security company, Palto, which emerged as Selebi's own dirty unit. According to the newspaper, on 24 November 2006, they were 'a vigilante squad of freelance operatives who used Selebi and the police as their cover. Balaclava-clad and flashing police identity cards, Palto members conducted cowboy-style raids for contraband goods. Invoking Selebi's name, they appeared untouchable.'

Officially, they were a VIP protection company but were employing former police Special Task Force members. Investigators found Stemmet's weak point – they had established that he had been responsible for dangerous crimes and, if he talked, he could shift the blame to Agliotti, leveraging complicity. The information had come from statements signed by former Palto employees – cops who were moonlighting for the company. Through committed and dogged journalism, the *Mail & Guardian* reported on the extent of the lawlessness:

According to an affidavit from Johannes Roux, then a member of a police crime intelligence unit in Johannesburg, he and others in his unit would moonlight with Palto on contracts to trace stolen computers and protect trucks transporting computer equipment. By 2000 and 2001, the affidavits allege, Palto was indulging in extortion and dirty tricks. Former Palto member, Chris Schutte, confesses in two affidavits how he and Palto members threw an explosive device at Microsoft offices in Sunninghill, Johannesburg. 'The purpose of this action was to convince Microsoft to use more protection services as provided by Paul Stemmet and not to injure or kill any persons.'

There were allegedly a number of similar 'operations' during this time. In one case, a prominent businessman wanted to 'scare' a debtor living in Bryanston, Johannesburg. An explosive device was thrown first into the wrong person's yard, and then into the correct target's yard where, according to Schutte, the businessman wanted to make 'sushi' of his debtor's koi fish. Roux describes another 'job' performed, his affidavit alleges, for Agliotti. He drove the car as a Palto member threw a hand grenade at a Randburg home where an Agliotti debtor lived.

There is evidence that already in September 2000, Palto conducted an 'operation' as if it was a police unit. In this case, the same prominent businessman mentioned above, allegedly wanted to get at a relative whom he said had 'molested' his daughter. According to Roux, he and Palto operatives gained entrance to the target's townhouse 'by showing our [police] appointment cards'. Once inside, Roux planted ecstasy in the target's home and he was arrested. Charges were later dropped. Schutte corroborates the incident (24 November 2006).

Throwing an explosive into the wrong person's yard? Making sushi out of a debtor's koi fish? Planting Ecstasy in a target's home? All this was done by Palto operatives abusing their role as police reservists and it was happening in suburban South Africa without any of us knowing anything about it at the time.

When I read this article for the first time, I could not help but think this bizarre story was morphing into something surreal out of a movie script.

It would be a massive R105 million drug bust in Kya Sands in Northern Johannesburg, involving a Chinese 'clearing agent' enigmatically referred to as Madame Cheng, that would become the flagship crime connecting Palto, Agliotti and Selebi.

The incident would form part of the basis of the 'defeating the ends of justice' charge which Selebi would have to answer to during his corruption trial and about which Agliotti would have to testify extensively. On 3 January 2002, photographs of the national police chief with a Cheshire-cat grin, his hands filled with seized contraband, featured on the front pages of the country's newspapers. The cops had recovered 1.5 million Mandrax tablets hidden in false tile boxes, packed in a lorry ready for shipment. Selebi was celebrating the haul and ensured that photographers were there to capture the moment for posterity. Those pictures would come back to haunt him.

What the country didn't know at the time was that Agliotti had asked Stemmet to arrange the transport, Stemmet had tipped off the cops and a 'controlled delivery' ensued. In his statement, Stemmet claimed he told Selebi, as early as 2002, that his buddy, Agliotti, was involved in the drug deal and that he was a crook. 'I informed the National Commissioner about Glenn Agliotti's involvement and the facts surrounding his request for an escort. Commissioner Selebi became very angry at Glenn's involvement. After informing Commissioner Selebi about Glenn's involvement in the drugs, he was never arrested.' It appeared as though Selebi chose to ignore the warning.

During his testimony in Selebi's trial, Agliotti asserted that police never even took a statement from him about the Kya Sands bust. Charges against the suspects were later dropped and a large portion of the Mandrax pills seized were stolen back from a police walk-in safe a year later. At the time, the *Beeld* newspaper (January 2003) reported that the haul was recaptured by what appeared to be members of the original syndicate in an 'audacious operation which ended in a shootout'.

But there is another intriguing twist in the tale.

During his testimony, Agliotti would claim that it was he who had, in fact, tipped Selebi and Stemmet off about the bust. Selebi had authorised a R500 000 reward payout for Stemmet. This meant that Agliotti had given the Police Commissioner a tip-off about the huge drugs haul 'for free' but Selebi nevertheless allowed him to sell the information to Stemmet, a registered police informant and reservist. Agliotti claims he was approached by handler Captain Nel and Stemmet and handed R100 000 in cash for the information. Instead of being interviewed and arrested for his involvement, he was paid a reward!

It seems this was one of the perks of having the country's top cop in your pocket. The indelible image of Selebi's grin on the front page of the newspapers, his hands overflowing with little white pills, sticks fast in my memory whenever I'm confronted by a news story. Things never are as they appear to be. As in this case, there may be complex forces at play behind the scenes and dirty men could be getting paid to commit crimes by the very officials we are paying to protect us.

A few days after pocketing his hot R100 000, Agliotti was signed up as a police informant with the pseudonym 'Picone', no doubt a tribute to his Italian heritage. He was paid a recruitment fee of R10 000. But his cameo appearance as an informant wouldn't be all that fruitful and he was deregistered as a source the following year.

WHILE THE SCORPIONS BAD GUYS TEAM WAS TURNING PAUL Stemmet in March 2006, the six-man SAPS unit, headed by Johan Diedericks, carrying out a parallel investigation into the Brett Kebble murder, was pulled off the case. Officially, police management strongly suspected they had leaked information to the *Rapport* newspaper, which could have jeopardised the case, and they had an idea that the investigators had put journalists in touch with a man who claimed Brett had paid him for sex. Unofficially, the police team was sniffing too close to Selebi and had to be sidelined before things became too hot for the Commissioner to handle.

Rapport published claims that the police had discovered that Brett was regularly paying a call boy named 'Vaughan' and other male prostitutes for their services. The paper tracked down Vaughan at a Randburg agency where he worked as a rent boy and printed an interview with him. A translation was published in the English sister paper, *City Press*:

> 'Brett Kebble was never alone with me when we were intimate. There always had to be a few other young men, to stroke his ego. And he enjoyed watching.'
>
> So said Vaughan, a 29-year-old male prostitute that the former mining magnate apparently had a 'soft spot' for. Vaughan (the name he uses with his clients) said he and Kebble, 41, met each other regularly over a number of years in Johannesburg and Cape Town and that their friendship developed into an 'intimate' one last year.
>
> Police had questioned Vaughan at the agency in Randburg, two weeks ago. They were interested in information about a threatening letter to Kebble that had been e-mailed to Vaughan's computer. He was also shown pictures of three men that have apparently been linked to the Kebble murder. Vaughan said he did not recognize any of the men.
>
> Vaughan claimed in the article that he had met Kebble at a massage parlour in Norwood, Johannesburg, three years ago:
>
> 'You recognise your clients by the cars they drive. We would say here comes "Mitsubishi Charles" or "Mustang Peter". Kebble was known as "Nugget Ricky", because he had introduced himself as Ricky and always had a nugget of gold in a handkerchief that the masseuses had to touch. And we knew him by his silver Mercedes. Later there was also a black

Porsche. He was always dressed in nice suits and shoes. He was always friendly and talked easily. The lights were always on in the room,' said Vaughan.

'He freely gave money and gifts, without expecting anything in return. He had a soft spot for me, but there was never any jealousy,' said Vaughan, who travels regularly between Cape Town and Johannesburg. He works in both cities.

When Kebble wanted sex, he wanted variety. 'Always four or more young men,' said Vaughan. 'He enjoyed sitting back and being pampered while he watched what the others were doing. And he was not "shy" to pay,' said Vaughan (26 February 2006).

Guy Kebble slammed the reports that his brother was gay, saying the media was conducting a reign of terror against his family.

I have always been unsettled by the rumours and speculation that Brett Kebble was gay – I suspected the rumours were deliberately stoked to tarnish his legacy and pollute the murder investigation. While I didn't make a concerted effort to find out, as I was indifferent to his sexual preference, I did mention it to those I interviewed in an attempt to uncover other possible motives for his murder.

'He had a double life. I think so,' says Laura Sham, Brett's PA. 'I really can't say it factually but I can say that he spent a lot of time around men. Ingrid and his marriage is just an arrangement. It makes sense, he went to a boys' boarding school, in business his whole life he was surrounded by men, perhaps he did enjoy the company of men.'

I hasten to add that while Sham was intimately involved in Brett's daily business affairs, she does not necessarily speak from a place of authority about his sexual preference.

It's a topic butler Andrew Minaar is eager to speak about, mostly because he has info which he's never revealed about Brett's sexual orientation.

'I wouldn't say gay, I'd say maybe he had a bit of a kinky side. I've heard from the staff here that there were boys here late at night. They used to come in a "Volksie",' he tells me, nonchalantly offloading his 'big secret'. 'I had just started with Brett and we were packing up his house in Houghton. The guys from Stuttafords came to me with some movies and asked me what they must do with them and when I looked at them, there was porn movies but they were all about boys. There were about three or four of them and I thought, "Oh God, what do I do with them?" But I'm thinking maybe he and his wife are kinky, you never know. I actually destroyed them. Brett always had blue movies with boys. When his wife used to come he'd call the driver to take a massive bag of movies away. At a stage it was locked in the safe upstairs here and Brett had hidden the key in a carpet rolled up in the garage.'

Journalist David Gleason also has an opinion. 'He was probably bisexual, ACDC. He struck me as being quite asexual. He and Ingrid did make four children so they must have done it, although the relationship with Ingrid was uncomfortable.'

Others told me they thought the rumours about Brett being gay had been planted in order to alter perceptions about him and mislead the investigators, reinforcing my suspicions. Whatever the truth, it was Brett's preference and I can't help but feel it didn't detract from the love he had for his family.

As a result of the *Rapport* article and the suspicion it had been leaked, a new police team was appointed to the case. Captain Johan Diedericks is still adamant that he played no role in leaking the information about Brett's sexuality to journalists. 'That is correct that information was leaked to the press but it was definitely not by me. I am too experienced to compromise an investigation in such a manner. The Rapport newspaper quoted a Captain and Commissioners Norman Taiwe and Richard Mdluli assumed it was me. That was bullshit. For all that I know it could have been Paul Stemmet as he was also called Captain and I know he was in contact with one member on the investigation team.'

At the end of 2006, Captain Johan Diedericks retired from the South African Police Service having spent over three decades as a cop.

'It was clear to me that I was closely watched. The team to assist with the investigation was picked by Commissioner Taiwe and they were unknown to me and were from other units. They were inexperienced and their purpose was unknown,' he says, his comments laced with cynism.

'During the investigation I visited Kebble's Cape Town office and seized some documents including a list of prominent ANC politicians who received money from Kebble. That list was handed to Commissioners Taiwe and Mdluli.' Diedericks suggests nothing ever came of that list. He also saw John Stratton in the office speaking to a high-profile ANC member at the time.

Despite being intimately involved in the initial investigations into the murder, Diedericks was never called as a witness in the murder trial.

'A strange thing in this was that not I or Superintendant Murray was called to testify in court or ever requested to submit scene statements as this is normal procedure. Superintendent Murray was never asked to confirm if Mikey Schultz pointed out the correct points on the scene.' However, he did receive some interest from the Scorpions. 'Soon after I retired, Gerrie Nel and Andrew Leask arrived at my office to discuss this case. To my surprise, they were more interested in Selebi.'

Two officers, PW van Heerden and Corrie Maritz, were appointed to replace Captain Diedericks and were tasked with probing the murder. Both men are career policemen who come from Afrikaner backgrounds. Van Heerden bares an uncanny resemblance to infamous 1980s policeman-turned-bank-robber André Stander, with his brush-cut hair and thick ginger moustache. He is a dedicated cop who spends hours on his job and also has a degree in law, although he's not shy to admit to indulging in more than a few beers after a day's work. Maritz is more refined, largely as a result of his English having less of an Afrikaans twang. He's a tall, dark-haired man with a goatee, and looks as though he would have made a good lock forward in the police's rugby side.

They would lead the parallel investigation to the one that was steaming ahead under Andrew Leask's and Gerrie Nel's authority. The two teams would develop a deep-seated professional hatred for one another and there would be little to no cooperation between the two units, which were effectively doing exactly the same jobs. In hindsight, it was this ugly animosity that would ultimately compromise any chance of a successful prosecution in the mining magnate's murder case.

B Y APRIL 2006, SCORPIONS INVESTIGATORS HAD STEMMET IN THEIR pocket but they needed more. That 'more' would come in the form of Paul O'Sullivan and an email that would throw open a whole new avenue of possibility.

O'Sullivan, an angry Irishman with a penchant for loud animal-print ties and a big axe to grind, was once the head of security at Johannesburg International Airport (now OR Tambo International Airport). An imposing man with a balding pate, droopy eyes and a near-permanent frown, he is a licensed fraud investigator and qualified engineer. He had emigrated to South Africa in 1994, having left his partnership in a lucrative London property business to buy up land in post-apartheid South Africa. He wriggled his way into the job at JIA after noticing how lax security was when his bag was stolen in a terminal. But in 2003, he was sacked – he says because Selebi was orchestrating a conspiracy against him, along with Airports Company South Africa CEO Monhla Hlahla.

The bitter war between security boss and police chief originated in 2001. O'Sullivan, in his capacity as the executive in charge of security at JIA, wanted to get rid of ACSA's largest private contractor Khuselani Security in an attempt to eradicate corruption and drug running through the national keypoint. Khuselani's guards were poorly trained and dirty, according to O'Sullivan, and he wanted to clean up the show. Evidence of this was seen in a R115 million daylight robbery of jewellery, diamonds and cash from a KLM flight. Despite having the backing of ACSA Chairman Mashudu Ramano, O'Sullivan's efforts were thwarted – National Police Commissioner Jackie Selebi summoned the Irishman to his office and subtly attempted to dissuade him from cancelling Khuselani Security's contract, which was worth R130 million. Selebi later admitted, in court papers, to being friends with Khuselani's owner, Noel Ngwenya.

An indignant O'Sullivan defied Selebi and went ahead with cancelling the contract. He claimed he then received death threats and tip-offs that Selebi and Ngwenya were conspiring to oust him and that the police would be taking over security at the airport. Ramano also feared for his safety at the time and even relocated to a hotel after unidentified men jumped the wall of his house. O'Sullivan later alleged that Gauteng police chief Perumal Naidoo and Hlahla bullied him into withdrawing a complaint of intimidation and attempted murder which he had lodged against

Selebi with police watchdog the Independent Complaints Directorate.

O'Sullivan had been a police reservist for years and his membership was terminated because of an apparent 'conflict of interests'.

He was suspended from his JIA position in 2002 after he handed the South African Revenue Service dirt that he'd dug up linking Ngwenya to major fraud. He was later temporarily reinstated before officially being sacked by Hlahla for what she cited as 'irreconcilable differences'. O'Sullivan had apparently flouted air traffic regulations by flying an unscheduled private aircraft.

And so began a seven-year crusade that would see the naturalised South African throw all his personal resources into building as much evidence as possible, tying the country's most senior police officer to a network of dangerous criminals. In O'Sullivan's version, the mission would cost him his marriage and his millions. His probe started with an investigation into the smuggling networks that used the airport as a gateway and ultimately led to the doorstep of the National Commissioner. O'Sullivan pursued witnesses, staked out suspects, took down statements and cultivated sources. By the time Kebble was murdered, the Irishman had already built up an arsenal of ammunition which he'd sent to the Scorpions. He hadn't received any reply from them. Investigators came knocking in March 2006 when they were searching for leads.

The information he gleaned he then fed to the Scorpions and leaked through the media, culminating in the so-called O'Sullivan dossier. He went as far as cuffing himself to the doors of a venue of an Interpol meeting in Marakesh, Morocco, in protest and distributing pamphlets trumpeting to delegates about Selebi's alleged corruption.

To many, these were the ravings of a disgruntled madman who would say anything to get his job back and Selebi's office capitalised on this, driving an aggressive spin campaign against the police chief's main accuser. Deputy Commissioner André Pruis and Senior Communications Officer Selby Bokaba were at the forefront of this attack. Bokaba claimed O'Sullivan was a British spy, an MI6 agent to be precise, with the intention of undermining the country's law-enforcement authorities. Selebi even said as much during a press conference; so too did then President Thabo Mbeki. O'Sullivan never entirely denied this – he admits he was an agent decades ago but that his speciality was counter-espionage and counterterrorism. Selebi also later suggested that his nemesis's campaign against him had its roots in the Commissioner's refusal to subject senior police officers in full uniform to full body searches at the airport. He maintained O'Sullivan had a vendetta and was doing all he could to smear him.

O'Sullivan was ruthless and bitter and the fight became very personal as he allegedly bombarded Bokaba's and Selebi's spokespeople, Sally de Beer and Vishnu Naidoo, with vitriolic emails. He allegedly threatened them and their families, calling them 'gutless pieces of excrement', even saying he hoped that their wives would be raped and their houses robbed. O'Sullivan, of course, denies this. At the time he was insistent that the emails had in fact been fabricated by Selebi's allies and that he had provided proof of this to the NPA after Bokaba and Naidoo laid a criminal charge against him.

It was one of the statements that O'Sullivan had taken down during his renegade search for evidence that landed in Scorpions investigator Robyn Plitt's inbox. The email contained notes from a meeting that O'Sullivan had had with a 'Casual Source' (CS) who was working in Nassif's company at the time. Leask and Nel would never identify who Casual Source was. The meeting had taken place on Tuesday 2 May 2006 between 09:30 and 10:30.

According to the statement, CS told O'Sullivan about attorney Tamo Vink who had been helping Nassif 'tidy things up by removing evidence in case they get raided by the Scorpions'. Vink is the lawyer operating behind the scenes for Nassif, attempting to get him the best possible deal from prosecutors. It was also revealed during Agliotti's trial how Nassif had to cover up for Vink after he allegedly shot his wife in the stomach during a domestic dispute while on an apparent drug binge. He told hospital staff she had shot herself.

CS revealed how Vink 'had a bonfire last week. Burnt everything, all the stuff that was mentioned in previous debriefs, such as cellphone records, investigation files, etc. They also burnt a lot of files on Wellesley-Wood. It was all the work done by Beukes and Diederichs at Kebble's request.' CS was referring to the ugly battle waged between the Kebbles and Wellesley-Wood. It seemed as though Nassif and his men were scrambling to get rid of any evidence relating to the mining brawl.

In the document, CS goes on about how Vink 'works with a guy called

Barry Roux. Together they got Beukes off on murder charges even though he was guilty.' Roux is the well-known advocate who had been hired on occasion by Nassif. He is also the prosecutor who dropped charges against Roger Kebble – the same charges that Nassif was paid to 'take care of'. Nassif has always maintained Roux was not bribed and he just 'got lucky'. Beukes was Henry Beukes, a former police officer who had been moonlighting for Nassif's security company, CNSG.

CS also referred to another freelance cop, Josh Diedericks, claiming he was getting paid R50 000 a month by Nassif, while accessing phone statements and movement control records from the cops.

CS then made a fascinating claim that supported the theory that Nassif's men had cleaned up the Kebble crime scene: 'Josh Diedericks and Beukes were first on the scene of the Kebble murder. A cop, Captain Johan Bothma, helped "clean" the scene; he picked up spent cartridges, etc, then CN [Clinton Nassif] had the car picked up and taken to Danmar Autos, as mentioned in previous debrief. Car was "cleaned", i.e. any evidence was removed.'

The information then became even more surreal as Casual Source recounted how one of Nassif's employees, Mohammed Mazibuko, went astray, needed some cash and stole twelve guns from him, including an Uzi and a 357 Magnum and then vanished. Nassif apparently sent Beukes and Diederichs after him. They tracked him down in KwaZulu-Natal, beat him up and left him locked up on the fifth floor of their office block. Mazibuko subsequently broke into a boardroom, 'drank lots of booze, then smashed the place up'. He was taken to the Johannesburg Central Police Station and thrown into the cells for his disobedience. But Mazibuko, an old and trusted employee of Nassif's, knew far too much. Nassif 'freaked and had Diederichs and Beukes go fetch him, drop the charges and get him out,' claimed CS. Mazibuko had only been inside for a few hours, but he had been 'singing' about 'how he could get them all into the shit'.

CS thought that Mazibuko had been killed and dumped but, ironically, it would be Mazibuko's testimony to the Scorpions that would sink his former employer down the line. Mazibuko would spill the beans about Nassif's attempts to commit insurance fraud and how he was sent to cash a cheque to pay Mikey Schultz for jobs.

There were more claims from CS about Roger Kebble's tax fraud and

Nassif's flamboyant lifestyle, but it was the second-last paragraph of the document that would have been most interesting for investigator Leask.

'Interviewer referred back to last debrief when CS mentioned taking an envelope to Nassif at a café in Sandton with Selebi. The envelope contained R50 000 in cash. CS saw Nassif give the envelope to Selebi. Asked how he knew the envelope had R50 000 in cash in it, CS said it was packed as if it could be money and later, Nassif bragged to CS that he had paid Selebi as he had Selebi in his pocket.'

From this interview with Casual Source, Leask had a lead that Selebi was taking cash bribes and that he was intimately involved with Nassif's circle. He also had other leads to pursue, which he could use as leverage against Nassif. The risk, of course, was that Leask didn't know who CS was and the credibility of the source could be questionable. All the claims could be fabrications.

The Casual Source interview would not be the last piece of critical evidence that Paul O'Sullivan would hand to investigators, steering them in the right direction.

I N MID-2006, THE SCORPIONS HAD SEVERAL IRONS IN THE FIRE AS they tried to find a crack in the cartel. They had Stemmet and Casual Source bubbling on the back burner. They had also been tipped off about a fraud case involving Nassif. An old police officer friend of Leask's was on the verge of arresting the spare car parts dealer. Nassif had been found in possession of R10 million worth of stolen BMW spares during a 2001 raid on one of his companies, JR Auto Spares. The incident caught the attention of international policing agencies but Nassif had never been convicted. According to O'Sullivan's Casual Source, it was because Nassif had bought his way out of jail. He claimed his colleague, moonlighting policeman Josh Diedericks, who was on suspension from the SAPS at the time, had bribed a sheriff of the court and paid him to make false statements against the investigating officer.

Leask's policeman friend told him about an insurance fraud matter involving Nassif. According to the cop, Nassif had his employee Mohammed Mazibuko drop his Mercedes-Benz from a forklift to increase the damage to the car after he had been involved in a minor accident. He had been on his way to play golf with Agliotti, it was drizzling and he hit a puddle which sent the car skidding into the pavement. Nassif subsequently claimed R500 000 from insurance after getting Agliotti to author an affidavit confirming the car had been extensively damaged. Nassif was worried insurance wouldn't pay out for the minor damage and he needed the cash because he was planning on emigrating to Los Angeles. He was wrapping up his business interests in South Africa.

But before the Scorpions could move on Nassif, O'Sullivan arrived on their doorstep again, this time with Anthony Dormehl in tow, the 'transport man' who moved the Kya Sands Mandrax haul and had previously done a fair amount of work for Agliotti. Dormehl owned a company called Premium Transport.

According to one person who has worked with Dormehl, he is a 'go do and go fetch' kind of guy. 'He is just a plain Jim and would always do what he is told, he works for anyone who will pay him, he does not ask questions, follows instructions and that's it. He did not care about the load he was transporting, he just did the job to get paid.'

O'Sullivan had found Dormehl and warned him that he knew about his past involvement in illicit contraband trafficking. Dormehl's company was often used by Palto for 'controlled deliveries' as part of pseudo-undercover operations. O'Sullivan turned him into a mole for the Scorpions by promising him indemnity and spent some time debriefing him before handing him over. Dormehl had showed him warehouses and other infrastructure that was being used in drug deals and began feeding the Irishman information about Agliotti. O'Sullivan even took Dormehl up in a chartered plane to photograph locations central to contraband trafficking. Then, on 26 April 2006, O'Sullivan called a meeting and introduced Dormehl to Leask and his team at the McDonald's fast-food outlet near the East Rand Mall in Benoni, at 20:30. Present at the meeting were Plitt, Dimpeng 'Slang' Maangwale and three others. Dormehl told the Scorpions that he 'was part of a syndicate trafficking a consignment of hashish'. A massive deal was about to go down and Dormehl was ready to sell out his accomplices.

I can't help but be amused at the thought of a plot to bring down a major, cross-border smuggling operation being hatched in a McDonald's as a snotty-nosed child scoffs his tomato-sauce-laden chips while a clown smiles from the netted plastic ball bin. It's all very surreal.

According to a Scorpion present at the meeting, O'Sullivan was extremely pushy as he explained to Leask that he had this source, Dormehl, who was going to give him what he needed. The Irishman, who is known to be obnoxious and difficult, insisted that all information would be passed on through him and that Dormehl would report to him. A heated argument ensued between Leask and O'Sullivan, with the chief investigator telling the self-appointed recruiter that things were not going to happen his way as the Scorpions were in control of the operation. The source says Leask told O'Sullivan that if he doesn't like him or the way he operates then he 'must walk', but Dormehl 'was going nowhere because he was a drug dealer and had half a consignment in his possession'. Leask won the standoff.

The Scorpions launched Operation Coffee, which formed a leg of the Bad Guys probe. Dormehl would make three signed statements detailing the activities of a major international smuggling syndicate that had tentacles in various countries and was using South Africa as a springboard to ship narcotics from Asia through to Europe and America. The contents of a 'Statement of Journal' which Dormehl signed under the pseudonym 'Bill Smith' would become the skeleton of his experience of transforming into a Scorpions mole and give the background to the syndicate's trafficking operations. His crucial revelations would lead to one of the biggest drug busts in the country's history – this bust would be the first domino to fall in the Scorpions' Bad Guys quest and would lead to Agliotti and Nassif coming under the control of the crack investigative unit.

In his statements, Dormehl alleged that he had met a man by the name of Steve Paparas through Agliotti. The fixer, Agliotti, had advised Dormehl that 'this guy will be coming to see you and you can just help him', which he did. That first meeting would lead to numerous 'jobs' which Dormehl would do for Paparas, driving trailers full of undisclosed contents and delivering boxes filled with contraband. Dormehl's Premium Transport had allegedly been used repeatedly by both Agliotti and Paul Stemmet to move contraband, so the work Paparas allegedly wanted him to do wasn't foreign to him.

Stefanos 'Steve' Paparas is in his early forties, has piercing eyes and is very good-looking in the boys-your-mother-warns-you-about type of way. He speaks loudly, with a working-class accent, and uses phrases like 'chicky' liberally. When he met Dormehl he was living in a nice house in Norwood in Johannesburg and was driving a Mercedes-Benz. His father Dimitrio, aka 'Uncle Jimmy', speaks little to no English, has bushy white hair and Steve affectionately refers to him as 'my old man'. He's always struck me as being a friendly grandfather, the type who runs the corner café. The fact that he has a dodgy ticker and has had to endure triple-bypass surgery while facing criminal charges has influenced my empathy for him.

After the meeting with Leask on 26 April, Dormehl agreed that he would fully cooperate with the Scorpions and handed over all the hashish that remained in his storage facility, keeping back two packs. The Scorpions unit swung into high gear as they began effecting a clandestine undercover operation – they had money to throw at projects like this. Dormehl's vehicle was fitted with a camera. Scorpions agent Dimpeng 'Slang' Maangwale, a lanky, genial man with a long history in law enforcement, was sent undercover to work as Dormehl's 'assistant' dressed in blue overalls.

Dormehl claims he was in phone contact with Steve Paparas over the following days as he and his father were allegedly struggling to find a way to fit hashish blocks into coffee tins for shipping. Dormehl took the two packs of hash that he had not handed to the Scorpions and went out to

Dimitrio's plot to test whether the blocks would fit into the coffee tins. 'Slang' was on the back of his bakkie, posing as a hungry, subservient employee named Eric. Submerging himself in his character, 'Eric' even obediently approached Dormehl in front of the elderly Paparas and said, 'Boss, I'm hungry,' and received a response to 'Go back to the car and sleep'. The entire visit to the plot was captured by the camera fitted to Dormehl's car and would be used as evidence in the drugs trial.

Through their mole and undercover operations, the Scorpions were able to establish that the drug deal had an international link. They had heard the name 'Bob the American' and knew that this character was in South Africa at the time. He had slipped the drugs into the country from Pakistan, hidden in stoves, and the hashish was then repackaged to resemble coffee packets. Half the consignment had already made its way out of the country to Holland and Paparas Jr had allegedly received a payout of nearly R1 million. The remainder of the stash was on the verge of being exported.

Finally, in late June, the deal was set to go down and Dormehl was to drive the consignment to the East Rand Mall where it would be handed over. In court, Dormehl would testify how 'Steve (Paparas) wanted everything delivered, apart from 28 kg and he said, "Keep 28 pairs of shoes with you."' But the Scorpions were worried that not all the international role-players were in the country at the time. They didn't want anyone to evade arrest as that would result in their simply shifting responsibility onto whoever got away. The entire plan would collapse because of an oversight.

With a massive drug bust in the balance, Leask and Nel took a gamble. They had Dormehl's truck pulled over by the Metro Police, who slapped him with a R1 000 fine for driving an unroadworthy vehicle. Dormehl had no clue that it was a set-up, but 'Slang', who was still operating undercover, did. As a result, the handover was postponed for another week.

On 5 July 2006, 'Bob the American' and an accomplice, Christiaan Alblas, were waiting for a truck to be delivered by Dormehl. When it didn't arrive, Alblas became suspicious and phoned an employee, Pedro Marques, to come and assist. The truck finally did arrive and 'transport man' Stanley Poonin, a local driver who worked for Bob, took the wheel.

Poonin is from Lenasia, a mostly Indian suburb in South-western Johannesburg, and is more often than not casually dressed in jeans and a cap that reads 'Jesus is King'. In jest, he later took to wearing a cap that bore the insignia of a scorpion when he made an appearance in court. Poonin drove to a storage facility in Alrode in Alberton, east of Johannesburg where Scorpions agents were waiting.

'Bob the American', Christiaan Alblas, Pedro Marques and Stanley Poonin were all arrested and 672 kg of hashish and 1 114 kg of compressed cannabis, packed into custom-made wooden boxes, were seized. The street value of the haul was a quarter of a billion rand.

But Steve Paparas, the suspected kingpin of the entire operation, was not there and had not been arrested. He was the one Nel and Leask were really after. The success of the operation was on a knife's edge. Dormehl had to keep on 'playing' Paparas so that the Scorpions could corner him. Dormehl claims he was in phone contact with Paparas and would later testify that 'he called me to say he was with his lawyers. He didn't know which way to turn and they had taken his father away. I feigned surprise and he told me not to worry. I asked him what I should do with the 28 pairs of shoes and he said I must get rid of it.'

Nel and Leask were anxious – they thought Paparas could be waiting at a nearby petrol station with hundreds of thousands of rands in cash for the deal to go through. It was Paparas they needed in order to leverage pressure on Agliotti.

At around the same time, Nel and Leask received news that Nassif was on his way to Los Angeles to lay the foundations for a new life there and planned to set up a call-centre business. The two Scorpions decided not to stop him from travelling to the States and agreed instead that it was more important to 'get the message to him' that they knew about his involvement in crime. The duo waited at the departures terminal for him and, although they had never met, Leask recognised Nassif immediately. It's not difficult as Nassif is striking, with his tall hunched frame and sharp jaw. He was walking past the check-in counters with his wife Kerry when Nel and Leask stopped him. The investigator introduced himself and told Nassif, 'I think you want to speak to me,' before handing him a business card. The burly security boss was so terrified that he fumbled the handing over of the card three times before peeling it off the floor.

Agliotti was also in the United States at the time on a working holiday. Both he and Nassif got the call telling them about the Alberton drug bust while they were in Los Angeles.

O N THE MORNING OF 5 JULY 2006, I RECEIVED A PHONE CALL from a fairly low-ranking police officer contact who worked in the forensics section on the East Rand. He'd been the source of a number of tip-offs, which generally proved to be on the money, leading to much-valued scoops. He was usually one of the first respondents called to a cash heist or shootout, as he was responsible for dusting for fingerprints and other arduous tasks. The cop told me he had just left a self-storage facility in Alberton where a massive drug bust had happened. He explained that the 'dagga' was stored in stoves and the lock-up garage was full of the stuff. The source had almost always been accurate in the past, so I immediately grabbed the keys of a marked 702 RunX, mobilised an intern and asked the source for directions. He explained that the location was in Alrode and gave me a vague explanation of how to get there.

It was a relatively quiet news day and the prospect of a multimillion-rand drug bust was a welcome interruption. The news rolled on the radio as I drove to Alberton. Then ex-Deputy President Jacob Zuma had his cursory hold on the day's headlines. He was bringing major defamation suits against several media organisations for publishing cartoons and columns about him while he was on trial for rape. The country was also preparing for him to return to court later that month on corruption charges. The Scorpions were also still celebrating a decision by Pretoria High Court Judge Ben du Plessis that week, ruling that search warrants used to raid the offices of arms company Thint were valid. The search-and-seizure operations were part of Zuma's corruption probe. Also making headlines: fourteen people had been injured in a taxi crash in Sandton; South Africans were recklessly losing their ID documents; and the quarterfinals of Wimbledon were underway following a rain delay ...

I navigated my way through the industrial landscape of Alrode, where every warehouse looks the same as the next, and finally stumbled on the self-storage facility the source had described to me. The trademark fleet of black VW Golfs, with red scorpions painted boldly on the bonnets, was the giveaway. I pulled my 702 car up on the pavement and walked through the steel gates, intern in tow. I could see activity in the distance outside two of the lock-up garages. In the forefront of the facility were two officious-looking men, leaning against the doors of one of the black cars. I didn't recognise the men but as they swivelled round in my direction, the alarm written across their faces was unmissable.

Despite having the naivety and over-eagerness of a cub reporter at the time, I immediately established that the duo seemed to be in charge of the scene. I excitedly queried, 'Oh, I hear there's been some kind of huge drugs bust here?' They looked at one another in horror and the colour drained from the rosy cheeks of the larger, bulkier one of the two. The shorter, sterner-looking one stretched out his hand and told me his name was Gerrie Nel and introduced his colleague as Andrew Leask.

Nel knew that news of the bust could not be made public at such a sensitive stage in the investigation. If it were revealed on the airwaves that five members of the syndicate had been caught, Steve Paparas would vanish. Agliotti and Nassif could also make a run for it. The success of the entire operation was at stake and the situation was desperate. I, of course, had no idea what was going on.

The men explained that, yes, there had been a drug bust, and yes, several people had been arrested. Please could I hold off on the story for 48 hours until the suspects appeared in court, as I could compromise a precarious investigation? Having sniffed the story, I was immediately reluctant but recognised that the scoop was not worth scuppering the operation. I agreed with Nel that I would hold off, on the basis that he would not leak the story to any other journalist.

The following day, I watched from the public gallery, the sole reporter on the wooden benches in the room, as the five suspects appeared in the dock. Scorpions agents milled around the gloomy passages of the small Alberton courthouse and there were whispers of tape recordings, undercover operations and links to something far bigger. But at that stage, all I knew was that it was the largest drug bust ever made in the country and an international syndicate was involved. I had just read *Mr Nice*, the sensational, gripping autobiography of notorious British smuggler Howard Marks, who used 43 aliases, 89 phone lines and 25 companies worldwide during the 1980s to deal dope. I was rapt and convinced that I was witnessing the downfall of yet another 'Mr Nice' right in my own backyard. The next morning, we broke the story on air and the NPA confirmed the bust.

Steve Paparas handed himself over a week later. I would only realise much later what I had been sitting on when I saw the front page of the

Mail & Guardian and how the operation had, in fact, flowed directly from the Bad Guys probe and was linked to Kebble and Selebi. The name of The Landlord – the kingpin of the syndicate – began to emerge. This did not refer to Steve Paparas, as it was a reference to someone who was still evading the law. There was immediate speculation that Agliotti held the title.

Staggering detail about the syndicate's clandestine contraband dealings would be revealed in court over the following few years. Arrests had apparently been made in Vancouver, Bangkok, Pakistan, Holland and across Europe since 1999, all linked to the South-African-based syndicate. In one operation, 550 kg of cannabis, which had been cultivated on a Free State farm, was transported to Canada, hidden in engine parts.

It emerged that 'Bob the American' was indeed a veritable 'Mr Nice', although he only received a relatively light sentence of ten years in jail, half of which was suspended in exchange for his testimony against Paparas, his father and driver Stanley Poonin. He would reveal that he had numerous pseudonyms, including 'Lesley Alan Curtis' and 'Christopher John Howells' but his real name is Robert Lottman. Ironically, he is a Canadian and not an American. He had been trading in drugs for decades and had travelled the globe on fake passports as he ran from the law. Lottman revealed how he had helped set up the operation by smuggling the drugs into the country from Asia and repacking the hashish into tins to resemble coffee. He admitted he was the middleman between suppliers in Pakistan and the recipients in Europe. After seeing Lottman in court, my colleague Adriaan Basson described him as 'more Al Gore than Tony Soprano', saying he looked like a 'private school dad at a school fête' in his blue striped shirt and chinos.

Lottman detailed how he was held hostage for ten days in 2003 by Paparas, allegedly on the orders of The Landlord after a shipment went missing. Thousands of kilograms of cannabis, heading to Germany, were stolen by corrupt customs officials in Holland. Lottman was allegedly ordered to hand over his passport and was kept in a container on Dimitrio Paparas's plot for a week, with only a mattress to sleep on.

Christiaan Alblas also received a ten-year sentence in jail, half of which was suspended in exchange for his testimony against the three accused. He'd later claim that he'd heard Lottman and Paparas speaking about The Landlord but he didn't know who the person was. He only knew that the individual was very powerful, with friends in high places, including police chief Jackie Selebi.

Pedro Marques, who worked for Alblas, received a jail term of five and a half years, three of which were suspended.

Paparas was placed under house arrest and granted half a million rand bail which was reportedly posted by his then friend Glenn Agliotti. In his bail application, it emerged that he had a previous conviction for illegal gambling and had been investigated for assault and possession of a stolen vehicle. He had failed matric and had held various jobs before becoming a director at a trucking company.

I've spent many hours with Paparas discussing his trial and the charges levelled against him. He can't speak publicly on the claims because his trial has not been concluded. It's been limping along for over five years and, as a result, Paparas is a very bitter man. There is so much he wants to say. 'Look at my poor old man, what they've put him through. Gerrie Nel, Andrew Leask and them. You'll see, there's lots on them that will come out,' he tells me in his noisy way. Paparas is angry that he's been left to face the music. 'All of them did deals to save their arses and I'm the one left standing,' he says. He's always been transparent about the fact that he too was offered a deal early on in the game but refused to take it. Now he says he's waiting his turn to come clean about his prosecutors and the way they've treated him.

Leask gave evidence in Paparas's bail application. During his time on the stand, the investigator repeatedly mentioned The Landlord, but not once did he reveal the identity of the 'big drug lord'. He knew that every member of the syndicate was cringing as he spoke from the witness box.

DESPITE GLENN AGLIOTTI NEVER HAVING BEEN FORMALLY identified as The Landlord, it seemed a given that he was the holder of the title. For weeks the Scorpions drove speculation about The Landlord's identity, fuelling our belief that it must be Agliotti. He really fitted the bill and all our sources were telling us it was so. All the players who were already in custody were referring to Agliotti by that name during their consultations with the Scorpions, fuelling the assumption that he held the title.

We were speculating furiously that he was the boss of an international smuggling syndicate and pressure was mounting on Jackie Selebi to resign, with calls also coming thick and fast for him to be sacked. We all wanted to know how the country's most powerful law-enforcement officer could be mates with a gangster so influential that he even had a Mafia-type nickname like 'The Landlord'.

Two months after the Paparas bust, the Scorpions cranked up the pressure even further. They launched raids on Agliotti's Bryanston townhouse and his Midrand business premises as part of the drugs investigation. Twelve people in total were named as suspects on the warrants used to authorise the searches, some of whom were employees of the dubious security unit Palto. They were suspected of being involved in crimes ranging from drug trafficking and money laundering to corruption and defeating the ends of justice.

While the raids were carried out on the pretext of being part of the drugs trial, Agliotti and Nassif knew very well that what the investigators were really closing in on was the Kebble murder mystery. Frequent articles in the *Mail & Guardian* linking them to Kebble would also have been adding to the heat and the Scorpions were playing off this media hype. According to a member of the investigating team, Leask and Nel 'didn't care if they broke Agliotti and Nassif on drugs, car insurance or murder, they needed to get them into a position that they would come clean on everything'.

Mikey

When Paparas and Glenn and Clint got caught for the drugs, I was going to go and see Ian Small-Smith, my attorney, about that because I wanted to tell Ian what had happened and get myself prepared because I thought that we had shit coming. Clint phoned me on the way and said, 'Don't you tell this oke nothing, nobody knows. Everything is going to be fine. Nobody knows anything, don't tell anybody.' So I said to him, 'Clint, Glenn's going to sing like a canary.' He said to me, 'There's no canaries on my shift.' Those were Clint's words.

Along with other colleagues in the media, I waited for the Scorpions to move on The Landlord, who we were convinced was Agliotti. We knew that the first move had been made and suspected it would all unravel shortly. We had worked out that the Scorpions believed the Paparas drug matter was linked to Kebble and a breakthrough on that case was imminent. We envisioned the scoop and the headline and we were salivating.

Clinton Nassif returned from his sojourn to the United States knowing he was now a hunted man. He had begun selling his assets as he prepared to emigrate. But he also knew that if he tried to leave the country again, Messrs Nel and Leask would be at the airport waiting for him. So he got his advocate, Barry Roux, to write the Scorpions a letter, effectively telling them that he was planning on emigrating and if they'd like to speak to him, the time was right.

The Scorpions responded by arresting Nassif on 26 October on a charge of insurance fraud relating to his damaged Mercedes E55. It was two days before he was due to leave for the States and the Scorpions had issued a warrant for his arrest, so he decided to hand himself over. Nassif was sent off to Johannesburg Prison, the so-called Sun City, before being released on bail of R300 000 the following day.

Versions of what happened to Nassif whilst in Sun City have been embellished somewhat, with Agliotti even claiming that the towering, churlish security chief was so terrified that he wet his pants. Another version is that he had spent just a few minutes in a cell before he cracked and scribbled down the names of the gunmen he'd hired to shoot Kebble and handed the piece of paper to Leask. Those more sympathetic to Nassif's position say he realised the game was up and there was no point in lying any longer, so instead he tried to save those he had roped in to do the crime.

Whatever the truth, Nassif agreed to dish up information and testify for the Scorpions in exchange for blanket indemnity for an array of crimes. Nassif had to come clean about every crime he had been involved in and, in return, he would tell investigators about the Kebble murder, as well as give details of Agliotti's relationship with the country's police chief, Selebi. Incredibly, Nassif also wanted indemnity for a long list of shady characters who were in his employ at some stage or another. He also asked for protection for Agliotti at first, but investigators obviously could not concede to that request.

Crucially, Nassif gifted the Scorpions with the names of Mikey Schultz, Nigel McGurk and Fiazal 'Kappie' Smith, finally confirming the identities of the men who had gunned down the desperate mining tycoon in Melrose in September 2005.

As retribution, the words 'King Rat' – the title of the James Clavell novel – were boldly spray-painted on the wall of Nassif's Bassonia home, marking him as a sell-out.

I F I, HYPOTHETICALLY OF COURSE, WERE A HIRED ASSASSIN AND were asked to gun down a very well-known businessman, I would want to be paid handsomely for the risk of facing a life behind bars and the torment of the public profile that would accompany the job. Mikey, Nigel and Kappie were promised R500 000 each for the hit and, for a long time, they weren't paid. You can imagine how unhappy they were.

When I raise the topic of Clinton Nassif and payment with the trio, it's immediately a burning issue. Nigel, with his hot temper, is the most emotional about it.

'After we done everything, it was a couple of weeks after that, we started to say "Where's our money?" We spoke to Mikey and he said it's a bit hot now.'

According to Mikey, Nassif was paying them in dribs and drabs, occasionally paying over R100 000 or R90 000 which he would split three ways.

'We waited a month, and then we got a bit of cash. I think he gave us about thirty grand cash to keep us going and to keep us quiet,' explains Nigel. 'We said fine. Then a month went by, another month went by. Now you must understand how Mikey works. Mikey was very close to Clint so Mikey battles to go and ask someone for money. He'll give the shirt off his back, he'll do anything for you, we also very similar that to go and ask for our money is the hardest thing in the world. That's just the way we are. And we started saying Mikes, me and Kappie put a bit of pressure on him, we said when are we going to get our money. This is a joke.'

Anxious and increasingly desperate, Nigel and Kappie went to see Nassif themselves to discuss the issue of payment as they knew Mikey wasn't making any progress. Nigel needed the money urgently as he had committed to buying a brand-new BMW and the money from killing Kebble was supposed to fund the car. What they heard at the meeting gave them little comfort and reinforced their suspicions that Nassif was going to 'knock' them.

'We went up to the office right on the top floor and Clint closed the door. He said, "You guys must understand something. I've got so much heat. I'm in so much shit I'm probably going to get arrested. I'm probably going to have to stay in jail for three weeks. But I'm going to stand vas and get out. They watching my bank accounts, they watching everything." This is what he was saying to us,' recalls Nigel.

Kappie is intuitive and astute when it comes to matters of the street and he immediately knew what was happening. 'I knew when we spoke to Clint to ask what's happening with our money, hey. I knew a problem was coming 'cause he was yellow. He's yellow, he's like a rat,' Kappie says, his accent emphasising the word 'yellow'. 'When me and Nigel was at his office, when we went to ask what's happening with our money, I said to Nigel that day, I said we got big shit coming. I think about two or three weeks later they came for us. I knew it was coming. I knew he was never loyal, even to Mikey all his life. Mikey could have been very wealthy today. He wouldn't need to work a day in his life. He was offered everything and then he went as a loyal friend and the guy still fucked him over,' Kappie tells me bitterly.

After Nigel and Kappie confronted Nassif, more signs started appearing that they were not going to be paid. Nassif dropped his employees' salaries by half, including those of Nigel and Mikey. He was scaling down his business and it looked as though he was preparing to emigrate to America. 'He wanted to buy a car from Aston Martin. We know the people that were selling the car and this Aston Martin was a left-hand drive. When they came they brought it in from England but they didn't know it was a left-hand drive. So Clint said he'll buy it 'cause he wanted to send it to America,' explains Nigel. 'Then the writing was on the wall that Clint was now getting ready to pack up and go.'

Nigel and Mikey had given CNSG their security contracts when they first went to work for Nassif. After he cut their salaries and began downsizing, they decided to take their contracts back. 'Clint wasn't happy about that but he was just going to drop everyone without no jobs and everything like that,' says Nigel. After months of badgering from Nigel and Kappie, Mikey could no longer ignore the truth – his close friend, who was like a brother to him, was trying to screw him. 'Eventually we called Mikey and we said, "Mikey, listen here, what's going to happen with our money?" And then Mikey saw the light, that his good friend Clint was going to knock him.'

Kappie gets worked up when he recalls what Nassif did to Mikey. 'That man had tears in his eyes. I promise you. He hurt him bad. He hurt him bad. And when that guy gets hurt we all hurt here. It's a bond we share. I can die any day next to that guy. Clint's a fucking arsehole. There's no loyalty there whatsoever. How can you ever? A man that sits with you every day and then turn around on you. Mikey dedicated his life to him, his heart and his soul to him, and this is what he'd done. We told him all the time. But he was blinded because this guy was disloyal and dishonest. This guy made millions and used Mikey like a rag doll.'

It was a difficult realisation for Mikey to come to. 'For the first like six months things were ok and we were falling out with Clint about the money and everything else. I realised what was going on. I believed everything was 100 per cent and I had a fallout with Clint and I took a step back and I realised, hey, "Open your eyes, you've got some serious shit coming" and I didn't realise that things weren't as peachy and rosy as I thought they were. But Nigel and Kappie had been warning me for a while. I just didn't want to see it. I didn't want to see anything wrong with Clint. And then I realised, "Ok, we got a bit of shit here." Then I started jolling, drinking, taking drugs, carrying on like a fucking lunatic because I wasn't sure then what was happening. You know, then I had got the feeling that this was definitely going to come out.'

Having realised that the money would not be forthcoming, Mikey arranged a meeting with Glenn Agliotti at the News Café restaurant in Fourways. Also present at that meeting was James Murray, a businessman who holds directorships of listed companies. In a sworn affidavit Agliotti claimed that Murray gave him R200 000 to pay Jackie Selebi to ensure his company Xantium Technology Holdings, which he owned with Nassif, received government contracts. The tenders didn't go their way and Agliotti said he repaid the money to Murray – the businessman has always maintained that the money was never intended to bribe the Commissioner and was paid to Agliotti as a consulting fee. James and his brother Jesse are good friends of Mikey and Nigel's – Jesse was also working for Nassif's CNSG at the time.

At the News Café meeting, Agliotti told Mikey that he had paid all outstanding money over to Nassif. He even told him that he had a KPMG audit report in his possession which proved that a total of R18 million had been paid to CNSG. It was this audit report that formed the foundation of the state's case against Selebi. Mikey also testified in court about how Agliotti asked him to help him collect money from Nassif which he still owed him. Agliotti had apparently pumped R900 000 into Nassif's company and there was the matter of a speedboat that they had bought together. Agliotti wanted his money back and he was going to Mikey to do his debt collecting. According to Mikey, Agliotti told him that he still had close ties with Roger Kebble 'who was so pissed off with Clinton Nassif that he would pay good money to see him fucked up in a bar fight'.

After the News Café meeting, Mikey phoned Nigel and told him that Agliotti wanted to speak to him and that he should meet them at The Grand, an upmarket strip club in Sandton. Mikey also warned his hot-headed friend that he should not hit or hurt Agliotti.

'I wanted to confront him. I wasn't going to really hit him. I wouldn't have minded it but I wanted to know where our money was,' Nigel tells me, although I'm not entirely convinced he wouldn't have thrown a big right hook if it came down to it. He really doesn't like Agliotti. 'Glenn knew we weren't happy with him. So he knew he had to calm us down because whatever was going on here, he can't afford to have us on his case. We went to the meeting at The Grand there by the sushi bar. We started speaking and I said to him what's happening with our money. Glenn said, "No, in fact I've paid Clint all of the money. In fact Clint owes me money." And I said … I did believe Glenn there. I must be honest. On that fact I believe that Glenn had paid Clint.'

If Glenn had indeed paid Clint, it would certainly look as though he was the paymaster for the Kebble murder. But during Agliotti's trial Clinton Nassif blew this piece of evidence out the water for the prosecution:

NASSIF: *You know, at the end after Brett's shooting and the money wasn't forthcoming, there was a lot of words and a lot of arguments between us [Mikey]. We weren't really friends for a long time, we still don't speak. I think he got pressure from Nigel and from Kappie. I don't think he knew where to go to, and obviously the pressure fell on me. At some stage they were going to go to Glenn and collect the money from Glenn. I told Glenn to tell them, if they ever do come – because I was speaking to Glenn still at the time. I said if these guys ever approach you for the money, tell them that you paid me to steer them away from him.*

ADV GCALEKA:	Why did you have to do that?
NASSIF:	I think to protect him, because I could deal with Mikey and Nigel, and I knew them well enough that they would never hurt me. But Glenn was another story.
ADV GCALEKA:	Do you know if they ever approached the accused?
NASSIF:	I think at one stage they – or I don't know who had a meeting. Somebody had a meeting with Glenn, he told them he paid, because it came back to me that Glenn said he paid and now, where's the money?

Mikey somehow coerced Nassif into signing an Acknowledgement of Debt admitting he owed him R800 000. Through his friend James Murray, he wangled payment for the Kebble murder. Nassif had put a R1 million deposit on Murray's property at the Pecanwood Golf Estate in Hartbeespoort but he never went through with the deal. Murray waited for Nassif to pay the remaining amount for two years but finally decided to sell the house to someone else. He wanted to pay Nassif's deposit back to him. Murray claims that Nassif sent him a letter instructing him to pay the R1 million over to three separate companies and carried out the instruction. The money was paid over to Mikey, Nigel and Kappie. Nigel used the money to pay off his BMW. Kappie tells me he used the cash 'wisely' to fund his sick mother's heart treatment. Mikey did what any self-respecting hit man would do. He went to Vegas!

CLINTON NASSIF HAD SUNG AND THE SCORPIONS HAD FOUND another crack. Leask and Nel knew they had to run with it before it was patched up. They kept Agliotti under surveillance and attempted to plant a bugging device on his vehicle. They approached Clinton Fouché, the golf director at Dainfern Country Club where Agliotti was a regular, to ask for his assistance. Fouché refused to cooperate and instead tipped Agliotti off that the Scorpions had attempted to second him. Agliotti phoned Selebi and told him about the device. Selebi instructed his friend to look under his vehicle for the piece of equipment, to take it off and hand it to his legal counsel, as what the Scorpions were doing was illegal. Agliotti testified in court that he looked for the device but never found it.

Leask had also begun chatting to attorney Ian Small-Smith, suggesting to him that his clients, Mikey, Nigel and Kappie, should come and speak to him. With two decades of experience, Small-Smith has a formidable reputation. He's a clean-cut Afrikaner from the Free State, with an endearing stutter, a wicked sense of humour and greying temples. Despite his easy nature, his critics are vocal about his allegiances and suspicious of his good-guy facade. He is a consultant at BDK attorneys (Botha, Du Plessis and Kruger), which has a reputation as *Die Lieg Fabriek* in legal circles. If there's a high-profile criminal case going on, it is highly likely that these lawyers are representing the accused.

Small-Smith agreed that a deal would benefit his clients, but the trio considered Nassif to be a traitor and weren't finding it easy to understand that telling the truth could be in their interests. Leask told the lawyer that there weren't going to be many chances and, when he came and kicked down their doors to arrest them, the opportunity would be lost. It was a cat-and-mouse game and Leask was looking for another opening.

Early in November, Jackie Selebi's office issued a statement through spokesperson Sally de Beer, saying that the National Commissioner is hopeful that a breakthrough will be made in the Kebble murder probe within days. Selebi had been briefed by the investigating team which told him that 'important information' was being followed up. Leask heard the soundbite of De Beer on Talk Radio 702 and cracked up laughing at the idea that the police team of PW van Heerden and Corrie Maritz was anywhere near closing the case. He knew that he had Nassif on side already and it was a matter of time before the three gunmen turned.

Shortly thereafter, the two police investigators working on the case, PW van Heerden and Corrie Maritz, left the country to follow what they believed to be hot leads. Van Heerden flew to Perth in Australia, along with Commissioner Norman Taiwe, to sit down and do a seven-hour recorded interview with one of the Scorpions' prime suspects, John Stratton. Maritz travelled to the United Kingdom with Deputy Provincial Commissioner Richard Mdluli to follow up a vague lead about Hummers and Zimbabweans.

Maritz and Van Heerden are not popular amongst Scorpions investigators, with some even referring to them as 'Tweedledum and Tweedledee'. Whether their overseas trips at such a sensitive time were the result of deliberate interference or plain incompetence, as Scorpions officials suggest, is difficult to determine. But it was not the first time that they had followed up a dead-end lead.

In September 2006, while both the police and Scorpions units were closing in on Agliotti and the three gunmen, they were all thrown a curve ball.

A 'witness' to Kebble's murder appeared out of nowhere. Twenty-four-year-old Lesego Amos Yekane claimed to have seen the shooting from his 'sleeping spot' in the James and Ethel Gray Park, which runs alongside the bridge where the magnate died. On the day after Kebble died, the website Moneyweb had run a story saying two homeless people had witnessed the incident but police immediately killed the rumour and nothing more was heard of it. The prospect of a witness coming forward wasn't entirely unreasonable.

Van Heerden and Maritz met with the man at the park on a Sunday afternoon after he was allegedly turned away from several police stations where officers told him to call the Crime Stop number. The duo arranged a follow-up meeting with him for the Wednesday.

In the interim, the 'witness' went to the media. He did an interview with journalists at the *Mail & Guardian* newspaper. He told them that on the night of the murder, after he had scrounged for food at a dumping site, he went to his sleeping spot at the park. As he was settling down, he heard the sound of cars on gravel. Yekane told the weekly that he saw three luxury sedans parked in the nearby park – a light-coloured Mercedes-Benz and two BMWs, one silver and one black. A man from the silver BMW went to lean at the Merc's window and then returned to the silver BMW which then sped off. Yekane claims to have then fallen asleep but was awoken by a loud bang. He said that he saw a 'huge man with a bald head walking from the Merc towards the BMW' and that the Merc crashed into the bridge.

The story got better. Yekane also claimed that he had seen the 'huge man with a bald head' later in newspaper photographs in the company of ANC Youth League members who had supported Jacob Zuma during his corruption trial. This claim fed perfectly into the political hit conspiracy theory. Then Youth League spokesperson Zizi Kodwa said at the time, 'This hobo is mad, he needs psychiatric treatment. He is a moron who is out to smear the good names of people.'

The so-called witness failed to pitch for his Wednesday meeting with the police investigators, because he was giving another interview to the SABC. Van Heerden and Maritz got word of this and blazed through to the broadcaster's headquarters in Auckland Park where they arrested him on a warrant relating to a housebreaking case in the Free State where he was from. That afternoon the investigators drove Yekane to Bloemfontein where he appeared in court the following day. It was merely a stalling device for them and the charges were withdrawn.

Van Heerden and Maritz were under severe pressure from high-ranking police officers and their phones rang off the hook while they were in Bloemfontein. Despite the intensity of the situation, they quickly realised that Yekane was playing games. They came to this conclusion through a fairly simple mistake from the 'witness'. He had given them a description of a canopy at the entrance to the park, without knowing that it had only been built subsequent to Kebble's death. He had successfully sent the police on a wild goose chase – he had not been in the vicinity of the James and Ethel Gray Park on the night of the murder. It seems as though he was simply after the attention and no story could guarantee him more attention than this one.

IN NOVEMBER 2006 ADVOCATE VUSI PIKOLI HAD BEEN IN HIS JOB AS head of the country's National Prosecuting Authority (NPA) for about a year. He had spent many years in government, though, having filled the position of Director General (DG) in the Department of Justice and Constitutional Development and other senior posts. Prior to the birth of democracy he was closely involved in the ANC's youth wing and received military training in Angola.

I personally have always found Pikoli to be a man of the utmost integrity, profoundly moral and loyal to his word – all traits that perhaps may have led to his downfall. What I like most about him, however, is the laugh that erupts from deep in his belly when his gappy smile spreads across his face.

Pikoli had the misfortune of inheriting the burden of the prosecution of Deputy President Jacob Zuma from his predecessor Bulelani Ngcuka. There was also another high-profile prosecution bubbling under and it was becoming Pikoli's problem. By November 2006, Pikoli had connected nearly all of the dots and had realised that his old friend from exile, Jackie Selebi, was in way over his head. He was fond of his comrade, whom he had come to know well during his tenure as DG in the Justice Department. Pikoli had told President Thabo Mbeki about his suspicions around Selebi's wrongdoing and Mbeki had encouraged the prosecutions boss to speak to Selebi about the allegations against him.

On 11 November Pikoli went to see Selebi and it was a highly charged, deeply emotional meeting. He would later recount to the Ginwala Inquiry into his suspension what had happened:

My meeting of the 11th was not an easy meeting for discussions with the National Commissioner because, there I was, sitting with the National Commissioner. I have known him from my days in exile, I worked closely with him when I was Director General of Justice, and now I had to ask him difficult questions based on allegations against him. I asked him about money he is supposed to have received and channelled through several accounts.

He denied it and he was convincing. At the time, I believed him. I cried in that meeting. He cried in that meeting. For me, it was a cry of relief because I never believed that he could be facing accusations of that nature.

We cried on each other's shoulders in that meeting and I told him
that I believed him when he said he never received the money.

Despite Pikoli being convinced that his old friend from exile was not em-
broiled in corruption, Leask and Nel continued doggedly building their
case against the country's most senior policeman. They were following a
long and torturous path but it was one that led to Selebi's door.

Mikey

Eventually, Ian phones me up and says to me, 'Listen boet, I need to see you urgently. I need to speak to you about something.' I thought fuck. I had a feeling it was about this. I went to go and check him in his office and I never said anything to him. I said to him I don't know what they talking about. I said to him if I know what happened to Brett Kebble then I know where Jimmy Hoffa is. 'Cause Jimmy Hoffa went missing too you know.

THE SCORPIONS WERE DANGLING A CARROT IN FRONT OF MIKEY, Nigel and Kappie. Their attorney, Ian Small-Smith, was doing his damnedest to convince the trio that what the authorities were offering was not just a carrot, but something far sweeter. They were so opposed to cooperating with officials that it was simply not an option for them.

For Kappie, who endured years of abuse from police during apartheid and after, talking to the cops was a completely foreign concept. 'I wouldn't. I would never. It's against the policy. That's why I was tortured all my life. Because I'd never speak.'

Mikey felt the same way but he was also not prepared to go to jail. 'If I know that I'm going to jail tomorrow or I'm going to be arrested, that's the end of it. Being inside four walls to me is like being dead so I've got nothing to live for. I'll have it out with the police and they'll shoot me. I've made a pact with myself and I'll stick to it, hey. And that was my plan all along,' he tells me.

After Small-Smith's approach, Mikey spoke to Nigel and Kappie about the deal on the table. 'They said, "Listen, we keep quiet." I said cool. Now the way the three of us have always worked is that there's three decisions. Every one of them must count. So if two make the same decision and the other makes another decision, we've got to come to a decision that we either all three go this way or all three go that way. We can't have two one way and one the other, that's not the way we work,' he explains.

Small-Smith was persistent. He tried a second time a few weeks later. 'He said to me, "Listen, come see me." I went to go see him. He said to me listen, there must be some kind of truth in this. This is the story. The Scorpions kept on going to him, telling him, "Tell Schultz to give us a statement and he'll walk out of court a free man." I said no.' Mikey was resolute and he wasn't even coming clean to his lawyer.

It was only on the third attempt that Mikey began to buckle. 'The third time, Ian called me and said, "These okes are busy building a case and they say they've got evidence against you. I think Clint's talking",' recalls Mikey. He tells me that he still wasn't convinced his friend Clint would sell him out. Small-Smith told his client that he was on his way to a meeting with Nassif's legal team – Tamo Vink and Advocate Barry Roux – at the Sandton News Café. He told Mikey to be available in case he needed him to go there. An hour after the meeting, Mikey received a call from his attorney and was told to go to the News Café.

'I got there, to the Sandton News Café, and as I walked in Tamo got up to walk away. I said to him, "Do I fucking smell?" He turned around and he said to me, "Mikey, please. Just listen to Ian. You got to listen to Ian about what's going on here." I said ok cool. I sat down with Ian and he explained to me that the deal was made. Ian's words to me were, "This boat's leaving. You want to get on this boat before it leaves."'

Whenever I speak to Mikey about his decision to turn state witness in the Kebble murder trial, he emphasises the argument he had with Ian Small-Smith at the Sandton News Café that day. It's crucial for him to stress just how much he didn't want to do the deal. In his world, it was an unthinkable thing to do but the deal was so sweet it was ultimately impossible to turn down.

'I argued with him for about two hours about what I was going to do,' Mikey tells me for the umpteenth time. 'He said he couldn't just take my word, he needed to hear from Nigel. I phoned Nigel, Nigel came there and me and Nigel both argued with him there for another hour. Eventually he convinced us,' Mikey says reluctantly.

But Mikey had the daunting task of trying to convince Kappie to take the deal. It was an all-or-nothing decision – either all three of them took it, or none of them did. It was serious business, but the story of him trying to talk Kappie into the deal made me laugh hard when I heard it the first time, with Mikey doing his best Kappie impersonation.

'He was driving and I said, "Listen bud, we got a bit of kak with the case." So he looks at me and says, "What case?" So I said, "Listen, we going to have to make a deal." He says, "What deal?" So I say, "On the case." He says, "What case?" So I say, "On the shooting!" So he says, "What shooting? I don't know what you talking about!" He says, "I don't want to hear about it." He says, "Please, please, Michael, I don't want to hear this shit." And then he drives around the block. He dropped me back at home and he left.'

Kappie refused even to admit there was a case to talk about.

Mikey and Nigel coerced their stubborn friend to meet with their attorney and to listen to reason. 'Ian sat him down and explained to him. I said to him, "Well, there's one of two things we've got to do here. If you don't want to do the deal and you are adamant you're not going to do the deal because you believe that we not going to get over this, then we all got to keep quiet and they must arrest us for the shooting and they are going to use Clint's evidence against us. Otherwise we do the deal." And Ian promised me. He said, "Mikey, I won't ever lie to you. I'm telling you this is the fucking best deal ever." He said, "Take this deal, it's not going to come around again."'

Reluctantly, they agreed in principle that they would take the deal. But first, they wanted to go home and tell their families what they had done.

Now, I'm not quite sure how one does this type of thing. The mystery of who killed Brett Kebble was high on the list of talking points at most South African braais or dinner parties, whatever people's social status or class. To have to go home to their families and tell them they had been keeping this gargantuan secret, that they had murdered Kebble, could only have been terrifying.

'It was like the hardest thing ever to tell my wife. It didn't go great,' Mikey says. An obvious understatement. 'I said to her, "Listen, I shot Brett Kebble." So she said, "Who's saying this now again?" Because every week-end there was a story when we were in the clubs about how we done this and how we done that and I said, "No, that's what happened. We shot Brett." She was quiet and very withdrawn. She started crying and said, "What's going to happen with the kids and that?" I was like, "Listen, we busy sorting it out. We are going to be fine." She obviously also didn't be-lieve that we were going to get the deal we got.'

The next day, Leonie, a demure blonde from a wholesome Afrikaner background, went onto the Internet and printed off every newspaper re-port she could find about the murder. 'When I walked past the room, she had a ream of paper like this,' Mikey says, using his hands for emphasis. 'I really think that she didn't believe me in the beginning because we kept quiet and she also never knew me like that.'

With his blue eyes, boyish grin and impeccable manners, it is difficult to believe that Mikey is capable of murder when first meeting him. He is polite and respectful, referring to those he respects as 'Aunty' or 'Mister'. He loves to tell cheeky jokes and proudly displays pictures of his children on the chat feature on his cellphone. It is only his tattoos that give any suggestion of another side. For his wife to hear that he'd committed such a high-profile murder must have been devastating.

Mikey also went to tell his sister Cathy and her husband Mark

Groenewald. He left his sister to tell his mother as he knew she could do a better job of giving his mother the news. What Mikey didn't count on though, was that his brother-in-law would phone his attorney and friend Gary Mazerham to tell him. Mazerham had his own connections to law-enforcement officials, and he phoned the police and the Scorpions.

'First he phoned Andrew Leask and said, "What about this deal?" Andrew's like, "What deal?" 'Cause nobody's supposed to know about it. Andrew phoned Ian and said to Ian, "Listen, I'll fucking pull this deal away right now." So Ian phoned Nigel, Nigel phoned me. So I pick up his call, Nigel's swearing at me, saying, "What the fuck you doing?" I was like, "What the fuck?" I said, "I never fucking told anybody. Did we or didn't we say we'd tell our families?"' Mikey recalls, doing his best to explain a complicated scenario.

The Scorpions were furious that one of the three had spoken out about their arrangement. Their deal was hanging in the balance as Leask could pull the plug at any stage. The Scorpions called an urgent meeting at BDK's offices on Anderson Street in the Johannesburg city centre. But the trio had a back-up plan, just in case the Scorpions decided to arrest them. 'When we went we said, "Ah fuck, Clint's the only one who's got any evidence against us," and we left Kappie waiting with a gun, very close to Clint's work. If we were arrested he was going to shoot Clint.'

Mikey tells me this quite dispassionately but I struggle to disguise the impact of the revelation. I ask Kappie if it really is true and would he have killed Clint if it came down to it. Yes, he tells me, slightly embarrassed. 'To save me and my friends' life. Yes. Something would have happened somewhere along the line and I'm sure that's what he would have done to us if it had been the other way around. That's why I still think we all three are still alive.'

O N THE EVENING OF 14 NOVEMBER 2006, AT IAN SMALL-SMITH'S office in the Johannesburg CBD, Mikey Schultz, Nigel McGurk and Fiazal 'Kappie' Smith signed their affidavits, effectively confirming their status as 'section 204' witnesses. According to section 204 of the Criminal Procedure Act:

> *(2) If a witness referred to in subsection (1), in the opinion of the court, answers frankly and honestly all questions put to him:-*

> *(a) such witness shall, subject to the provisions of subsection (3), be discharged from prosecution for the offence so specified by the prosecutor and for any offence in respect of which a verdict of guilty would be competent upon a charge relating to the offence so specified; and*

> *(b) the court shall cause such discharge to be entered on the record of the proceedings in question.*

> *(4)(a) Where a witness gives evidence under this section and is not discharged from prosecution in respect of the offence in question, such evidence shall not be admissible in evidence against him at any trial in respect of such offence or any offence in respect of which a verdict of guilty is competent upon a charge relating to such offence.*

Despite killing Brett Kebble, they would not go to jail if they testified truthfully in a court of law about the crime. It would be up to a judge to decide if they would 'get' their 204s.

Their fears about Leask pulling the deal were set aside. Mikey says he gave the Scorpions investigator an assurance that he could trust him. 'I said to him, "Listen, if that's how this relationship's going to be, if you need me, then I'll be your best fucking witness," I said, "I'll tell you exactly what's going to be and what's going to happen."'

During the meeting Leask received a call from a police officer asking if he knew where the three men were. Massaging the truth, he said not exactly, obviously not wanting to give away the location of his witnesses. As a result of the call, the investigator's defences were immediately up and he was worried about the safety of the trio. He issued them with an ominous warning.

'We were walking out the meeting and were at the elevator,' Mikey tells me. 'We had just signed our first little statements. Andrew Leask said to us, "Be careful tonight, these okes might want to arrest you, lay low. Do you need us to come and protect you? We don't want to give it away yet that yous are witnesses because we haven't arrested Agliotti yet." We said, "No, we'll be fine, hey."' Leask's instincts were spot on.

Later that night, Small-Smith received a phone call from Commissioner Johan de Beer from the police, telling him that 'he'd like to have a word' with him. Small-Smith agreed and asked him where they should meet. De Beer responded by saying, 'I'm on your pavement, sir.' De Beer, Sharon Schutte and grey-haired Director Martin Naude, from the police's organised crime unit, were waiting for the lawyer at a petrol station around the corner from his house in Northcliff.

It was not an everyday occurrence that such an influential representation of the SAPS showed up for a late-night meeting at a petrol station around the corner from an attorney's home. They were looking for Small-Smith's clients and wanted them to turn themselves in. The ever sharp-tongued lawyer told the high-ranking police officers that if that's what they wanted, then the 'fucking queue ends around the corner'. He told them what they did not want to hear, that a deal had already been struck with the NPA.

This news would have come as a death blow to the senior police officers as they knew exactly what was at stake. They were under severe pressure from an irate Commissioner Selebi and his right-hand men as the Commissioner's own freedom from justice was hanging in the balance. Information was being filtered up to the top and back down again, with clumsy effect. Just as concerning was the fact that the police were losing the embittered, acrimonious race against the Scorpions. The two separate law-enforcement arms were engaged in a hostile rivalry that underpinned the entire case.

Selebi had got wind that there had been a major move and, according to those in the know, he began to panic. He may have realised that if the gunmen turned, pressure on Agliotti would be leveraged beyond his control and in all likelihood his erstwhile friend would be forced to sell him out. Or, alternatively, the police chief wanted justice to be done and knew that if the Scorpions got to the shooters first, they would be indemnified and the killers would walk free. It depends on who you believe.

Selebi's wingman, head of Crime Intelligence Mulangi Mphego, mobilised officers and hunted for Mikey, Nigel and Kappie.

Mikey's account of that night is eyebrow-raising and reads like a crime thriller. He, Nigel and Kappie spent two days playing a cat-and-mouse game with the police, hiding in hotels and movie theatres and jumping walls in desperate attempts to escape.

'That night when I got home my mate John [Kruger] phoned me and he's got some friends in Pretoria in the cops. He said, "Get the fuck out of Jo'burg, boet!" He said they coming and they coming hard. He said to me his friend had phoned him and said to him that Selebi and the commissioners and that Tata Zonke, his little mob, they were on their way to Jo'burg. He said to me, "Get rid of your fucking phone." He wouldn't even phone me on my phone. He phoned me on my sister's phone. He said to me, "They got the triangulator box, they're coming. Get off your fucking phones, they going to find you."'

Mikey's voice and gestures added emphasis to the drama of the story. 'Look, we were worried. They were going to kill us. They were going to kill us. It was made clear that if there was any kind of resistance, to "shoot to kill". It was made clear in Pretoria. Shoot to kill because we were dangerous people.'

Mikey immediately phoned Nigel and Kappie to alert them about the warning call but, true to form, they weren't perturbed. 'I phoned Nigel and I said, "You got to get out of there." We got into an argument and then eventually he agreed he'd meet me. I dumped my car, I took my mom's car, met Nigel and we fucked off and we booked into a hotel under a false name. Michael Smith or something. I got hold of Kappie and Kappie said to me, "No, I'm not going." I said, "We have to go, you got to be careful." He said no, he's not going.'

While Mikey and Nigel were holed up in a hotel hiding from the cops, Kappie was being blasé, chilling at his wife's house. He had given authorities his girlfriend's address so the police went to the wrong house. But they were moving in and finally they hit the house next door to where he was staying.

'They sent people to come and bump us off that night,' Kappie tells me in astonishment. 'To come and shoot me! I had to jump the wall by the neighbours. They tried to grip us.' With the police closing in Kappie phoned the Scorpions and they met him on the side of the road. 'I don't know who they phoned but, well, I'm still alive now,' he says with a chuckle.

According to one officer, who doesn't want to be identified, 'They were running around in black cars, Mphego's guys, visiting houses, banging down doors, picking people up. They called in policemen working on other cases and asked them if they had photos of "Schultz" to identify him with. They were under immense pressure because Selebi was ranting and raving.'

A senior Scorpions member who was part of the Bad Guys team says he's convinced that the police wanted to shoot and kill the trio that night. 'I still believe today that the police would have gone out publicly and said that they'd received good information. They went to these houses where guys were heavily armed, there was a shootout and the guys who shot Kebble had been killed. The public would have loved that.'

Mikey and Nigel spent the following day hiding, much to my amusement, in the movie theatre at Eastgate Mall. And no, he can't remember what they watched. They did move around, though, making sure that the police couldn't pin them down.

Late in the day, Mikey put his phone on and called Ian Small-Smith. The attorney told him it was finally safe to come out of hiding. Agliotti had been arrested and the Scorpions had made it public that the shooters were their witnesses and not the accused. The next morning, Mikey, Nigel and Kappie awoke to find their faces splashed all over the daily newspapers.

'They never had photos of us and never knew who we were but the next morning we woke up and they had found like some old photos and shit. The next morning it was "Schultz", "The Killers". That Sunday, that *Sunday Times*, I remember it was full-up, hey. They had photos and everything like that, that we were the shooters and stuff like that.'

Their secret was finally out. The killers of Kebble had been publicly identified. Their faces were there for everyone to see. But they would not be the ones on trial. Instead, they would be witnesses in a criminal trial. Mikey didn't care.

'I didn't give a fuck because, to be honest, having the deal that we had meant more to me than worrying about how people think of me and how to feel. I don't give a shit about what people think of me,' says Mikey.

He knew that he would have to deal with the reputation of being a publicly recognised killer, and his feelings about it don't exactly feed into one's perception of a hit man. 'People that know me know that I've got good intentions, I've got a good heart, and people that don't know me, they talk the biggest load of shit about me. I didn't really give a fuck what the people were going to say. I did worry about my kids because I know that they were a bit bigger and stuff like that and being in school and that and other kids are ugly to them but you know. My younger daughter had shit with other kids saying, "Why did your daddy shoot that man?" I took her out that school.'

Mikey comes across as profoundly genuine when he speaks about people's reaction to the news and how it impacted on his family. It gives me unique insight into the complexity of his character and the sensitivities buried beneath his hard-man facade.

ARLY ON THE MORNING OF 16 NOVEMBER 2006, PROSECUTOR Gerrie Nel was gearing up for a particularly big day. There would be a crucial development in the Bad Guys matter which had occupied his mind and diary for nearly a year and it would be a turning point in his team's attempts to prove that the country's most senior police officer, a highly regarded stalwart of the nation's struggle against the apartheid regime, was corrupt.

As he walked out of his Silverton office, briefcase in hand, he told his colleague Andrea Johnson to draw up an indictment for charges relating to a conspiracy to commit murder and murder. Only later that day did it become apparent that the charge sheet she had drafted was actually for one Glenn Agliotti. She had used the charge sheet for the Chris Hani murder, which Nel had successfully prosecuted, as the template for the one she drew up.

That morning, Andrew Leask and his investigative team arrived at Glenn Agliotti's Bryanston townhouse at the exclusive complex The Savoy in Mount Street just as Agliotti was getting ready for gym. Leask had not been there before when his team carried out search-and-seizure operations two months previously. This time he walked through the front door and introduced himself to Agliotti and his family. He informed him that he was under arrest, read him his rights and suggested he phone his lawyer. His exact words to Agliotti were, 'Pack a bag. You won't be home tonight.'

Nel spoke to Advocate Laurance Hodes on the phone and they decided, by agreement, that Agliotti would be taken to the Sandton Police Station holding cells where he would be detained.

News of the arrest began to leak out and Eyewitness News received a tip-off from a lawyer close to Agliotti's circle at the time. Colleague Regan Thaw and I immediately deployed to the Johannesburg Magistrates Court and began the customary wait on the pavement along with a bevy of 'snappers', camera people and hacks from various publications. We split up, each taking an entrance to ensure we captured Agliotti's arrival.

The Scorpions made an expected Hollywood-style entrance in their fleet of black VW Golfs, sirens blaring, and Agliotti, dressed in a striped pink-and-purple collar shirt, was rushed into the building, his hands in cuffs. He appeared before the red-and-black-robed magistrate, Lukas van der Schyff, in a courtroom stuffed with journalists. There was instantaneous scribbling in notebooks as Van der Schyff remarked, 'You look vaguely familiar,' to Agliotti, recognising him from a previous appearance in the court on the cobalt-smuggling matter.

An unusually subdued Agliotti responded, 'Yes, sir.' Within five minutes, one of the most anticipated court appearances in the country was wrapped up – a new magistrate would have to be allocated. Van der Schyff couldn't hear the matter as he had previously presided over a matter involving the accused.

Agliotti would be kept at the Sandton police cells until 8 December, when he would bring a formal bail application. He was led down the stairs to the holding cells in the bowels of the courthouse. The metal door clanged shut behind him.

The Scorpions issued a statement through spokesperson Makhosini Nkosi:

> There will be more arrests which would be best dealt with in a cooperative relationship between the Directorate of Special Operations [DSO] and the South African Police Service [SAPS]. Agliotti was identified by the DSO as a role player in the Alberton drug bust earlier this year. Communication between the DSO and the detective service of SAPS last night [Wednesday] and earlier this morning shed light on the status of the SAPS investigation. The SAPS has given its full cooperation and has dedicated two investigators to the DSO. This was done so that the two agencies could ensure a dedicated and focused approach of the ongoing murder investigation as well as prosecution.

Those 'two investigators' were Corrie Maritz and PW van Heerden, the police officers who were sitting in the UK and Australia respectively, at the time of Agliotti's arrest. This was the ultimate defeat for the two cops. Not only had the Scorpions won the race to the shooters, but now they would have to serve in a unit with the very same officers they were competing against. Added to this was the deep resentment entrenched between Scorpions investigators and SAPS officers as a result of the ongoing rivalry between the two law-enforcement arms. Their styles were different, they had opposing views on the witnesses and they had a deep dislike for each other. Life for Maritz and Van Heerden was going to be difficult under the authority of Andrew Leask.

THE STORY MOVED QUICKLY AND EYEWITNESS NEWS CONFIRMED that Clinton Nassif had turned state witness against Agliotti and also broadcast the names of the three shooters. We confirmed that all three had been talking to the Scorpions in the 48 hours leading up to Agliotti's arrest and that they were associated with Nassif's company, CNSG.

There was enormous pressure on Selebi to step down in the wake of Agliotti's arrest but the police chief stood defiant. Instead, he gave an exclusive interview to my Eyewitness News colleague Nomsa Maseko on the night of Agliotti's arrest. He revealed that the Scorpions had kept him completely in the dark about their plans to arrest Agliotti, despite his announcement two weeks previously that the police were on the verge of a major breakthrough.

He was also only told of his friend's arrest at 9:00 that day – three hours after the Scorpions had been at his Bryanston home. Selebi confirmed that when the police went to arrest suspects, their lawyers told officers that they had already been given immunity in exchange for becoming state witnesses. Maseko asked:

Why is it that the Scorpions made the arrests?
It is simply because we had an approach that is slightly different. We went for other people, there are about five people who we were aiming at. And when we got to those people, it became clear to us that they had entered into some arrangement with the people who had finally arrested them. So it was no point, it would have ruined everything if we went ahead with those people.
Now people are calling for your resignation, what is your reaction to this?
Give me one reason why I should resign, just one. There is no reason for me to do that.
Maybe one reason is because of your friends: Agliotti is your friend and he has been implicated in a high-profile murder. Are you saying that you didn't know that Agliotti was involved?
I said to you that he never discussed any matter or any of the allegations with me. Even if he was my son, if my son got arrested for whatever allegations, it does not make me an accomplice.

You mentioned four other people that were a part of the SAPS investigation. What happened to the other four?

You can't ask me that because we never arrested them. I said to you that they arrived at a certain arrangement with those who arrested them.

Is one of them Clinton Nassif?

I don't know.

The fact that the Scorpions made the breakthrough, surely at a personal level it must be demotivating for you that another law enforcement agency made the breakthrough?

When I spoke (two weeks ago), I said to you, 'Two weeks' time,' isn't it? And on Monday, the police were out looking for some of the people. And on Tuesday, they did that. When they got to the people, they were told by their legal representatives that these people had reached an agreement with those that ultimately arrested Glenn. It couldn't have been that police could have gone ahead with the arrests when there was such an arrangement. It just doesn't make sense. It was a matter that we couldn't find them on the two days that we were looking for them.

In the days after Agliotti's arrest, pressure on Selebi to resign was at an all-time high. His friend was behind bars and the picture was not becoming of a police chief who was meant to be beyond reproach. President Thabo Mbeki continued to deflect criticism, with complaints mounting that he was failing to act against his friend in order to protect him. At a meeting at the Union Buildings in Pretoria, Mbeki asked religious leaders to 'trust him' on Selebi after they had suggested a Commission of Inquiry into the police chief's relationship with Agliotti. He told them he had no grounds to suspend his police chief on the information he had received but if anyone had any more information they should come forward with it.

Selebi was also present at that meeting but didn't speak on the topic. Mbeki always maintained that he did not have actual evidence before him which could force him to act against the Commissioner. However, down the line it would emerge that Mbeki was regularly updated on the investigation into his police chief's alleged corrupt activities and he was fully briefed on the extent of the evidence against Selebi.

G LENN AGLIOTTI IS A SURVIVOR, MANIPULATING SITUATIONS TO suit himself. While in the Sandton Police Station holding cells, he did what he needed to do to make himself as comfortable as possible. 'When I was arrested, I stuffed R2 000 cash into my underpants for "ice cream",' he tells me during a long lavish lunch at Bellagio.

'Ice cream' was the slang term for bribe money which he liberally dished out to officers to ensure he could maintain his 'private suite' at the cells, his stash of cash regularly topped up by his fiancée on her frequent visits. The obvious irony, of course, is that he had bribed the most senior police officer in the country and effectively got away with it.

His 'private suite' was well maintained. Every day Lani or his ex-wife Vivian would bring him fresh white roses to place at his bedside and he had pictures of his kids pasted on the walls. He didn't sleep on just one mattress as the other prisoners did, instead convincing officers to supply him with a stack of mattresses to make a bed. Agliotti never once ate prison food and proudly tells me that he lost a fortune of weight while behind bars – fifteen kilograms in thirty days. This despite his fiancée bringing him hard-boiled eggs, mortadella sandwiches and boerewors for meals. He told the police this was necessary because of dietary requirements stipulated by his doctor. For entertainment, he recounts, there was the weekend show of the drugged-up, eccentric Nigerian prostitutes who were brought in on Friday nights, screaming and hysterical. He had a supply of good books and if there was one he particularly liked, he would recommend it to the policemen, which is what he did with Spencer Johnson's motivational book *Who Moved My Cheese? An Amazing Way to Deal with Change in Your Work and in Your Life*.

Despite all he had done to ensure his comfort, prison remained a horrible place for him. He was detained over his fiftieth birthday and missed a celebration that had been planned in his honour. Over this period, Agliotti waited for some kind of message to come from his friend Jackie Selebi, certain that he would somehow be saved by his influence. The message never came.

While he was incarcerated, Vivian, with whom he still enjoyed a close relationship, received a phone call from restaurateur Alexis Christopher late one night. Christopher was the man who had dined with Agliotti the night before Kebble was killed and who testified against him in court.

Versions of how a clandestine parking garage meeting came about, who was present and what was discussed vary according to who is telling you. Christopher says he told Vivian that Nassif would be waiting for her and that he did not mislead her into meeting him. Agliotti's version is that she was terrified, crying hysterically and fearing for her life when she saw Nassif's imposing frame as he stepped out from behind a pillar. According to Agliotti, the point of the meeting was to get him to 'dovetail' their versions about the murder. Nassif sent a message to Agliotti through Vivian, telling him to speak to his attorney, Tamo Vink, because he would be able to negotiate him a deal. The idea, it seemed, was that they could all enter into plea bargains with the state.

'When Agliotti heard Nassif had turned, he shat himself,' says a lawyer close to the case. 'Nassif had always assured him he wouldn't drop him and by asking Viv to tell him to dovetail their versions, he knew that Nassif had turned, so he said fuck him.' The lawyer explains that Agliotti realised he would have to talk to secure his freedom. However, Agliotti insists he never 'shat himself' as such.

Agliotti's decision to talk was not popular with his attorney Robert Kanarek. 'I had a big fight with him and I told him that I don't act for snitches,' Kanarek tells me. It would be the first of many fallouts Agliotti would have with his lawyers. Despite his unhappiness, Kanarek requested a meeting with prosecutor Gerrie Nel on Agliotti's behalf.

Instead, Nel sent Leask to see Agliotti in the cells on a Sunday afternoon. Leask explained to him that he would 'have to work his arse off' and give him exact details of payments he made to Selebi, full names, dates, everything. The investigator told him he didn't care if he wrote on 'shit paper', he had to write every single detail down. Agliotti disputes this claim and tells me Leask was actually 'very kind' to him and assisted him. Leask left the police station and rendezvoused with Nel, who was waiting for him at a nearby location. Leask told his colleague, 'This man is going to take us, we're going somewhere.'

The duo then travelled to Pretoria to inform their bosses about the development and Leask excitedly filled them in on what Agliotti had said. But he was concerned that the police would try to shut up the star witness and he told them, 'We've got to look after this guy so that he doesn't get killed.'

Cooped up in his cell, Agliotti began to write and write, making hand-written notes. According to a member of the Bad Guys team, 'He was spitting out information like a computer, like a printing machine. He started talking about NIA reports and about travelling to the UK with his daughter. He was finished, finished, finished. He was on his knees and was just spitting out the info.' Agliotti disagrees with this version, calling it 'bullshit'. 'We were negotiating. We knew they needed us,' he says, assuring me that he was not forced into a corner.

He made three handwritten affidavits in total and their contents were explosive. He spoke of cash payments made to the Commissioner at his office at Mavericks in Midrand in brown envelopes stuffed with money and how he regularly purchased clothing for him and his family from stores such as Grays, Hugo Boss, Louis Vuitton, Harrods and Lacoste. Agliotti scribbled notes about how 'JS' showed him confidential reports 'emanating from England' which detailed his trips to London and came clean about bank accounts Misty Mountain (Pty) Ltd and Spring Lights (Pty) Ltd, which were used to channel funds from Kebble to Selebi and Nassif. He revealed how Selebi's lover, Ntombi Matshoba, with whom Selebi had fathered a son, had been recruited to work at CNSG with Nassif in the hope of 'securing business with the SAPS'. He detailed his relation-ship with Stemmet, Madame Cheng's alleged involvement in drug deals and how he came to know former Hyundai boss and fugitive from justice Billy Rautenbach.

Agliotti's notes were voluminous and exhaustive and displayed his phe-nomenal ability to recollect names and details. He was precise, listing the exact amounts paid over on specific dates and supplying astonishing de-tails about meetings and incidents. It is one of the characteristics that most impresses those he meets. He does acknowledge that there was 'coaching by the DSO' as well.

But he also used the platform to alert the Scorpions about the dubious approach in Hyde Park that had been made to him by his former ally, Clinton Nassif.

In his handwritten statements, Agliotti says, 'Because of the importance of telling the truth, I will not be coerced into doing so, but rather under-take to tell the entire truth and nothing but the truth.' He had the opportu-nity to collude with Nassif but he realised he was being offered indemnity for bribing the country's Chief of Police. He wasn't going to compromise that deal and turned his back on Nassif.

While in the Sandton holding cells, the Scorpions also offered Agliotti a plea-bargain deal for Brett Kebble's murder. 'They offered us whatever we wanted,' reveals his attorney Kanarek. 'Just as long as we gave them a plea of guilty. Many, many times and he wouldn't take it.' Agliotti refused to admit any guilt in the mining tycoon's murder.

I N MID-DECEMBER, AGLIOTTI RETURNED TO THE JOHANNESBURG
Magistrates Court where he was formally charged with murdering Brett
Kebble and conspiracy to murder. This time, a Scorpions team armed with
R5 rifles and handguns stood guard outside the room. The Scorpions were
legitimately concerned that Agliotti could be killed. They asked him to
wear a bulletproof vest as they transported him to court in downtown
Jo'burg. 'No one was allowed to know which car I was in and they would
say "The package has arrived" when we got to court,' Agliotti jokes, mim-
icking a police radio. During the trip, the Scorpions would pump Talk
Radio 702 in their cars at full volume to torment him as he was forced to
listen to news reports about himself.

Magistrate Chris Eksteen granted Agliotti bail of R500 000 and he was
placed under 24-hour house arrest. As part of his bail application, Agliotti
presented a supporting affidavit in which he described himself in glowing
terms, claiming to be a philanthropist who supported numerous charities
and how during his school years he was a house prefect, first-team rugby
player and head chorister in the choir.

He also dropped a startling bombshell, claiming for the first time in
open court that Brett Kebble had had a hand in his own murder:

> [Kebble] initially, and before I became involved, planned to provide the
> pilot of his aeroplane with a tablet placed in a drink that would have
> caused his death and the consequent fatal crash of the plane, with the
> late Brett Kebble being killed as a passenger thereof.
>
> After I became involved, it was decided to rather make his death look
> like a carjacking. After numerous dry runs and plans, he was killed in
> this manner by persons who have been identified by the state and ap-
> parently granted section 204 indemnity for the roles they played.

In this bail affidavit Agliotti effectively makes an admission. He says that he
'became involved' in the planning of Brett's murder. Agliotti's camp says this
was only done because they were bullied into doing so by the NPA. They
claim Nel insisted on full sight of the statement before it was presented to the
court or else bail would be opposed. At that stage Agliotti's legal team also
did not think the prosecutors would be able to cut deals with the shooters.

Agliotti made another important revelation in the statement, that the state was also about to charge John Stratton for the murder and begin the process of extraditing him from Australia:

> *I have been advised that the state intends to add another suspect, Mr John Stratton, who is currently living in Australia. I have further been informed that it is anticipated that it will take approximately one year to secure his presence.*

Prosecutor Gerrie Nel did not dispute Agliotti's claims about an assisted suicide and the imminent charging of Stratton. Instead, he told the court that he agreed with the contention that the murder could be 'termed an assisted suicide' and that the shooting was 'exceptional and not a normal contract killing'. The prosecution was clearly buying the theory.

But there was a crucial error made on that day. Magistrate Chris Eksteen failed to warn Agliotti properly that this bail statement could be used against him during his trial. Because of this oversight in procedure by the magistrate, the statement would not be admissible during Agliotti's trial, despite his saying in the affidavit, 'I became involved' in the murder.

Just over a month later, the Scorpions decided they needed to turn the screws on Agliotti and Selebi. It was still speculated that Agliotti was The Landlord but no formal charges had been brought against him in connection with the Paparas drug bust. On 18 January 2007, Agliotti made his first appearance in the tiny, obscure court in Hardach Street in an industrial part of Germiston, which would be regularly frequented by journalists and members of the international crime syndicate. It was an unlikely venue, which seemed not to carry the gravitas required for the scope of the events which it hosted.

I and a pack of other journalists loitered on the street outside for hours on days when they were expected to appear. Some would chain-smoke while others chatted away on their cellphones. I've always found those waits agonising but an inherent part of the job of a journalist. Hurry up and wait. After several hours of waiting on that particular day, Agliotti finally arrived, was formally added as an accused and appeared in the dock with Steve Paparas, Dimitrio Paparas and driver Stanley Poonin. It now seemed to be official that Agliotti was The Landlord.

MONDAY 24 SEPTEMBER 2007 WAS A PUBLIC HOLIDAY, HERITAGE Day, to be exact. I'd spent the day taking a break from the rolling news cycle. It had been a fairly gruelling few weeks and I'd had my nose to the grindstone. At around 15:00, I was driving with my mother after a shopping expedition in Fourways and I flicked on the car radio to listen to the news update. My hand flew over my mouth as I heard the lead story: 'National Director of Public Prosecutions, Vusi Pikoli, has been suspended with immediate effect. President Thabo Mbeki has released a statement saying the decision was taken on the basis of what he's calling an irretrievable breakdown in the working relationship between the Minister of Justice and Constitutional Development and the NDPP.'

My immediate thought was Pikoli had been sidelined to protect Selebi. The sentiment seemed to be shared by others in the media, analysts, opposition party politicians and the general public.

In the subsequent days the media would attempt to piece together the events leading up to Pikoli's suspension. What had he done to precipitate the President issuing such a shocking statement on a public holiday? Pikoli was a largely popular man and public perception was on his side. If indeed it were true that he was a casualty of prosecutorial interference then it would be a travesty.

The truth of the sequence of events that led to the public holiday statement would be fully ventilated in an inquiry set up by Mbeki to probe Pikoli's 'fitness to hold office' and the alleged 'breakdown in his relationship' with Minister Bridgette Mabandla.

The inquiry was headed by Dr Frene Ginwala, a stern, august character with a regal presence and impeccable struggle credentials. She had been the Speaker of the National Assembly and she was seen to be aligned to Mbeki, although he had effectively sacked her as Speaker a few years previously.

Part of her mandate from Mbeki was to look at whether 'when deciding to prosecute offenders, Pikoli took sufficient regard to the nature and extent of the threats posed by organised crime to the national security of the Republic'. By including this in her mandate, Mbeki was directly referring to the section 204 indemnity deals that had been signed with Nassif and the trio of gunmen. Mbeki had read the sentiment of the police and the public, realising there was much outrage that guilty men were being allowed to walk free and national security was being compromised as a result. But despite this there was still a groundswell of support for Pikoli as the perception was that Mbeki was flagrantly abusing his power to protect his friend Selebi.

Significantly, Ginwala's inquiry was not a 'judicial commission', which meant her findings would merely be recommendations to the President, who had no legal obligation to follow them. She could tell him what she liked but he didn't have to listen, which is ultimately what did happen.

The inquiry was held in the auditorium-like council chamber of the Johannesburg City Council offices, an authoritative-looking grey building perched on Braamfontein Hill. It was a surreal affair which journalist Jeremy Gordin aptly summed up at the time in a column in the *Sunday Independent*:

> It is as though we have all been living through a local version of Alice's Adventures in Wonderland, *the story of a girl who falls down a rabbit hole into a literally fantastic realm populated by strange creatures.*
>
> *To begin with, because Pikoli is the national director of public prosecutions, he has had the ultimate responsibility since 2005 for the corruption case against Zuma, the president-in-waiting of South Africa. Given the divisions between the government and the ANC that are numbing the country at present, this is a serious matter.*
>
> *Yet we seem to take it in our stride that the person in charge of this case – our equivalent of the United States' attorney-general – should have to face an inquiry into his competence.*
>
> *And make no mistake. The inquiry might not be a trial. But a public inquiry, during which all sorts of insinuations, true or false, are made, is by its very nature the equivalent of being pilloried in public.*
>
> *Pikoli, who has not been charged with doing anything illegal, has effectively been put on trial. But Pikoli is not on trial in the usual sense. An anonymous poet once wrote: 'What a funny bird a frog are'. And the Ginwala inquiry is a funny, or unusual, bird: it being carried out in terms of the National Prosecuting Authority Act (section 12.6) – and not in terms of labour or commissions law (13 July 2008).*

It was a bewildering experience listening to the testimony of the witnesses who took their seats in front of Ginwala and her two assessors in what was effectively an impromptu courtroom. The detail which emerged about that period in September 2007 gave rare insight into the country's corridors of power. It was intriguing to find out just what skulduggery and manipulation occurs behind the veil of state security.

Pikoli took the stand at the inquiry and was led through his evidence by his advocate, the brilliant Senior Counsel Wim Trengove, recounting the events that led to his suspension on a Sunday night in the President's residence in Pretoria. Together with subsequent developments we have a fairly good handle on the sequence of events.

Throughout 2007, the Scorpions continued building their case against Jackie Selebi. Agliotti made a wide-ranging, detailed affidavit based on the statements he'd written while in prison and he led them to his ex-fiancée Dianne Muller and her father Martin Flint, who was the accountant at her events marketing company, Mavericks Maseputsula. Their evidence, particularly Muller's, would play a vital role in buttressing the state's case. Investigators sourced further witnesses and carried out a forensic analysis of Selebi's bank accounts through the auditing firm KPMG.

Throughout this period, Pikoli regularly updated Justice Minister Bridgette Mabandla and President Mbeki about the progress of the unit's investigation into the police chief's alleged corrupt activities. Pikoli claimed that between March 2006 and September 2007, he briefed Mabandla thirteen times and Mbeki ten times, both verbally and through written reports. Pikoli complained to both of them about the constant difficulties the Scorpions' investigating team was having in getting any kind of cooperation from the SAPS. He explained that it was an extremely frustrating battle to get documentation and evidence from the cops' top guard. This was at the height of the feud between the two units and the fact that they were refusing to help one another was not surprising at all.

In late June, the Bad Guys investigating team met face to face with Minister Mabandla and personally briefed her on the status of the probe. At that meeting, they told her that they had taken a decision to prosecute Selebi and the DSO was 'essentially tying up loose ends in the investigation and preparing for an arrest coupled with a search of Mr Selebi's residence and the SAPS head office'.

Pikoli was warning the country's Justice Minister that the National

Commissioner of the South African Police Service was going to be arrested for corruption – it was a massive development.

On 31 August, Pikoli took the decision to arrest Selebi. He also decided to go ahead with search-and-seizure raids at Selebi's home in Waterkloof and at Wagthuis, his official office and police headquarters. This meant that one law-enforcement arm of government was going to raid the offices of another – both sides were armed and the consequences could be disastrous. He gave the investigating team the go-ahead to secure warrants and instructed them to report to him as soon as they had done so, so that he could brief the President before the warrants were executed. By taking this decision, Pikoli had set in motion a series of events that would ultimately lead to his sacking.

A warrant for Selebi's arrest was obtained on 10 September and Pikoli told Mabandla about the development a day later, requesting a meeting with Mbeki. It was the type of news the President really needed to know from his prosecutor in chief – after all it was his Police Commissioner who was going to be handcuffed. The search warrants were secured just three days later on 14 September.

The following day, a Saturday, Pikoli met the President and his Director General, Reverend Frank Chikane, and briefed them about the warrants. He told them that he had no choice but to raid the SAPS head office because police top brass simply were not cooperating with investigators and were withholding documents and evidence. Despite being briefed regularly on the progress of the case, Pikoli said Mbeki was 'shocked'.

'The President appeared shocked and was not happy with the fact that we had obtained these warrants because he felt the process was still under way.' Mbeki was of the belief that Pikoli had spoken to Selebi and the police were handing over whatever documentation the Scorpions investigators requested, or so he said.

At that meeting came the now infamous 'two week, one week' conversation between Mbeki and Pikoli. It's an exchange of dialogue that the public is not often privy to and hearing it made me feel as though I was watching an episode of *West Wing* set in Pretoria instead of Washington, DC.

Mbeki asked Pikoli to hold off on executing the warrants for two weeks, but the prosecutor would only agree to a delay of one week to create what he called an 'enabling environment' for the Police Commissioner to be arrested. Mbeki said to him, 'Vusi, do you know how angry the police are? Do you know there are police officers who are prepared to defy any court order?' implying that if the Scorpions raided Wachthuis, it could end in violence.

Pikoli, ever principled, stood his ground and would allow only a one-week delay. 'My mind also went back to 2005 when we had ugly stuff at the residence of Mr Jacob Zuma. And considering the fact that we were now going to have warrants executed against the National Commissioner of Police, who had men under arms, there could be a potentially explosive situation.'

After Pikoli told Mbeki about the warrants, the President must have considered his options. He could suspend Selebi in the interim so that he would not be in command of officers at the time of his arrest or he could facilitate a meeting between the two law-enforcement authorities about the warrants. Chikane requested that a report on the issue be drawn up, which Pikoli did overnight. He delivered it the following morning, on Sunday 17 September. At that meeting, Mbeki informed him that he would call a meeting of the National Security Council so that they too could be briefed about the developments.

Pikoli agreed to brief the members on the basis that he was not seeking their approval to proceed with the execution of the warrants. He was unswayed, insistent that as the National Director of Public Prosecutions he did not need any political consent to charge a suspect.

Over the next few days, a series of letters on official government letterheads crossed the desks of Pikoli, Mbeki, Mabandla and her right-hand man, then Justice Department Director General Menzi Simelane. Simelane is a bureaucrat, a party man with firm allegiance to the ANC. With his manicured goatee, soft voice, small eyes and supple backbone, I have never found him to be a likeable character. All the letters were made public during the Ginwala Inquiry and it was fascinating for me, and other journalists, to publicise them, giving readers/listeners/viewers that unrivalled behind-the-scenes perspective on government.

The first letter was penned by Mbeki and addressed to the minister, saying he deemed it 'appropriate that you obtain the necessary information from the National Director of Public Prosecutions regarding the intended arrest and prosecution of the National Commissioner. This would enable me to take such informed decisions as may be necessary with regard to the National Commissioner.'

Mabandla took her lead from Mbeki's letter and the very next day handed a communiqué of her own to Pikoli. It emerged that, controversially, Simelane had actually drafted the letter which Mabandla had simply signed. At the end of the inquiry into Pikoli's suspension, Dr Ginwala would find that that letter amounted to prosecutorial interference in violation of the country's laws. The letter, essentially, was an instruction not to arrest or prosecute Selebi.

In the letter Mabandla requested 'all of the information on which you relied to take the legal steps to effect the arrest of and the preference [*sic*] of charges against the National Commissioner of the Police Service', effectively demanding all the evidence that had been gathered over an eighteen-month period. She told Pikoli that she 'must be satisfied that indeed the public interest will be served should you go ahead with your intended course of action'. She then instructed Pikoli not to proceed any further: 'Until I have satisfied myself that sufficient information and evidence does exist for the arrest of and preference [*sic*] of charges against the National Commissioner of the Police Service, you shall not pursue the route that you have taken steps to pursue.'

Pikoli considered the instruction to be a clear violation of the principle of prosecutorial independence as entrenched in the NPA Act. Mabandla had no authority to tell Pikoli who he could or could not prosecute. As NDPP he was independent of the political principle and was not answerable to Mabandla. Pikoli, of course, refused to comply and told Mabandla as much. He also told her, that if he were to comply, it would be a breach of the oath of office he took and of his duties under the Constitution.

On that Sunday night, as I and many other South Africans were in all likelihood reluctantly winding up our weekends to the soundtrack of the requisite *Carte Blanche* episode, Pikoli was making a dreaded trip of his own to Minister Bridgette Mabandla's house in Brooklyn.

The meeting was to go as badly as it possibly could. The minister asked him to resign. She said she was making the request because 'there had been a breakdown of trust between them'. Pikoli was taken aback by this claim, as he always believed there to be a cordial relationship between them. However, it was a strange comment she made in parting that stuck with him. 'She said, "Vusi, it's all about trust, no it's all about integrity. I will talk one day".' He refused to resign.

From there Pikoli travelled to the President's residence Mahlamba Ndlopfu. He probably drove the tree-lined road that led past the Union Buildings, the impressive Herbert Baker structure on the hill, taking in the view of the purple jacarandas in flower at dusk in spring. He must have pulled into the estate where cabinet members reside fully aware of what would greet him when he arrived at Mbeki's palatial home.

Inside the elegant Cape Dutch-style house, standing amid the ornate antiques, the President told him straight that he would be suspended if he did not resign. Pikoli asked Mbeki to tell him why. He claimed the President said to him it was 'about plea bargains and you entertaining the possibility of granting immunity to criminals'.

Pikoli responded by saying, 'Mr President, I think you are on thin ice because these issues touch on the core competence of the National Prosecuting Authority.'

Mbeki, of course, was making direct reference to the deals struck in the Kebble case. He used those agreements as justification for the suspension of the NDPP. After all, how could the country's chief prosecutor allow self-confessed killers to go free, all in the reckless pursuit of bringing down an adversary heading up a rival law-enforcement agency?

Pikoli didn't see it like that. 'I believe, and honestly so, that there is only one reason for my suspension and that is the investigation and prosecution of the National Commissioner of the police service,' Pikoli told the Ginwala Inquiry.

Mbeki had a letter drawn up confirming Pikoli's suspension which he handed to him that Sunday night. The irony was that the warrants for Selebi's arrest and the search of police headquarters were due to be executed the very next day and Mbeki had succeeded in delaying that action.

I N THE SAME WEEK VUSI PIKOLI WAS SUSPENDED, DETECTIVE PIET Byleveld was promoted. He was called to police head office in Pretoria to be surprised with the rank of Director. Jackie Selebi's spokesperson Sally de Beer made a comment to the media at the time. 'For once Byleveld did not have a clue about what was to happen when he was called to head office in Pretoria under the guise of briefing top management on recent serial killings. He was taken completely by surprise.'

Normally, police posts are advertised and the officers are required to apply for promotion. That was not the case in this instance. Instead, it was done by police management without him applying.

'Piet Byleveld has rendered exceptional service to the SA Police Service and in turn, top management fully supported by the Minister of Safety and Security, decided to take the exceptional step of appointing him to serve at a higher level,' said De Beer. Byleveld had occupied a fair amount of media space with his investigations which led to the convictions of the Nasrec and Wemmer Pan serial killers as well as the conviction of Donovan Moodley in the Leigh Matthews murder case and the arrest of Andrew Jordaan for the murder of schoolgirl Sheldean Human.

However, a number of law-enforcement officials questioned the timing of the decision. Byleveld had skipped a rank. The move also came on the very day that it was revealed that an arrest warrant for Selebi had been issued. The detective had also been given a new task – to investigate Mikey Schultz, Nigel McGurk and Kappie Smith. He was probing a series of crimes relating to the bouncer underworld. Amongst them was the shooting of Red at The Glen, Renier Groenewald's death and the Hazel Crane murder.

This was Selebi's fight-back strategy. He was putting pressure on the Scorpions and their Project 'Bad Guys' by going after the foot soldiers. 'Bad Guys' relied on the gamble of negotiating successful deals with the shooters. At the same time, Agliotti was wavering about what course of action he should take. Sources were saying that he was retreating from a deal with the Scorpions because Selebi appeared to be untouchable.

Unsurprisingly, the police strongly denied that Byleveld's promotion had anything to do with the charges against the Commissioner. 'It is indeed a sad day when a media organisation chooses to question the credentials of a detective of the stature of Piet Byleveld and to insinuate that he was not appointed to a higher rank on merit,' De Beer told the *Mail & Guardian* (12 October 2007).

Mikey Schultz claims credit for Byleveld's promotion. He hates the detective and insists he would never have been made a director were it not for him.

I warily ask Byleveld about his promotion and tentatively mention that Mikey thinks he's responsible for the honour. There is nothing delicate about the policeman's response.

'That's a load of crap, man! Crap! You tell him, jus, he's talking crap. I was promoted because of Mandela. After the Sheldean Human case Mandela called me to his house. There I met Mandela, then he took it up with everyone. It was through all my cases, not through Mikey Schultz please. They must rather demote me to a constable! Tell him that please,' Byleveld implores. 'You must tell him that's what I'm saying. I don't want to be promoted because of a scumbag like this. Then I give my rank back and be a constable. I don't want to be associated with crap. I'm getting the moer in. Scumbags.'

In an attempt to counter 'Bad Guys', the police's crime intelligence arm launched 'Operation Destroy Lucifer'. The phones of senior Scorpions officials were bugged, including those of Leonard McCarthy and ex-NPA head Bulelani Ngcuka. Mounds of tapes would be collected, the contents of which would prove to be explosive and invaluable. It was all part of Selebi's plan to solidify his defence and fight for survival.

As part of Clinton Nassif's 204 agreement, he was required to come clean about every single crime he had committed or been somehow implicated in. He failed to mention his role in the Paparas drugs matter. The Scorpions had discovered that Nassif had indeed played a part – that he assisted with transport and storage of the hashish that was held at T-Bond, a company partially owned by him. The information had come from Agliotti, who took revenge on Nassif for selling him out. He told the Scorpions about Nassif's involvement under the guise of telling them the full truth.

Details were also revealed in a statement signed by Nassif's right-hand man Mohammed Mazibuko, who had been 'singing' in prison after running off with his boss's arsenal of automatic machine guns.

In his affidavit, Mazibuko revealed how Nassif 'called me to his office and instructed me to go to a warehouse to collect a box. I knew that this warehouse belonged to Miros (Mauro) Sabbatini, a close friend to Nassif.'

He says that once he'd collected the sealed box, he took it back to Savika House and went up to Nassif's office, where he found his boss sitting with Sabbatini and Mikey Schultz. 'I opened the box in Nassif, Mikey and Miros' presence. The box contained slabs sealed in silver glossy paper, similar to those that they use to seal Cremora. Nassif then instructed me to rip open one of the slabs and I took the contents out. I did not know what it was, but it was dark in colour compressed in a block. Nassif then asked me if I knew what this is, and I replied, "No." Nassif then informed me that it was hashish, a compressed dagga drug. There was in total 25 slabs of hashish in this box.'

After reading this statement, Leask and Nel went to Nassif in mid-October and put it to him that the omission could not have been accidental as his involvement was blatant. He could not receive indemnity but he could enter into a plea agreement and receive a ten-year prison sentence suspended for five years. In exchange, he would have to testify for the state in 'other matters'. This meant he was selling out his old friend Agliotti and he was confirming he would testify against him in the Kebble murder trial. It also meant the Scorpions were cranking up the pressure on Selebi.

After pleading guilty, Nassif walked out of the small court, his shoulders hunched and his eyes darting over the top of his square glasses. He is not one for media interviews and would rather grunt than tell a journalist how he's feeling. All he would tell reporters on Hardach Street was that he was 'relieved'.

I wasn't surprised by that emotion – he had again avoided going to jail for a crime he was implicated in. However, he would have to testify against a man he had shared breakfast with almost every day for the past five years. Agliotti had become his friend and his business partner – they golfed together, had bought a boat together and 'King Rat' had agreed to sell him out to ensure his own security.

A WEEK LATER, A GIFT LANDED IN MY HANDS. IT WAS THE 'DEEP throat' stuff journalists dream of. A clandestine meeting in an obscure coffee shop, a brown envelope, a threat never to expose the source. Inside the envelope was Nassif's unsigned 204 affidavit. The contents were jaw-droppingly sensational. For the first time, we had a blow-by-blow account of the circumstances surrounding Brett Kebble's murder, although we were very aware that this was 'a version' and not necessarily the truth. Even so, it was spectacular. We were also privy to Kebble's psyche at the time of his death and his apparent motive for wanting to die in an assisted suicide. If, of course, it was true.

In the statement, Nassif asserted that he had been approached by Stratton asking him to find a tablet that could induce a heart attack. He also claimed that Agliotti 'continuously asked him about an instant-death tablet'. He then claimed that Brett had phoned him weeks before his death and had told him that he 'owed it to him' to arrange his murder.

'Brett said he wanted it in a way that he would go out like a hero, being a martyr for the black people, as it would appear as if he had been assassinated by the government. Brett said it was just too much for him to come back to, meaning that things had happened in JCI or Randgold or Western Areas which he had to answer for. Brett said the Kebbles had been taking a beating over the last two years and they could not manage anymore.'

Dramatically, Nassif claimed that he 'struggled with the idea' of arranging the hit and spent days 'praying and crying with Brett' in an attempt to change his mind. 'I struggled with the idea and in fact I still struggle with it. I still have difficulty to sleep because I thought there was definitely a way out for Brett, other than what had been proposed and what had happened. After days of trying to convince Brett, sitting, praying and even crying with Brett, trying to convince him that it was not necessary, he started getting upset with me and told me that he could not manage the pressure anymore.'

Nassif divulged how he contacted Mikey Schultz and offered him R750 000 to do the job. The business end was sorted out and a date and time were confirmed.

Then Nassif dropped the clanger, revealing for the first time just how excruciatingly agonising Brett's last moments must have been.

After we confirmed the veracity of the document with numerous sources, we decided to broadcast the contents of the affidavit despite the statement being unsigned. Nassif's camp immediately rubbished the authenticity of the document, saying whoever was leaking the statement to the media was attempting to 'stitch him up'. It was all gamesmanship at the time – Nassif had already signed that exact statement and, retrospectively, we did the right thing to run the story.

B Y EARLY DECEMBER, THE SCORPIONS HAD KNOCKED OVER MOST of the dominoes in their quest to prosecute Jackie Selebi, although they had lost their captain Vusi Pikoli in the process and were rudderless. We were watching and waiting to see what would happen to Glenn Agliotti. Was he really a major drug dealer of international repute or was he just a wannabe local fixer with Mafioso ambitions?

There had been murmurings about him entering into a plea agreement, similar to that of Clinton Nassif's, in exchange for his testimony against Steve Paparas and his cooperation in 'other cases'. 'Other cases' of course meant against Selebi. But the idea seemed unlikely as he had been painted as the kingpin of the drug syndicate, The Landlord. Agliotti was still trying to orchestrate the best possible deal for himself, to ensure he had a get-out-of-jail-free card.

Just after 08:00 on 5 December my phone rang when I was driving to work through the backstreets of Athol, ironically just two or three blocks away from Brett Kebble's Inanda home. I had suspected the call would come. Agliotti's deal with the Scorpions had been confirmed. He would enter into a plea bargain on the Paparas matter, receive a suspended sentence and, in exchange, would testify against his ex-friend Steve Paparas. He was selling him out. But what this also meant was that for the very first time, Agliotti was publicly agreeing to testify for the Scorpions 'in other matters' too – he was making it official that he was turning on Selebi and would be the state's star witness against him.

That afternoon, a smiling Agliotti strolled from a silver Mercedes-Benz CLK320 up the usually desolate Hardach Street in industrial Germiston with his attorney Robert Kanarek and advocate Laurance Hodes. The media pack was already getting to know Agliotti from his appearances in the Johannesburg Magistrates Court and the charisma offensive had begun. He posed for photographers alongside the two-door sports car and chirped reporters. He was in a good mood, it seemed – we were just learning that Agliotti was almost always in a good mood.

Inside the pokey building, Magistrate Jan van Wyk sentenced Agliotti to a suspended ten-year prison term, fined him R300 000 and ordered that he pay an additional R200 000, considered the proceeds of crime, into the asset recovery account. As a result of the plea, Agliotti would have the unwanted title of 'self-confessed drug dealer' to go along with the 'Brett Kebble murder accused' when he was referred to in the media.

According to a statement signed by Agliotti and read out in court by Hodes in his accented drawl, Agliotti was not The Landlord after all. 'There is no basis for this label and it was a ruse employed by Paparas to cover his intricate involvement.' The prosecution did not dispute this. Agliotti was never really The Landlord – Paparas had embellished Agliotti's role and had given him a sexy mob name to make it sound as though he was the kingpin.

Paparas gets worked up when I ask him about this and retorts with an answer along the lines of 'Ag bullshit, man, Glenn was involved.'

The statement explained that Agliotti met Paparas ten years previously at the wedding of mutual friend, Martin Wingate-Pearse, in Mauritius. They began doing business in the late 1990s by dealing illegally in cigarettes. According to Agliotti, Paparas developed a relationship of trust with him and told him that he dealt in drugs and that he had dagga in Swaziland. Agliotti introduced Paparas to Anthony Dormehl as Paparas required a transporter and a warehousing facility for his drugs and other goods. He alleged that Paparas was smuggling drugs at the time and spoke about the contraband as 'hash', 'black' and 'mandrax'.

Agliotti claimed that towards the end of 2005, Paparas asked him for advice on how to smuggle hashish into South Africa from Iran. It was decided to use gas stoves to disguise the shipment as similar products were manufactured in Iran. It was also agreed that they would use the name Ophirton Hardware, a business situated in Booysens, as the delivery address. Paparas allegedly made all of the necessary arrangements and the container landed in Durban and was sent to City Deep Container Depot. Paparas then met Agliotti and gave him the shipping documents that were required to clear the consignment. Agliotti asked Nassif for help and he agreed to use a company called Tony's Logistics to fetch the container and transport it to T-Bond. Agliotti said that he later told Paparas that he had been informed that customs were inquiring about the consignment and Paparas allegedly said the goods should be moved as quickly as possible. He claims they were then moved to Paparas's father's plot on the East Rand.

Agliotti dished the dirt on Paparas, who he had been friends with for years, in the same way that Nassif had turned on him. The Scorpions were quickly proving the old adage that there is no honour among thieves.

Agliotti was fingerprinted before leaving court. Opening the door of the silver Merc in Hardach Street, Advocate Hodes told us enquiring journalists that we would 'have to wait and see' about whether Agliotti's link to Selebi had been resolved. What we wanted him to say was that Agliotti had agreed to testify against Selebi but he was far too cunning to fall into that trap. Agliotti echoed the words of Nassif. 'I am very relieved I think. At least the truth is out, but they will have to call me something else (other than) The Landlord.' He was sure to leave us with a quality quote for our stories.

I N THE LAST QUARTER OF DECEMBER, THE NEWS CYCLE WASN'T winding down as it usually does when what we call the 'silly season' starts to kick in. This particular year it was just gearing up and rolling into full swing. The country was teetering in a state of flux. Its prosecution boss had been sacked, the Chief of Police was on the verge of being charged with corruption and the former Deputy President Jacob Zuma was also facing the prospect of having corruption charges reinstated against him.

All of this was playing out against the most dramatic background – the ruling ANC was at war with itself. A watershed political event which would change the face of the nation's leadership landscape was drawing near – the ANC's highly anticipated 52nd conference in Polokwane. Mbeki and Zuma, who had forged a brother-like relationship while in exile during apartheid, were contesting the position of President of the ANC and the party was being torn apart in an ugly fight for power.

In the aftermath of Pikoli's suspension, Mbeki appointed Advocate Mokotedi Mpshe as acting head of the National Prosecuting Authority.

One of Mpshe's first acts as NDPP was to appoint a four-member panel to review the case against Selebi. The panel was comprised of Frank Dutton, who was instrumental in setting up the Scorpions; former Judge Mbuyiseli Madlanga; KZN Director of Public Prosecutions Shamila Batohi; and ex-policeman and forensics expert Peter Goss.

Another of Mpshe's immediate tasks was to cancel both the arrest and search warrants issued for the National Police Commissioner as part of what the *Mail & Guardian* (18 January 2008) called at the time 'Mbeki's mad dash to save Selebi'.

The NPA issued a statement 'clarifying the status' of the warrants, confirming that an arrest warrant was secured from the Chief Magistrate in Randburg on 10 September and a search warrant was issued by the Deputy Judge President of the Witwatersrand Local Division on 14 September.

The statement said that Mpshe, upon his appointment, had decided to conduct a review of the matter and decided it would be prudent to make an application for the cancellation of the warrants. He approached the Randburg Magistrates Court and the magistrate agreed to the cancellation. He also approached the Deputy Judge President, who was not as obliging and indicated he was not prepared to retract the warrant. The

NPA stated that, pending the outcome of the review process, it would not execute that warrant.

What the statement didn't say, however, was that President Mbeki's legal adviser Mojanku Gumbi had requested that Mpshe cancel the warrants, that Simelane had drafted the affidavit asking for the cancellation and that Mpshe had made a late-night visit to Magistrate Stanley Mkhari's house to have the warrants squashed. We only learnt this through media reports and bits and pieces that came out in the Ginwala Inquiry and press conferences months later. It started to look more and more as though Mbeki was moving to protect Selebi.

By mid-December, the review panel had finalised its report and reached a decision that was not immediately made public. The Polokwane conference was in full swing at the University of Limpopo on the outskirts of the city which I had grown up in. Zuma was wrestling control of the ruling party from his old comrade and ally Thabo Mbeki, a final decision was being made to dismantle the Scorpions and Jackie Selebi was strolling about in his baggy shorts and police cap looking for friends. I was knee-deep in mud, holed up in an outside broadcast van and ridiculously sleep-deprived.

On the final day of the conference, Mpshe went on Talk Radio 702 and told show host Bruce Whitfield that the NPA had enough evidence to charge the newly elected ANC leader, Zuma, and his prosecution was imminent. Journalists at the conference, including me, exhausted and mud-encrusted, went into overdrive. The conference had been a momentous apogee following months of political hype and now the leader of the ruling party and the most senior policeman in the country were both about to face criminal charges of corruption. The international media were lapping it up.

On New Year's Eve, Mbeki was seeking solace after being publicly deposed and embarrassed at Polokwane, and hosted a party for close friends in Pretoria. According to then *City Press* senior editor Makhudu Sefara, who attended as a guest, Mbeki 'emerged from the hallowed halls of power with a camera around his neck. Clad in a cream Cuban shirt, khaki pants and black shoes, this was vintage Mbeki!' Amongst the guests was Jackie Selebi.

For some reason known only to him, Mpshe chose that evening to phone the President to inform him that the NPA was ready to charge the police chief. Mbeki's legal adviser Gumbi would later tell journalists including myself, at a press conference at the Union Buildings, how she took the call, dragging herself off the dance floor and then pulling Mbeki aside at 03:00 'after all the dancing', to tell him about Mpshe's decision.

Gumbi is a slender woman with long braids and hard features who owned Mbeki's ear for much of his time in the presidency. There were few decisions that he took without consulting the former Azapo activist from the Free State.

According to her, Mbeki immediately acted on Mpshe's news on New Year's Day and began to activate 'the government machinery' looking for a replacement for Selebi and calling meetings with ministers in the security cluster and police management.

I N THAT FIRST WEEK OF JANUARY 2008, AS MANY SOUTH AFRICANS were making their way home from their annual coastal retreats and digesting the political ramifications of what had happened in Polokwane, a series of astonishing events was occurring in the upper echelons of government as some of the most senior members of the security fraternity scrambled to protect one of their own. There was flagrant abuse of position and of power.

On 4 January, Glenn Agliotti was 'lured' from a boozy lunch at his new home in Pecanwood near Hartbeespoort to an office park in Rivonia by senior intelligence official Dennis Kekana. Agliotti was approached by Tanya Volschenk, who acted as a conduit to the powers who were running the country. She suggested he speak to the National Intelligence Agency. Forever seeking the best possible deal for himself, Agliotti agreed. He was already sitting comfortably with the NPA, but if the NIA or any other agency had something more lucrative to offer him he would take it. He was disgruntled and aggrieved, having been under house arrest for over two years. He also realised that the Scorpions were on the verge of being disbanded, the Polokwane conference having sounded their death knell, and he was worried about long-term security.

Volschenk was also at that office park meeting with Kekana. She typed up a statement on her laptop that was duly signed by Agliotti. In the affidavit, Agliotti made a number of claims, which were potentially devastating to the Scorpions' case against Selebi. He insisted that he had consistently maintained that he had never bribed the police chief, that the Scorpions' 'prime objective was to save its existence by bringing down Selebi' and that he was 'targeted in a political game that involved the intended demise of Zuma and Selebi amongst others'. Agliotti repeated conspiracy theories which he'd often heard at Brett Kebble's dinner table and which he still believes in today. He told the NIA that the Scorpions were controlled by 'outside forces, namely the CIA and FBI' who were targeting Selebi and Zuma in order to destabilise the country by overthrowing law-enforcement and intelligence agencies.

With his devastating statement in hand, Agliotti went with Kekana to another meeting, in a room in the Balalaika Hotel in Sandton. Present at that meeting were National Intelligence Agency head Manala Manzini, Manzini's deputy Arthur Fraser and police Crime Intelligence head Mulangi Mphego.

Manzini looks and sounds like a bullfrog, the big whites of his eyes set deep in his rotund face. The spy chief once admitted to beating his politician wife because she wouldn't cook and iron for him. Mphego also has a moon face and is short and squat – he emerged as Selebi's go-to guy, his fixer when times turned tough. He would later face a charge of defeating the ends of justice and appear in court for his role in procuring the statement from Agliotti.

At that meeting, Agliotti, disillusioned and desperate, 'told the NIA what they wanted to hear'. Unbeknown to Agliotti, Mphego was recording the meeting and a copy of that video landed in the hands of a *City Press* journalist midstream during Selebi's corruption trial. According to the newspaper (18 October 2009), the video shows Agliotti hugging the man he affectionately referred to as 'Mphegs' and handing the statement to Manzini.

The turncoat affidavit would come to be known as the 'drunken affidavit'. Despite the name, Agliotti still maintains that most of the contents are truthful. It made its way to the fax machine of Selebi's advocate Jaap Cilliers courtesy of the legal head of Crime Intelligence at the SAPS, Director Pikkie van Vuuren. Three days later, Agliotti met Mphego and NIA Deputy Director General Arthur Fraser at the Villa Via hotel in Sandton.

Their meeting was also recorded by Mphego and later flighted during Selebi's corruption trial. Dressed in a blue striped shirt and sipping water, Agliotti is seen telling the Crime Intelligence boss that the Scorpions were behind an 'obsessed plot to bring down Selebi'.

In the video, Agliotti recounts what Scorpions investigators allegedly said to him: 'They said, "Glenn, unfortunately you got involved in the middle of a political game." I said, "Fuck off. So you are targeting me because I am associated with the National Commissioner as a friend?"'

On the tape, Agliotti again reiterates the claim he made in the 4 January drunken statement that he never bribed Selebi. 'I never bribed the Commissioner. He is my friend. I never asked him for anything. I respect his position.' He also launches into a tirade about the deals the Scorpions cut with the hired hit men and Nassif, calling him a 'fucking liar' and complaining, 'How many people have they murdered? Where is the justice?'

Agliotti's own legal team was incensed when they heard about the statement and the series of secret meetings in dimly lit hotel rooms. Robert Kanarek was particularly irate about Agliotti's claim that he had paid his attorney legal fees in the amount of R3 million. The Scorpions were beyond seething.

While giving evidence in Selebi's corruption trial about this tumultuous time, Agliotti broke down in tears in the witness box as he attempted to justify why he flip-flopped, saying that at the time he was under house arrest, had been in prison for a month and Nassif was brokering deals:

> I wanted somebody to hear my side of the story and what I had read in the press continuously for an ongoing amount of time and my theory. I came to make this statement in order to try and secure a deal for myself as I was never offered anything like Nassif and the others had been offered by the DSO and I was led to believe that this may be possible through the NIA … this I did for my interest and at that time for the accused … he did not even know about it, but I thought it would be in both our interests to give NIA a version that they wanted to hear, and that is how this statement came about.

After watching his erstwhile friend sobbing in court, Selebi, a sardonic smile on his face, quipped to journalists in the public gallery that Agliotti would need a box of tissues for cross-examination. When Agliotti heard me report this on the radio later in the day, he sent me an SMS jokingly asking if he could get an advertising deal with Kleenex. I couldn't help but laugh at the thought of Agliotti sniffing out an opportunity even when he appeared to be broken and bruised.

Above left: Glenn Agliotti leaves the Johannesburg Magistrate's Court on the day of his arrest for Brett Kebble's murder.
(CHRIS COLLINGRIDGE, INDEPENDENT NEWSPAPERS)

Above: Glenn Agliotti, 15 kilograms lighter, in his cell at the Sandton Police Station. Note the white roses and decorative photographs.

Left: Gerrie Nel leaving his house in custody after police investigators searched the premises following his shock arrest.
(ETIENNE CREUX, INDEPENDENT NEWSPAPERS)

Below: Jackie Selebi is protected from the media by bodyguards as he arrives at the Randburg Magistrate's Court on 26 June 2008.
(SHAYNE ROBINSON, INDEPENDENT NEWSPAPERS)

Above: Gerrie Nel (left) and Andrew Leask arrive at court during Jackie Selebi's corruption trial in 2009.
(MUJAHID SAFODIEN, INDEPENDENT NEWSPAPERS)

Centre: Jackie Selebi's chief accuser, Irishman Paul O'Sullivan.
(ANTOINE DE RAS, INDEPENDENT NEWSPAPERS)

Left: Vusi Pikoli arrives at the South Gauteng High Court to testify in Jackie Selebi's corruption trial.
(CHRIS COLLINGRIDGE, INDEPENDENT NEWSPAPERS)

Left: Jackie Selebi arrives at the South Gauteng High Court for judgment in his corruption trial.
(SHAYNE ROBINSON, INDEPENDENT NEWSPAPERS)

Below: Brett Kebble murder accused Glenn Agliotti with his advocate Laurance Hodes SC during his trial.
(DUMISANI SIBEKO, INDEPENDENT NEWSPAPERS)

Above: Mikey Schultz and Fiazal 'Kappie' Smith leave the South Gauteng High Court following Kappie's testimony. (CHRIS COLLINGRIDGE, INDEPENDENT NEWSPAPERS)

Right: Nigel McGurk makes a call following his testimony. (CHRIS COLLINGRIDGE, INDEPENDENT NEWSPAPERS)

Top: Clinton Nassif arrives at the South Gauteng High Court to testify against Glenn Agliotti. (CHRIS COLLINGRIDGE, INDEPENDENT NEWSPAPERS)

Centre: Judge Frans Kgomo handing down his ruling in the Brett Kebble murder trial. (CHRIS COLLINGRIDGE, INDEPENDENT NEWSPAPERS)

Below: Glenn Agliotti talks to journalists outside the South Gauteng High Court while on trial for Brett Kebble's murder. (BONILE BAM, INDEPENDENT NEWSPAPERS)

Left: Glenn Agliotti laughs during an adjournment on his judgment day.
(CHRIS COLLINGRIDGE, INDEPENDENT NEWSPAPERS)

Quiet before the storm: Mikey Schultz mentally prepares himself before his title bout against Zimbabwean Tineyi Maridzo. (ANTOINE DE RAS, INDEPENDENT NEWSPAPERS)

Mikey Schultz hits the mat 1 minute and 11 seconds into round three of his title fight against Tineyi Maridzo at the Wembley Arena. (ANTOINE DE RAS, INDEPENDENT NEWSPAPERS)

Fiazal 'Kappie' Smith and Mikey Schultz in Pepe's tattoo parlour in Parkhurst. (MANDY WIENER)

JUST DAYS AFTER GLENN AGLIOTTI HAD DEPOSED TO THE 'DRUNKEN affidavit' and a day after the Villa Via meeting, there was another shock development. On 8 January, Gerrie Nel, the prosecutor leading the case against Selebi, was dramatically arrested.

I received a midnight phone call, alerting me to the fact that twenty armed policemen had taken Nel into custody in front of his wife and children, on what overwhelmingly appeared to be trumped-up charges. Bleary-eyed, I rushed into the newsroom to begin digging up what I could about the bizarre move.

According to the warrant, Nel was arrested on five charges, including corruption, perjury and defeating the ends of justice for crimes apparently committed four years previously. Two of the complaints against him were made by one of his own investigators, who had helped expose alleged corrupt members of their unit, Cornwell Tshavhungwa and Geophrey Ledwaba.

In an affidavit filed by Nel following his arrest, he claimed that the two police officers from Potchefstroom, who were seeking an arrest warrant for him, had admitted that there was not sufficient evidence to charge him and that they were carrying out instructions from 'higher up'.

The day after Nel's arrest was a surreal one as journalists, Scorpions agents and a group of German students loitered around the then Pretoria High Court befuddled about what was going on behind the scenes. The long wait was broken by a moment of amusement for me as I received an SMS from Agliotti: 'Ask Nel if he wants me to bring him a McDonalds happy meal. J'

Eventually, by mid-afternoon, as the courts were shutting down for the week, it was decided Nel would make an appearance in the Magistrates Court up the road. En masse we all traipsed the few blocks to the court for the next instalment of the strange programme. Following another lengthy wait for us journalists in the dark, abandoned passages of the court building, Nel finally appeared, looking out of sorts in his patchwork jeans and short-sleeve casual shirt. Looking even more out of sorts was prosecutor Matric Luphondo, who arrived in shorts and slops clutching a brown file. With his black gown making a desperate attempt to hide his bare legs, Luphondo called the matter before the magistrate as Nel stood in the dock with a bevy of police officers looking on. Nel was released on bail.

Nel's arrest was a manifestation of the increasingly ugly turf war playing out between the Scorpions and the SAPS, which had sparked fears of a security threat. ANC Secretary General Gwede Mantashe even warned 'we have got a potential crisis on our hands'. Mpshe was alarmed by the nature of Nel's arrest and claimed that the SAPS were so desperate to get the prosecutor behind bars that they had flouted policy by failing to get his permission to execute the arrest and they had ignored the advice of at least four advocates.

The arrest had come just two weeks after Nel had secured a fresh warrant for Selebi's arrest from Randburg Magistrate Cheryl Loots.

The move was undoubtedly a desperate bid by Selebi's lieutenants to thwart his imminent prosecution. The upshot of their efforts was that they only succeeded in infuriating an already determined prosecutor, who became even more impassioned about bringing down a corrupt cop. The fight was now personal.

But during that saga Nel made a decision which, arguably, tainted him in the eyes of cynical journalists and his detractors. He turned to Ian Small-Smith to represent him in court following his arrest.

Small-Smith was the same attorney representing the hit men with whom Nel had negotiated 204 agreements. It may have been innocent, but a question mark lingers. What exactly was the relationship between Nel and Small-Smith? Had Nel cut the deals with the shooters only to help out his mate? Had the decision to give them indemnity been pre-arranged by the two men for their own benefit? The prosecutor, who had to ensure he was beyond reproach, was tarnished. However, in his mind, he had appointed a lawyer who was known to fight for his client's rights, a lawyer who was tough and who knew when the police and prosecutors were misleading the courts about an accused.

Two days after Nel's dubious arrest, Jackie Selebi made his move. He brought an urgent application in the Pretoria High Court, asking for an interdict preventing any criminal prosecution against him. He also wanted more information about the charges that the NPA was planning on levelling against him, as well as details of those who had given statements against him.

Effectively what he was saying, in my opinion, was, 'Stop talking about charging me, show me your evidence and go to hell.' Agliotti's 'drunken affidavit' was the cornerstone of Selebi's application but the NPA was prepared and had a rebuttal affidavit signed by Agliotti as part of its answering papers, in which its star witness retracted most of the claims he'd made to Mphego and Manzini.

I still maintain that Selebi's decision to launch a pre-emptive strike was short-sighted. All he succeeded in doing was forcing the NPA's hand. With storm clouds gathering over the capital and a summer thunder shower brewing, the mood in the vicinity of the Palace of Justice was ominous.

Just after lunch the NPA's spokesperson Tlali Tlali released a bundle of documents to the salivating press pack, which comprised the prosecuting authority's submissions to the court, the bulk of which was an affidavit by acting NPA head Mokotedi Mpshe.

In the statement Mpshe dropped the bombshell that had been two years in the making. He confirmed that Selebi would be charged and an indictment served on him later that day. 'The charges against him are based on a strong *prima facie* case supported by the testimony of a range of witnesses and corroborated by real evidence,' he explained. In the court papers, Mpshe said Selebi would not be arrested but rather asked to appear in court, a marked difference from the dramatic way in which Nel had been taken into custody. 'I have undertaken that if he is to be charged, he will not be arrested and an arrangement will be reached with his attorney for a date on which he has to appear in court.'

I grabbed my bundle and ran outside onto the buzzing pavement and, with raindrops falling all around me, broke the news – the National Police Commissioner was to be charged with corruption.

The following day, a Saturday, President Mbeki addressed a press conference at the Union Buildings, announcing that Selebi would be placed on extended leave, at his own request. Deputy Commissioner Tim Williams would be acting in his position pending the outcome of his trial.

On 1 February Selebi made his first appearance in the Randburg Magistrates Court, oozing arrogance, flashing a big smile and throwing thumbs-up signs to policemen lining the courtroom. He told the court he was innocent and intended pleading 'Not guilty'.

Mikey

They had a bigger picture. I think the bigger picture was Jackie Selebi. Clint sold it to the Scorpions that he was going to give them Agliotti and Agliotti was going to give them Selebi and Selebi was the Police Commissioner of South Africa. He was corrupt and he was taking money. But let's face it, the whole government is corrupt. We live in Africa. That's just the way it works here. That was that bigger picture. I asked Piet Jonker the one day, how is it that you can get us immunity on murder? He said to me yous okes are such a small piece in this big puzzle. He said it's like so far looked over. He said but when the puzzle's finished and you see the bigger picture, then you'll be able to understand what it is. By that condition of getting Jackie Selebi I think that's what the bigger picture was. That's what the whole thing was about.

IT IS 28 JULY 2009. JACKIE SELEBI SITS SLUMPED ON THE BEIGE couch in the TV room of his Waterkloof Ridge home, propped up by animal-print scatter cushions listening, enthralled, to a piano composition reaching a crescendo. Incongruously, an image of 'Yanni – Live at the Acropolis' is on the TV screen. Selebi's eyes are closed as he follows each note, savouring the escape that it brings him. A pile of books is arranged on the table, displaying his affinity for autobiographies and an apparent curiosity about white-collar crime. Not entirely surprising for a person who has spent the past few years enforcing the law and apparently attempting to dismantle major crime syndicates. The collection also again reveals that glimmer of the 'everyman' as well as his diversity of character. John Perkins's *Confessions of an Economic Hit Man*, Jake White's *In Black and White* and *Peeling the Onion* by Nobel laureate Günter Grass all appear well read. I imagine him pausing Yanni for a few seconds to flip through the pages of one of the books to check a quote or a fact that has escaped him momentarily.

This was a unique perspective on the enigmatic character who had been grabbing headlines in South Africa for three years. The interior of his home had never been seen by the prying eyes of the media, who had scrutinised the bottom line of his bank accounts and the relationship between him and his friend Glenn Agliotti. He had granted me and then Primedia Head of News and Programming Yusuf Abramjee a rare interview. Even during his tenure as the country's police chief he was reticent to speak to reporters and was more likely to grunt at journalists than provide detailed insight into police activity. I had been closely monitoring developments around his case for over three years and was grateful that he felt comfortable enough to speak to me.

Having opened the door for me and shown me in, Selebi's wife, Anne, politely asked whether I would like a cup of tea. She delivered it on a tray and disappeared, not to be seen again until I left. I thought for a fleeting moment that her behaviour was true to my perception of the mould of an exile wife married to a powerful organisation man. To all appearances, she was the type of woman who seemed to accept forgivingly that her husband's secretary from his days at Shell House, who became his lover and with whom he sired a child, continued to hold a presence in their lives for years after. In my mind there were two types of ANC women – the ambitious, successful, self-sufficient kind like Nkosazana Dlamini-Zuma or Nosiviwe Mapisa-Nqakula and the subservient, resigned type like Anne Selebi. But on further consideration over a few sips of tea, I acknowledged that was a rather narrow perspective and this would become clearer as the dynamics of their relationship would be revealed, to an extent, during Selebi's testimony in his trial.

Selebi and I spoke about the personal and about politics. It was the day before his successor as National Police Commissioner was to be named by President Jacob Zuma and Selebi was resigned to the fact that his attempts to cling to power had come to naught. Zuma had been elected President of South Africa in the April poll, just weeks after corruption charges against him were spectacularly dropped. This was in direct contrast to the outcome against Selebi who was awaiting trial on very similar charges. Speculation was swirling that the no-nonsense, abrasive KwaZulu-Natal MEC for Transport and Community and Safety Liaison, Bheki Cele, had been hand-picked for the job even before Zuma swept to power in the elections two months previously. As is so often the case with political speculation, the denials would soon turn to celebratory confirmations as the man known for his fedora hats and trench coats would be appointed to the position at the Presidential Guesthouse in Pretoria the following day. His mantra 'Shoot to kill' would soon occupy the banners of broadsheets countrywide and spark a debate about the requisite force needed to respond to armed criminals.

Cele was in the ANC's underground structures with Zuma in the 1980s and the President would want a close ally in the position. Something Selebi was blatantly not, although not for a lack of trying. On the day that corruption charges were withdrawn against soon-to-be President Zuma in April 2009, it was claimed that, in a bid to ensure his political survival, Selebi had fed crucial tapes to Zuma's lawyer, Michael Hulley, through right-hand man Mulangi Mphego. In the recordings, former National Director of Public Prosecutions, Bulelani Ngcuka, and Leonard McCarthy, the head of the Scorpions, have detailed discussions, suggesting the case against Zuma is the result of a conspiracy. The tapes were the result of 'Operation Destroy Lucifer', apparently put into action to find evidence to bolster Selebi's own defence. The ANC leader's prosecution would turn on the emergence of those recordings and provide sufficient will for the charges to be withdrawn. The charges were dropped sixteen days before the elections and the timing of the leaked tapes was critical. At a press conference at the NPA's Silverton offices, acting NDPP Mokotedi Mpshe indicated that the decision was based on an abuse of the prosecuting process by McCarthy and not the actual merits of the case. Mpshe quoted from the tapes, divulging details of phone calls and messages between Ngcuka and McCarthy. The two men used pseudonyms for politicians, referring to Selebi as 'Ouboet' and Zuma as 'Oujan'. Mbeki was given the code names of 'the man' or 'the fellow'. In one particular text message conversation, McCarthy and a private intelligence man known as 'Luciano' discuss a 'political solution' to Zuma's case.

Ironically, the claim of the manipulation of the prosecuting authority was the very same conspiracy theory put forward by Brett Kebble as he publicly accused Ngcuka of abusing state resources to attack Zuma's power base. Businessmen Saki Macozoma and Kebble nemesis Mzi Khumalo also apparently featured in the recordings – Kebble had motivated that Ngcuka was the NPA's puppet master, driving the Zuma prosecution as kingmaker, in order to anoint Macozoma as President. The emergence of these tapes gave credence to Kebble's 'pie in the sky' claims years after his death. Selebi would also revert to the conspiracy theory defence, pointing to the recordings as evidence that he was being maliciously prosecuted. So too would Glenn Agliotti. Agliotti also points to the tapes saga as evidence that the contents of his submission to the NIA in the so-called drunken affidavit were accurate – that he was 'targeted in a political game that involved the intended demise of Zuma and Selebi amongst others'. He still maintains he was unfairly targeted and the Scorpions only went after him to get to Selebi and ensure their own existence.

It was valuable weaponry for any accused – they were being prosecuted purely for personal political gain. Shortly after the tapes were made public, Selebi's lawyers made an application to acting police chief Tim Williams to declassify them. For some unknown reason, the tapes were never used as evidence in Selebi's trial.

Mention of the explosive tapes reminded me that there was a time when the man who sat on the couch in front of me, looking tired and resigned, was indeed politically powerful. From 1987 he served as a member of the African National Congress's influential National Executive Committee and was the comrade responsible for assisting members of the ANC who had been exiled during apartheid to return to South Africa in the early 1990s. The eminent personalities who had fought in the struggle abroad would have passed through his office in Shell House and it would have been his duty to settle them in, in a land which held haunting memories for many. He then made a name for himself in diplomacy, serving as South Africa's ambassador to the United Nations, a powerful position. He returned home to fill the post of Director-General of Foreign Affairs before being appointed the country's first black Police Commissioner in 1999, a job that Selebi, by his own admission, never really wanted. His star rose even higher when, in 2004, he became the first African president of international policing body Interpol. Although largely a ceremonial position, Selebi was seen as the most potent cop in the world.

He was also a long-time friend of the country's President, Thabo Mbeki. The kind of friends who would bring in the New Year together at Mahlamba Ndlopfu, the official residence of the head of state in Pretoria. Mbeki may have had a glass of fine whisky in hand but Selebi probably would not – he always insisted he was a teetotaller. That friendship would become a point of contention for both men as it became increasingly apparent that Mbeki was protecting Selebi from prosecution and refusing to dismiss him in the face of mounting accusations that he was involved in corruption. It did little for public confidence in government's ability to fight crime, both domestically and internationally.

It was a year and a half since Selebi had made his first appearance in court and he was philosophical about his six and a half years as the country's chief of police. 'No regrets, absolutely no regrets,' he said. 'There could very well be mistakes but there are no regrets whatsoever.' After all, he had spent eighteen months at home reflecting on his time in the position.

'Well, it has taken its toll emotionally. You know, children go to school and come back and they still find you at home and say, "When is this coming to an end?" In that sense, it has taken its toll,' a melancholic Selebi told me. 'But it has been a period of reflection. I have reflected on almost everything that I have done over these two years and generally trying to look at whether I would have done things differently. And in the majority of cases, I would have done the same things.' When he spoke about the burden of the claims on both himself and his family, I got the first hint of sadness about the man. Over time, as he endured a lengthy, gruelling trial, my empathy and pity for him grew as the sadness pushed its way to the fore.

I had always been struck by Selebi's arrogance as police chief and this was a tenet that permeated his every action throughout his corruption trial. This arrogance was evident as Selebi told me, in the safety of his securely guarded home, that he did have an impact on the fight against crime. This from the man who once infamously said, 'What is all the fuss about crime?' 'It's for others to evaluate but I think that there has been an impact. An impact on the working conditions of the police, in dealing with problems of crime which was a permanent feature of our lives. Twenty-four hours a day we were sitting and saying, "How do we work out this problem?" I think there was an impact, there must have been.' During his time at the helm of the SAPS, South Africa developed an international reputation for having one of the world's highest murder rates and millions of citizens lived with the horrifying reality of violent crime. According to crime statistics released in 2004, a total of 21 553 people were murdered in the country in 2003 while Selebi was Commissioner. That translates into an average of 400 citizens killed a week. Victims were also left enraged and infuriated by the lack of acknowledgement from Mbeki's administration as high walls and electric fences became ubiquitous in the suburbs.

I asked him what had been the most valuable lesson he had learnt while running the country's police force and his answer was a reminder of his history in the ANC and the emphasis placed on the collective. 'One thing that it has taught me is that there is nothing that replaces working with other human beings. No single individual can do anything except by working as a team.' The three separate images of Nelson Mandela in his lounge became more prominent.

Selebi warned his successor that he would have to be politically savvy if he was to survive. 'They have to walk through that as if they're walking on a field full of landmines because you've got to avoid all of those things that have nothing to do with policing. Your job is to do policing, not to do any other thing other than that.' Perhaps Selebi could have benefited from his own advice. Ironically, a year after Cele's appointment, he would also be dogged by allegations of maladministration over the controversial R500 million rental deal for new headquarters for the police.

At the time of the interview, it was just three months before Selebi was due to go on trial in the South Gauteng High Court in October, and when I raised the subject of his court case his deflated demeanour automatically adjusted. His eyes became fierce when I asked if he ever took cash for favours and if he had a case to answer to. 'I don't! They know that I don't! But let them have the courage to come on the fifth of October to place whatever they say they have there outside in the open so that we can deal with it. I don't have a case to answer to.' Besides, Selebi insisted, he hardly had contact with shady 'business consultant' Glenn Agliotti, who used to be his friend, 'finish and klaar'. 'I haven't spoken to him for a long, long time. I haven't spoken to him whatsoever.'

He was equally defiant when asked if former President Thabo Mbeki ever protected him from prosecution as Vusi Pikoli has always claimed. 'My relationship with him is a very good relationship and it is untrue for anyone to suggest he was protecting me so that I can do crime. He has never done that and he wouldn't do that.'

When I had pulled into his driveway, I had immediately noticed the three uniformed cops in the gatehouse, assigned to protect the country's most senior law-enforcement officer. But soon they would be packing up as Selebi would become an ordinary citizen the following day. Dressed in tracksuit pants and ankle-high hard boots, Selebi was visibly muddled about his identity – a regular citizen who once wore the polished uniform of a power-wielding National Commissioner. From the following day, he would technically be unemployed and unemployable.

A snarl appeared on his face as he vociferously denied rumours that he has asked Zuma to redeploy him as an ambassador. 'I have not asked him for anything! For anything! Nothing! Why would I go back? I've been there already. I've been an ambassador. I've been a DG of Foreign Affairs. I have not asked for anything!' The eclectic clutter of mementos around the house, from the multitude of elephant figurines to the Asian coasters, bore testimony to his years as a diplomat.

So what would he do with his time then? His reply belied his claim that he was not bitter about how his life had turned out. 'I've been thinking about what not to do when people have levers of power in their hands. That's what I want to think about.' After a moment he chuckled and tried again: 'Maybe I'll sit down with a few colleagues and see if we can't write a book.' An attempt, I think, to convince himself he would not be spending the next few years in and out of the country's courts, fighting for his freedom.

After Anne Selebi graciously showed me out and the electric gate rumbled closed behind me, I was left to consider Selebi's curious remarks. What does happen when people have levers of power in their hands? Do they succumb to the enticing lure of greed and fall victim to corruption? Do they abuse that power by manipulating state agencies to drive personal vendettas? Or do they retain a steady course, humbly accepting the responsibility of that power and the office which they've sworn to uphold? Selebi surely knew and would not have to spend much time thinking about it.

NATIONAL COMMISSIONER OF POLICE AND PRESIDENT OF INTERPOL Jackie Selebi famously stated to the *Mail & Guardian*'s Nic Dawes that he was just friends with Glenn Agliotti 'finish and klaar'. He also arrogantly waved his palms at a cynical media pack and stated laconically that 'these hands are clean'. He had repeatedly shouted from the rooftops that he wanted his day in court so that he could shed his tainted reputation and prove to his detractors and vilifiers that he was innocent of corruption and a victim of a horrible, political conspiracy. On 5 October 2009 he was finally granted that opportunity and walked up the stairs of the South Gauteng High Court and made his way to Courtroom 4B, flanked by his advocate Senior Counsel Jaap Cilliers, his junior Fanus Coetzee and his attorney, Coetzee's wife, Wynanda. Cilliers had made his name by successfully defending 'Dr Death' Wouter Basson, the former head of the apartheid government's secret chemical and biological warfare project.

Pritchard Street had been shut off for the event, with Metro Police officers patrolling the area and orange beacons deterring motorists from gaining access to the thoroughfare. Officials controlling security had long memories and it was only a few years previously that another high-ranking, powerful figure walked into this building as an accused and thousands of impassioned followers saturated the area outside the courthouse, shimmying up lamp poles, climbing atop armoured Nyalas and burning traditional herbs on the pavement. But Jackie Selebi did not carry the same political clout as Jacob Zuma and the crowds would not be coming out to show their support for this stalwart of the ANC's tenacious battle against apartheid.

Despite the lack of toyi-toying protesters, there was still a sense of event about the place. Photographers had turned out en masse to capture for posterity the sight of the country's most senior police officer being hauled before a judge to answer to charges of corruption and defeating the ends of justice. Every inch of the hard wood benches of the courtroom were filled with Selebi's relatives and friends, journalists hungry for headlines, and that curious throwback of society, voyeuristic court-watchers who spend their days strolling from one room to another with the sole intent of watching justice being dispensed. This case promised to be the sexiest soap opera in town, and their experience told them to stick around.

Also in the public gallery was the implacable Paul O'Sullivan, Selebi's nemesis, foe and chief accuser. Seeing Selebi in the dock was sweet vindication for the eccentric Irishman. Sitting at the opposite end of the courtroom, exchanging acerbic looks with O'Sullivan, was police officer Selby Bokaba, a member of Selebi's spin brigade.

The metaphoric stage was set for one of the most hyped and highly anticipated trials of South Africa's young democracy. It promised political intrigue, insights into the country's corridors of power, details of top-level corruption, abuse of state agencies for personal gain and tales of deceit, duplicity and dirty tricks. The bull terrier Gerrie Nel and his team of investigators and analysts were in place, stage left, with Andrew Leask tapping away on his tablet computer. Cilliers and his support staff were seated, stage right. Selebi, having spent some time preparing in a consulting room outside, took his seat in the dock. Judge Meyer Joffe's clerk, who would be awarded the title 'Lady Gaga' by the regular media fraternity, had laid out her principal's ever-present pencil case and black legal files. The squat, uniformed orderly asked everyone to rise and in strode Joffe in his officious red-and-grey robe, his hands clasped behind his back and his shoulders hunched.

Selebi stood and answered firmly to the charges put to him, entering pleas of 'not guilty'. Cilliers rose from his seat, pushing his elbows out behind his body in his trademark mannerism, and began to read from the ten-page plea statement. As he stood, I recalled what his junior, Fanus Coetzee, had said to me on the phone the previous afternoon. I had made a cursory call to the legal team in anticipation of what would be happening on day one of the trial, hopeful of gleaning any morsel of information that could be included in a morning preview piece. Coetzee had assured me that the plea explanation would be 'newsworthy' and astonishing, and urged me to be in court. I was baffled as to where he thought I might rather be on the day. I also spoke to Selebi the day before the start of the trial. He told me that he was 'feeling strong'. I had also asked him, for the benefit of photographers, whether or not the accused would walk into court through the front door of the building. He had insisted that he is the kind of man 'who always walks through the front door'.

The plea statement was what many of us on the press benches anticipated – a blanket denial from Selebi, who immediately launched an offensive, taking a swipe at the men he believed to be the puppet masters orchestrating the malicious prosecution against him. He went straight for the jugular – suggesting former NPA heads Bulelani Ngcuka and Vusi Pikoli had launched a campaign against him, because they were the ones who had become implicated in corruption and Selebi had discovered their dirty secrets.

Selebi fired the first salvo in the trial, which would get uglier and dirtier as it unravelled. He argued that he was only being prosecuted because Pikoli and his lieutenants were fighting to keep the Scorpions alive and who better to target than the head of the opposing unit, the Chief of Police. He even suggested that Ngcuka maintained strong influence over the Scorpions and exerted huge pressure on the head of the organisation, Leonard McCarthy, to proceed with the campaign against him. This campaign, Selebi continued, involved leaking information to the press on an ongoing basis in an attempt to destroy his credibility and providing cabinet and the President with misleading and untested information. He lambasted the NPA's decision to cut deals with criminals to build a case against him:

> The NPA/DSO also approached a number of people with a history of criminal activities and offered them indemnities against prosecution on serious crimes ranging from murder, attempted murder, drug trafficking, racketeering, money laundering, fraud, theft, intimidation, defeating the ends of justice etcetera in exchange for false statements implicating the accused.

Selebi finalised his plea statement saying, 'The accused therefore pleads that the case against him was manipulated with *mala fide* intentions in an attempt to discredit him for the reasons as set out above and to ensure the continued existence of the DSO.'

EVIDENCE IN JACKIE SELEBI'S CORRUPTION TRIAL LASTED FOR well over fifty days with eighteen witnesses taking the stand for the prosecution in the stuffy, wood-lined courtroom. The personalities who featured in the case traversed the full spectrum – from lovable rogues to feisty blondes, ex-armed forces soldiers to secret sleuths, designer clothing store stewards to spectacled accountants.

On most days during the one-hour lunch adjournment, Selebi sat alone on a bench outside the court or in a nearby consultation room. He would be bent over, his elbows resting on his knees, his hands clasped together and his droopy, yellow eyes peering down his nose. On many of those days he would beckon me with a jerk of his head and I would sit with him as he ate his lunch of one apple. I never saw him eat anything other than that and when I enquired why, he would pull up his nose and simply say he had no appetite.

During those lunchtime chats, Selebi ranted about the prosecution's conduct and how the campaign against him was vindictive and malicious. His lip quivered and his brow furrowed as he complained about Paul O'Sullivan's involvement in the investigations and Gerrie Nel's questionable motives. He insisted that Judge Meyer Joffe, who was affectionately referred to as 'The Sandton Shul' by the media pack due to his position on that shul's committee board, didn't like him from the start and didn't like his legal team either.

But these rants were always imbued with arrogance – he was 'confident, very confident'. Selebi told me how his defence team was going to 'tear Agliotti apart during cross-examination, you'll see'. He pre-empted how tapes and audio recordings talking about judges' allegiances would be showed to the court. 'You'll see, when they start bringing TVs and video players into court, then you'll see,' he warned me. Some of these tapes were played, to my surprise, but others were not.

He also let on what his own legal team's strategy was with the state's star witness Glenn Agliotti – 'Jaap Cilliers is "getting him on side", being nice to him, getting Agliotti to say, "Yes, that's correct, yes correct," and then we trick him and we get him. He rolls over and gets his tummy tickled, plays into the hands of Jaap and gives him what he wants.'

I asked him why he didn't make representations to the recently appointed National Director of Public Prosecutions Menzi Simelane, who had taken over from Mokotedi Mpshe, and he replied, 'I don't want to bother Simelane with this, I want it to be sorted out here. Otherwise the DA and the media all think I'm trying to get out of this thing.' He was consistent with his line that he wanted his day in court. Selebi promised great revelations from the witness box, assuring me, 'The things I will say will be explosive, about everything.' He insisted, 'I cannot wait to get in there and finally talk.'

As an aside, we also debated the state of the country's politics, how Julius Malema was 'a young hothead who knows nothing'. Selebi was once the President of the ANC's Youth League, the position Malema was in. We also discussed the murder of AWB leader Eugene Terre'Blanche, who was killed mid-trial. I asked him his opinions about the crime and the racial undertone of the murder and, without missing a beat, Selebi invoked the words of former Police Minister Jimmy Kruger upon hearing about the death of Black Consciousness leader Steve Biko: 'It leaves me cold.'

Inside the courtroom, Gerrie Nel, the meticulous strategist, was slowly constructing a case against the erstwhile Police Commissioner. His first witness was Selebi's ex-friend, the 'corrupter' Glenn Agliotti, who had agreed to incriminate himself in exchange for indemnity. Agliotti's testimony was illuminating – he detailed how the two men would meet in the Sandton City shopping centre and would go on buying sprees for designer labels like Aigner, Hugo Boss and Gucci, with Agliotti always picking up the bill. He revealed how Selebi would visit his ex-fiancée Dianne Muller's Midrand office in full police regalia to collect envelopes stuffed with cash and how he had the country's most senior cop at his beck and call to attend meetings at a finger snap. There was also testimony about how Selebi had shown Agliotti top-secret intelligence documents in the parking lot of the Makro Retail Centre in Woodmead and at the boardroom table of his own office. Amongst these documents were top-secret UK reports and Paul O'Sullivan's Casual Source report, which was amongst the first pieces of intelligence used by the Scorpions in their investigation. TV screens were rolled into the courtroom, transforming the staid, serious environment into a movie theatre. On screen, we saw Agliotti meeting with policeman Mulangi Mphego, denying his 'bribing' of the National Commissioner.

The Kebbles featured prominently. Agliotti recalled how he had effectively sold Selebi to Brett and John Stratton during a time when they were mid-brawl with Wellesley-Wood and fighting criminal charges. They had a complaint which they wanted addressed at the highest level possible in the SAPS. Agliotti approached Selebi and a meeting was arranged. Judge Willem Heath and Stratton presented the complaint to Commissioners Mphego and Rayman Lalla. Agliotti had successfully bought Selebi's influence. He realised this could be a long-term business prospect:

AGLIOTTI: *They [Brett Kebble and John Stratton] wanted the accused to be onboard and to have access to the accused and I said to them that it would cost them a million US dollars, which was my consulting fee and they agreed to that amount.*

ADV NEL: *They would pay you that amount to do what?*

AGLIOTTI: *Well, as part of my consulting fee and obviously in their minds to keep the accused onboard, he was basically onboard our team.*

ADV NEL: *Now you said that they wanted access to the accused, they paid you a million US dollars. Did this happen, was access granted?*

AGLIOTTI: *Well, not initially. That only came with time or later in time.*

ADV NEL: *What happened?*

AGLIOTTI: *Well, after quite a time they insisted on meeting the accused. I tried to prevent this but there reached a time where they insisted and if this did not happen they would terminate my services with them, so I arranged a dinner with the accused, myself, Brett Kebble and John Stratton, which then took place in Illovo, 65 Fifth Street, because by this time they had moved to the address which I have just mentioned.*

ADV NEL: *You said that you resisted. Why resistance?*

AGLIOTTI: *Well, I did not want them to have easy access to the accused because then they would no longer need me or my services. So it was a decision that I took, a business decision.*

In order to receive his payment of US$1 million, Agliotti had to set up a company through which he could be paid. He turned to his fiancée's father, Martin Flint, an accountant, who supplied him with a shelf company called Spring Lights. This account effectively became a slush fund used to finance Brett's shady, illicit campaigns. It was used to pay Agliotti, Clinton Nassif's security company and Judge Willem Heath's consulting firm. A total of R40 million flowed through this company to pay for dirty tricks and clandestine operations and a fabricated loan account called 'Misty Mountains' was also created as a conduit. During cross-examination, Agliotti confirmed just how badly JCI was fiddling with its finances:

> ADV CILLIERS: *So you have assisted by actively assisting them to cook their books?*
>
> AGLIOTTI: *Mr Cilliers, they cooked their own books and they did a lot of it, it was not me that was cooking their books, believe me. They cooked it themselves.*

Selebi listened to all this evidence from the dock, where he sat on the black 'Luciano Pavarotti – Live in Africa' cushion he brought with him daily.

Ultimately, Judge Meyer Joffe would not find Agliotti to be an honest and truthful witness. I suspect because Agliotti did confirm from the witness stand that, 'I do lie from time to time,' and defence advocate Jaap Cilliers did label him 'one of the worst, if not the worst witnesses ever to testify in a South African court'. Joffe decided he would only accept Agliotti's evidence where there was corroboration. That corroboration would come in the form of Muller, his ex-fiancée, who counted out cash for Selebi and witnessed it being paid over; her father, Martin Flint, who cashed cheques for Agliotti; and KPMG auditor Dean Friedman, who drew up a forensic audit report on Selebi's financial affairs. Joffe was also pointed to cash cheque stubs inscribed with words like 'JS' and 'Cash Cop'. Because payments from Agliotti to Selebi had always been in cash, there was no paper trail so the prosecution had to build a case based on inferences and credible witness testimony.

Many a time during our lunchtime chats, Selebi stretched out his thumb and index finger, shaping them into a gun. He confidently blew on the barrel of his 'pistol' and said to me, 'Where is the smoking gun?' However, a very wise advocate explained to me during the trial that the prosecution did not always need a 'smoking gun' – that crucial piece of evidence which shows direct involvement on the part of the accused. 'Sometimes it's just the weight of all the feathers together which is enough.'

The weight of the feathers, all the pieces of evidence that the state constructed into a case, may not have been enough to prove beyond any reasonable doubt that the Commissioner was guilty of corruption. But the prosecution was gifted something far stronger – this gun may not have been smoking, but it sure as hell had Selebi's fingerprints all over it. The ex-police chief's own evidence from the witness box ultimately sank him and was a pivotal contributor to a guilty verdict.

At the time, I was told that Selebi's legal team tried hard to keep him out of the box. They even asked his wife, Anne, to try and convince him, but he refused to listen. Selebi is an arrogant man and he wasn't going to let his opportunity to shine slip away from him. He had waited many years to put his version across, to lambaste his accusers publicly. It would prove to be a devastating decision.

The ex-Commissioner spent most of his time in the witness box standing, his hands insolently stuffed into his pockets. His expensive suits, which were once tailored to his body, hung around his diminished frame, looking cheap. Selebi adopted what my colleague Adriaan Basson labelled 'the Swiss Army Knife Defence'. He flatly denied receiving any money or gifts from Glenn Agliotti, except for one present of a Swiss Army knife. Agliotti's retort was that he was not so cheap as to buy anyone such a gift.

Selebi claimed that he was meeting with Agliotti regularly because the man was a police informant who used to feed him intelligence about crimes:

SELEBI: *He gave me lots of information. He is like an Encyclopaedia Britannica. If you said to him and this is what I did if I go to him and say, 'Who is John Almond,' I will get a story about John Almond that I had not intended to … If you say you know Mr Cilliers, he will give such an explanation that you never know how he came across. So, he gave me lots of information about contraband cigarettes*

and who was involved. He gave me lots of informa-
tion about the Chinese. He gave me lots of infor-
mation about people who were bringing electronic
equipment into the country illegally. He gave me
information about people who were bringing shoes
illegally from China into the country. He gave me
information about the car racket.

Selebi reinforced the perception of Glenn Agliotti as a sweet-talking, charming corrupter, who manipulated situations to his own benefit:

SELEBI: *He was someone who was looking for recognition*
in the circles that he moved around. They needed
to look at him and you know and he is talking to
the National Commissioner was such recognition. I
am saying this because we would be sitting and sip-
ping coffee in any place and he would receive a call
and instead of saying, 'I am sitting and drinking
coffee,' he would say to the caller, 'I am busy sipping
coffee with the National Commissioner,' which was
unnecessary. I think on numerous occasions I said
to him, 'Can you not leave me out of this?' but he
is a sort of person who was in search of recognition
and will use whatever relationship or whatever
meetings that he had with me. So he is that kind of
a person, very flamboyant and very convincing if
you talk to him, charming, that is my experience of
Glenn Agliotti.

ADV CILLIERS: *At that stage that we are talking now it seems to me*
2002 and onwards what was your understanding of
the business that Mr Agliotti was involved in and/
or conducting?

SELEBI: *I can never tell you. I think I always knew that he*
was a hustler trying to make ends meet. This day
he is dealing with export and import. This day he
is now dealing with mining and the other day he is

dealing sports promotion, you know, those kinds of things.

Selebi sprouted forth from the witness stand, attacking the prosecuting team and its motives and conducting a general demolition job on the Scorpions, subscribing to the adage that 'the best defence is a good offence'. But it wouldn't be long before he was backed into a corner during cross-examination by Gerrie Nel. On the back foot, Selebi became cantankerous and belligerent – the downhill slide began. He started contradicting his evidence, changing his versions and evading questions, cocking a snook at the court process.

Nel forced Selebi to admit that he had indeed gone to dinner with the Kebbles at Agliotti's request but he insisted there was no sinister motive for the visit and there was no talk of business at the table:

ADV CILLIERS: *Now Mr Agliotti was very emphatic that the conversations on these dinners related to political type of conversations and conversations of that nature. What was your version on this issue, what type of conversations took place?*

SELEBI: *It is true it was like, you know, it was like here is the boss and here is his lieutenants and he led discussions about political issues to try and show how much he knows about the political situation in the country. I remember one incident in this discussion, now I am meeting this person for the first time and he says to me 'comrade'. Now not many people called me comrade, very few. He said 'comrade' to me.*

ADV CILLIERS: *Did you at any stage receive anything from the Kebbles, apart from maybe the food at the dinner?*

SELEBI: *I was just going to say the only thing that I received from them was food not even their wine, I do not take alcohol. If receiving is that then that would be the food that they served at the dinner nothing, nothing more. Nothing about them discussing with me about their business.*

In summing up Selebi's testimony, Gerrie Nel described the former Commissioner's 'Big Five Lies', playing on the South African tourist attraction of the Big Five animals. Judge Joffe went further, suggesting there was even a sixth big lie.

For me personally, there were two events that stood out during Selebi's evidence – events which made me cringe with embarrassment and pity for the once deeply respected struggle stalwart who carried himself with dignity and pride. Both incidents would provide ample fodder to cartoonists as they comically caricatured a dishonest Selebi, his nose growing longer and longer.

The first was a 'cut-and-paste document' that Selebi presented to the court as evidence. He initially claimed it was this 'sort of document' which he had shown to Glenn Agliotti but that later changed to being the actual declassified document which he had shared with his friend. Selebi was sent home to find the original and bring it back to court the following day. What he produced the next day was unbelievable and many of us watching from the public gallery looked on with big eyes in astonishment as Selebi tried to get away with it. The 'original' report he presented to the court had the wrong font, logo and colours. It was clear for all to see that a cut-and-paste job had been done overnight as Selebi scrambled to create a document that supported his evidence. Nel accused him of forging the report.

The second incident was the shredding of the receipts or, as I like to refer to it, the 'the dog ate my homework' incident. Selebi, who was once one of the most powerful men in the country, responsible for a massive police budget, told the court that he was not in charge of his household financial affairs. Rather, it was his wife who ran the family's money matters. Selebi testified that she had kept every one of the receipts they'd received over several years and she had used these slips to draw up a document to assist him with his evidence. Advocate Nel asked the ex-Commissioner to bring these receipts to court as evidence. The following day, Selebi told Nel that Anne had shredded them the day before! After having kept the slips for more than seven years, she just happened to shred them a day before they were needed in court. Selebi claimed she had done so because 'she had found better evidence, bank statements'. While his astonishing version on the receipts was dismantled by Nel, Anne Selebi stood staring out of the window in the corridor outside the courtroom while her brother-in-law, George, filled her in on developments inside. She had been removed from the room by attorney Wynanda Coetzee as she may have been called as a witness. In retrospect, it may also have been to save her from the shame of watching her husband's collapse.

I found Selebi's implosion on the witness stand tragic. To watch a man of such stature fall apart like that was difficult. Part of me believed that he was a victim of the system. He was part of the culture of entitlement. Having given his entire life to the struggle against apartheid, how could he be rewarded with criminal charges? Why shouldn't he receive gifts and money from a friend when he had sacrificed so much? After all, other politicians had done the same and got away with it. I could just imagine him saying, 'How dare they!' The system also saw to it that he was being paid R30 000 a month. Was that fair remuneration for the most powerful police officer in the country?

Our lunchtime discussions came to an end when Selebi took the witness stand. Instead, he spent the breaks alone, not speaking to his legal team as he cut a solitary figure in the corner of the consultation room, eating his apple.

A member of Selebi's camp confirmed to me what I suspected. They had an inkling that he was in poor health. I had heard that he was seriously ill but that he had refused to admit as much. 'The old man doesn't remember what he's saying or what is going on. He can't remember what he had for dinner last night and we think there might be early onset Alzheimer's. He's such a macho man, he was a flagship for our country and now that's all gone. We've tried to get him to a doctor but he won't go.' For me, it was a possible explanation for his incoherent statements from the box.

I ran the theory past another journalist who responded, 'It is a sickness. It's a sickness called arrogance.' In the end, I had to agree. One of the Scorpions investigators described it as 'Kort Kombers Syndrome', which translated into English is 'Short Blanket Syndrome' – if the blanket is too short you can cover the head and not the feet and vice versa. Selebi couldn't hide all his lies all the time.

Midway during Selebi's testimony, fate would have it that Glenn Agliotti had to make an appearance as an accused in the Brett Kebble murder trial in the very same courtroom as his erstwhile friend. It was a picture that spoke a thousand words. Standing in the bare wooden dock was Agliotti, the charming corrupter who had allegedly conspired to have a mining magnate killed in an extraordinary assisted suicide. Next to him stood the country's former police chief, the improper beneficiary of Agliotti's largesse, fighting for his dignity in the face of corruption claims. Behind them in the public gallery sat Guy Kebble, churlishly heckling Agliotti. Outside in one holding room were Mikey Schultz, Nigel McGurk and Fiazal 'Kappie' Smith, the hired guns who had shot the tycoon in the still of the night. In another holding room nearby was the ostracised Clinton Nassif, Brett Kebble's ex-security boss, who had given the instruction for the job to be carried out.

It was an unreal sight. It brought the entire sordid story home for me to see it played out in such stark reality. How did we get here? How is it that the country's most senior policeman is standing in a court of law as an accused along with a cast of such unsavoury characters? What drove him to meddle in this underbelly? And what pushed Brett Kebble, a cultivated tycoon, into this dark world?

During the midst of the 2010 FIFA Football World Cup, Judge Meyer Joffe found Jackie Selebi guilty of corruption and sentenced him to fifteen years in jail. Unfortunately for Selebi, the world's media was in town to capture the moment. It was an awkward, incongruous event for the country, to witness the dramatic downfall of one of its greatest men at a time when the nation was celebrating itself.

In handing down the judgment, Joffe dismissed Selebi's theory of a malicious prosecution and claims that he had not received a fair trial. In fact, he was critical of the SAPS's abuse of power and questioned the prosecutorial interference that led to Vusi Pikoli's suspension. He pointed to the series of events at the beginning of January 2008, during which Agliotti met with the country's intelligence bosses and deposed to the drunken affidavit and when Gerrie Nel was arrested:

The reason for this flurry of conduct was not determined nor is it the task of this court to determine it. Suffice it to say, without so finding, and it is stressed without so finding, the activity appears to have been designed to assist the accused and in making available the affidavit did assist the accused. If that is indeed so and in so far as a member of

SAPS and another government agency were involved therein it is to be deprecated.

Joffe also found Agliotti's evidence about Selebi's meetings with the Kebbles 'had the ring of truth to it' and that Selebi's version could not be 'reasonably possibly true'. He ruled that Selebi did not attend these meetings at Brett Kebble's home 'out of friendship, but because the accused was obligated to go by reason of the payments made to him by Agliotti'.

The judge reserved his most scathing and critical remarks for sentencing. Staring Selebi directly in the eye, Joffe told him that he had been an embarrassment to the office of National Commissioner of Police, an embarrassment to those who had appointed him to the position, an embarrassment to the members of the South African Police Service whom he had led, an embarrassment to all right-thinking citizens of the country and finally, an embarrassment to the court for thinking that his 'mendacious and in some respects manufactured evidence' would be believed.

Selebi left the courthouse with his eyes downcast and his cheeks puffed out. An embarrassment to all.

Selebi has since been granted leave to appeal the judgment and the sentence. The appeal is expected to be heard in mid-2011.

D ESPITE BEING THE ARCHITECTS OF THE INDEMNITY AGREEMENTS
with the shooters and the case against Glenn Agliotti, Gerrie Nel,
Andrea Johnson and Andrew Leask would never prosecute the matter.

In March 2010, at the height of the Selebi trial, Nel and Johnson were
unceremoniously yanked off the case. This development was only made
public in May of that year, a month before Glenn Agliotti's trial was due
to start. The team was also removed from former Crime Intelligence boss
Mulangi Mphego's defeating-the-ends-of-justice case. Mphego was facing the charges for his role in the clandestine 2008 Agliotti interview in
a Sandton hotel room during which an affidavit was procured from the
state's witness. The team was allowed to continue with the prosecution of
Steve Paparas, his father Dimitrio and driver Stanley Poonin, in the drugs
matter in the Germiston Magistrates Court.

Changing the prosecuting team so close to the start of the trial was
an inexplicable move by National Director of Public Prosecutions Menzi
Simelane. The official line from Simelane's office came in the form of a
statement through his spokesperson Mthunzi Mhaga, in essence saying
Nel's team had too much on its plate:

> Two months ago the DPP South Gauteng took a strategic decision in
> the interest of justice to replace the prosecution team in both cases.
> Mr Mphego made representations to the NDPP for a permanent stay
> of prosecution and therefore it is not fair to overburden the same team
> with so much work when we have many equally capable prosecutors.
> Hence the decision that they concentrate on the Selebi case so that it
> doesn't affect other cases where they are involved.

In the statement, Simelane suggests the decision was taken by the Director
of Public Prosecutions in the South Gauteng division, who at the time was
Advocate Gladstone Maema. When the news broke, I phoned Maema and
he was equally adamant during my interview with him that the decision
was his alone. Maema also told me that Nel's team had been extensively
consulted and their opinions about the decision were canvassed.

On 26 March 2010 at 07:00, Nel, Johnson and Leask met with Gladstone
Maema in his office. Also present at that meeting was Advocate Dan
Dakana, a senior prosecutor who would be taking over the cases. Assisting

him would be Lethabo Mashiane and Kholeka Gcaleka. At that meeting, Maema told them that in his opinion, the prosecuting team should not change and the decision had been made by Simelane alone. He was simply fulfilling an instruction. Nel stressed the complexity of the matters and recommended the handover be done during a two-day workshop so that he could give the new team insight into the entire project. Nel told the meeting that he believed Glenn Agliotti was guilty of conspiracy to murder and the case against him was strong.

The *Mail & Guardian* also published extracts from the letter that Simelane had sent to Maema on 20 March, giving him the order to change the prosecuting team. Simelane writes:

> *I have noted that you have made very little progress in dealing with the above matters [the prosecutors for the Glenn Agliotti and Mphego cases]. You will recall that I instructed that new [sic] prosecuting team be appointed. To date I have not been advised of the new team.*
>
> *As you are aware, these matters are already in court and a new team will have to be briefed on both matters urgently so that it can be equipped to handle the cases. The delay is naturally very regrettable (14 May 2010).*

Simelane tells Maema that he has 'personally' decided to appoint state advocates Dan Dakana, Lethabo Mashiane and Kholeka Gcaleka to prosecute Agliotti and Mphego.

Menzi Simelane and Gerrie Nel have a deep dislike for one another, largely as a result of their respective positions during the Ginwala Inquiry into Vusi Pikoli's suspension. Nel fought in Pikoli's corner against the government at the inquiry while Simelane was the state's main witness. Ginwala vindicated Pikoli but he still came out of the experience smelling bad. During the hearings, Simelane lambasted Pikoli and Nel's decision to grant indemnities in the Brett Kebble matter. He was extremely unhappy that 204s had been given to the three shooters and that plea bargains had been struck with Nassif and Agliotti in the Paparas drugs trial. There was definitely no love lost between Simelane and Nel. Simelane had motive to pull Nel's team off the cases. If the prosecution failed, he could turn around to Vusi Pikoli, Nel and Leask and say, 'I was right. You never should have cut deals with criminals.'

But that wasn't the only deciding factor for Simelane. While the Selebi trial was underway, Roger Kebble made representations to him, motivating that the prosecuting team should be changed. Kebble's attorney, Kim Warren, met with Simelane and communicated the family's concerns that the prosecuting team had a conflict of interest because of their role in Selebi's trial. At the time, Warren said that the family felt the prosecutors needed to keep Glenn Agliotti 'on side' as a state witness against the ex-Commissioner and it would affect their judgment in prosecuting him for his role in Brett's murder. This was a legitimate concern for Simelane – could the same team use a man as a witness in one trial and then prosecute him in another matter as an accused? Simelane decided it was a direct conflict and changed the team.

It would ultimately be a decision that would cost the state any chance of a successful prosecution against Agliotti. The new team was inheriting a massively complex case and had almost no time to prepare or consult with witnesses. It would be a difficult challenge for the most astute of advocates, let alone the little-known team that had been appointed. At the time, Maema assured me they would do the matter justice: 'They have received a briefing from the previous team. They have read the docket and they will be able to deal with the matter with the same ability as the previous prosecution would have done so.' I wasn't convinced.

The revelation that Nel and his team had been replaced happened to come on the same day that the head of the NPA's Integrity Management Unit, Prince Mokotedi, told the Selebi trial that Nel had been investigated for allegedly siphoning off funds for informants from a Scorpions slush fund. Mokotedi claimed that Nel's name had been connected to an R80 000 claim for a payment to an informer who had provided information about an impending drugs shipment. The ship never reached South African shores and the informant was paid. However, Simelane confirmed at the time that the NPA's integrity unit was not investigating Nel around that incident.

Nel and Leask would be targeted later though. After Selebi's conviction, the ex-Commissioner laid charges against both men, providing ample excuse for their critics to launch an investigation into their conduct during the Bad Guys probe. The NPA confirmed it received complaints from Selebi and from the South African Revenue Service (SARS). I understood that Nel and Leask had refused to give SARS access to Agliotti's tax documents as they believed that would compromise their case against Selebi. It would also have been a violation of Agliotti's rights. SARS didn't see it that way.

Life at the NPA became a living hell for Nel and his team as they were pushed into a corner, watching from their Silverton offices as Dan Dakana's team floundered spectacularly in Courtroom 4C of the South Gauteng High Court.

It's 8 July 2010, two weeks before the trial is scheduled to start in the High Court, and the country is buoyant, awash with a renewed patriotic spirit, as the FIFA Football World Cup is reaching its zenith. The cars ramped up on the pavement outside the Wembley Indoor Arena in Turffontein are still dressed in rainbow mirror socks looking decidedly tatty and dirty, having been tied on at the start of the tournament a month previously. Germany had played Spain in the second semi-final of the competition in Durban the previous night and the world was now gearing up for a Spain vs Holland showdown at Soccer City in Soweto in just three days' time. But tonight, with no soccer on the go, the focus is on a high-velocity rematch of a different sort: Tineyi 'Marstak Power' Maridzo vs the challenger, Mikey Schultz, for the WBO Africa Super Middleweight title.

Eight months previously Maridzo, a little-known Zimbabwean prize fighter, sent Schultz, the hired hit man, crashing out in just 86 seconds to win the interim title. Now Schultz and his passionate followers are hungry for revenge. There's a sense of expectation in the dirty South and the pressure is on.

I have the night off from exhaustive World Cup coverage, unaware of the fact that I'll be rushing off to catch a plane to Madrid the following day in expectation of Spain's euphoria at winning the trophy. I convince my brother-in-law, a keen boxer, to pick up some tickets from Nick Durandt's gym in Norwood for the night's fight, in exchange for his entrance price. It's been years since I've been ringside and I'm looking forward to witnessing the raw energy first-hand.

We take our seats on the floor with a square-on view of the ring, right behind the scorers and alongside the passage down which the boxers will bounce later that evening, bobbing and weaving, waving their fists to the crowd. Already, dancers in leotards and knee-high boots are gyrating against the ropes, their green and blue tassels jiggling to the beat of what sounds like elevator music. My brother-in-law, who seems to know a bit about this business, points out my ignorance and explains that it's 'boxing music'. Wembley Arena and the crowd it pulls on fight night is a parody of all the stereotypes Jo'burgers have of the Southern suburbs and the 'rough, dodgy' types who live in the area. Turffontein and the surrounding neighbourhoods have a rich immigrant heritage, with a strong representation of people of Portuguese and Lebanese descent and working-class culture. Its reputation precedes it, most notably because of the punters who frequent the nearby Turffontein racetrack. On fight night, the bleak concave concrete building becomes a magnification of the community and any preconceptions about the culture are reinforced and amplified.

They all seem to be caricatures of themselves, none more so than the hairy bikers proudly parading the colours of their clubs, most prolifically 'Satan's Saints'. Many wear that haggard scruffiness of a panel beater or a mechanic, and the scars on their faces bear testament to the many rounds most have gone in a lifetime of street fighting. Aspirant boxers are dressed in jeans and 'Title' or 'Everlast' shirts, with the real groupies lucky enough to get their hands on 'Team Mikey Schultz' gear.

There's an abundance of mullets – business in the front and party at the back – but this is the mullet reinvented, sculpted and styled. The first thing that strikes me is that the majority of men in the arena are dressed almost identically, but they find expression through their hair. It appears as though they've spent hours carefully manicuring their tresses. Some have one side shaved or guide their mohawks in a particularly obscure direction, all with the ultimate intent of making their hair look 'messy' and not done.

My second overwhelming observation is that just about everyone knows everyone else. This is a close-knit community and handshakes are being dished out as readily as spanners at a tow-truck convention. Many have long histories with the man sitting alongside them, whether it be chequered or not, and have done some kind of work together in the past, whether clean or not.

The crowd is peppered with familiar faces too, some infamous rather than famous. There's former professional soccer striker and hell-raiser Mark Batchelor, with his spiked white hair, affectionately known as 'Batch' in these circles. He'd been pulled off air as a commentator for sports broadcaster Supersport three years previously after allegedly beating a gym instructor with a knuckle duster at a restaurant. Also in the expensive seats is James 'The Bullet' Dalton, ex-rugby player and Mikey's cousin, who comes with a mean reputation. In the same year that Batch was getting involved in pavement punch-ups, Dalton was standing in the dock, accused of attempting to murder his wife. She claimed he'd tried to drown her in the bath and smother her with a dress. The couple subsequently reached a confidential interim settlement.

Sitting spitting-distance away from them is the stocky, diminutive Pauli Simpson in his weathered brown leather jacket, smiling broadly with cheerful eyes. Simpson is one of the city's top private investigators and has deep tentacles in this network. Behind him is Piet Jonker, a Scorpions investigator who is part of the team probing Operation Bad Guys, the investigation into Brett Kebble's murder. His presence here is incongruous – after all, he is on 'the other side', prosecuting the star of tonight's show, Mikey Schultz. But Jonker is a regular at Mikey's fights and was even spotted wearing a 'Team Mikey Schultz' shirt at his previous face-off against Maridzo. The fashion blunder made front-page news in a national paper the next day and Jackie Selebi's legal team even raised it in his trial, as proof that his prosecution was tainted and malicious. But Jonker explains to me that he's known these guys for years, from the days when he too was a professional fighter. Chatting to Jonker, curiously, is Kappie, flashing his gappy grin at admirers who come past to shake his hand. He's part of the Mikey Schultz legend and sheepishly smiles when somebody comments that he's 'causing kak' again. He's come to support Mikey, who he refers to as his 'brother from another mother'.

The bell rings, announcing the start of the night's first bout. A colleague has told me to keep my eyes peeled as his trainer is first up. It's an uneventful fight and I'm far more fascinated by the match that follows – it's a ladies' fight and, despite my feminist inclination, I'm astounded by the beating that the two competitors unleash on one another. Probably the best contest of the evening comes next – Shaun Santana, who happens to be a brother of a good friend of mine, is slugging it out with Daniel 'Billy the Kid' Bruwer in a junior heavyweight bout. Bruwer splits Santana's weak left eye and the white tassels on Bruwer's camouflaged silk shorts are quickly streaked with blood. He recovers from a heavy knock-down in the third round and in the eighth the referee stops the fight because of Santana's split eye. TKO.

Shouts of 'Go Jazzy!' resonate around the cave-like arena as the stringy, wiry, King David boy, Jared 'Hollywood' Silverman, dances into the ring. He looks scrawny in his spacesuit silver shorts with a huge blue Star of David on his left leg and top-of-the-range Adidas boots. But despite appearing as the kid who'd be pummelled behind the bicycle sheds by the Highland's North boys, his sprawling, long reach is too much for his competitor and he rewards himself with a juicy Nando's burger at the end of his victorious bout.

While Jazzy Hollywood is in the ring, Jonker, the Scorpions investigator, calls me over and offers to take me backstage to say howzit to Mikey. We walk up the stairs to the so-called VIP section, which, in this rundown corner of Turffontein, is an empty room furnished with a scattering of office chairs. I open the door and am taken aback when I see Mikey. His tattooed torso is slathered in Vaseline and he is already gloved up, his bony fists sheathed in black. He's hopping from one foot to the other, smacking his fists together. He's obviously not wearing his glasses, which lend him an air of respectability, and his stubble is long, adding to the intimidating impression. Bizarrely, there are ten or so people sitting in the room, their seats lining the walls, staring at the show of the boxer psyching up.

The only person not watching is a sweaty 'Billy the Kid', who is recovering in the back corner of the room, his head hanging between his knees. I recognise one of the seconds who has been working the ring during the night and Mikey's sister, Cathy, who he refers to as his 'boss'. It takes Mikey a few seconds to register who I am, he's so in the zone; his piercing blue eyes have the glare of concentration. I immediately feel like an intruder, like being in a Springbok change room before a big test, but Mikey assures me he's so psyched that I'm not causing a problem at all.

Flexing his biceps, he quips that his 'guns are loaded'. The irony is not lost on me. I leave him to shadow box and nod his head as one of his sparring partners feeds him a stream of advice.

Minutes later and the atmosphere in the arena shifts – we're getting to the business end of the evening and the punters, some of whom have been humorously discussing their figures, are now scrambling to their seats. The lights dim and the ominous beat of Eminem booms over the PA system. Through the flare of flashing spotlights, Mikey walks out in a black gown, bearing the word 'Affliction' in Gothic script on the hood. He looks every bit the professional boxer; his seconds, who have been assisting other fighters from his stable throughout the night, have changed their shirts for the title bout to an imposing black. Durandt, his trademark scruffy blond mane restrained by a bandana, kisses his charge on the cheek before stepping out the ring. Mikey stares towards the entrance as his nemesis, Maridzo, makes an understated arrival. He has no entourage, barring the one person carrying a Zimbabwean flag on a pole. I can see a glint in Mikey's eye that I have not witnessed before and, for a brief moment, I recognise the hit man in him. It's as if a cognitive switch has been flipped and he's morphed into the killer. As the anthems play, Pauli Simpson, the private investigator, remarks that tonight is different from last time, when Mikey was sent reeling back to the change room in the first round. This time the crowd is baying for blood as revenge for that knockout. The week preceding the fight has been marked by a debilitating episode of bronchitis for Mikey and claims that Maridzo has taken a massive payment to throw the match, which is vehemently denied all round. It's clear this rematch is taken very, very seriously by both sides.

The opening bell rings and Maridzo comes out fast but Mikey starts solidly. The Zimbabwean relies heavily on the overhand right that floored his competitor in their previous match but Mikey dodges it successfully. In the second round, Mikey starts to take command and scores well, likely even winning the round. The crowd is relieved that at least this time he's gone beyond 86 seconds and his prospects of success are encouraging. I turn to chat to Pauli briefly as he remarks that he's been watching Maridzo train this week and he just hasn't been looking good. His gum guard has been out of his mouth and he's been breathing heavily, he tells me. As he suggests that the titleholder doesn't stand a chance, I hear the hollow, nauseating sound of a solid punch connecting and I flip my head around.

Maridzo has landed his big overhand right and Mikey's lights have gone out. The challenger doesn't stagger or stumble; he rocks back on his heels and slams onto his back on the mat. The room goes deathly quiet for a split second. As the crowd comes to, there is pandemonium as photographers elbow one another to get the picture of the hit man sprawled unconscious across the deck. I recognise many of them and, instantly, my news instincts kick in and I rush to try and snap a pic on my phone to tweet. In my boxing naivety, I am convinced Mikey is dead and the state has just lost its key witness in the Brett Kebble murder trial. There is panic as his trainers battle to revive him. It feels as though minutes are rushing by and I became more and more convinced that the headlines will read 'Hit man dead'. Finally, Mikey shakes his head and struggles to his feet, oblivious to his surroundings. He later confessed to me that he doesn't remember one bit of that fight and he only woke up in the change room later that evening, yelling at his sister that he didn't want to be late for his rematch.

As the referee lifts Maridzo's arm, James Dalton quips in his heavy, unsophisticated accent, 'I think we've just witnessed a career-ending punch, boet.' The reality of the outcome sets in and a photographer remarks, 'Well, his life is pretty much screwed now. Been knocked out twice solidly and you're up on a murder rap. That's pretty kak.' In three weeks' time, he'll feel the flash of cameras on his face once again as he walks up the stairs of the South Gauteng High Court.

Mikey

It went against everything that we believe in because we believe that you don't talk and stuff like that. And Clint, who was supposed to be in our team, he fucking went and he left us out to dry basically. And it was the only choice that we really had and it was a new experience for all of us. Having to stand in front of the judge and fucking say everything, it was a shit experience to be honest because standing there and telling the world what we had done, it wasn't easy. But thank God it had the right result at the end of the day.

THERE ARE SOME THINGS IN LIFE YOU THINK YOU WILL NEVER SEE. Mikey Schultz, Nigel McGurk, Fiazal 'Kappie' Smith and Clinton Nassif in a courtroom, ties wrapped uncomfortably around their necks, is one of them.

And so it is on the morning of 26 July 2010 in the corridor of the fourth floor of the increasingly decrepit South Gauteng High Court. Mikey, Nigel and Kappie sit together in a holding room, anxiously bantering about the strange circumstances they find themselves in. A little way down the passage, pacing up and down in his Hugo Boss suit, avoiding eye contact, is Clinton Nassif. Alone. The pariah who has sold out his friends.

Inside Courtroom 4C, milling about with the confidence of a proud cockerel, dressed in a navy suit, pink shirt and Gucci tie, is the 'accused'. Vintage Agliotti, he is jesting with journalists and charming the court orderly.

Setting up on the defence's side of the room is the familiar smooth-shaven, strong face of Agliotti's advocate Laurance Hodes, wearing the silk robe of a senior counsel. It was only bestowed on him a few months prior. Hodes comes from solid litigious stock. His father, Max Hodes, is a well-known senior counsel and acting judge, a master of his craft with a famous palate for garlic.

Hodes Junior did not always want to follow his father's path. His mother committed suicide when he was young and he was a difficult child. He considered a career as a.vet or a psychologist, but a two-year tour in the army settled his mind and he chose law. After completing an LLB, Hodes went straight to the Bar, he admits as a result of his father's guidance and influence. He did his pupillage at the Innes Chambers with Advocate Dennis Fine, specialising in commercial law, the theory being that he would learn the art of criminal law from his father whose office was housed in the same building. Hodes cut his teeth doing *pro deo* cases, saving two clients from the death sentence. He emerged as an exceptionally capable advocate, with a sharp intellect, remarkable memory and one of the driest senses of humour I have ever encountered. I have never known Hodes to be wrong on a legal prediction and have experienced him as a man of his word. Some others in his profession may disagree, but such is the industry. Hodes had first met Agliotti when his father acted for him during his cobalt-smuggling case. Laurance also did the bail application for Madame Cheng's men in the Kya Sands drug bust, and Laurance's and Agliotti's paths crossed often in subsequent years.

Assisting Hodes is the eccentric attorney Robert Kanarek with his odd spectacles strung around his neck. In his early sixties, Kanarek is a veteran of the law and of life. He grew up in Lichtenburg and tells me that all his life he 'fought to overcome difficulty'. He admits to loving conflict and challenges. As a young lawyer, he set up a practice in Soweto during the height of apartheid, an unheard-of venture for a white attorney. He also hosted a radio show on a Soweto station educating people of the township about their rights. However, most lawyers are motivated by money and I would expect nothing less of Kanarek who jokes that his mantra used to be, 'Have cheque, will travel!' He spent much of Agliotti's trial hobbling about on crutches as a result of a foot operation. As the case wore on, the deep division between Kanarek and Agliotti would also bubble to the surface.

Gerrie Nel and Andrea Johnson are absent from the prosecutors' bench. Instead, they are replaced by three unfamiliar faces. Gauteng Deputy Director of Public Prosecutions Dan Dakana, an unremarkable, soft-spoken man with a permanent look of bewilderment etched on his face, leads the team. His deputies, senior state advocates Lethabo Mashiane and Kholeka Gcaleka, provide what he lacks in fire and passion, and one can't help but get the impression that Dakana has only been placed on the team to lend it respectability.

Gcaleka is a controversial character. With only six years of prosecutorial experience, she was elected as the chairperson of the Society of State Advocates in 2010. Her appointment resulted in an outcry from a sector of the NPA, with many questioning the process by which she was elected. She also came out publicly backing Menzi Simelane, saying that the society unequivocally supported him in his transformation agenda at a time when he was making very unpopular decisions within the NPA. Gcaleka is seen as being extremely close to Simelane and her appointment to the Agliotti prosecuting team was met with raised eyebrows – she is perceived as something of a diva in prosecuting circles. According to her biography, the only matter of real substance that she has prosecuted was the case against seven men who raped Buyisiwe, a rape survivor. Buyisiwe's trial received publicity for the incompetence of the justice system and constant delays in the trial – hardly something for the prosecutor to trumpet about.

Lethabo Mashiane, a short, combative fellow, has somewhat more courtroom experience than Gcaleka and was named the Best State Advocate by the Society of State Advocates in 2009. He did his law degree at the University of the North before going to work at the Legal Aid Board and the National Department of Agriculture. Mashiane joined the NPA in 2000 and was involved in the successful prosecution of a number of matters. He was part of the team in two trials involving the Chinese Mafia – four life sentences were handed down to a Chinese national who killed his uncle, wife and two children and buried their bodies in shallow graves in Tarlton near Krugersdorp, while in a separate incident a Chinese man received a life sentence for killing a fellow countryman at a casino. Mashiane also has experience of the media and high-profile matters – he successfully prosecuted the men responsible for killing world-renowned reggae icon Lucky Dube, and argued appeals in the Max the Gorilla case as well as Jackey Maarohanye's trial – Mama Jackey, 'The Angel of the Soweto', the principal of a Soweto charity, was sensationally found guilty of kidnapping charges amongst others.

During Agliotti's trial, Mashiane sat between Dakana and Gcaleka, pointing out facts and errors, often appearing to be the only one of the three with any semblance of interest in the case.

Also absent from the courtroom is Andrew Leask and his investigating team. This is strange as Leask was supposed to have stayed on the matter despite the fact the prosecutors had been removed. Only Corrie Maritz and PW van Heerden are in court. They are now members of the Directorate Priority Crime Investigation – the Hawks, the police unit created to replace the Scorpions. The situation has come full circle. They were the two police officers who investigated the case before being seconded to the Scorpions. They are now back at the police and are again in control of the matter.

With the scene set, I take my standard seat in a courtroom, second row from the back next to the door and the plug point, and set up my impromptu office: laptop, recording equipment, microphone, headphones, downloading cable, 3G and lunch. I log on to Twitter – I have decided I will be 'live-tweeting' the trial for Eyewitness News. I did some tweeting during Jackie Selebi's trial and the innovation was a success. To my surprise, the updates from the Brett Kebble murder trial will become quite popular over the next few weeks, largely because the content of the case is so sensational. It is made-for-Twitter stuff. For me, the real challenge in covering a complex legal matter has always been condensing the information into 40-second radio updates. Getting it all down into 140 characters for a tweet proves to be a real battle. To borrow from my colleague Cathy Lund at *Cosmopolitan* magazine, news reports coming out of this trial were never going to be 'vanilla' …

> *#Kebble And so it begins. Nassif strolling about. Mikey and others came in earlier in suits. What will happen?*

> *#Kebble Agliotti in Gucci tie. Three 'gunmen' in holding room outside. Were very friendly when I greeted them, smiles and jokes.*

> *#Kebble NPA says investigating team was replaced because they have 'other matters'. Bollocks.*

Hearing the trial is Judge Frans Kgomo, not to be confused with his namesake, the controversial Northern Cape Judge President Frans Kgomo. This Kgomo is meticulous and by the book, keeping a firm hand on his courtroom while providing light-hearted humour when necessary. With his brush-cut 'Mr T'-style hair and tendency to stare over the top of his glasses when making a point, he endears himself to almost everyone in the courtroom and is perceived as balanced and fair. He is progressive, allowing cameras and microphones in court when others would probably have not.

Agliotti rises and the charges are put to him. Initially he was only to face a charge of murder and another of conspiracy to murder Brett Kebble. However, when Dakana's team took over the matter, they altered the charge sheet. Just five days before the trial was due to start, Hodes received an amended charge sheet and a brand new affidavit signed by Clinton Nassif a few weeks before. The prosecution had decided to add charges:

1. Conspiracy to murder Mark Bristow, Jean Daniel Nortier, Mark Wellesley-Wood and Stephen Mildenhall
2. Attempted murder of Stephen Mildenhall

3. Conspiracy to murder Roger Brett Kebble
4. Murder

Gerrie Nel's team had chosen not to add these charges as they were try-ing Agliotti without John Stratton as his co-accused. They had not yet been successful in extraditing the elderly Stratton from Perth and felt they could not prove all the charges without both men standing in the dock together. Dakana's team clearly felt differently. It was a real risk.

With his head cocked to one side and with the experience of an old legal hand, Agliotti pleaded 'not guilty' to all four charges.

Under Count Three, the peculiar charge sheet read as follows:

In that during the period August and September 2005 and at or near Illovo in the district of Johannesburg and/or at places unknown to the prosecution, the accused conspired with John Stratton, Roger Brett Kebble, Clinton Ronald Nassif, Michael Donovan Schultz, Nigel McGurk and Fiazal Smith to aid to procure the murder of Roger Brett Kebble.

It was not the kind of indictment one is used to seeing – Brett Kebble con-spired to kill Brett Kebble.

The state's first witness is Mikey Schultz, his dark suit covering his tat-tooed arms, lending him an air of respectability. His beautiful wife Leonie and her mother watch nervously from the back row of the public gallery as he testifies awkwardly and hesitantly, not trusting his words.

#Kebble Mikey Schultz takes the stand. No tattoo's or boxing gloves in sight.

#Kebble Gripping stuff. Twice Schultz aimed at Kebble and pulled the trigger and twice the gun failed to discharge.

#Kebble Schultz: I pulled the trigger, this time the gun fired. I kept fir-ing. I'm not sure how many times. It was more than five times.

#Kebble Schultz: Nassif told me that Brett had more balls than me as I'd never be able to go through with that.

#Kebble Schultz: Stratton said 'thank you for a job well done'.

#Kebble Schultz still pointing out photographs of the murder scene. Kappie and Nigel in coffee shop waiting for their turn.

Polite as ever, Mikey stays calm during his evidence and sticks to his statement in cross-examination. He isn't taking any chances. But Hodes gets what he needs out of him.

#Kebble Cross Exam! Hodes is going for it! Schultz concedes Agliotti never conspired to kill Kebble or any of the others.

#Kebble Hodes is eating Schultz up. He concedes Agliotti had nothing to do with Kebble's murder and in fact told him to 'call off the boys'.

#Kebble Schultz: Agliotti told me Roger Kebble would pay good money to have Nassif f@#*ed up in a bar fight.

Mikey's testimony is riveting and the twitterverse is gripped.

HartleyR [Ray Hartley, editor of the *Sunday Times*] *Jammed guns, assisted suicides, testifying in court ... SA's mafia is an embarrassment. They are laughing at us in Sicily.*

KevinMcCallum [sports reporter from *The Star*] *As a hit man, Mikey Schultz is about as good a boxer as he is an assassin.*

Mikey steps off the stand and lopes out of the room, a bounce in his step. He has said little to incriminate Agliotti.

#Kebble Schultz leaves the courthouse punching the air. Like a boxer.

Nigel McGurk walks down the stairs of the room looking visibly nervous. His temper is notorious. Plus, he doesn't like Agliotti at all. It's a volatile cocktail. Nigel also can't rely on himself to articulate his thoughts and emotions properly.

#Kebble Schultz is off McGurk is on. Tall, strapping, well built, balding. Owns a tyre fitment center now.

#Kebble McGurk: Mikey and I did dirty work for Nassif. Collecting money and 'intimidating' people. We had a reputation as 'heavies'.

#Kebble McGurk: I wasn't fond of Agliotti. He would always say 'Show me Love, Show me Love'.

#Kebble McGurk: We didn't look very professional...you don't say.

#Kebble McGurk: Nassif was arrested. The beans were spilt. Thats why I'm here.

Hodes plays on Nigel's dislike for Agliotti, teasing out his temper. He forces Nigel to stray from his written statement, a no-no in court procedure. On two issues, Hodes catches Nigel. One is the meeting at The Grand strip club, when he confronted Agliotti about payment for Brett Kebble's killing; the other is about the 'call off the boys' phone call from Agliotti.

#Kebble Things are hotting up here between Hodes and McGurk. McGurk says Agliotti controlled the finances for the Kebble hit.

#Kebble Hodes to McGurk: You have memory like red wine. You never mentioned meeting with Agliotti about payments at The Grand but do now.

#Kebble McGurk: Agliotti said we could continue working together. Work like intimidating people, shooting people.

#Kebble How rough. McGurk: I would have hit Agliotti if he didn't pay me my money. I didn't like him. I would have hit him.

#Kebble McGurk is starting to wip [throw his toys] himself now. Getting proper grumpy with Hodes who has accused him of fabricating a meeting with Agliotti.

#Kebble Quote of the day. McGurk: Kebble had the biggest cahoonas I've ever seen. He wanted to die. I realize what we did was wrong.

Nigel is released from the witness box battered and bruised. His indemnity from prosecution dangles in the balance. He has lost his temper and contradicted his evidence. He may not have been entirely truthful.

Before Kappie takes the stand, former Alan Gray executive Stephen Mildenhall jets in from his new home in London for a morning to testify. At least that's what the prosecutors told the court. He actually flew in from Cape Town for the day.

#Kebble Welcome to the show tweeps. Mildenhall due up next. Mikey Schultz in coffee shop across the road. He's here to support Kappie.

#Kebble Mildenhall takes the stand. Pinstripe suit and briefcase. Softspoken. He looks like an auditor.

#Kebble Mildenhall: I was shot three times. Twice in right shoulder and arm and once in left. My wife rushed me to hospital.

#Kebble. Mildenhall: I certainly have no gripe with Agliotti. I want to put this behind me.

Kappie, looking uncomfortable in a purple-collared shirt, sits on the bench in the corridor waiting his turn. Testifying in court goes against everything he believes in. It is an inexcusable transgression of his beliefs. He takes the stand nonetheless and his testimony is over nearly as quickly as it begins.

#Kebble Kappie: Mikey told me Brett wanted to go. I asked... go where?

#Kebble I cut up the gun used to kill Kebble with a torch and threw the pieces into the Klipriver.

#Kebble Kappie: I don't have a relationship with Clint Nassif. We don't talk. (Maybe cause he sold you out?)

#Kebble Kappie: I fully agree that Agliotti wasn't involved.

#Kebble. The worlds shortest cross examination. Kappie done and dusted. He looks proper relieved.

'IT WAS A HELL OF A EXPERIENCE. SOMETHING I'VE NEVER BEEN through in my life. It wasn't easy to cope with it. We were very nervous.' Kappie, a reformed gangster with a notorious reputation, was terrified of the witness box. 'Ja, in all my life I'd never done that. I'd rather go to jail. I never do that. I've been tortured all my life, my teeth has been pulled out of my mouth, I've been shocked three days in a row to come speak the truth and I never did. I'd rather die or go to jail and that's how I am. A lot of people know that about me and that's why, you know, I didn't have much to say.'

As Mikey, Nigel and Kappie reminisce with me about their experiences testifying in court, it is easy for them to find humour in the situation retrospectively, teasing Kappie about being the 'star witness'. Although at the time, things were not so funny.

'I never want to go through that experience again in my life. It was a rough ride, hey,' Nigel remarks. He had the most difficult encounter of them all. 'I must be honest, I don't wish that on anyone. It was hard. For us to go and talk about what we've done, we've got a code amongst us that we don't talk, but we got a deal which turned out to be a great deal. It was winning the Lotto, if you want to call it that. Oh no, it was the Powerball!'

Mikey feels much the same way about the experience of testifying. 'Horrible. I've never ... fuck it!' he exclaims.

In the run-up to their appearances in court, the trio were extremely concerned about the change in prosecuting team. They admit they didn't feel that they would be protected by Advocate Dan Dakana and his associates as state witnesses. 'When we were working with Gerrie and Piet Jonker and Andrew Leask and that you know, we felt like we had a team, we felt like we had backup. Then what happened was that they changed the prosecution and we started with this Dan Dakana and them. I'm not joking or being funny or anything but my five-year-old little boy is more fucking bright than that. It's like talking to a wall,' Mikey says flippantly.

A major scoring point for Laurance Hodes was how witnesses disclosed information in court that had not been included in written statements. In most instances, the new details had emerged during consultations with the prosecuting team in the days prior to their testimony in court. Hodes was firm on this – if they were going to talk about it in court, it had to be included in an affidavit.

'A lot of things came out in consultation and I could have put Glenn in a lot worse light but Gerrie and them were there for us, these other guys didn't give a fuck about us,' says Mikey. 'I said to Nigel that morning I was going into the box, I said, "You know what Nige, I'm sticking to my statement" as I was advised and Ian also advised me. I said, "I'm sticking to my statement" and Nigel turned around and said to me, "Well why you want to do that now?" I said, "Listen boet, I'm not willing to take the rap and put my 204 on the line here for them." I said they don't give a fuck about us. At the end of the day it's better for them, so I'm sticking to my statement and that's why I stuck to my statement fucking word for word. And Nigel unfortunately, it's in his make-up that he was going to say what was happening and stuff like that.'

Mikey studied his affidavit for weeks prior to the trial, with his friend former policeman John Kruger helping him. 'I knew that I had to stick to my statement but I fucking didn't want to even. It's not that I was lying, but I didn't want to even get put in a corner once by Hodes,' he says, unsurprisingly invoking a boxing analogy.

Nigel acknowledges he let his emotions get the better of him to an extent. 'Mikey said, stick to your statement. Giving a truthful and frank statement was exactly what I did. I didn't like Glenn, it was the truth that I told. They never came to me and said to me "say it like this" or "say it like that". It came up in consultation and Mr Hodes did a great job. He had to do what he had to do and I understand that, but it was my truthful and frankful version of exactly what happened and I got the hard end of the stick there for sure,' says Nigel, getting slightly worked up again as he relives the experience. 'It was hard because I had to be discredited, be called a liar, you know, and it angered me. I wanted to jump out of that box, hey, and seeing Glenn look at me as if I ... he knows damn well what we were talking about,' Nigel adds, emphasising his point by tapping on the table.

All three of them were worried that Nigel had gone too far and had compromised his indemnity deal. 'We were very worried about the outcome,' admits Kappie. 'We were and we were more worried about Nigel. We knew we would get mine and Mikey's, but Nigel was the one we were really worried about.'

THE SHOOTERS HAVE DONE LITTLE TO IMPLICATE GLENN AGLIOTTI. Only Nigel's evidence, that Agliotti had told him at The Grand that he had paid the money for the murder to Clint Nassif, could count against 'the accused'. The idea for the prosecution is to create the impression of a criminal 'hierarchy' – the shooters implicate Nassif, who in turn implicates Agliotti and Stratton. That is the idea. It's now up to Nassif to do his part and implicate Agliotti.

But first, there are fireworks. Restaurateur Alexis Christopher takes the stand and Hodes goes to town with him on his version of what happened at the Hyde Park parking lot meeting between Nassif and Agliotti's ex-wife, Vivian.

#Kebble Hodes is gunning for Christopher now. Why didn't he include details in his statements.

#Kebble Christopher: On meeting between Agliotti's wife and Nassif – 'She was howling and I was like "what is going on here"'.

#Kebble: Court in hysterics. Hodes: Nassif stepped out from behind a pillar for clandestine meeting. Agliotti's wife was in tears.

#Kebble Judge has to step in and tell Christopher to calm down. He's bouncing around the witness stand. Hodes on form.

#Kebble Journo in public gallery: This is like watching seals being clubbed. Its kak.

#Kebble Hodes to Christopher: You tried to be a big shot deal broker. Judge: Jy is 'n twee gat jakkals.

Christopher flees from the witness stand. He too has done little to implicate Agliotti and his testimony appears to be littered with lies and contradictions.

As a brief reprieve from the tedium of court testimony, everyone becomes distracted by the story of a 145 kg pet tiger that has gone walkabout. Panjo, a seventeen-month-old Bengal tiger, somehow escaped from his owner Goosey Fernandes's bakkie and is roaming between Groblersdal and Delmas. From the bizarre to the sublime. Thankfully Panjo is tracked down, largely due to the assistance of some Woolworths chicken, a celebrity animal tracker and a team of sniffer dogs. Panjo's escape provides fodder for courtroom humour.

> EmpathicWarrior Anyone else get the feeling that panjo got this much attention cos no one involved in the kebble murder is going to jail.what a farce!

> #Kebble Bwahahaha. Hodes: Glenn's lucky he was in court. He had an alibi for stealing #Panjo.

With Agliotti and his legal team confidently in the driving seat, it's the turn of Clinton Nassif, the state's 'star witness'. I can't help but feel they should have led his evidence first if they had any hope of constructing the impression of a hierarchy and implicating Agliotti. He takes his seat in the witness box, clutching a bottle of water. His muscular frame fills every inch of his dark suit, stretching his jacket at the seams.

> #Kebble King Rat himself is here today. Clinton Nassif in the consulting room outside

> #Kebble Nassif very nervous and jumpy. Prosecutor asks him to speak up. Going through how he knows Agliotti.

The petite Kholeka Gcaleka leads him through his evidence as he details his relationship with Agliotti, the shooting of Stephen Mildenhall and Brett Kebble's murder.

> #Kebble Nassif: Glenn and I decided we weren't killing anyone. We spun them stories and ran them around.

> #Kebble Nassif: Brett pleaded. He was at the end of his wits with JCI trouble. Said he'll either end up in prison or a mental institution.

#Kebble Nassif: Brett was a desperate man. We thought John Stratton would arrange the finances.

The weakness of the prosecution and a lack of proper consultation begins to show – Nassif doesn't even wait for cross-examination before torpedoing the state's case. He explains away the one piece of evidence from Nigel McGurk the prosecution could use. He tells the court that he instructed Agliotti to tell the shooters he had paid the money for Brett Kebble's murder because he didn't think Agliotti could handle Mikey, Nigel and Kappie. This absolves Agliotti of involvement.

#Kebble Nassif: I told Glenn to tell Mikey and Nigel that he had paid me. I wanted to protect Glenn from them.

#Kebble Nassif is single handedly destroying the states case here. He basically says Agliotti never paid for the murder. Booooom.

#Kebble Nassif: I could handle those guys (Mikey and Nigel and Kappie) Glenn couldn't. Thats why I told him to say he paid me.

#Kebble Nassif: I've been humbled by the past five years. I apologize to Kebble family and to Mildenhall. If I could change it I would.

#Kebble Lunchbreak. Hodes and Agliotti have massive smiles on their faces. This could not have gone better for them.

Hodes begins his aggressive cross-examination that will last five gruelling days. Early on, Nassif drops a bombshell, suggesting Roger Kebble knew about his son's assisted suicide plot before it was carried out.

#Kebble Shocked about Nassif's claim that Roger knew about the assisted suicide before. Family always said 'why didn't Glenn tell us'.

After court I phone Roger and he is incensed. I record a four-minute rant during which he colourfully lambastes the incompetence of the prosecuting team and angrily denies Nassif's claim.

#Kebble Roger Kebble is furious about Nassifs claim that he knew about the assisted suicide plot. Listen on @Radio702 and @CapeTalk 567.

#Kebble He's also slammed the new prosecution calling it 'a bloody shambles'. He says Hodes is having 'a ball' because theres no opposition.

The following morning, Hodes continues his offensive while Mikey Schultz and his friend ex-policeman John Kruger watch from the public gallery. Nassif is obliterated as Hodes destroys his evidence, forcing him into contradictions.

#Kebble Classic awkward moment. Mikey asks Agliotti for his copy of The Times so he can read the headline 'King Rat Trapped'.

#Kebble Woah! First five minutes and Nassif slams the box in anger. 'I'm not a liar. Your accused is a liar. I've taken responsibility'.

#Kebble Hodes to Nassif: You do not qualify for a 204 by any stretch of the imagination. Nassif: Why not?

#Kebble Hodes to Nassif: We're going to collect your lies as we go along. Nassif speaking about insurance fraud.

#Kebble Hodes: You sunk other people instead of taking responsibility. Nassif: Absolute rubbish.

The situation escalates and the tension in the room is tangible. Nassif squirms as he tries to evade Hodes's line of questioning. Nassif refuses to answer questions and instead replies 'no comment' or his memory conveniently fails him.

#Kebble Hodes: Mr Nassif you are a dishonest, evasive witness.

#Kebble Nassif: I'm prepared to be here for weeks. Hodes: Wonderful. Ignore my questions for weeks and a credibility finding will be made.

#Kebble Nassif: I've taken blame for what I've done. That's why I'm here. Hodes: No you haven't. You're trying to worm your way out.

#Kebble Nassif losing it now. "I'm not worming my way out. Are you crazy?".

#Kebble Judge is very good. Wants Nassif to calm down 'in the interests of justice'. "If you're going to burst, tell me".

#Kebble Hodes: The state's case stands or falls by your testimony.

#Kebble Hodes to Nassif: You have absolute contempt for this court. You don't want to be here.

#Kebble Journo in public gallery: Feel like I'm watching a dog been hit by a freight train. Just want someone to come shoot it.

Nassif's jaw begins to jut out and his body language tells a story. He slouches back in the box, his arms folded, as he shrugs off Hodes's questions.

Another bombshell. It emerges that before the trial started, Nassif's lawyer approached Glenn Agliotti's attorney in this very courtroom, in an attempt to convince Agliotti to plead guilty to the charges against him. Nassif wanted them to enter into a plea-bargain arrangement – he and Agliotti would plead guilty in exchange for suspended sentences. His attorney Tamo Vink even wrote a letter to 'Uncle John' Stratton in Australia in an attempt to cut a deal. Hodes produces the letter, to the dismay of the witness.

#Kebble This revelation is bad bad news for Nassif. He was very naughty.

#Kebble Nassif offered Agliotti a deal for both of them to plead guilty so that he could 'help Glenn'.

#Kebble Nassif's lawyers also went to Australia to try and offer John Stratton a deal. Without any knowledge or consent of the prosecutors.

#Kebble Hodes provides emails from Stratton's lawyers confirming the approach and Nassif brokering a deal with NPA.

#Kebble Nassif: I was ready to plead guilty. I considered it.

#Kebble Hodes: This is becoming farcical. Nassif: Look I don't know whats going on here.

Prosecutor Gcaleka attempts to regain some ground but fails dismally.

#Kebble Re-examination. Very difficult to follow. All over the place.

#Kebble Prosecutor wants more questions about Tamo Vink incident. Judge warns her she's opening can of worms for herself.

Mikey's friend, John Kruger, tweets me from the row behind.

jongotti13 @MandyWiener as if nassif's hole he dug isn't big enough, the prosecutor is now helping him dig it deeper!

OVER THE NEXT FEW DAYS, HODES BRINGS AN APPLICATION to approach Menzi Simelane, the National Director of Public Prosecutions, to get the charges thrown out. He tells Kgomo 'the wrong man is standing in the wrong box'. Kgomo dismisses the application, saying the state may still have an ace up its sleeve. We wait and see.

In an attempt to introduce cellphone records as evidence, the state calls three separate experts from cellular companies. Vodacom's Petro Heyneke, Nashua Mobile's Charl Naude and MTN's Hilda du Plessis. Hodes destroys the evidence of all three.

> #Kebble Hodes says can't trust the analysis if people were using 'throw away' phones or pay as you go's.

> #Kebble Judge: You would supply the records of the President of RSA if requested. Heyneke: Yes, if we received a directive.

> #Kebble MTN lady says I can't legally access my own cellphone records. Has to be done through Access to Info Act. Somethings not right.

> #Kebble Judge is flabbergasted that he can't access his own phone records. He wants proof.

> #Kebble State is implying that Hodes manipulated the disk with his cellphone records from MTN. This is very messy.

> #Kebble Hodes: You willy nilly hand out information and then justify it later. Hilda: Only in high profile cases.

> #Kebble Oy Hilda. Its been a long day in your grey suit, under that perm. Almost there.

> #Kebble Hodes establishes that Nashua guy used to be a cop in the same unit as Investigating Officer PW van Heerden.

> #Kebble Nashua man wasn't properly subpoenaed by his mate and he doesnt have proof to back up his evidence.

#Kebble Hodes: You were doing a buddy a favour. You were rushing. There are three different dates in your statement.

And then a massive victory for Agliotti.

Judge Frans Kgomo hears legal argument about the admissibility of his 2006 bail application affidavit. This is the statement in which Agliotti implicates himself in Brett's 'assisted suicide', saying 'when I became involved'. Kgomo rules it cannot be admitted as evidence because Agliotti was not properly warned by the magistrate.

#Kebble The great irony is that the one thing that could sink Agliotti is his own statement.

#Kebble Kgomo: In my view whether the accused is represented by an experienced advocate or not, the court still has a duty to warn him.

#Kebble Judge refuses states application. This means Agliotti's crucial 2006 affidavit can't be used against him.

#Kebble This is a big victory for Agliotti. This statement is probably the strongest piece of evidence against him.

Their case obliterated, the state asks for a postponement. They want to call Roger Kebble as a witness but he is allegedly due to undergo knee surgery and can't travel for eight weeks. In a mad scramble, the state produces a doctor's letter but it all looks suspiciously like a cover-up. There are holes in their story. The judge suggests travelling to Cape Town to hear Roger's testimony and Hodes offers to compromise. It's clear from early on that Roger Kebble will do whatever is necessary to stay out of the witness stand. Perhaps he has too many skeletons in the closet to keep hidden? There is also the four-minute ranting interview he did with me during Nassif's testimony. He will have to explain his comments about the prosecuting team when Hodes no doubt plays it in court.

#Kebble State: We can't close our case without calling Roger and he cant travel for eight weeks after knee surgery.

#Kebble Judge: Won't we be closing the stable door while the horse is already running in the meadows.

#Kebble ooh the doctors letter says Roger's surgery will be in Joburg. So why can't he testify while he's in Jozi?

#Kebble Roger is in Johannesburg and the operation will be in Johannesburg. He can't climb stairs and struggles to 'get oxygen'

#Kebble Roger Kebble's got an advocate to fight the state.

#Kebble State: Roger wants to testify. He's not ducking and diving. But he's not well.

#Kebble Wow. Judge says he's seen Roger Kebble on TV complaining about delays in the trial. But he doesn't know if it's the same Roger Kebble

Remarkably, the judge grants an eight-week postponement to allow Roger Kebble to recover from his impending knee surgery. During the trial Agliotti has discovered Twitter. He posts a message about the decision.

GlennAgliotti Justice delayed is justice denied. Going to enjoy a good glass of wine.

During the eight-week hiatus, Agliotti enjoys many glasses of wine and posts many more tweets. In October, when the trial resumes, it's evident for all to see that 'Roger the Dodger' will not be making an appearance. The knee operation never happened, but he has apparently discovered he has a heart problem.

#Kebble Adv Lethabo Mashiane handing in a letter from a cardiologist explaining Roger Kebble's condition.

#Kebble According to the doctor Roger Kebble will need a 'couple of months' to recover. State is at a 'cul de sac'. Wants postponement!

#Kebble Clever judge: At RK's age there will be one condition after another which will ensure he never testifies in this court.

#Kebble Judge: My view is that we are dealing with peripheral witness. What justice will be served if delay to satisfy his anger.

#Kebble Judge rules No Postponement. No further postponements because of Roger Kebble. State must lead other witnesses and then Roger.

The state has just one witness left to call: Investigating Officer PW van Heerden. Andrew Leask watches from the public gallery as Van Heerden lays the blame for the shoddy case against Agliotti firmly with the previous prosecuting and investigating team. Gerrie Nel, Andrea Johnson and the other investigators follow my tweets from their Silverton office, their blood boiling at Van Heerden's claims. He alleges Nel's team never cared about the Brett Kebble murder trial because they were solely focused on the prosecution of Jackie Selebi.

#Kebble Investigating officer PW van Heerden next up. Crew cut, moustache and all.

#Kebble PW: I was sidelined by the Scorpions on this case.

#Kebble I didn't have access to the boardroom. Had to conduct meetings in passage. Statements were kept from me.

#Kebble PW: The DSO milked me for info on Selebi's conduct during Kebble murder investigation.

#Kebble PW says statement of Paul Stemmet (Selebi whistleblower) was removed from docket and not given to defence.

He voices the opinions of many members of the SAPS and the public regarding the granting of indemnities to Mikey, Nigel and Kappie.

#Kebble PW: Selebi and other senior cops were very upset that the

shooters were granted indemnity from prosecution.

#Kebble PW: Granting the actual shooter, puller of trigger indemnity, does not sit well with any old police officer nor the public.

Van Heerden had spent weeks carefully preparing spidergrams and plotting graphs of cellphone records. Hodes anticipated he would be on the stand for at least a week as he constructed a picture of the whereabouts of all the characters based on their cellphone usage. Hodes opposes the introduction of these records and, astonishingly, Van Heerden capitulates without a fight.

The investigating officer then makes another incredible claim as he explains why the state fought so hard to call Roger Kebble as a witness.

#Kebble Well this is remarkable. PW says they wanted to call Roger Kebble to dispell suggestion he had a motive to kill his son!

#Kebble Hodes shocked by 'startling revelation'. PW can't remember which witness made the claim that Roger had a motive.

Journalists in the media pack are baffled. None of us recalls any witness during the trial suggesting Roger Kebble had a motive to have his son killed. But we've come to expect the unexpected in this trial. The state has failed dismally. They are all out of witnesses and there's very little on record implicating Agliotti. They have failed to produce the figurative ace up their sleeves. So Hodes does what we expect him to. He brings an application in terms of section 174 of the Criminal Procedure Act so that Agliotti does not need to launch a defence.

#Kebble State Closes Case. Agliotti is going to ask for the charges to be thrown out! No surprise there.

I gauge public opinion and sentiment is with Agliotti:

DoronBlock@MandyWiener He should get the S 174 discharge

Craigep: @GlennAgliotti aint guilty from what I have read and heard. What about indemnity for the 3? off? *I reckon

evanssethokga@MandyWiener @GlennAgliotti is not guilty. The state sucked in this case. Big time.

THE JUDGE SENDS BOTH LEGAL TEAMS off for a week to go and prepare 'heads of argument', a written summary of the points of their argument for and against a discharge application.

When they return to the courtroom, Hodes admits that uncharacteristically he hasn't handed in his 'heads' but explains this is due to his client's financial constraints. In other words, Agliotti has not paid his lawyers and they had refused to hand over the documents until he handed over the cash. For the duration of that week, Agliotti had strung his lawyers along, promising them tens of thousands of rand and the money was simply not forthcoming. Robert Kanarek stood his ground and refused to release the 'heads'. Agliotti was doing to his lawyers exactly what he had done to Mikey, Nigel and Kappie – he was trying to knock them. Agliotti is under immense pressure from the taxman – SARS has recently auctioned off the contents of his house for a little over R33 000 as the revenue service attempts to recoup R78 million he owes them in outstanding taxes. Agliotti eventually pools together enough money and the heads of argument are handed in. Oral arguments are heard.

#Kebble We're underway. Hodes arguing for a discharge. Microphones and cameras allowed in. Get to hear the drama yourselves!

Hodes focuses on the conduct of the prosecution and the manner in which Agliotti was treated. He complains about evidence not being handed over to the defence, particularly Paul Stemmet's affidavit.

#Kebble Hodes slamming state for not leading IO PW van Heerden on cellphone records as promised. States' biggest capitulation.

#Kebble Hodes clever about relying heavily on constitution. Judge Kgomo has always shown strong commitment to constitution.

#Kebble Hodes: State ought to have come to court with clean hands my lord.

#Kebble Hodes: They will do anything to incriminate the accused, anything to point a finger at him. Thats what they're not supposed to do.

He then directs his attack at Clinton Nassif and the failure of the shooters to implicate Agliotti.

#Kebble Hodes: Even a five-year-old child could see the similarities in affidavids of McGurk and Smith. Its cut and paste.

#Kebble Hodes: If they want to rely on Nassif, they've shot themselves in the foot because he removes accused from conspiracy.

#Kebble Hodes: We thought they had an ace up their sleeve. If it was Mr Nassif, then it wasn't an ace. It was a joker! Wow

#Kebble Hodes: Nassif was annihilated, obliterated, smashed to pieces. Judge: He was pulverized. Laughs. Shoowee! Judge agrees.

The judge is clearly with the defence as he agrees the state's main witness was 'pulverized'. After a day and a half on his feet, Hodes sits down and prosecutor Dan Dakana starts his argument.

#Kebble Prosecutor Dan Dakana says 'Brevity is the soul of wit'. Lets hope so.

#Kebble Judge peppering Dakana with questions and he's floundering. Hodes was hardly asked any questions.

#Kebble Judge getting annoyed with Dakana. Wants page references and proof. Like watching car crash in slow motion.

#Kebble aah so embarassing. Dakana makes completely the wrong submission. Realizes its wrong. And then closes argument. Oy vey.

#Kebble Hodes is flipping out.

#Kebble Judge: Tame your language Mr Hodes. I will decide who is lying. Hodes: I will tame my language and my temper my lord.

Dakana wraps up in less than an hour and we in the media pack cringe at the inadequacy of his argument. A discharge should be a walk in the park for Agliotti.

JUDGMENT DAY. GLENN AGLIOTTI IS STANDING WITH HIS LEG UP ON one of the wooden benches in the full public gallery schmoozing reporters as technicians run around the courtroom laying cables and connecting microphones. Agliotti calls it 'being friendly'. The judgment will be broadcast live on television. Photographers have also been allowed into the room and they're snapping away as I attempt to duck out of shot. Robert Kanarek jokes with Kholeka Gcaleka, cajoling her into looking depressed for the cameras. She laughs and shakes her head. Agliotti has chosen a charcoal tie for today. I ask him why he isn't wearing a 'power tie, like Jacob Zuma always did on big court days'. The President and his bodyguards would always wear bold red ties on days when important decisions were being handed down. Agliotti responds that he's wearing a charcoal tie because 'you can't be too cocky'. My phone vibrates across the bench. It's Mikey wanting to know what's going on and has the judge started yet? His messages continue to stream through all day.

Judge Frans Kgomo strides in and takes his seat. Oblivious to the TV cameras, he starts his judgment with a preamble:

For the first time, I watched the TV in connection with this matter. Normally, I refrain from watching news and TV so that I should not be influenced. I realised and heard about me taking about an hour or so to deliver this judgment. I don't know how long it is going to take. It would depend on the circumstances.

As soon as Kgomo makes that statement, I know which way the judgment is going. He would never have watched the news about this matter if he knew that he would continue to preside over the case. He's going to grant the discharge application. The rule of thumb is also that if the judgment is long, it's usually going to be granted as he has to provide justification. The ruling is long and takes up much of the day. Kgomo makes it clear from the outset that he is aware of the gravitas of the case and the implications of his decision:

At a glance, or in the eye of the uninitiated, one may be excused of thinking or saying that this is a run of the mill case of murder and conspiracy to commit any other offence. This is not so, in my view, in this case. This case is about hidden and/or sinister agendas perpetrated by shady characters as well as ostensibly crooked and/or greedy businesspersons. It is about corrupt civil servants as well as prominent politicians or politically connected people wining and dining with devils incarnate under cover of darkness.

Kgomo has realised that what he has encountered is the South African Mafia at play in his courtroom. He invokes the analogy of Mario Puzo's trilogy, *The Godfather*, relating each of the players in Brett Kebble's world to those in the books and the movies:

I revisited the book after listening to the evidence that was led so far in this matter because it is my view that some of the trickery and shenanigans that were practiced by the Cosa Nostra, that is the mafia in the Sicilian parlance as demonstrated in that book, was also practiced in this particular family of the Kebbles. For example, what was happening within the Corleone family was not very unlike what was happening within the empire presided over by Brett Kebble. The evidence sketched out by Clinton Nassif about this empire was based on skimming money from the JCI Group of companies, RandGold as well as others like Western Areas mines and then buying patronage with it from the high ranking police officials, prospective directors of public prosecution, politicians at the highest levels and all or any person in the position of authority from whom a favour may or could be obtained.

Kgomo advances the comparison between the Corleone and Kebble empires. According to him, The Don or 'godfather' was Brett Kebble.

The Consigliore, described as the counsellor, the right-hand man, his closest companion, his auxiliary brain, was John Stratton. He quotes from *The Godfather*: 'The Consigliore was one man in the world who could bring The Don crashing down to destruction but no Consigliore had ever betrayed a Don, not in the memory of any of the powerful Sicilian families who had established themselves in America. There was no future in it and every Consigliore knew that if he kept the faith, he would become rich, wield power and win respect.'

Kgomo explains that between The Don, who dictated policy, and the operational levels on the ground, there are three layers of command or buffers so that nothing can be traced back to The Don. Under the Consigliore is the Capo Regime, a divisional head who controls a specific territory and enforces obedience and discipline within that territory. A Capo Regime is in charge of soldiers who execute The Don's orders and in Mafia terms they are referred to as 'button men'. The term originated from the fact that once an order is issued to them to push the button, meaning to shoot to kill, they have to push the button without asking any questions.

Kgomo decides that the Capo Regime in Kebble's empire was Glenn Agliotti and the lower Capo Regime was Clinton Nassif. The button men were Mikey Schultz, Nigel McGurk and Fiazal 'Kappie' Smith, and the soldiers were the other employees in the security groups as well as any other person who could be enlisted for a fee to work and execute a plan.

#Kebble I think the judge is quite taken by the mafia idea. Now using mafia references to detail evidence.

#Kebble This judge is hysterical. Comparing Kebble family trickery and shenanigans to The Godfather's Corleone family.

#Kebble Agliotti must be lapping this up! Kgomo giving full review of The Godfather.

While Agliotti might be loving the Mafia analogy, I suspect he may be put out that Kgomo has not referred to him as The Don and has placed him lower in the Kebble hierarchy. When Agliotti signs off tweets, he often calls himself 'Don' or 'Capo Di Tutti Capi', which translates into 'boss of bosses' and is used in Mafia circles to refer to a supremely powerful crime boss. He also signs off tweets with 'Grazie' and 'Ciao', feeding into his perception as an Italian gangster. He insists he only uses those words because he really is Italian.

Kgomo's analogy reminds me just how surreal this entire scenario is. My colleague at eTV, Karyn Maughan, tweets me.

karynmaughan: @MandyWiener is this really happening? Or did I eat a Hillbrow cookie?

I get another tweet from 'Bad Brad' Wood, a former reality TV star who moves in the same circles as many of the characters featuring in the trial.

BadBradza @MandyWiener mandy is he going to walk?

The NPA had announced that morning it would be charging Wood with four counts of murder after he allegedly shot illegal miners underground at the Aurora Grootvlei mine in Springs where he is the security manager. He had foolishly gone on Talk Radio 702 admitting his involvement. I responded to his tweet, cheekily seeing the irony in the situation.

MandyWiener @BadBradza Brad, at this rate there's more chance ur going to jail :)

Kgomo sums up the evidence before him. He is extremely critical of Nassif.

#Kebble Nassif is in trouble. Kgomo going through some of his contradictions. Re payment, sushi knife meeting, instructions.

#Kebble Kgomo: When Nassif was caught out, which was 80% of the time, he would say 'no comment'.

#Kebble Kgomo: Nassif obviously tried everything in the book to avoid testifying in this court or in any trial.

#Kebble Kgomo: Nassif was proven to be an untruthful witness who changed his version without batting an eyelid.

He then zeroes in on the prosecution's conduct. Kgomo is astute and acknowledges far more was at play behind the scenes than he ever knew about:

As the trial unfolded, especially from the evidence of the 13th and last State witness, the current investigator Colonel Van Heerden, it became clear that some power play or absence or lack of common unanimity of purpose was the order of the day, within the Directorate of Special Operations or the DSO amongst themselves, the DSO and the South

African Police proper, as well as the DSO operatives and the Directorate of Public Prosecutions on the other hand.

He questions why John Stratton, the common denominator, was never extradited to stand trial alongside Agliotti.

#Kebble Kgomo: Why the accused was not prosecuted with Stratton may have been one of the biggest injustices to come out of this trial.

#Kebble Judge hits nail on head. Where is Stratton? He was the 'common denominator'. Agliotti would have had 'uphill battle'.

#Kebble Kgomo: It is clear the DSO wanted Agliotti so badly it didn't matter what they did to get him here.

#Kebble Kgomo: At the end of the day there was no credible evidence left on record on which a court could convict.

Kgomo reaches the tail end of his judgment. We all know exactly what is going to happen, but the suspense is intense nonetheless. Kgomo reads on:

Coming to Mr Michael Schultz, he was the person who pulled the trigger. In actual fact, he was supposed to have been sitting in that dock as an accused person but somehow, for reasons unknown to this Court, he was promised and offered a section 204 indemnity. As I have indicated, this prosecution team was not involved in that decision, it was the previous team. However, as it may, he was forthright in his testimony about what actually happened. He received his instructions exclusively from Nassif and he delegated and disseminated those instructions to his fellow travellers in crime. My considered view is that he testified truthfully about all the unfortunate and bloodcurdling acts that he committed.

Nigel is also granted indemnity, although 'he was a difficult witness' for Kgomo:

He displayed an above average hatred for the accused. I could see his face darken and contort with scorn and hate or rage at the mention of the accused's name. He contradicted himself during cross-examination and, after careful assessment, I have come to the conclusion that those contradictions were not per se as a result of being untruthful, he was so blinded by hatred of the accused that whenever the latter's name was mentioned, he would puff up and start retorting things that ultimately contradicted what he had said before that stage. However, looking at the totality of the evidence, I am satisfied that regardless, he also corroborated his partners in crime. He knew nothing else other than the instruction that he received from Schultz to go and execute this dastardly deed.

Kgomo seems to have had far less trouble granting Kappie his 204:

He testified in a flowing and convincing manner, indicative of a person who was there when the crimes were committed. His evidence dovetailed and was similar to that of Schultz. He also should have been an accused person because he was kop in een mus with all the people who were doing all these funny things. He was, however, honest and truthful about his part in the dastardly deeds.

Kgomo has ruled that all three testified truthfully and honestly. They are free.

Clinton Nassif is not so lucky:

He was evasive, slippery and unconvincing about what he wanted to tell this Court. He was present during the planning of all this that happened. I distinctly formed an impression that he was not telling this Court the whole truth. He contradicted himself and also contradicted his bedfellows. He was a woeful witness who acted with emotions when expected to answer simple questions. Why he was never discredited by the prosecution, I do not know.

Nassif's indemnity is denied. This means he could be charged for Brett Kebble's murder.

Agliotti breathes deeply. We all do.

Having listened to all the evidence led through all the 13 State witnesses herein and having carefully considered the law and the facts, it is my considered view and finding that the accused herein should not remain an accused in the dock longer than this moment, as the State has not led evidence upon which the Court, acting carefully, can convict him on any of the charges he is facing in this court. If he is called upon to testify that would be unconstitutional and unfair. It is my further finding that the State has not made out a prima facie *case against the accused at the end of its case. The manner in which the prosecution was conducted, from the time it was handled by the prosecution team that was replaced by this present team, violated, in my view, the rights of the accused to a fair trial.*

Agliotti is told to stand. He is acquitted. Bedlam.

#Kebble Agliotti wins! He's free. No longer 'Brett Kebble murder accused'.

#Kebble Agliotti hugs AND KISSES Hodes. Scrum of photographers around them.

#Kebble Chatted to Mikey Schultz – he's over the moon.

#Kebble Also spoke to Guy Kebble. He's furious - says its 'indictment on justice system and country'.

Mikey

We hit the jackpot. We won the lottery, hey. If you told me take this deal or hit the lottery I'd rather take this deal because you can never put a price on anyone's freedom hey, and I don't do well locked up at all. It's bigger than winning the Lotto. I'd rather have this than win the European Lotto because this has just given us a new lease on life and there's no passing on life now.

M IKEY SCHULTZ WAS IN CHURCH WHEN HE HEARD HE HAD effectively got away with murder.

On the morning of 25 November 2010, Mikey, Nigel and Kappie met for breakfast at the Food Lovers Market in Stone Ridge shopping centre in Eastern Johannesburg. Together, over the past five years, they had shared a unique life experience and the day would be acutely important in determining their freedom and their future. They had asked the restaurant manager to turn the TV onto the live feed of Judge Frans Kgomo delivering his judgment and over breakfast they watched and listened.

After eating, Nigel went to work, Kappie went home and Mikey went to a funeral. Boxing publicist and writer Terry Pettifer had died a few days earlier from a heart condition and was being buried.

Nigel was too nervous to watch or listen. 'I could see by some of the stuff on TV that I was going to get a rough ride here and I was nervous about it. I just didn't want to listen. I knew in my head that I'd just told the truth and that it will come out alright, but if worst comes to worst and I didn't get my 204 what was going to happen then? I knew my friends weren't going to testify against me and all the evidence that I did give was all truthful and frank, so good luck to them finding new evidence. I knew in my heart, but I didn't want to put myself through the torture of watching it on TV.'

Kappie watched Kgomo grant him indemnity at home with his son. 'I had tears in my eyes. I was sitting with my son and I had tears in my eyes. I was so happy and relieved. It's unexplainable, because in this world it doesn't happen. Whatever you admit, you go to jail for today, and we got a chance in hell, hey! God, I'm grateful.'

Mikey's phone beeped as he sat in a pew of the Baptist church in Glenvista, telling him his 204 had been granted. 'I was sitting in the funeral and then when I got the message, it was the wrong thing because I was so happy and so full of joy and a colleague of ours from the boxing world was busy getting buried. His funeral wasn't lekker. When I walked out of there, that evening and the next day the realisation of actually getting this off our shoulders made me realise how much pressure we were actually in because you don't actually realise when you in it. You just take it in your stride and you take it day by day and then when we got the verdict that we were set free, that we had got off, it was like the world had been lifted off our shoulders.'

Mikey and Kappie both phoned Nigel – Big Ears had got his 204 as well and all three of them could relax. 'I battled to get my head around it. To have killed someone and been involved with an attempted murder with someone else, I battle to get my head around it. It's … to come clean like this, it's unheard of. I don't think it's happened before ever.' Nigel was a relieved man.

Their celebrations were surprisingly muted. There was no wild drunken night out. No raucous party as one might expect of these men. That Saturday night, the trio took their wives for an understated dinner before going past the nightclub Taboo for an hour. 'We just sat there, the three of us, to say sorry for putting my family through a hell of a thing. There was a lot of people out there who supported us that we have to thank,' Kappie tells me.

The trio had survived, to live on for another day. 'When we went to celebrate it was the three of us. It's always been the three of us, it will always be the three of us,' Mikey says, as his two 'brothers' nod in agreement.

ТHE MORNING AFTER THE DAY BEFORE.

I am horribly sleep-deprived and at my desk in the Eyewitness News newsroom by 04:30. I still have what my colleagues refer to as 'my big story booties' on. Figuratively speaking, of course. It has been a roller-coaster ride since Glenn Agliotti was acquitted – a haze of radio reports, interviews, analysis, tweets, messages and phone calls. All of this is compounded by the fact that it also happens to be my birthday.

Through the course of Agliotti's trial I have discovered what an effective gauge of public opinion Twitter can be, and it provides me with a fairly good indication of the country's impressions of the acquittal:

paulvecchiatto1 @MandyWiener I think it shows that institutionalized incompetence plays into the hands of criminals

PyperK @MandyWiener this result wasn't very LeadSA. I have no more faith in our justice system. Money buys freedom. Am so pissed off.

angelo2711 @mandywiener have a good 1, despite the travesty & miscarriage of justice.

ovayoavu @BonganiMshibe @MandyWiener #Kebble The issue here was not Agliotti-it was Selebi of which he's bin delt with. Eish-wh r w going as a country?

tshepo87 @MandyWiener A deaf person would have told you @ GlennAgliotti was innocent

BwanaChris @MandyWiener question for our teflon don - can he look into the eyes of the Kebble widow and children without shame ? #Agliotti

kwansen1 @MandyWiener this trial reminds me of the "usual suspects", Glen Agglioti really played the NPA

karens2000 @MandyWiener he with the biggest cheque book always wins

SoopaJuice_46 @MandyWiener Wow, I don't know how to react or what to say. The real killers got off. What a joke.

comradesipho Jesus take the wheel. RT @MandyWiener: #Kebble Agliotti wins! He's free. No longer 'Brett Kebble murder accused'.

PyperK @MandyWiener the Law is an ass.

jskapanga @MandyWiener it was like watching a movie, a funny one what a waste of our time, he made our justice system look like fufus [fools]

A court of law has found Glenn Agliotti innocent, but in the court of public opinion the view appears to be somewhat different. There is also widespread condemnation of the National Prosecuting Authority and the decisions to grant indemnity to all and sundry. This has effectively meant that everyone has walked free and no one has stood much chance of being convicted. This view has been fuelled by Judge Frans Kgomo's ruling, criticising the 'power play' within the prosecuting authority.

Mid-morning I get an SMS from a member of the Bad Guys investigating team: 'Hi Mandy. The DSO was also on trial in S v Agliotti, but without representation. Regards.' I receive another, which I find equally profound: 'Justice was bludgeoned to a pulp by the state who is supposed to uphold and enforce it.' Emotions are running high and Guy Kebble is all over the radio and TV news calling Agliotti a 'bag of puss' amongst other things.

Just after 09:00 Agliotti and Robert Kanarek arrive at Primedia Place and are ushered into a boardroom. Agliotti has agreed to a live press conference and the media has been invited to attend. Already the cameras are in place and the photographers are on their haunches in preparation. I have a long chat to him in the 'holding room' about the hundreds of messages of congratulations he has received and how his family has been taking the news. Before long he takes his seat on the podium and looks smug. I am not surprised that he's oozing confidence. Today Agliotti is the hottest news ticket in town and we all know it.

At 10:00 Editor-in-Chief Katy Katopodis starts the briefing by quoting some of the reactions that have been circulating on Twitter and on air. 'Glenn, emotions have been running high since the judgment, people have been calling in, they've been tweeting saying … "It's a travesty of justice", you've been described as a "Mafioso", a "gangster", a "murderer", "Glenn has played the SA justice system like butter plays toast", "Five years of rubbish", "How does it feel to get away with murder?" … What is your response to that?'

Agliotti's reply is cool and measured. 'Simple. I didn't murder the man. The judge found me not guilty and that is what I have to say about that in a nutshell.' He stops there and then realises he finally has an opportunity to stick the boot in to his accusers. 'It's been a long road, a difficult time for my family. Everyone focuses on me but I think we have to focus on how this all originated and look at the beginning of it and I think when people actually take themselves back in time and see how this all started off I think it will answer a lot of people's questions. I've been called many things. I just listen and take it all in. You can never please everybody. People are going to have their own opinions. I was painted this by the so-called Scorpions, the DSO at the time. It suited them, it suited their case and what they wanted to achieve. That's how it came about.'

Katy wants to know if he has spoken to the Kebble family and if so, what he has had to say to them. Has he apologised? Agliotti is dismissive of the question.

'No, I haven't spoken to the Kebble family, and I have no reason to apologise to them.' Agliotti shifts his offensive onto Guy Kebble, making reference to the ex-rugby player's 'attempts' to speak to him during a court appearance earlier in the year while Jackie Selebi's trial was underway. 'Guy Kebble was on eTV news this morning and made a comment that he tried to approach me and I didn't want to talk to him. Well, he's got to be open and honest about it and not lie about how he approached me in the High Court. He sat behind me with his father's attorney Kim Warren and was very derogatory and swore and cursed and if that's the way you're going to approach me, to discuss anything with me, I will not stoop to his level and entertain his comments.'

Katy interjects and ambushes Agliotti with a sound bite – a pre-recorded question from Guy Kebble himself. Agliotti looks flabbergasted and even expresses his surprise at hearing Kebble's voice boom across the room. The sarcasm seeps through the speakers.

'Hello Glenn, Guy Kebble here. You're off the hook now it seems. I don't think you really feel that good about it but be that as it may. If you claimed to be as innocent as you are right through this process, why didn't you ever think of picking up the phone and calling Roger? You seemed to spend sufficient time hanging around his coat-tails etc. sucking on wine and eating his food so why didn't you just pick up the phone?'

Agliotti starts his reply diplomatically before upping the ante. 'Basically, we tried to contact Roger. My wife Lani did on a number of occasions. We bumped into one of his acquaintances Julie Adler at various places and it was clear they wanted nothing to do with me or discuss anything with me. I wasn't "hanging on Roger's coat-tails" as he puts it. It's very sad. He must ask himself how much he cost his father in botched business deals if he really wants to be honest.'

It's my turn. I have spent a considerable amount of time with Agliotti over the past few weeks and most of my questions have already received answers, but the one I ask seems appropriate considering the circumstances. I comment that Agliotti has become something of a celebrity as a result of this trial and ask him if it is appropriate that he's soaking up this new-found fame and using it to his benefit. It seems to me that he's riding the wave, parlaying it into a money-making device.

Agliotti shrugs his shoulders and responds easily although, I suspect, not entirely authentically. 'Mandy, I am who I am. I've always got on with people, I'm a people's person, I've always believed that I've got nothing to hide, therefore I won't try and dodge the press. It's been a long time, four years I've built up friendships through this court case with a few of the members of the press. I don't believe I'm a celebrity, I don't believe that it's any claim to fame. The people that put me in this position are the Scorpions and they must take all the accolades.'

One of the reasons I ask the question is because of the way Agliotti has taken to social media, in particular Twitter. I have to admit my role in converting him to the practice, having set up his account for him on his Blackberry during a slow court day and having given him a crash course on Twitter etiquette. However, I never suspected his use of the medium would become so intense. I have realised it is the perfect platform for him – it allows him to entrench the public perception of a gangster and a Mafioso. It also enables him to interact with random strangers, growing his network and impressing the public with mentions of other pseudo celebrities and visits to illustrious restaurants. For Agliotti it has always been about perception morphing into reality.

A combative Yusuf Abramjee stands up and addresses the elephant in the room. It is what most have been thinking but struggling to articulate quite so directly. 'You might not have pulled the trigger, you're a self-confessed murderer, part of a conspiracy, you're a convicted drug dealer, you're a corruptee, you corrupted the National Commissioner. Which in facts means you're a free criminal. You sit here with a straight face; how do you sleep at night? Can you explain to the South African public how you sleep at night, a free man, while other people who commit crime are behind bars?'

Agliotti seems only slightly put out by Yusuf's direct approach. 'I sleep very well. You know, I've had to endure, four, five years and the murderers got indemnity. So if that answers your question, I sleep very well at night. Thank you.' Question dismissed.

Only weeks later did Agliotti let on just how angry he was with that question. 'Ask that clown Abramjee where he comes with that "self-confessed murderer"! Put that in your book!' he told me.

Katy tees up Agliotti with a more inviting question and he unleashes half a decade's worth of stored-up wrath. He is deeply angry with the NPA about the way he has been handled.

'I've had to endure house arrest, I was treated like a child. There were times that if I wanted to go anywhere I would have to refer to my attorney Robert Kanarek and we'd have to write and request going to the doctor or going anywhere. It was a form of control, which was frustrating, annoying. I couldn't attend a lot of things I wanted to with my family. My daughter, her school, certain activities. It's been very trying and testing, on them more so than me.' He becomes increasingly angry as he hits his stride. 'They had a hidden agenda and that's why I keep saying to people, if you just go back, and everybody's knocking me and I'm the Mafia and the drug lord as Yusuf said and I don't sleep at night. Go back to the beginning. Ask the NPA and the Scorpions, how well do they sleep at night? They are all laying the blame at Menzi Simelane's doorstep. He was handed this hot potato, this case. You've got to go back and ask Pikoli, who convinced him to hand out the 204s, and who convinced him, as the judge yesterday said, not me, not me, the judge said yesterday, how did they arrest this man on this evidence? They should be held accountable.'

Agliotti restates his suspicion that he was the victim of a political conspiracy and echoes Jackie Selebi's sentiments. He is somewhat cryptic as he suggests there were far greater powers at play, referring to the so-called Zuma tapes. 'I said it from the word go. In my submissions to National Intelligence and to Commissioner Mphego at the time. I made it very, very clear that this was a political conspiracy because Mbeki wanted a third term. It was clear and evident with the Polokwane conference. The tapes that came out, where Ngcuka was speaking to Leonard McCarthy about arresting Zuma, and if that's not a political conspiracy then I don't know. And those tapes involve Selebi, Zuma and I'm sure myself because we never heard what the tapes consisted of.'

There is a theory that the prosecuting team only wanted Glenn Agliotti on side in order to secure the downfall of Selebi. Once they had succeeded in doing so, they 'let him go' and intentionally sabotaged the case against him. It was a 'reward' for his cooperation in testifying against the ex-Commissioner. 'No, what walk free?' he exclaims when Katy poses the hypothesis. 'I should never have been charged in the first place. The judge said so, not me. I'm not the judge. I should never have been charged.' He admits he is considering legal action against the NPA for his wrongful prosecution and reiterates that Nel and Leask must be 'held accountable'.

Now that he's a free man, who, in his opinion, should be prosecuted for Brett Kebble's murder? Agliotti doesn't take long to think about his response. 'I think by his own admission Clinton Nassif, who wanted to cut 105 plea-bargain deals just before we started this case, that should be evidence itself that he should be prosecuted and if they need me to testify I will do so.' Clearly, there is no love lost between those two former friends.

What about Stratton? If he had been present, would Agliotti have had an 'uphill battle to apply for a discharge, as the judge said in his ruling?' asks *Mail & Guardian* reporter Ilham Rawoot. 'I'm not sure. I'm not a legal eagle. I don't profess to know much about the law but they've never tried to extradite Stratton. The DSO lied to us by saying the application is in, they're bringing him back, but that was all just hogwash from the DSO.'

Agliotti is visibly seething as he tears into the DSO, using every possible opportunity to tarnish Gerrie Nel and Andrew Leask. I can't help but ask the next question to keep the momentum going as we reel in the quotes. What would he say to Gerrie or Andrew if he saw them now? 'I'm not sure how I would react but somebody has to have an inquiry into how this whole thing was handled. I sincerely hope that will happen. I think the first question I have for them is "Are they pleased with themselves?" Clearly the Kebble case was not high on their agenda. They dragged us out in court for almost four years and they postponed and delayed the case all the time until the Selebi matter was completed. So, yes, I've got a lot to ask them.'

Agliotti is capitalising on the opportunity, redirecting any criticism aimed at him towards his accusers. Some might say he is even playing the sympathy card. But then, another ambush, and I literally see Agliotti's jaw lock and jut forward. It's a habit of his when he tries to mask irritation and anger.

Paul O'Sullivan's Irish drawl pierces the air. There are two recorded questions. The self-appointed investigator has requested to be at the press conference but was refused access. O'Sullivan carefully enunciates each word for dramatic effect:

'In July 2006, you had a meeting with Jackie Selebi in the car park at the Value Mart in Woodmead and Jackie Selebi handed you a bunch of papers which included intercepted emails of mine which implicated you, by intelligence reports, in the murder of Brett Kebble. The following Monday you called an urgent meeting and present at that meeting were John Stratton, Clinton Nassif, Mikey Shultz and Nigel McGurk and you chaired that meeting. The purpose of that meeting was to make sure everyone had the story straight in case my document led to further investigation. Can you explain your role in convening that meeting?'

Could it be possible that all the role-players had sat together in this meeting and carefully hatched the entire story of the assisted suicide once they knew authorities were onto them? Were Mikey, Nigel and Kappie all lying about what happened the night Brett Kebble was shot? That would mean they've all secured their freedom despite being intrinsically involved in orchestrating the murder. Ingenious, but a travesty.

Before O'Sullivan's question is even finished, Agliotti is already answering. His composure cracks. 'Firstly that's a lie. There was never a meeting between Stratton, myself, Nassif and whoever else he says was at that meeting. That's an absolute lie and Mr O'Sullivan must stop using these platforms to enhance his own abilities. He did so in the Selebi matter, using the NPA and the DSO for his own agenda and to get back at Selebi, so in response to his meeting, that's a lie.'

The second question raises an issue I'm extremely concerned about: Agliotti's new-found friendship with Czech billionaire Radovan Krejcir, the new Mafia boss on the block.

O'Sullivan's voice rings out again: 'A few months ago you received several hundred thousand rand from a wanted fugitive by the name of Radovan Krejcir. Can you explain why you, a convicted drug trafficker, are receiving several hundred thousand rand from a person who is on the run from Interpol?'

Krejcir arrived in South Africa in 2007 from the Seychelles and was taken into custody at OR Tambo International Airport on an Interpol red notice. He was sentenced in absentia in his home country to six and a half years' imprisonment for tax fraud. He is also reportedly being investigated on charges of conspiracy to murder, counterfeiting, abduction and extortion. He lent his financial backing to an opposition political regime and insists he cannot return home out of fear for his life. He has been fighting extradition and has even applied for political asylum. He has entrenched himself in Johannesburg's underworld, the new boss in town, with millions at his disposal to buy favours. Krejcir is the real deal with murmurings that he even had a hand in his own father's murder, which he, of course, denies. He has set up headquarters at the Harbour Fish Market restaurant in Bedford Centre and has even installed bulletproof glass on the outside patio after a Russian hit squad allegedly tried to kill him.

The billionaire occupied headlines after South Africa's 'King of Tease' Lolly Jackson was murdered in Kempton Park in early 2010. The murder exposed Krejcir's relationship with strip club owner Jackson, his alleged killer Cypriot national George Smith, self-confessed money launderer and bank manager Alexos Panayi, and Gauteng head of Crime Intelligence Joey Mabasa. After Jackson's death, Smith allegedly phoned Mabasa to tip him off about the killing before heading to Krejcir's HQ at the Harbour restaurant. Smith was spirited out the country, apparently fleeing to Cyprus. Krejcir employed the expertise of Ian Small-Smith to defend him and immediately turned state witness, assisting the police with the probe into Jackson's death. Small-Smith, of course, is the attorney who secured deals for Mikey, Nigel and Kappie.

I know that over the past few weeks Agliotti has been meeting with Krejcir, discussing business deals and borrowing money. I'm not entirely sure how he'll dance around this question. I also know that Mikey has befriended Krejcir and speaks highly of him. It all makes me very uncomfortable and seems disturbingly ominous. It feels as if somehow Krejcir has replaced Brett Kebble as the money-laden 'Don' and the cycle is repeating itself, replete with a high-ranking police officer at their disposal.

To my surprise Agliotti admits his involvement with Krejcir. 'Firstly I met Radovan through Jean Meyer who has been in the news. I was there with an attorney. We were looking at doing a gold deal through Zambia which never transpired.' Meyer, a gold refiner and suspected smuggler, was arrested in Sandton while transporting R20 million in gold bars which were destined for Hong Kong. As a result of his arrest he employed Paul O'Sullivan to assist him, who set about probing Krejcir's relationship with Jackson, Smith and Mabasa. The Irishman is driving a campaign against Krejcir and Mabasa in much the same way as he targeted Agliotti and Selebi.

So what exactly is Agliotti's involvement in this murky state of affairs and what is he doing cavorting with these underworld characters? 'Radovan, I have nothing against him, I've heard and read what he's done in the press. The business I do with him is nothing to do with anyone else. It's a business transaction. It's open and transparent.' That's all he will say and many of us in the room are left unsatisfied. I know this matter will come up again.

The focus returns to Brett Kebble, and eTV reporter Karyn Maughan wants to know if Agliotti really believes Kebble actively participated in his own murder. 'I think it's evident and clear that he did have a role to play. With all the evidence that's been led, I'm convinced of it, yes,' responds Agliotti. Karyn pushes on. 'Do you feel any kind of moral culpability that you could have stopped him from participating in this bizarre scheme?' she asks. 'Not really, Karyn. I had no role whatsoever to play. I had no influence in those decisions. It wasn't for me to answer for it or try and convince him.' Despite admitting his involvement in the assisted suicide in a signed statement, Agliotti is still refusing to admit his role publicly.

He reveals he has been placed under financial strain as a result of five years' worth of legal fees. I wonder if he had to borrow money from Krejcir in order to pay his lawyers. 'Yes, absolutely, it's been very difficult, I'm not going to kid you. Everyone was under the impression there were millions hidden and there was millions here and the Kebbles' millions and that's all hogwash, it's nonsense. It's been trying and difficult financially,' Agliotti confirms.

As the press conference winds up, Agliotti turns up the charm. He jokes in response to another direct question from Yusuf that he'll give him 'the inside scoop' if he plans on committing any further crimes and quips at me that I 'will miss him' as he won't be making any further appearances in court.

So what next for the man no longer labelled 'Brett Kebble murder accused'? 'Nothing is going to change the public perception. People who know me and know me well, know what sort of person I am. Nobody's perfect but I just want to get my family back on track. I have lovely kids, a lovely support system and I have so many people to thank. I don't know what the future holds. I just want to concentrate on my family. Try and get my life back together again, try and get business back on track. It has been very traumatic. I've been pulled through the mud. It's going to be a difficult road ahead. Not easy but I don't know where it's going to take me.'

Katy closes the press conference and I put out a tweet asking people what they think about Agliotti's performance.

Joseph_Shaw @MandyWiener: a charming gangster - the worst kind you get!

dapye @MandyWiener shocking to know that we have to share the planet with people like that. god help us all. if you have money you are untouchable

BrendonNell2204 @MandyWiener There has to be a movie in this. Ooh, even a trilogy. The Good, the bad and the incompetent #NPA

PyperK @MandyWiener I loved the questions. He's such a smug fucker.

As Agliotti leaves the building and the microphones are dismantled, I can't help but feel that this will not be the last we see of him. He has had a tantalising taste of fame. His relationships with known criminals disturb me and he is making enemies of the wrong people.

Maybe he will surprise us all. Perhaps he has been right all along about the fact he was unfairly targeted by the Scorpions. He has been elevated to a crime-land boss when in truth he is just a small-time player. Having seen the potential repercussions, maybe he will go off and live a quiet, sedate life with his young children at home in Pecanwood with a view of Hartbeespoort Dam. Maybe he will be a good and generous friend and father, grateful for the support he received at his most trying time.

I reflect on the past five years and wonder what Agliotti has learnt from it all. I suspect, if given a second chance, he would do it all over again. I believe he would still bribe a powerful policeman, he would still knock his paymaster and he will forever be a fabulous raconteur, spinning everyone a story. And he will be doing it all in a well-cut suit and with a smile on his face.

TIME HAS NOT BLUNTED VUSI PIKOLI'S DEFIANT COMMITMENT TO the truth and his deep-rooted obedience to his steady ethics and morals. For me, Pikoli has always been the vanguard of integrity and something of a moral compass. Having been sacked as the National Director of Public Prosecutions, effectively for rumbling along with the prosecution of Jackie Selebi, he fought the President and government for many years purely on principle. Ultimately, he agreed to take a settlement and was paid out several million rand, although he will always insist that he never compromised his principles to take the money.

Pikoli came out of the skirmish with ex-President Thabo Mbeki largely untainted in terms of public perception but it would be foolish to think he was entirely untarnished in reality. Some criticised him for being overly accommodating, others for being too politically naive. After the collapse of the state's case against Glenn Agliotti and the indemnities being granted to the shooters, fingers are collectively being pointed at the ex-prosecutions boss and whoever else was involved in offering the immunities. Comparisons are being drawn with another highly publicised murder filling newspaper column space at the time, that of Swedish model Anni Dewani. The tourist, who was on honeymoon in the country with her husband, was shot in what initially appeared to be a hijacking in Cape Town township Gugulethu. Taxi driver Zola Tongo had just been sentenced in the Western Cape High Court to an effective eighteen years in jail for the murder as part of a plea-bargain agreement. In exchange for the 'lesser sentence', he implicated the husband Shrien Dewani in the murder. The public wanted to know why in the Kebble case the shooters walked free in exchange for their testimonies while Zola Tongo had to go to jail for eighteen years. Also, Tongo was paid R15 000 while the Kebble shooters were paid R1.5 million in total. Where is the justice?

Pikoli has been forced to defend the deals cut with Mikey, Nigel, Kappie, Agliotti and Nassif on numerous occasions, most notably before the Ginwala Inquiry into his own suspension when flamboyant prosecutor Seth Nthai labelled them 'flawed', 'unlawful' and 'reading like a fairytale', suggesting there was a flagrant dereliction of duty on Pikoli's part.

I now have many questions for him too. Why were the section 204 immunities offered and why were plea bargains not negotiated instead? This would have seen the shooters pleading guilty and receiving lenient sentences rather than walking free entirely without any semblance of a criminal record. Was the requisite attention given to the Brett Kebble murder trial or was the primary focus on the case against Selebi? Was that prosecution motivated by malice and a personal agenda as the former policeman claims?

Pikoli agrees to meet me at a Cuban restaurant in Menlyn in Pretoria during his lunch hour before rushing off on holiday. It's a swelteringly hot day in the capital and the mist sprayers on the shop's canopy are working overtime. Pikoli is now head of forensics at Gobodo Incorporated, a private consultancy firm. Ironically, he's still investigating corruption in the public sector but is probably being paid a great deal more to do the same job. A youthful Fidel Castro, puffing on a fat cigar, stares out at me from a poster on the wall as I ask my first question. What does he think of the state's capitulation against Glenn Agliotti?

'Obviously I am disappointed that the state's case sort of collapsed, because it was dismissed at the level of a section 174 application,' he says, lamenting the fact that Agliotti was not even forced onto his defence. 'So it shows that there were problems. Not that they didn't have a strong case. I believe they did, otherwise I would not have authorised the investigation to go on. I really believed the state had a strong case when Agliotti was arrested and still believe they have a strong case, then and now. Perhaps what could have made things go wrong for the state was the change of teams,' he says pre-empting my next question.

Pikoli has a tempestuous relationship with current NPA head Menzi Simelane and I want to know if he thinks Simelane intentionally scuppered the prosecution against Agliotti, for political reasons. Pikoli picks his words carefully.

'For me it would be difficult to say it was a deliberate attempt to try and botch up the case. I don't know. He might have had his own reasons. In the absence of anything that clearly shows there was such an intention, I cannot say it was deliberate. Also I am saying this being cautious of the fact that so much has happened between me and Menzi so I would want to remain objective when I talk about him and not perhaps be seen to be clouding things according to my own prejudices. I'm careful, so I can't say it was deliberately botched. I don't know what made him to change the team but clearly there was a weakness then in the preparations.' He has said what I suspected he would say without actually saying it.

The original prosecuting team of Gerrie Nel, Andrea Johnson and Andrew Leask are protective of Pikoli and he, similarly, of them. He implies that things might have worked out very differently if they were still leading the case against Agliotti.

'I think the first team – Andrew, Andrea, Gerrie, all these guys – they knew what they were doing and I had confidence in them. I trusted their judgment. Of course I would question them, I didn't accept everything they said to me. We had endless meetings and I would interrogate them. I did challenge them. Like for instance when they told me they intended offering these guys a section 204, I wasn't quite happy. I didn't readily accept that,' he says, becoming more animated. For the first time, Pikoli reveals that he was reluctant about the decision to grant immunities to the shooters. To my surprise, he also attempts to shirk some responsibility, pressing home the point that he was no longer the NDPP when the deals were actually signed with Mikey, Nigel and Kappie. I point out to him that the indemnities were negotiated while he was still in office and the deal with Nassif was signed by him. The shooters signed their agreements in Ian Small-Smith's office in November 2006. Pikoli was only suspended in September 2007.

'I was really worried about the actual shooters, my point would have been of perhaps a section 105(a),' he says, suggesting that plea bargains should have been negotiated instead of immunity. 'I think the argument was more that these are just the people who pulled the trigger. The real masterminds here are the guys who have got to be charged, given your general organised crime syndicates and how they're operating,' he insists, pursuing his line that cutting deals with the 'button men' of organised crime is consistent with international practice. It's the same defence he employed during the Ginwala Inquiry. 'Your normal runners – even if you can arrest as many runners and have them convicted, if you don't deal with the guys at the top, the syndicate will continue operating, the enterprise will continue working. So the issue was really to go for the guys at the top. That's what happens normally when you're working with organised crime syndicates. Of course it does not belittle the murder itself, that they killed a human being whether he wanted it or not; the fact is they pulled the trigger when he was driving the car,' Pikoli assures me.

I ask him a difficult question and he answers it with his trademark hearty laugh. I'm not quite sure why, perhaps he finds it absurd of me to ask. If Mikey Schultz goes out and kills someone else now, will Pikoli bear the responsibility for that person's death? Is it 'on him'? After all, Mikey is a free man because of the decision that originated in Pikoli's office.

'It's not necessarily on me,' he says, smiling. 'Of course, perhaps the little comfort, whether it is cold comfort or not, at least I never signed off on the final deals. Perhaps, who knows, I might have changed my mind in the course of the investigation. I don't know that, nobody knows that. But at least I didn't sign the final offers of indemnities. It happened after I was gone. Little comfort. Cold comfort,' he trails off before stating indignantly, 'I'm not happy with the fact that nobody has been prosecuted. I don't like it. It is something that I will always think about it.'

In the wake of Agliotti's acquittal, the Scorpions have come in for a considerable amount of criticism for the way they conducted themselves during the Bad Guys investigation. Agliotti has accused them of abusing his rights, even asking if they sleep well at night. Guy Kebble has slammed them for prioritising the Selebi prosecution over that of Brett's death, saying they used the murder case to leverage complicity against the former National Commissioner. I ask Pikoli if enough emphasis was placed on the Kebble murder.

'For me, the Kebble murder … we knew there were other allegations about him and how he did his business. We were also involved in the JCI investigation, Empire K, but also … this has also been like a story out of the movies!' he says, sounding astonished. 'Truthfully speaking, even the first time I heard the names Agliotti and Clinton Nassif and when I was told that Kebble had organised his own death, it was simply unbelievable to me, you know? Now the question you asked directly, about whether the Scorpions perhaps paid too much attention on the Selebi matter, I would not have done that deliberately because a murder case is still a murder case irrespective of who is involved in the murder case. For me the fact that Stratton and Agliotti were being charged with the murder and the fact that both of them are people higher up in this criminal case, for me it showed that the emphasis then was more on those who were actually involved in organising the death of Kebble rather than those who actually shot him, without belittling the role of the shooters.'

Judge Frans Kgomo was critical of the state's failure to prosecute Agliotti along with Stratton and I have always been baffled by the NPA's ineffectual attempts to extradite Stratton. As far as his lawyers are concerned, no effort was really ever made and I can't understand why. Agliotti always maintained that the Scorpions were stalling his trial so that Selebi's trial could be run first. That way they could keep Agliotti 'on side' as a witness against the Commissioner.

'I don't know what subsequently happened on the extradition application with Stratton but for me, when I was there, I was looking forward to the prosecution of Agliotti *and* of Stratton,' he says, placing emphasis on the word 'and'. 'That never happened so far as Stratton is concerned but I don't know what happened after I left about the application for his extradition.' Charging both Agliotti and Stratton would have been sufficient justification for letting the shooters off the hook. 'I sort of relented in my thinking about also having these guys [the shooters] either charged or being granted plea and sentence agreements, then to have Stratton and Agliotti, it would not necessarily have meant that the Scorpions didn't really care for the murder of Kebble. You would have two guys being prosecuted, being indentified as the guys to be involved. That's why I'm saying I'm disappointed in how this whole matter ended.'

My position in my coverage of Agliotti's acquittal is that the case against him was a 'victim' of the breakdown in the relationship between the SAPS and the DSO. In fact, a member of Agliotti's legal team even snidely remarked to me, 'As fat as he is, Agliotti fell through the crack between the police and the Scorpions.' Judge Kgomo had also pointed to the 'power play' within the unit as a reason for the crippled case against Agliotti. I float this all past Pikoli. He responds with a history lesson on the relationship between the two organisations, clearly making the point that the animosity came from the police and not the NPA. It's a very emotive issue, one he feels strongly about.

Pikoli tells me he tried to improve relations between the two organisations by using police VIP personal protectors and always opening his office doors to SAPS investigators when they were probing the conduct of prosecutors. 'As far as I'm concerned there was never any time when I did anything to undermine the functioning of the police in any way. The nearest perhaps then would have been around the time of the arrest of Agliotti, but even then I went to the President so that the police could give us the docket. I had a meeting with the police and the National Commissioner and asked for the docket. I made it an official request. Personally I can never say I did anything aimed at undermining the functioning of the police.'

He goes as far as throwing down a challenge to anyone who can argue otherwise. 'There's nothing anyone can come up with that says I frustrated a police investigation. If you come across that please come to me and confront me with that.' On the contrary, he says the police weren't exactly gushing with cooperation. 'When we started having investigations against Jackie, things were really ... we thought our phones were being bugged! When we wanted documents from the police we didn't get it.'

My mind wanders back to Selebi's comments to me in the corridor of the High Court and the clandestine video recordings taped by Mulangi Mphego.

It has been a long journey for Pikoli. As he sips on his mango juice, the mist of the cooling sprayers floating across his face, he looks far more relaxed than I've ever seen him, free of the politics of public service. I ask him to reflect on this entire episode which has characterised his legacy and he is true to his commitment to principle.

'Look, this was never a nice experience for me. I have come to accept that in life you never know where you will end up anyway. There are things that are perhaps beyond your control but also in terms of one's values and principles, that at least you are in control of. I'm happy that I have not lost any of those as far as I am concerned. As I said from the outset, I am disappointed with the collapse of the state's case against Agliotti. Not that people don't get acquitted, even if you think you've got a good case, people do get acquitted. But the way it turned out, clearly it showed that there's a problem within our criminal justice system. I feel bad about it.'

Philosophically, I ask him if he regrets the Bad Guys docket ever landing on his desk. He gives me one last trademark laugh and says no, 'I don't regret it, it is just a matter of how things were managed, perhaps by all sides.'

THE GLISTENING AZURE SEA SPARKLES THROUGH THE FLOOR-TO-ceiling glass windows of the Ambassador Hotel in Bantry Bay, as the spray from the waves crashing onto the rocks below flies skyward. I'm sitting on a couch in the restaurant, waiting for Roger and Guy Kebble to meet me. It's two weeks since Glenn Agliotti was acquitted of Brett's murder and they have agreed to 'spew their poison'. It's a magnificent day in Cape Town and already the city is beginning to heave with the December crowds flocking in from Gauteng. Roger and Guy have chosen the venue – a luxury hotel perched on prime property on the exclusive Atlantic seaboard. It represents all that is monied and pretentious.

As I wait, I browse through a copy of the morning's *Cape Times* newspaper. It features an interview with Vinod Hindocha, the father of murdered tourist Anni Dewani. The headline reads 'Go back Shrien – Anni's Dad' and the article conveys a request from the mourning father to his son-in-law, imploring him to return to South Africa to 'tell the world what happened'. It is the story of a desperate father, mourning the loss of his child in a suspicious, convoluted hit apparently orchestrated by someone very close and familiar. The similarity between the Dewani and Kebble stories is unmissable, and it strikes me that in Brett Kebble's tale there is also a sad, desperate father looking for answers. The personal tragedy has been overlooked in favour of the salacious and scandalous.

Roger and Guy arrive and are friendly and polite but seem slightly out of place in the posh surroundings. Guy promises that if I push the right buttons, I will hear 'some interesting stuff'. Having never met Roger before, I am curious to determine for myself if he really is 'as rough as a goat's knee', as he has been described. Over the course of the interview and subsequent lunch at a boutique restaurant in the city, I find both their characters surprisingly complex despite coming across as fairly simple men. They discuss truffle hunting in France and call someone a 'bloody poes' in the same breath. They dine only in the finest of restaurants and sip on the most expensive wines, while discussing whether to keep their box at Newlands rugby stadium for another season. They are concerned about my breeding and what school I attended as they talk about their close-knit clique of who's who in society. Conversation ranges from corruption to politics to pasteurised milk.

I have heard a great deal of second-hand commentary on Roger and

Guy's relationship with Brett and I want to hear it from the source. Was their relationship as fraught with acrimony as everyone likes to believe? 'He cut us out of his life almost totally,' Roger admits. 'We were never invited to his house. He was always buying things we couldn't work out how and he just tended to keep us away. In hindsight it was because he didn't want us in his presence where he couldn't discuss things socially, where somebody might have exposed him.'

Guy, the former professional rugby player, has a hard-man facade but the extent of his emotional hurt from his failed relationship with his brother is evident. 'We used to have running telephone battles. There was a stage where there was a total blackout on Brett. He wouldn't take any calls, we couldn't see him. The number of times when I did bump into him I'd say, come on, let's get together on such and such time and occasion,' Guy says, relaying his exasperation. He turns to Roger to emphasise his point. 'I mean, you remember the time, hey, you were in Canada and Brett phoned you because I wanted to go and take his bloody head off. I'm serious.'

One incident in particular pained him deeply and he raises it more than once during our meeting. 'I remember on his birthday the one time, nine years ago in Cape Town, I said we're going to have lunch tomorrow. I went and bought some CDs and you know, put a little package together for him, only to be called as I was driving up Edinburgh Drive by his secretary, Rita, just to be told we would have to take a rain check. Two minutes before my arrival I'm being told this.'

Guy and Roger agree that the distance came from Brett and not them. I propose the theory that the two of them ostracised Brett and didn't like him because he was not as hard as they were and didn't share their interests in rugby and other similar things. He was more sensitive and arty. Guy immediately dismisses this out of hand. 'That's so crap. That's absolute crap. I spent I don't know how many years it would be now, trying to get this whole family unit together and Brett and his family just weren't there. Brett made no effort whatsoever to try and bond. We were like on our hands and knees trying to be as comforting as we could but there were times when I would call him, he wouldn't take my calls so I would leave voicemails, saying "Brett, if you don't call me back, I'm going to come through from here, I'm going to kick you down in your office, like a brother should do", says Guy, speaking deliberately, his voice getting louder with each word. He recounts another incident when Brett blew him off on Father's Day, cancelling a family lunch to celebrate with John Stratton instead.

Roger admits that Brett never thought his family intellectual or superior enough. 'He regarded Guy and I as fools,' Roger confesses, the cadence of his voice softening as he discusses his son's merits. 'Of course, the other thing about Brett was that he was extremely talented in people skills when he had to make an impression for his benefit and he was very musical. He was the sort of guy who could walk into a bar and open a piano and entertain people. So he had that. He really had the world as his oyster and some people came into his life and just totally buggered it up.'

In their version, Brett rarely made time for his brother and father as he was too busy fulfilling his ambitions, moulding himself as a modern-day Randlord. 'Brett played huge corporate games,' admits his father. 'He used to have this vision in his mind that he would become a Barney Barnato and somebody said in the press that Brett was a new Barney Barnato and I think in a way that affected him. He played that role and it was almost impossible to get through to Brett and to talk any logic. He never had time. I very seldom ever got a meeting with him, if ever, by himself. He always had somebody there. We had to wait and see when there was nobody around and then walk in.'

The last time Guy saw his brother was in May 2005, four months before he was killed. There is a sense of regret in Guy's tone as he relays the events of that day. 'We just couldn't get close to Brett. The closest I got to Brett, at the end and the last time I spoke to him, was on my birthday, the second of May. It was a Sunday. For some or other reason I think he started to feel pressure. Suddenly we were praying at the table. You remember?' Guy says to his father in astonishment. 'We never did that with Brett. This religious thing had come in and Brett had then become over the top.' His comments trigger my memory about Brett's odd baptism in his friend's swimming pool in the run-up to his murder.

At that last lunch, Guy issued a warning to his brother, one which he did not heed. 'That particular day, I was sitting there with Brett saying, "You know, what's going on? Are you in control of what's taking place?" and he sat there with Ingrid and they held hands like and he said, "Nah, it's fine, what are you worried about?" I said, "No it's not, it's not the information that I have, alright. I've seen your people, they tell me stories. People are stealing stock, converting it into cash, etc. There's evidence of it." He said, "Oh, who told you that?" so I started to rattle off some names. I said, "Brett, John Stratton is going to kill you." I'm serious, I said that. I said "John Stratton will kill you." I never heard from him again.'

Brett was dismissive of his brother's concerns about John Stratton. 'All he said was John Stratton's fantastic. He's energetic, he's 72 years old. I said to him, "Brett, he's an arsehole." They clammed up alright. The next time I heard from Brett was a reply to an SMS because he just shut us out again. On the second of August I sent him a text and he said "*thanks boet*". That was it. Never again. Not one word.'

I find this story fascinating as two other close friends of Brett had issued similar warnings to him about Stratton and received an equally dismissive response. Journalist David Gleason confronted Brett about his business dealings with Stratton after hearing from an Australian colleague about his 'reputation'. 'On the number of occasions I met Stratton, I profoundly disliked him,' Gleason told me. 'I was looking at some accounts and phoned a journo friend in Perth. I called Brett and said to him what are you doing with this Stratton. He said, "Mind your own business, it has nothing to do with you," which is perfectly reasonable, but I am a journalist so everything is my business.' Dominic Ntsele's story is much the same. He also questioned him about the wisdom of cavorting with Stratton after speaking to an Australian reporter. 'The same journalist who told me about Stratton's MI5 connections actually told me that Stratton had stolen from the Kebbles. I told Brett that. Brett's answer was a very unusual, short, "That was then." It was odd. And typical of me, I asked the question in Stratton's company,' Ntsele recounted.

Guy and Roger share a deep disdain for Stratton. Ironically, neither man can actually remember how the elderly businessman arrived on the scene and they spend some time deliberating the issue.

'Look, certainly Brett was the guy that negotiated all the things with Stratton. I mean I had very little to do with Stratton business-wise,' Roger tells me. Guy is uncouth as ever as he recounts meeting 'The Turtle' for the first time. 'You told me before I even met Stratton, that this guy was a menace,' he says for his father's benefit. 'I remember seeing him at your office one day. I came in and I said, "Who's that piece of biltong standing outside?" and you said, "It's this poes Stratton." The next time I saw him was after your arrest. That was the first time I heard his voice, in your study at your house in Houghton. They were all running. All they ever did in life was make it more difficult for anybody to see through the shit that they had in front of them. To keep everybody confused. It's a state of chaos. It's a great war, to keep people running in every direction.'

Guy agrees Stratton was key to Brett's involvement with sinister characters and suspects he may have even been playing both sides, feeding Mark Wellesley-Wood information about Roger to keep him under pressure. Roger is hugely critical of both Stratton and Wellesley-Wood. Both Roger and Guy surmise that what happened to Brett was that he got 'meat-hooked' – he got caught in a situation he simply could not fight his way out of.

Roger also believes Stratton was simply too intelligent to leave a paper trail. 'I think he's had huge experience and I think he's very patient,' he tells me and then uses a rugby analogy to explain his thinking. 'He's like a rugby player these days. You know, be patient and then crash over for a try. He had those skills and the moment he saw a gap in a system he put his wedge in there and he wedged Brett in there.'

Father and son are similarly opinionated about Glenn Agliotti and need little invitation to spew criticism about him. 'The first time I met him, I couldn't wait to get away from this guy. If I heard the words "china", "my bru", "my this", "my brother", I really wanted to be sick,' Guy tells me. 'I did abuse him in court. I said, "Glenn, turn around and face me, dipstick" and everything else. He could not look me in the eye. I said all you have to do is turn around and tell me you had nothing to do with this. That's all I was hammering about.'

Roger had been particularly close to Agliotti, travelling abroad with him on numerous occasions. Visuals of Brett's funeral and Agliotti comforting Roger confirm this. 'Agliotti and these guys could see the stress that we were going through after Brett's death and that's when they sidled up to us,' says Roger. 'I used to speak to Stratton and Agliotti almost every day and according to their affidavit they planned this suicide,' he adds in disbelief. He's referring to Agliotti's inadmissible affidavit in which he 'admitted' being part of the planning of Brett's death. 'You couldn't hear them enough,' adds Guy. 'From the start I did not like him. He was a liar from the start. All we would have expected, if Glenn was the person that he claimed to be and if Brett was suicidal or whatever, he should have said, "Listen Rog, Brett's this and I've been offered three bars or ten bars or whatever." We would have said Glenn, for that, for your honesty, something could have been done.' Roger chips in for dramatic effect. 'He was born a liar. He was born a turd, but a lying turd.'

Both men now say that in retrospect, it was clear that the police investigation into Brett's death was being fiddled with. To my surprise, they recount a meeting that took place shortly after the murder – Jackie Selebi came to see them and Clinton Nassif was very nervous. At the time they didn't know why.

'Selebi arrived after Brett's murder and he wanted to find out everything, and Nassif couldn't stop smoking those cigarettes and hovering. I've never seen cigarettes go down like that. I mean he had a magnum pack and Selebi was there shitting himself,' Guy says laughing dryly. 'Selebi knew everything that was dirty, filthy and that gave him money.' Roger picks up. 'Selebi rocked in there with his driver. He had bad manners. He was hardly worthwhile speaking to. He said, "President Thabo Mbeki has told me personally as the Commissioner of the South African Police Force to make sure we bring this case to a successful closure as soon as possible." So we said well, yay, here we go. And he's busy dealing in drugs and Christ knows what. It's there for you to see what kind of people these are,' adds Roger. It was after that meeting that Roger agreed to pull former Judge Willem Heath off the case and forensic investigator David Klatzow was sidelined. Roger told the police they had confidence in their abilities.

Now with hindsight, it's clear that was a bad idea as the police investigation limped along. 'Agliotti and the rest of that gang, they were putting up a smokescreen around this whole murder. They knew exactly what had happened and they sent Detective Diedericks to see me. He used to come once a week,' Roger recalls. 'They couldn't even tie up the telephone calls. Diedericks was a buffoon and he knew he was doing wrong. He led us astray about Brett going to a gay boys' club on a Thursday in a Bentley and all that shit.' Guy and Roger vehemently quash any suggestion that Brett might have been gay. 'No, not at all. I'd get all this crap and stuff. So for a year we went through all this crap,' Roger adds crassly.

Guy reveals the extent of disinformation that was spread. 'The whole thing was so well handled by the cops,' he says sarcastically. 'They had collected the rounds in a pile in the middle of the road, that sort of crap. I flew to De Aar one day to interview some dumb prick of a prisoner that apparently had seen Brett doing a deal with a Chinese for diamonds,' he recalls incredulously. 'This was it! Five million rand was the story, the thinking was that Brett hadn't paid the Chinese and this is why they had done it. Russians, Chinese, gay issues, child pornography, whatever. Outside of the hardship of losing a brother we got this.'

Guy Kebble had previously said to me that the failure of the state to properly prosecute his brother's murder is an indictment of the country's justice system. So how exactly does Roger feel about the way the trial went then? 'It's shocking. It's a fucking mess,' he says, eloquent as ever. 'It's a disgrace that a guy like Tony Yengeni goes to jail because he got a discount on a Mercedes-Benz, and these buggers, there were three killers, and there were three in the planning division, and all of them walked away scot-free. On a technicality, they won't allow Agliotti's bail affidavit!' He is enraged and I see the angry, mourning father who has lost his son much like Anni Dewani's dad.

It was largely due to Roger's intervention that the prosecuting team was changed. He had approached Menzi Simelane, complaining about Gerrie Nel's conflict of interest. Does he regret that decision? 'Well, I don't know which one would have been worse. Gerrie Nel had a lot more experience and maybe they might have conducted themselves in a more professional way, but I mean this prosecuting team just ... to become a senior prosecutor you've got to have ten years of this ugly stuff in jails and courts. Here's this little poppie that walks around like some film star. No, no ...' he says in reference to prosecutor Kholeka Gcaleka.

A court reached a decision on the matter. Do they believe justice was ultimately done then? Guy certainly does not believe so. 'There's no justice whatsoever and justice will never be served on this issue. It's just gone too far really. The pain and aggravation and all the running around, all the money, etc. Who gets compensation for that? The only people that have gotten compensation are the people who have gotten away with the crime. That's the real compensation. And to be honest with you, at the end of the day, it makes me so unpatriotic, really. I'm not proudly South

African. I don't have much time for what's left here. The country's in a lot of shit.'

If the family wanted justice so badly then why did Roger make such a fuss about testifying in court? He delayed the judicial process unnecessarily and dodged repeated requests to enter the witness box. I broach the subject and the topic is not up for discussion. 'I'm not going to answer that,' he says sharply, shutting me down. I notice that he seems to be walking alright and isn't having too much difficulty with his knee. He also doesn't give any indication whatsoever that he was behind his son's murder, as hinted at in court by the investigating officer PW van Heerden.

Clinton Nassif had claimed in court that Roger did know about Brett's plan to commit suicide. He had personally told him about Brett's desperation to die. Is this true? Roger believes Nassif telling him about Brett's wish to kill himself was the first strategic step taken by the cabal of people who planned his murder.

'It was obviously a little part of evidence that they could refer to. To dream up this thing and fall back onto it to say, "Ja, ja, I told his dad. I spoke to Brett about it." Of course Brett said, "What are these people doing? You tell them anything you like and they make a mountain out of a molehill" and he was actually very cross.'

Despite his lack of cooperation, Roger is annoyed that there is no closure. 'We want it closed. If the court had decided that Brett had committed suicide, we would have thought that's closure. If the court had decided that he was murdered and they can't find the person that murdered him, we would have closure. If they said he was murdered and that's the person we would have complete closure. For the children, they don't know. Those children are going to live for the rest of their bloody lives with this cloud hanging over their heads not really knowing what took place. Now the situation is getting to the point where I don't believe what any bloody court says. I think the judge in this case was a good judge. He sat there and he was fucked by the lack of evidence, by the prosecution and by Hodes.'

At the risk of sounding too saccharine or being too sensationalist, I remark that obviously the entire experience must have taken its toll on the family. It's a clichéd question but one that needs to be asked. It's not lost on Roger. 'Your answer to your question is obvious. Of course it's affected us. I mean, my daughter is destroyed by this. She absolutely cannot believe that what has happened here has happened. She would also have accepted a court decision. My wife will never ever recover from it. Guy, outside of his strong brick-wall attitude … it's hurtful. And for me, ja, you lose a soldier. It's a balls-up. Brett's dead, there's not much we can do about that. But Christ, let's bring things to closure in a dignified and just way,' says Roger, in a rare display of sensitivity.

I have often thought about Brett's mother, who has lost a son and how so little has ever been said about her. I'm not surprised in the least that she is struggling to cope with such a public, difficult loss.

Of course, there is also a widow, Ingrid, who has steadfastly kept out of the glare of the media spotlight. She has never spoken publicly and ignored my requests for an interview.

Roger has never had a good relationship with Ingrid. According to one of Brett's friends, the family thought that, as a schoolteacher, she was beneath his standing and that he should have found someone more 'commensurate'. Ingrid's life was plateauing while Brett's was on the up and up. Roger admits his relationship with his daughter-in-law is not a good one. 'We've got an ongoing lack of communication with Ingrid. Ingrid tends to be, as we say, a "Rissiepit"; she's obviously protecting a whole lot of issues herself. She has been anything but helpful in this whole thing. She tended to bump us away.'

In 2008, Roger brought a R15 million civil lawsuit against John Stratton and Glenn Agliotti in the Cape High Court. The claim was for the upkeep of Brett's four minor children. In papers filed in court, he said that his son's estate was insolvent and therefore unable to contribute to supporting the children. He also said that their mother was unable to support them 'to the full extent of their needs' for expenses such as school fees, allowances, medical costs, transport and clothing. 'Accordingly I, as the grandfather of the minor children, am obliged to maintain the minor children insofar as these aspects are concerned. I am entitled to recover these amounts from the persons responsible for the murder of the deceased.' Roger reached an undisclosed, out-of-court settlement with Stratton and it's unclear what ever happened to the claim against Agliotti. I'm told that when Ingrid heard about the lawsuit 'she flipped out' and did not support Roger whatsoever in the matter.

'You know, it wasn't only that issue,' says Roger. 'She just kept on staying away from everything. "Don't go further, don't create more publicity." Her excuse was to not have more publicity for the children's sake. I mean every time we make a statement, we know the banners are going to be up and they probably going to be more subtly put so that it looks more sensational. Ingrid used to flip every time something went out on the wires and you know, I just wrote her a very factual, kind letter to tell her I don't want to deal with you any more because of the way you behave.' Despite this he still has a close relationship with his grandchildren.

Roger tells me that Brett had told Ingrid to trust only John Stratton and nobody else. There are suspicions she may still have a close allegiance to him and be regularly in touch with him in Australia. 'She said to me, on one or two occasions, there are certain things I'll never tell you about Brett. I said, "Ingrid, I don't want to know about Brett's idiosyncrasies. I want to know what you know. How was he? I mean, you lived with the guy. It went from week 12 to week 22. There must have been changes taking place. Did he ever mention that somebody was looking at putting him away?" And she won't say a word.'

Guy says she even tried to dissuade him from pursuing a probe into his brother's murder. 'Ingrid said to me after the murder, we met privately, she said, "Please don't investigate this. Please leave it, let it go, there are a lot of difficult people involved." So I said ok fine, but I haven't really spoken to her other than in an altercative way.'

As the surf crashes ever harder onto the rocks below and the summer sun climbs higher, the interview is drawing to a close. Lunch is calling for these two hungry men. I ask about Brett's legacy and what they think it might be. Has the state's failure to properly investigate his death tainted his memory? Guy believes it has. 'It affects the memory of him. At the moment it's only Brett that's in the firing line and he's not here to defend himself.' This explains why Guy has been on a public crusade to defend his brother whenever possible, despite their diminished relationship. 'He's dead and that's the sad thing. Everybody's forgotten about it, everyone on the radio's discussing "Brett Kebble, the mining magnate" etc. Just refer to him as a person. But then also understand that he's not the only party. We understand he was wrong.'

Roger interjects. 'We understand he made mistakes, but he did them with an ulterior motive of coming right. People have jumped onto the bandwagon and they're utilising all this sensational stuff. I think his legacy is probably, in a way, in changing the old mining structures of this country. I think another legacy is he gave to the planet four kids that are going to be hugely successful. If you analyse Brett, basically he was a person that was intellectually bright, he was very talented in so many ways and he could also charm the pants off everybody. But he just missed a bloody step somewhere and they killed him.'

'KILL ALL MY DEMONS, AND MY ANGELS MIGHT DIE TOO', PENNED Pulitzer Prize-winning playwright Tennessee Williams. It is a quote that, for me, embodies Mikey Schultz, Nigel McGurk and Kappie Smith. I have come to know all three of them well, and to unpack their personalities is a complex procedure. They have never been anything other than polite, well mannered and respectful in my presence. They are good-humoured, light-hearted and entertaining. As Nigel had said to me in the past, they may have been 'bad' and 'naughty' but not necessarily 'evil'. Having covered this story for half a decade I am not naive. I am cognisant of the fact that they are, after all is said and done, willing to kill. I have heard terrifying stories of their escapades; there are horrific incidents, murders, which I am told about and cannot necessarily corroborate or verify. I know that where there is smoke there is fire. And I struggle to reconcile these two aspects of their personalities.

I still have many questions and they agree to sit with me one last time and reflect on all that has happened. Are they at least remorseful about killing Brett Kebble? If they are, then it proves their humanity is overriding.

Mikey doesn't see it that way. 'I'm not remorseful about Kebble at all because I know that man was in a bad place, he wanted to die. I didn't murder the guy. I didn't go there out of malice, because I felt like it. I didn't just wake up one morning and say, "Hey fuck it, Brett must die." It wasn't like that,' Mikey insists. 'This man planned his own death. This man was in a bad place. I seen it for two nights in a row. I seen it when the car overheated and I seen it when the gun didn't go off.' Mikey simply does not feel as though he has done any kind of injustice. 'I feel very sorry for his family. I don't feel like I've done an injustice because he was in a bad place and he wanted this more than anything and, fuck, it was a wrong thing to have done, as Nigel would call it, it was an "immoral business decision", but that man was not in a right place.'

Nigel shares Mikey's sentiments. There is no remorse about killing Brett. 'Morally you can look at it and in law it's not right, but in this circumstance it was very different. I've done things, other things, and been involved in things. But this, man, if you'd seen the desperation on his face ... he wanted to go so bad,' says Nigel, emphasising the point. 'Like I said in court, he had the biggest kahunas I've seen. For a man to come and anticipate that you're going to die, you can't explain that, hey.'

For me there is some solace in the fact that they acknowledge they are sorry for other 'bad' things they have done. Ironically, Kappie, who probably has the most to atone for, readily speaks about this. 'Yes, ja, I do. Well what can I say? There's certain things I regret doing. Like the stuff I put my family through and stuff. I got a new start to life and I want to make good use of it.' Mikey and Nigel nod in agreement and echo what Kappie has said. 'Hundred per cent, correct.'

These men are under no illusion that life has thrown them a second chance. The question now is what they will do with it. Having won the lotto, will they simply gamble it away again?

Kappie repeats how grateful he is, in response to just about every question I pose. 'We glad we were given the opportunity to come out and speak the truth, otherwise if we didn't get that opportunity I think today we would be in jail and we are really grateful,' he says time after time.

Mikey doesn't believe the trio would have landed up behind bars had they not been offered this deal of a lifetime by the DSO. 'I believe that the three of us have always had a pact – that we would always keep quiet and if the one made a decision the other two had to go with on the decision. It was all or nothing. I believe if we all were quiet, they had no evidence. It was Clint's word against ours. I believe that it would always be hanging over our head. The way it happened now it set us free. It basically gave us a new lease on life that we can move on with life and it's a fresh start basically. It would have been a rough ride, we would have all been arrested, but I believe that if the Scorpions didn't have us, they had less of a case than what they had.'

Mikey adds an afterthought, which reminds me of what I'm dealing with here. 'Who knows if Clint would have even made it to court …'

What would have happened if just one of them had been offered indemnity to testify against the others? I know the answer to this question before they even formulate a word. Absolutely not. And what about a plea bargain, as has been suggested by many commentators as what should have happened?

'That's why we took the deal, because we weren't going to do time,' says Nigel adamantly. 'That was what was explained to me. Who wouldn't take that deal? Anyone in their right minds would.'

Mikey agrees. 'We would have gone through the motions, hey.' Kappie chips in. 'It was either all three together, no plea bargain just for one person. It would rather be all three of us.'

Again, I am struck by the unique bond of loyalty this trio shares. They are brothers and vow never to sell one another out at any cost. 'We suffered for four years and the only thing we had was the three of us together and we made it, no matter what it was. It was tough at times, but we stuck together. And I'm just happy it's finished,' says Kappie.

Mikey adds, 'What we've got, money can't buy. That's the point what I was trying to make when I was saying about winning the lottery. To me this means more to me than the freedom we got, and my brothers here, means more to me than money could ever buy.' I wonder, if it really came down to their own individual survival, whether they would still be so loyal. What would their price be for selling out their 'brothers'?

Had they not been offered the deals they had been, they would have taken their chances against the law, much in the same way Agliotti did. Chances are they too would have emerged victorious. 'The same way that Agliotti walked it, we would have walked it,' says Mikey, confirming my suspicions. 'With Ian in our corner. We would have had the right people in our corner and we would have walked exactly the same way as Agliotti. Clint was the only person that I ever dealt with and if Clint had made it to the court it would have been a different story,' adds Mikey.

There was a very real risk that they could be killed for testifying against Agliotti. It is a consequence they had thought long and hard about. The way they speak about what could, hypothetically, have happened to Nassif drives home the point that there was a very real risk that they could have been assassinated in their cars as they made their way down Pritchard Street. 'I think we was also lucky,' says Kappie. 'There's also a chance that they tried to hurt us probably in between and then maybe we also wouldn't have made it to court. I'm just happy everything's finished. I'm not proud of what I done, but I'm just glad,' he adds again.

Knowing all that they do about the way the situation turned out, would they take the job of shooting Brett if it were offered again? Nigel speaks for all three when he answers.

'No ways. Not to go through all of this and being involved in something so high profile. I didn't really know Brett or know what he was about. You must remember we did something and maybe it wasn't right but we all agreed to it and that's something we've got to live with. But to get the implications of Jackie Selebi and then it goes to Thabo Mbeki and then the Scorpions being disbanded … it's a joke. No, I wouldn't go through it again.'

Killing Brett Kebble was not just murdering one man, it was so much more. The implications were immense. Nigel continues, 'I regret going through the trauma of being in the public eye all the time. That I really battled to handle. But as far as the other stuff … in a way it's given me a chance to clean my slate. It's given me a chance to come clean. It's almost redemption and to clean up my life. I can't regret anything. I can't regret the friends I've got because they are like family to me. I've got a good wife, I've got two healthy kids. I can't regret anything like that and I've got to protect it. But there's a code of how you do things and I think that's what also got me through everything. And it's brought my friends and I even closer. We're stronger because we've gone through a lot and we still here. We can still walk around with our heads held up high. People always want to be a part of what we are. But if I knew what I know today, no, I don't think I'd do it. I won't be doing it again.'

True to form, Kappie lightens the mood. 'Ja, sometimes I say we shot the wrong person, hey!' he chimes in, chuckling.

When I ask the trio their opinions on Glenn Agliotti's acquittal, their mood shifts. They become angry and vitriolic. I know that there are two sides to these men. I always imagine some kind of cognitive switch that gets flicked, transforming them into hired hit men. In this instance, Agliotti's name could be that trigger that flicks the switch.

'He's a piece of shit. He sold his best friend down the river. He's a liar, a deceitful little fucking piece of work,' spits Mikey. 'A con artist,' adds Kappie. Nigel goes off on a tangent on the topic. 'I wanted to jump out of that box seeing Glenn. He knows damn well what we were talking about. I don't care what anyone else says, he knows in his heart exactly what we spoke about and he knows what his involvement was. He owes Mr Hodes his life for doing a great job defending him and basically he also won the lottery. He came out there clean and he owes it to Mr Hodes but he knows in his heart a hundred per cent he's as guilty as all hell. He knows. If he can say he can go and sleep at night and he knows everything, then he's the yellow man that he's always been and he'll be the worst father that he's ever been because his daughter must look at him and say: is this a father? He can thank his lucky stars, hey. If we had got the go-ahead from someone else I wouldn't be in this situation,' Nigel adds enigmatically.

Mikey responds. 'Ja, Glenn can thank me. It's ... it was close, very fucking close. I want to throttle him when I see him 'cause he's a motherfucker.'

Would they have considered killing Agliotti for not paying them for the job? Was there something else at stake? I think twice about asking the question, but do so anyway. Would they kill Glenn Agliotti now, even though their slates have been cleared?

Nigel laughs off the suggestion. 'Would we be that stupid? Now that we have a clean start? A leopard never changes its spots. Mark my words. He's riding this, thinking he's a Don. Thinks he's this big man. He thinks he's changed the law, he's made history. He's got off with something, he's made a mockery ... believe me, he's going to dig his own hole and he's going to bury himself with all that.'

I struggle to tell if Mikey is joking or not when he responds to my question about whether he would consider killing Agliotti. 'If there's a 204 on the table, yes.' His is a dark and dry humour. 'No, he's a cunt. I wouldn't kill him, but assault him, I'm not going to promise anything, hey, because he's a fucking prick. He owes me money and besides all that, I don't like him. I don't like what he's about, I don't like what he stands for and when I do see him I will have my say with him and if he's got a lot to say back he's going to find himself with a bunch of fives in his mouth. But kill him? I wouldn't go that far. Because it's actually a waste of a fucking bullet. He's a piece of shit.' For extra effect Mikey adds in one more dark comment, triggering belly laughs from the two others. 'Well, we definitely not going to be doing nothing with Clinton Nassif, that's for sure. That motherfucker's got the biggest mouth in the world and this time, if we had to do anything, the whole thing would be not to be caught.' He assures me he is joking.

When I tell Agliotti about the trio's comments, his response is similarly colourful. 'That's rich coming from them. They have a lot to say about me but nothing about Nassif. Shows you how a dumb fuck like Nassif fucked over the dumb, dumber and dumbest. What a fucking joke. They got away with it, not me.'

Being in the media spotlight has bolstered their reputations as strongmen in the circles they move in, despite having been given the 'bumbling assassins' title. They are now notorious and are celebrities to a degree, Mikey more so than Nigel and Kappie. Their infamy precedes them and being at a boxing match or extreme fighting tournament with them is evidence of this as everyone wants a handshake and acknowledgement. Mikey tells me that 'some young crack addict' is even going around using his name, claiming to be 'Mikey Schultz' and stealing cellphones. Another 'young doos' used his name when threatening to kill a police officer. The cops took the threat seriously and put together a team to arrest him. The confusion was cleared up but Mikey was enraged.

For this reason, the trio were furious that they were painted as bumbling, incompetent assassins by the media during their appearances in court. When *Sunday Times* reporter Rowan Philp wrote a story headlined 'Dumb, Dumb and Dumber' (1 August 2010), they went mad. They admit they weren't exactly slick and professional in the execution of their jobs but being labelled outright dumb doesn't bode well for their street cred.

With their names cleared, Mikey says they are now 'back with a bang'. It's a statement that, I have to admit, unnerves me.

'We've always made our living off the street and stuff like that. We move and do what we do and when this came, it put shackles on our hands. Everybody out there who had a problem with us now knew this and they took full advantage of this. I mean, the shit that people were talking about us and stuff like that, we lost ground. People did move into our space and I believe this has made us stronger now and we're back. There's a lot of people, a lot of insignificant little fools and clowns out there who used this to their full advantage.'

However, Nigel vehemently assures me that it doesn't mean they're going to go out and break the law again. 'No, we've got a network and we've got a very good network. We've got a network that's bad and we've got a network that's good. Now, with all of this that's come out and everything, we must use it to our advantage in the right way. Mikey prefers that celebrity status a bit more than me and Kappie I'd say, but yes, it is a celebrity status and we must use it to our advantage. Because of our code and everything we don't knock people. We do business and everyone thinks, even if we go for a collection, we won't take a person's money and not do anything about it. We're not going to take it to another level and anything like that. But with my celebrity status I can make a phone call and say, "Listen, you owe this person money, can we sort it out." Exactly. That's what I'm going to say. That's what I'm talking about. We'll use it to our advantage.'

Nigel attempts to justify the work that they do, saying it's a necessity because citizens in the country simply cannot rely on the law-enforcement system. It's too laborious and time-consuming. 'The system doesn't work here. You can say what you want to, it doesn't work here. The law takes too long. You know, in America, someone writes a cheque and it RDs, three days later there's a sheriff there. It doesn't work. Here, you got to go to court. It takes one, two, three years. It's too late. The person is out. That's what's wrong. That's why they need to come to people like us and yes, we are violent. But like I said, there's evil, there's bad and then there's naughty. I mean, you know, to go into a house and shoot a person for his cellphone. I mean, come on man, that's evil. You know? That's completely evil. I know there's a lot of people that say killing is killing, and in law that is right. There's black and white and that's how it works. We in that grey area where we can help.'

It's a fine line they will walk and it's difficult to determine if it's a line they will cross in the future, having seen the potential consequences of their actions. There is an overwhelming sense of gratitude and acknowledgement that they have been given a second lease on life. They are also acutely aware of the burden that their families have had to bear as a result of the wrongs they have committed.

'This must have been one of the best things that's happened to us,' admits Mikey. 'None of us drink because of it, none of us go out and get involved in shit like that any more and it's shown us that there is another side to life other than being in clubs and drinking and stuff like that. I've been given a new chance and this has been a hell of a rough ride, more for my family. I'm a man, I can take my shit, but it was hell of a hectic on my kids. When I look at my mother and I see what I put my mother, my wife and my sister through, it's not worth it, it's not worth going through it again. This has just given us a new lease on life and there's no passing on life. I'm very blessed, I've got four beautiful kids, I've got a beautiful wife that supported me and stood by me through this whole thing and she has really shown me character.'

I know exactly how difficult it has been for Leonie, Mikey's beautiful, naive, 'plaasmeisie' wife. She has spoken to me about it, although she has requested not to go on record. It's a chapter she wants closed. She has just this to say: 'I love him with all my heart! I will stand by him through thick and thin. One thing he has taught me is the meaning of loyalty. I know a different side to him and that is the side I fell in love with. I've travelled a long road with him and I wouldn't change a thing.'

Nigel can't stress enough how his children have changed his life. They have forced him to grow up and take responsibility. 'Having your kids changes your life. You got other responsibilities, whereas before, we were reckless. You didn't have to think about anyone else. You just thought of yourself. Now, having kids is a different responsibility and everything like that. I have to protect my family and I have to be around and with all of this, this has been a good start if you want to cleanse yourself, clean your slate and move forward and learn from it. I don't want to be in another situation.'

Kappie, with his brood of half a dozen children, feels much the same way. 'Ooh, no, I love my kids. I'd never want them to do and go through what I've been through and stuff like that. No, I love my kids. I've got good kids and I thank the Lord every day. My son is nothing like me, more brighter. You know, he's a good child and I hope he stays like that.'

Kappie's son has had a brush with the law. His driving skills aren't as good as his father's and he didn't manage to get away from the cops. It's a problem all three of these men will face. What will they do when their children grow up and start doing what their fathers did in the reckless abandon of youth?

Mikey has thought carefully about this. 'One thing we can say is that the three of us are very streetwise. We've learnt from our mistakes. I don't want my kids to pay the same school fees that I paid. I'll make sure that my kids get a good education and I'm going to push them to study and stuff like that and just to do well in life. Just teach them that there is a right way to live and there is morals and standards that you have to keep. I'll fucking make sure that my sons won't try and be heavies.'

They all have plans for the future. Nigel works at a major tyre-fitment centre and Kappie still has his panel-beating shop. Mikey is considering a return to the boxing ring. He also has various business interests and, to my surprise, he is also talking about starting Elite again. He wants to put the old crew back together but says this time he won't be on the front line.

He will get other people to do the dirty work instead. Mikey believes he is invincible.

As I walk away from our last meeting, I wrestle with what the trio have said. Do I really believe their 'new lease on life' sentiment? They are such compelling characters, charming and invigorating to be around. I grapple with this, struggle to reconcile it with the anger and rage they display when talking about those who have wronged them. Are they truly not evil? What have they done to show me they are good?

I badly want to believe them, that they won't break the law again, that they won't do anything stupid. Yet I know that passion or a lapse in thought may push them over the edge. Something or someone will flick that trigger, leading them down that dangerous path. It could be a nebulous remark in a parking lot, or an attempt to reclaim lost ground and restate their power. It could be something far more sinister, involving a billionaire Czech fugitive or a move by the police to finally bring them to book.

I wonder if they have the character to withstand temptation. Or a rush of blood to the head. Have all their demons been killed and do their angels remain? I so want to believe that.

WHAT THEN IS THE TRUTH?

At the end of it all, I am left with a hollowness, an uneasy sense of not knowing. Someone must be lying. Perhaps everyone is. I consider whether I am dealing with a cast of sociopaths, attempting to blind me with their superficiality, charm and wit, living in a world of high drama and risky thrills.

Was Brett Kebble, millionaire, magnate, modern-day Randlord, really an active participant in his own death? Could the bizarre idea of an assisted suicide be genuine? Or was he the fall guy, killed in an ingenious plot orchestrated by those closest to him in order to save themselves? Was there a pot of Brett Kebble's gold, hundreds of millions of rand stashed overseas, waiting for his murderers? Had Brett Kebble really asked Clinton Nassif and Glenn Agliotti to smuggle R50 million offshore, undetected, by buying uncut diamonds, as some claim to be true? Could they have taken him out and kept the money for themselves? Maybe a political assassination by a government institution driven by personal vendetta and power?

Well, it all depends on who you ask and whether you believe they have the capacity to lie or not.

ROGER KEBBLE

My theory is that Brett said the game is up because there was nowhere to go. All his options were wiped out and I think then he said to these people, 'The game's up, I'm going to go, guys, I've cocked up here a bit badly, let me sit down and give you the story.' Stratton would have obviously seen where he landed up in that thing and he was in control of that security stuff. He paid them, he spoke to them, he organised them. Brett would never do that. So he had Nassif and Agliotti and Mphego and Selebi himself.

Brett never once got to the point to say, 'Jeez, Dad, I'm not sleeping well at night. I don't know where to go.' He never said that. He would have said to them, 'Listen guys, the game's up, I'm finished, I can't carry on like this.' I mean, Brett loved his kids. Brett wasn't the sort of person that was going to go and dive off a cliff.

Look, I don't think that he ran the company in any efficient way, but jissus, he wasn't going to go and kill himself.

GUY KEBBLE

Brett's not the sort of person that would take a bullet. Ever. Brett was very, very sensitive to pain. Trust me. He was not a rough guts. He was a softie. He was a naff. Brett got klapped at school, I had to protect him my whole life, you know. You know, when they talk about misfiring the first round, you don't go back for a second. Your life's been spared. No, it's impossible. You hit somebody you hit them once with a bullet. Not seven times in their body. If you look at the scene, Brett's car had skidded to a halt. Had he gone on any further he would have hit that bridge head-on. But the cops are standing there telling us these are pull-off marks.

Stratton's sitting and there's no extradition, they're going to battle to get him. He'll appeal it on health grounds. The timeline, you know when Brett got stripped of his title as CEO, that's exactly when he sort of sat and thought, 'Look, I've got to ...' he's lost control of the treasury. This is going to get exposed, now let's go do it. All that would have happened is exactly that, they would have all been brought to book. Now, at the moment, everyone points a finger at Brett. Brett's wrong, but there's a whole lot of other people who should be brought to book, and that's part of the campaign, that's to bring them to book.

It would be speculation but there was a large amount of money that was taken out of JCI. It's gone somewhere. You can't ask somebody where it's gone and now I can't understand. These things go through banks. It wouldn't take much of a forensic auditor to find out. But the whole thing's been washed away. And it wasn't going to be that assisted-suicide theory at first; that was the next theory. It was going to be this failed hijacking. Then they investigated the books and that and they pointed fingers at Brett Kebble.

ANDREW MINAAR

What's on the table points to assisted suicide but still, I don't know. I think Brett must have been coached or someone was preparing him for that or he was set up. I think Brett would have taken too many people down with him, whoever he had corrupt business dealings with. I just think Brett would have squealed on everyone about what was happening with the fraud and that, and I think he saved a lot of people's bacon. What doesn't make sense is why would anyone do it without having cash upfront? Why would Nassif or Agliotti kill their own business? Who knows. I can't see it being assisted suicide. Factually it may point to it, but to me there's a piece in the puzzle that's missing, that doesn't actually gel.

David Gleason

It's simply out of character for the man. You have to be considerably bonkers to contemplate suicide.

Initially, I thought he had been murdered. He gave me the understanding that government institutions had been pressed by a faction serving the interests of Thabo Mbeki. He believed they would stop at absolutely nothing including removing people permanently if they proved to be an obstacle. Initially, I thought it was a political hit. When I heard it was an assisted suicide, I said, 'Absolute crap'.

There are two possibilities. One, he was taken out by a group of his business associates who have stolen upwards of R400 million. They parked it in places where it couldn't be got at. The other is that it was an institutionally organised hit. Government hit him. I am beginning to think that's rather remote.

It was not an assisted suicide. I don't think he was deranged, disturbed or mad enough to do it.

Laura Sham

If Brett went to jail, and Brett wasn't prepared to go to jail, they would all go down with him. Do you think for one minute Brett would keep quiet in jail? It was the only way out. I just cannot fathom in my mind how Brett accepted that from somebody because I knew him to be a strong person. How do you willingly plan your own death? And I cannot believe Roger did not know about it. I'm convinced of it. He could have done something. Not scream at Brett. Maybe show him some affection.

Dominic Ntsele

It was not assisted suicide. If it was assisted suicide, Brett would have found an elegant way to kill himself. He's not going to go for a botched hijacking, using idiots.

I don't think Agliotti was involved. Agliotti did not have the access to Brett which Stratton had. I actually cannot think of Agliotti and Brett in a room discussing anything with that importance and significance. Agliotti wasn't as important to Brett as everyone thinks he was. He might have been important in other businesses. To the extent that he becomes such a business associate and gets involved in the thinking and the strategy and whatever ... nah. No. I asked Brett who Agliotti was and he said, 'Some strong man helping with security.'

It's not often in my life that I meet people who are about to kill themselves, but he didn't seem any different to any other day. He was good. He was singing 'Summertime'.

Nigel McGurk

If you'd seen the desperation on his face. He wanted to go so bad. For a man to come and anticipate that you're going to die, you can't explain that, hey. That man was in such a desperate situation and I know his family doesn't believe it and his brother doesn't believe it but I can look at him in the eyes and I can tell his father and his family that he wanted to go. And I believe he also did it for his family. Whatever wrong he also did, I can't answer. But he took the fall. And I saw that with my own eyes.

He definitely came to his death. Without a doubt. That guy came. He knew exactly where he was going to be. We found the car, we followed him, the car overheated, we had to go home. He carried on driving around, waiting, thinking it was the wrong car. He came to his death. The following night we were told exactly where to be. He was there. The gun goes and jams not once, twice. Please, you know what Mandy, at the end of the day it worked out to our benefit because that is the truth. That's how badly the man wanted to go. Now you ask me was it suicide? I don't know what more you want me to say. Without any doubt, the expression on his face the night when it happened. The horror when he looked and the gun jammed. I can never ... you had to be there to understand it.

It's an image that will never come out of my mind.

Fiazal 'Kappie' Smith

I looked at him and jeesh, it was just ... when you looked in those eyes, I don't know what he went through every day. Twice in a row, especially the third time when the gun did go off, oh it's unexplainable. What could be so bad? What could you have done that you want to kill yourself like that?

For what?

Everyone has their own opinion. They look at you today, especially us, and they think this guy just shot him, it wasn't assisted suicide. The more you try and tell them the more they don't believe you.

Mikey Schultz

Fuck you. How can you ask me if it really was an assisted suicide? What am I supposed to say? I know what happened. If they're trying to imply that Clint had set it up to look like Brett had come to meet us and was shot, that's not the truth because the gun didn't go off on the first time and didn't go off on the second time and it didn't go off the third time. I'm willing to take a public polygraph test and they can ask me about Brett, if the gun ever went off, and stuff about the case and I will sit there and answer it for them in the public.

That's exactly, exactly what happened, hey. You know, Mandy, we got told it doesn't matter what happened. We got told, tell us the truth, it doesn't matter, implicate yourself. Because that's how you're going to get off here. I didn't have to lie about it. If the gun had've gone off the first time, I would have said it went off on the first time but it really didn't. It just didn't. That's the true fact of it.

Judge Frans Kgomo never made an outright finding on whether or not Brett Kebble was killed as part of an assisted suicide. However, he did grant the shooters indemnity for telling the truth. And he also acquitted Glenn Agliotti whose defence was 'assisted suicide'. Ingrid, Brett's wife, is silent on the topic, ignoring repeated calls and messages. Clinton Nassif has failed to reply to a list of questions sent to him.

John Stratton, the man discussed heatedly by many of those interviewed, responded via his attorney Rael Gootkin at Webber Wentzel:

As you are aware the NPA has on more than one occasion since November 2006 announced that they will be applying for our client's extradition from Australia with regard to the murder of the late Brett Kebble and the attack on Stephen Mildenhall. To date, as far as we could ascertain, no such request has been made. In the light of the total lack of credibility of Clinton Nassif, the main witness in the Agliotti trial, who is also the main witness incriminating our client, and the manner in which the investigation was done, as found by the court, it should now be clear to the prosecuting authorities that a prosecution of our client has no reasonable prospect of success. That may explain why, after more than four years, the threatened request for extradition has not been made.

In the letter, Gootkin goes on to question the prosecutors' conduct, saying:

[T]he court found that the Scorpions wanted to convict Agliotti 'so badly that it did not matter how evidence was procured to prosecute him' and suggested there could have been collusion between witnesses and the compilers of statements.

I had also sent Stratton and his attorney verbatim extracts of those I interviewed. The allegations were dismissed as 'devoid of any factual basis and … nothing more than pure speculation' which they found to be 'highly defamatory'.

Our client instructs us that Brett Kebble was a highly intelligent individual who made his own decisions and who was fiercely independent in his views and his actions. To suggest that anyone could have influenced him to have himself killed or have Mildenhall shot is, in our client's view, utter nonsense. If Kebble took such a decision, it would have been his decision alone and our client denies being a party thereto. Our client has on more than one occasion denied any involvement in the death of Kebble or the attack on Mildenhall. He also agreed to be interviewed by senior SAPS detectives. This interview, which was recorded and took place in Perth under the auspices of the Australian Federal Police during mid November 2006.

So what, then, is the truth? Which one of this gallery of rogues do you believe?

In my opinion, only one person can ever know what truly happened on that secluded, tree-lined road in Melrose on a crisp spring night in September 2005. Brett Kebble.

'PRAY TO YOUR GOD,' SAYS PEPE IN HIS THICK YUGOSLAV/MACEDONIAN accent as the hammering needle breaks flesh. Mikey's nerves tingle as the pigment seeps through his dermis. The strains of The Boss rock out of a portable CD player in the corner of the shop, fighting against the incessant buzz of the tattoo iron. The orange walls in the underground parlour are adorned with images of the artist's work, a display of his skill and ability.

A young man looks on. His T-shirt reads, 'My heart is black, cry no tears for me'. Mikey winces in pain as he endures the consistent rapid-fire of the vibrating needle, sending Kappie into fits of laughter.

'He has his poes face on. It's like an addiction. He can't come to the shop and not have something done. We think Pepe's putting heroin in the ink or something.'

Mikey's canvas is almost full. Another memory indelibly catalogued. His body reads like a memoir of his turbulent, hell-raising life.

Acknowledgements

While I personally covered the evolution of this story from the day Brett Kebble was murdered in September 2005, I must acknowledge the work of my colleagues who were filing alongside me. I have used their reports to fill the inevitable gaps in my memory and corroborate my reports and notes. In other instances, where they have broken exclusive aspects of the story, I have relied solely on their work and credit them as is appropriate.

The full extent of this story would never have seen the light of day were it not for the formidable journalistic work of the team at the *Mail & Guardian* newspaper. Erstwhile editor Ferial Haffajee, Nic Dawes, Sam Sole, Stefaans Brummer and later Adriaan Basson, were pivotal in exposing the underbelly of the country's business and political spheres. Through gritty perseverance, they pieced together this saga of corruption at the very highest of levels, of insatiable greed, unpalatable political interference, the abhorrent abuse of state agencies and the downright dirty and dangerous tactics employed by agents hired to scare and kill. I relied heavily on the weekly instalments published by the newspaper and its investigative arm amaBhungane, the Centre for Investigative Journalism.

I also made extensive use of the news reports in the Independent Newspapers group's publications, most notably *The Star* and the *Sunday Independent*. I discovered the search function on www.iol.co.za to be a remarkable resource. Similarly, background was also gleaned from www.ewn.co.za, www.news24.com, www.timeslive.co.za, www.sabcnews.co.za and the South African Press Association's website www.sapa.org.za.

Thank you also to the editorial staff at *The Star*, who graciously gave me permission to use their photographic archives, and to the individual photographers whose images appear in the picture sections.

Thank you to those authors and organisations that have generously given me permission to use excerpts of their publications in this book. These include the Independent Newspapers, the *Mail & Guardian*, the *Sunday Times*, *City Press*, *Carte Blanche*, *The Property Magazine*, *Noseweek*,

NewsTime, Miningmx.com and Zebra Press.

Regular points of reference were provided by the descriptive profiles and obituaries of Chris Barron of the *Sunday Times*, Andrew Meldrum of the *Guardian*, *NewsTime*'s Rod Mackenzie and David McKay, editor of Miningmx.com.

I must also acknowledge other sources that I looked to for information and background: Jingo Journalism www.jingo.co.za, *The Herald*, Moneyweb, the Australian Broadcasting Company's Four Corners, KeyNews, Ever-fasternews.com, Fightnews.com, timesSAguardian.com, haaretz.com, iafrica.com and theage.com.au.

A number of previously published books also served as resources. These include *Hazel Crane: Queen of Diamonds* (David Kray – Spearhead Press), *Brett Kebble: The Inside Story* (Barry Sergeant – Zebra Press), *Steeped in Blood: The Life and Times of a Forensic Scientist* (David Klatzow, as told to Sylvia Walker – Zebra Press) and *Finish & Klaar: Selebi's Fall from Interpol to the Underworld* (Adriaan Basson – Tafelberg).

Reading the books of Peter Harris, Jacques Pauw, Jonny Steinberg, Anthony Altbeker, Richard Calland and Andrew Feinstein served as guidance and inspiration when I was blinded by ignorance and bewildered by doubt.

*   *   *

If there is anything I have learnt during the process of writing this book, it has been the inherent value of the concepts of loyalty and trust. For many of those I interviewed, the value placed on a person's word far outweighs that of a legal document or a signature. Most have placed their faith in me on the basis of my undertaking that I would handle their stories with objectivity, rectitude and integrity. I hope I have achieved that.

Speaking to me transgressed the fundamental beliefs of Mikey Schultz, Nigel McGurk and Kappie Smith. In their world, you do not trust a journalist who will invariably land up sensationalising or bastardising your words. I am exceedingly grateful to all three of them for looking upon me differently and for giving me custody of their stories. They have allowed me into their inner circle and their lives, and that has been a rare privilege. Thank you for your trust.

Leonie Schultz and Stacie McGurk also took the time and care to read the manuscript and were generous in their assistance throughout the process. Thank you.

Over the past few years, I have spent many hours with Glenn Agliotti, both in the confines of a courtroom and across the white linen of a restaurant tablecloth. He has regaled me with his life experiences and can hold court like no other. I am grateful for the many hours he has given me and for the access he has granted me, on many occasions on the basis of exclusivity. I also take sole responsibility for getting him hooked on Twitter.

Many others have given me their valuable time and were willing to forgo their trepidation in granting me interviews. Thank you to Roger and Guy Kebble for speaking to me at a time when all they wanted was for this burden to disappear. Guy has always been approachable and willing to speak, a trait most valued by those of us in the fourth estate.

Andrew Minaar, Laura Sham, John Kruger, Charlene Voget, Sandy Caetano, Tinky Love, Mike Bolhuis, Piet Byleveld, David Gleason, Rod Mackenzie and David McKay have each contributed to the accuracy, authenticity and integrity of this book. I appreciate their efforts and their patience. Dominic Ntsele's guidance has been invaluable. Up the Bucs.

Vusi Pikoli's conviction in speaking truth to power is astounding. I hope this 'depressing dialectical exposition' does not keep him awake at night.

To those who have chosen to remain anonymous, their courage is profoundly acknowledged.

I am indebted to Laurance Hodes SC, for always, always making the effort to assist me in any way possible. Thank you for the careful explanations and for steering me in the right direction. He is yet to be wrong on a legal prediction, although I suspect he might argue otherwise. Thank you also to Rob Kanarek for all the help along the road.

Over the years, the assistance of debatably the most successful criminal attorney in town, Ian Small-Smith, has been priceless. He has always been ready with a comment and a bad joke. Good luck on the farm.

David O'Sullivan, Alex Eliseev and Gerald de Villiers had the task of reading the manuscript in its rough state. Thank you for treating the text with such care. Their input has been a major contribution in moulding this book into its final form. Thank you also to Hugh Melamdowitz for the legal read.

Sarah-Jane Olivier has held my hand throughout this entire process. Her inspiring emails gave me perspective when I had none and she indulged my doubts and insecurities when I needed her to. Thank you also for handling my work with such finesse and circumspection.

To The Desh, for painstakingly transcribing hours upon hours of interviews. And for taking all my money. She is going to be a great journalist and she owes me biriyani now.

I had the good fortune of sharing the benches of the South Gauteng High Court with a fabulous group of colleagues who made the experience bearable. To Sally Evans and her blanky for making me cry with laughter and entertaining the occasional rant. To Karyn Maughan and her obtuse, warped sense of humour and the yummy snackage we shared – we will forever have the frog. Ilham Rawoot, Kalay Nair, Kerryn Stapp and Magdel Fourie made up the rest of the back-corner cabal. I had such fun searching for wedding dresses and mocking clerks during legal argument. Let's do it again one day.

Thank you also to Marga Ley, Mirah Langer, Gill Gifford and Candice Klein.

Adriaan Basson is so wise – I have learnt so much from him. Thank you to Antoine de Ras for the use of his powerful image on the cover of this book and to Lisa Skinner for the author's pic and for being such an anorak. She is a great friend.

@TheTwitterverse and my followers – in 140 characters:
Thanx 4 the RTs, the #FFs and all the support during #Selebi + #Kebble. Together we have created a precedent. It's been an honour. Thank u.

It was a series of tweets, SMSs and Facebook messages that instigated the writing of this book. A post on my Facebook wall from Jenny Crwys-Williams, the queen of literature in this country, pushed me over the edge. 'Book! Book! Book!' she wrote on my status mid-trial. How could I say no to that? Jenny was the catalyst and I am so grateful to her for her direction and backing.

This rookie author could not have asked for a better publishing team. I am still certain Terry Morris, the MD of Pan Macmillan, had 'crazy' running through her head at our first meeting when I told her, 'I want to write a book about bad guys.' Unbelievably, she agreed, and I am grateful for her faith and for being willing to take the risk. Andrea Nattrass, my publisher, has the patience of Job and the longest whip I've encountered. She has carefully steered me through this journey, leading me when I was overwhelmed and clueless. She has invested as much as I have in the final product, spending long hours tweaking, correcting and providing wise counsel. For that, I am truly grateful. I apologise for all those times I sent her scurrying up her climbing wall and the incessant BBM conversations. Through it all, when she must have been grumbling at her screen and cursing at her phone, she maintained a remarkable level of professionalism. It has been a real pleasure working with her. Thank you to the rest of the team at Pan Macmillan, especially Wesley Thompson, Tarryn Talbot, Laura Hammond and Kelly Ansara, as well as Valda Strauss, Kevin Shenton and Michiel Botha, for being so excited about this project and for taking up the challenge.

A journalist is only as good as his or her editor. I have little doubt that I would still be writing traffic updates were it not for Katy Katopodis, Editor-in-Chief of Eyewitness News. Katy has grown me, guided me and mentored me over the years. I know how very difficult I can be to manage and her ability to do so with such success has been admirable. I am indebted to her for allowing me some time away from work to write a book. It was something she did not have to do but she chose to believe that I could. Thank you.

To all my colleagues at Eyewitness News, I apologise for the deadline tantrums and the post-court grumpiness. Contrary to popular belief, radio is a team sport and I could never produce the work I do without their intervention. I have such fun sharing an office with them all. Thank you also to Primedia Broadcasting and in particular Eyewitness News for supporting this venture.

Writing this book has been an extremely taxing undertaking. I have endured long hours in isolation staring at a computer screen, something I am not accustomed to. I could not have done this without the support of my friends and family who accepted that, for a period of time, I had dropped off the radar.

To my girls Lou, Mand, Nades and Jade: I love them all so much. Thanks for celebrating me when I am reluctant to and for being so excited about my achievements. They are the very best fan club.

Thank you to the Meisel clan – they have so willingly accepted me into their family and it has been such a joy for me to be a part of that. I cherish Friday nights and the escapism that loud, crazy dinners around the table brings. I'm sorry, but I'm not changing my name!

To my family, thank you for a lifetime of love and support. Elian's perfection classes on the tennis court really paid off. I so value his advice and his often peculiar, yet insightful, perspective on things. Janine is the most caring and generous sister ever and I relish our Skype conversations and long email chats. I am so proud of what they have both achieved. Parental unit, thank you for teaching me to love news and books so much and for teaching me the value of breaking bread with all men. It can't have been easy raising such an independent, *hardegat*, obstreperous child but they did a fantastic job. While their *meshugas* sometimes drives me mad, I do love them for it.

Grey and Horatio comforted me in moments of sheer terror and arresting panic. At times they told me to just get over it and snuggled up in a beam of sunlight but occasionally they would trample on my keyboard, reminding me to keep perspective.

Finally. Sean – this is what I've actually been doing, locked away in the study for the past few months, while you have been doing everything else. Somehow we have managed to build a house, plan a wedding, change jobs and publish a book, simultaneously. One day, when we are old and weathered and sitting together on a bench in our sunset years, we will reflect on this insane period of our lives and smile. It has been one hell of a ride and I would not have wanted to share it with anyone else.

Mandy Wiener
February 2011